ALSO BY JOHN GROSS

The Rise and Fall of the Man of Letters
James Joyce
The Oxford Book of Aphorisms (ED.)
The Oxford Book of Essays (ED.)

Shylock

A Legend and Its Legacy

JOHN GROSS

SIMON & SCHUSTER
New York · London · Toronto
Sydney · Tokyo · Singapore

SIMON & SCHUSTER
Simon & Schuster Building
Rockefeller Center
1230 Avenue of the Americas
New York, New York 10020

Originally published in Great Britain in 1992
by Chatto & Windus Ltd. as
Shylock: Four Hundred Years in the Life of a Legend.

Designed by Edith Fowler
Manufactured in the United States of America

10 9 8 7 6 5 4 3 2 1

Library of Congress Cataloging-in-Publication Data

Gross, John J.
Shylock : a legend and its legacy / John Gross.
p. cm.
Includes bibliographical references and index.
1. Shakespeare, William, 1564–1616.
Merchant of Venice. 2. Shakespeare, William, 1564–1616—
Characters—Shylock. 3. Shylock (Fictitious
character). 4. Jews in literature. I. Title.
PR2825.G76 1992
822.3'3—dc20 92-35672 CIP
ISBN 0-671-70707-8

Particular illustrations are reproduced by courtesy of the following: The Board of Trustees of the Victoria and Albert Museum for Sir John Gilbert's drawing of The Merchant of Venice; *the Theatre Museum for Johann Zoffany's painting of Charles Macklin and the photographs of Henry Irving, John Gielgud (with Peggy Ashcroft), Laurence Olivier (with Jeremy Brett), and Ellen Terry; The Hampden-Booth Theatre Library at the Players, New York, for the drawing of Edwin Booth; The Shakespeare Centre Library, Stratford-upon-Avon, for the sketch of Charles Kean's production, and the photographs of the set of Komisarjevsky's production and of the Japanese production; and The Museum of Modern Art, New York, for the still from Lubitsch's* To Be or Not to Be.

Excerpt from "Dirge" in The Waste Land: A Facsimile and Transcript of the Original Drafts Including the Annotations of Ezra Pound, *copyright © 1971 by Valerie Eliot, reprinted by permission of Harcourt Brace & Company.*

Excerpt from "Burbank with a Baedeker: Bleinstein with a Cigar" in Collected Poems 1909–1962 *by T. S. Eliot, copyright 1936 by Harcourt Brace & Company, copyright © 1964, 1963 by T. S. Eliot, reprinted by permission of the publisher.*

Contents

PART THREE *A Citizen of the World*

Preface

The earliest printed text of *The Merchant of Venice* is the First Quarto of 1600. On the title page the play is described as "The most excellent Historie of the *Merchant of Venice.* With the extreame crueltie of *Shylocke* the Jewe towards the sayd Merchant, in cutting a just pound of his flesh: and the obtayning of *Portia* by a choyse of three chests."

"Extreame crueltie": one might well feel that there was not much more to be said. But Shylock, a villain who makes his appearance in a mere five scenes of a romantic comedy, has captured the imagination of the world. As a stereotype, he has undergone countless mutations, and for nearly two hundred years there have been claims that he is much more than a stereotype, that he is meant to engage our sympathies in ways that would have once seemed inconceivable.

The present book opens with an account of the elements that went into his making, but it is primarily an attempt to trace his subsequent fortunes—in the theater, at the hands of critics and commentators, as an inspiration to other writers, as a symbol and a source of debate. He belongs to literature, and his greatness can only be properly appreciated in literary terms; but he belongs equally to the history of folklore and mass-psychology, of politics and popular culture.

Each of Shakespeare's plays is a self-contained world. It has its own interconnections, its own atmosphere, its own balance of forces. To concentrate on a single character is to risk losing sight of this: who would want a whole book on King Lear rather than *King Lear,* or on Prospero rather than *The Tempest?* But Shylock is a special case. Not only does he stand out from his surroundings in peculiarly stark isolation; his myth has often flourished with very little reference to *The Merchant of Venice* as a whole, quite often with none at all.

In the first part of the book I discuss his origins and his development within the play itself (in relation to the other characters, I need hardly say, since his fate is not finally separable from theirs). I have also tried to look at him in the light of Jewish history. The actualities of that history may not have much bearing on what Shakespeare wrote, but the play is important enough to be worth considering in a more-than-Shakespearean perspective.

Part Two is devoted to Shylock's interpreters in Britain and America, down to the Second World War—"interpreters" meaning both the actors who played him and the critics who wrote about him. Part Three ranges more widely, through his role in English culture at large and his history outside the English-speaking world. There are chapters on the very varied responses that he has elicited from Jews, on the uses to which he has been put by those who see him as a symbol of capitalism, on the psychological interpretations he has attracted, and on the part he has played in the demonology of anti-Semitism.

The Second World War constitutes a decisive break. A full account of what has been made of Shylock since 1945, both in the theater and beyond, would require a book in itself—a book which I leave to others; but I have tried to sum up what seem to me the most significant developments in my concluding chapter.

•

I would like to thank the following for their advice or assistance: Chaim Bermant; T. J. Binyon; C. S. L. Davies; Ted Hughes; Dan Jacobson; P. J. Kavanagh; Neil Kozodoy; Douglas Matthews; George Watson. I owe a special debt of gratitude to Miriam Gross for her encouragement, and to both her and Gina Thomas for help with translations from the German.

JOHN GROSS

PART ONE

Shakespeare's Shylock

CHAPTER ONE

Where Does He Come From?

· I ·

Shylock has a long ancestry, and a short one. In creating him, Shakespeare drew on ancient traditions, but he also made use of more immediate sources.

It is generally agreed that the plot of *The Merchant of Venice* derives in large part from a story in the fourteenth-century Italian collection *Il Pecorone* ("The Simpleton"), the tale of Giannetto. No English translation of *Il Pecorone* was published until long after Shakespeare's death, which means that he must either have read the tale of Giannetto in Italian (assuming he knew enough of the language) or in a translation circulating in manuscript; but the similarities between tale and play, first pointed out by the eighteenth-century scholar Edward Capell, are too great to be a coincidence. Both works weave together the story of a pound of flesh, the story of a rich lady and her suitors, and the story of a ring which a lover swears to cherish forever and then finds himself forced to give away.

The lady in *Il Pecorone* lives in a town called Belmonte, but she is a less morally elevated character than Portia, and the story of her wooing is a good deal less edifying. In order to win her, a suitor has to spend a night making love to her, forfeiting his wealth if he fails. Those who offer themselves are invariably duped by being given drugged wine: an ardent young Florentine, Giannetto, falls for the trick twice, and it is only after one of the lady's maids has warned him about the wine that he finally succeeds.

When it came to the pound of flesh story, Shakespeare stuck much closer to his original. Giannetto's three forays to Belmonte are financed by his godfather, a wealthy Venetian merchant called Ansaldo, who is under the impression that they are trading expeditions. In order to pay for the third of them, Ansaldo is forced to borrow money from a Jew, pledging a pound of his flesh by way of surety. Giannetto, having won the lady, is too busy enjoying himself at Belmonte to remember the bond until the day it falls due. He then hurries to Venice with the necessary funds, but it is too late: the Jew is more interested in taking Ansaldo's life than in getting his money back, even though Giannetto offers to repay him ten times over.

Help is at hand, however. The lady of Belmonte arrives in Venice, disguised as a lawyer, and advises the Jew to accept the tenfold repayment. When he remains obdurate, she tells him that he is indeed entitled to collect his pound of flesh, but that if he sheds a single drop of blood in the process he will forfeit his own life. Taking fright, he says that he is willing to settle for the money he has been offered, or even for nine times the original sum, or eight times, or five times, or even for the sum itself ("and a curse be on you all"). Now it is her turn to insist that he must take a pound of flesh, or nothing. In a rage, he tears up his bond, and that is that.

The most striking thing about Shakespeare's use of *Il Pecorone* is how much he made out of how little. This is particularly true of the story of the pound of flesh. In the tale of Giannetto it only takes up two thousand words or so (about a quarter of the text), and for the most part it is told in the barest outline. Once or twice you can see how it might have stirred Shakespeare's imagination—in the account of the moneylender in court, for instance, advancing on

Ansaldo with a razor; but the moneylender himself remains a completely flat character. He doesn't even have a name.

Still, the gist of Shylock can be found in *Il Pecorone,* and we can learn something about Shakespeare by considering what were the main elements that he thought worth adding. In the first place, while there is no suggestion that Ansaldo and the moneylender have had any previous contact, Antonio and Shylock know each other well, and Shylock has strong personal motives for seeking Antonio's destruction. The moneylender, by contrast, offers a wholly generalized (though hardly less sinister) reason for persisting in his course: "he wished to be able to say that he had put to death the greatest of the Christian merchants." Secondly, Shakespeare deepened Shylock's motives by adding the entire subplot of Jessica and Lorenzo. Finally, Shylock is held accountable and punished for his misdeeds, and compelled to become a Christian. The moneylender, on the other hand, simply tears up his bond and fades out of the story.

It is possible, no doubt, that there was another major source for *The Merchant of Venice* which has since been lost. In particular, a great deal of ink has been spilt speculating about a reference in Stephen Gosson's pamphlet *The School of Abuse* (1579) to a play called *The Jew,* "shown at the Bull." Gosson, an unsuccessful playwright turned puritanical critic, took a harshly disapproving view of the stage, but there were a few plays he was prepared to exempt from his strictures, and *The Jew* was one of them: he praised it for the seriousness with which it laid bare "the greediness of worldly choosers, and the bloody minds of usurers." This has sometimes been interpreted in terms of the two main strands in *The Merchant of Venice,* with the bloody-minded usurer representing an early version of Shylock, and the worldly choosers foreshadowing Portia's rejected suitors, the Prince of Morocco and the Prince of Arragon. But strong arguments have been put forward on the other side. Can Morocco and Arragon, whatever their faults, really be described as worldly or greedy? Would any dramatist writing in the relatively primitive era of the 1570s have had the skill to sustain a sophisticated double plot?

The one thing Gosson's reference makes clear is that Shylock was far from being a complete theatrical novelty. A villainous Jewish usurer was being portrayed on the London stage some twenty years before *The Merchant of Venice* was written (and nearly 300 years after the Jews were expelled from England by Edward I).

Were there other plays on which Shakespeare might have drawn? There are references in theatrical records to an unspecified "Venetian comedy" presented in 1594, and to an otherwise unknown work by Thomas Dekker, *The Jew of Venice.* A number of "Jew of Venice" plays were also performed by the English companies which began touring Germany at the end of the sixteenth century. One of them has survived in manuscript under the title *Komoedia gennandt Der Jud von Venezien* ("Comedy called The Jew of Venetia"), and although the central character is closer to Marlowe's Barabas, whose name he shares, than to Shylock, the closing scenes feature a Shylock-like bond, a trial and what contemporary playbills called *Dass wohl Gesprochene Uhrteil Eines Weiblichen Studenten* ("The Well-spoken Judgment of a Female Student"). There is no forced conversion to Christianity, however. Barabas ends up by being thrashed and thrown out of court.

Possibly this work derives from an unknown play which also served as a source of *The Merchant of Venice.* There is no way of telling; but it seems much more likely that its borrowings come direct from Shakespeare.

There are also what look like a few echoes of *The Merchant of Venice* in a contemporary broadsheet balled, *The Ballad of Gernutus*—or is it the other way around? Gernutus is a Jewish moneylender who lives "in Venice town." Like Shylock, he ensnares an innocent merchant with "a merry jest"—the bond; like Shylock he whets his knife in the courtroom, only to be thwarted in the usual manner. Possibly the ballad was written before the play, and possibly Shakespeare had read it. But if so, it didn't offer him anything as a source that he wouldn't have done better to get elsewhere. It is a crude affair, and its chief interest is in suggesting the kind of loathing that a Shylock figure could inspire in the popular mind. Gernutus, even before the story starts, is compared to a hog, of no use until it is slain, and to a "a filthy heap of dung"—

His mouth is almost full of muck,
Yet still he gapes for more.

For good measure he has a wife who practices a little usury of her own on the side.

With other sources, the literary detectives are on firmer ground. It seems certain that Shylock's arguments in the trial scene owe something to a set speech on a similar theme in *The Orator,* by the Frenchman Alexandre Sylvain, which was translated into English in 1596. There are clear anticipations of the flesh-bond (though the usurer isn't a Jew) in Anthony Munday's romance *Zelauto* (1580), and the same work contains at least a hint of Jessica and Lorenzo. The ultimate source for the Jessica story, on the other hand, was probably the fifteenth-century Italian author Masuccio.

But these are questions for scholars rather than ordinary readers. Only one work that influenced *The Merchant of Venice* still qualifies on its own account as living literature—*The Jew of Malta.*

• 2 •

Marlowe was born in the same year as Shakespeare, but he got off to a quicker start. He was only twenty-three or so when he astonished his contemporaries with *Tamburlaine*—around 1587, at a time when Shakespeare was still completely unknown. *The Jew of Malta,* which was probably written in 1589, was almost equally successful, and its continuing popularity may have been one of the things that prompted Shakespeare to attempt a Jewish theme himself. There were revivals in 1594, the year following Marlowe's death, and again in 1596; *The Merchant of Venice* is now generally agreed to have been written sometime between 1596 and 1598.

What is certain is that Shakespeare knew Marlowe's play well, and that he learned from it. The most obvious parallel between Shylock and Barabas, apart from their villainy, is that they both have daughters; the most obvious verbal link between them is the one between Shylock's lament over Jessica—"My daughter! O my ducats! O my daughter!"—and Barabas's cry as Abigail retrieves his money-bags: "Oh girl! oh gold! oh beauty! oh my bliss!" But there are at least half a dozen other distinct echoes. Barabas anticipates

Shylock when he talks about the multiplying of money, and when he invokes the prosperity of the biblical patriarchs. And one of his comments yielded Shakespeare a Familiar Quotation, though only after it had been reassigned from Jew to Christian. When the Knights of Malta make pious noises to justify their confiscating his fortune, he retorts: "What, bring you Scripture to confirm your wrongs?" In *The Merchant of Venice* this becomes a shaft directed at Shylock by Antonio: "The devil can cite Scripture for his purpose."

But points of detail do not tell us very much in themselves. It is as well to remember, as Lionel Trilling once observed, that the idea of "influence" had its origins in magic. Any artistic influence that goes beyond mere imitation is something that cannot readily be broken down into small discrete units. It probably involves a degree of negative influence as well; the lessons an artist rejects are no less important than those he incorporates.

If you were to judge *The Jew of Malta* purely by its plot, you would wonder how much it had to teach any serious writer. Barabas's career is one of unbroken infamy. He cheats, robs, betrays, murders, poisons an entire nunnery. He is a monster, and he meets a monster's end, tumbling into a cauldron of boiling oil. Yet within this utterly melodramatic outline, Marlowe has created a compelling, at times almost sympathetic, character.

It is not just Barabas's wit and energy that produce this effect, but the play's whole underlying thrust, its savage view of human nature. Most of Marlowe's Christians turn out to be as unscrupulous as his Jews, and hypocrites into the bargain. We are in a harsh, self-serving, double-dealing world, and within such a jungle Barabas at least has the appeal of being more agile and more clearsighted than his enemies. Time and again he makes telling points against their pretense of virtue; and in stripping him of his wealth, they have of course given him an excellent reason for hating them.

The Jew of Malta offered Shakespeare the precedent of a Jew who was articulate, who dominated the action, who had his own point of view and his own grievances. With such an example in front of him, it would have been a very retrograde step to have gone back to a Jewish villain who was a mere offensive blob, like Gernutus in the ballad.

There are nonetheless profound differences between Shakespeare's Venice and Marlowe's Malta. The role assigned by Shakespeare to his Christian characters is far more extensive, and altogether more positive; his Jew, on the other hand, has been scaled down and domesticated. Where Barabas plays at high politics, Shylock pursued a limited personal feud, and he has none of the insatiable ambition that makes Barabas, for all his grotesque aspects, a superman in the line of Tamburlaine and Faustus. Nor is he a systematic machiavellian—unlike Barabas, who is introduced to us in the prologue to *The Jew of Malta* by Machiavelli himself. This side of Marlowe didn't pass Shakespeare by, but it was to make its influence felt in Richard III rather than Shylock.

According to the government informer Richard Baines, one of the blasphemous opinions with which Marlowe used to divert his friends was that "Christ deserved better to die than Barabas and that the Jews made a good choice, though Barabas was both a thief and a murderer." It is hard not to recall *The Jew of Malta* when reading these words, just as it is hard not to feel that Marlowe put a good deal of himself into Barabas—his power fantasies, his dynamism, his scorn for received opinion. Unfortunately the play grows coarser as it proceeds, and by the end we are left with little more than a comic-book ogre, an Elizabethan Goldfinger or Dr. No. But in the early scenes Barabas is someone who demands to be taken seriously, and his self-aggrandizement is not just a form of private megalomania. It coincides with a great historical moment, with the sense of capitalism unleashing its full power for the first time.

His attitude towards wealth is both voluptuous and severely businesslike. Thrilling to the thoughts of sapphires, amethysts, "fiery opals," "grass-green emeralds," he remains firmly at home in the world of account-books and bills of entry. Above all, he knows how to make money work for him at long distance. He trades with Egypt, Spain, Greece; his webs of credit extend to half the commercial centers of Europe:

In Florence, Venice, Antwerp, London, Seville,
Frankfort, Lubeck, Moscow and where not,
Have I debts owing: and in most of these,
Great sums of money lying in the banco . . .

A bold vision: it presupposes a European economy with ever-widening interests and ever-tightening links. But there is something more. Barabas also takes pride in being one of a select group of international plutocrats, all of them his coreligionists:

They say we are a scattered nation—
I cannot tell—but we have scrambled up
More wealth by far then those that brag of faith.
There's Kirriah Jairim, the great Jew of Greece,
Myself in Malta, some in Italy,
Many in France, and wealthy every one—
Ay, wealthier far than any Christian.

Here, already full-blown, is the myth that was to be presented more than three hundred years later as sober fact (though it was still a myth) in a once-celebrated book on the subject by the German economic historian Werner Sombart—the Jew as the driving force of modern capitalism.

The Merchant of Venice also reflects a world of expanding commercial horizons, but there is a significant variation in the picture Shakespeare draws. When Barabas talks of one of his ships as an "argosy," he is using a glamorous new term—derived from the Adriatic port of Ragusa—which had only just established itself. (The earliest example cited by the *Oxford English Dictionary* dates from 1587, though in the form "ragusye" it can be found a little earlier.) In *The Merchant of Venice,* on the other hand, it is Antonio, not Shylock, who owns argosies, who sends out ships to regions as far apart as Mexico and Lebanon. Shylock, sticking to dry land, seems a very cautious creature in comparison. And there is nothing to suggest that his financial dealings are on the same scale as those of Barabas, either: no holdings in Antwerp or Lubeck or Moscow.

But if Barabas is in some respects the more modern figure, in others he is far more medieval, a survivor from mysteries and miracle plays. His name alone was enough to guarantee that at every turn an Elizabethan audience was reminded of his depraved spiritual status, just as surely as if he had been called Judas. It sent out a signal that, whatever else he was, he embodied the same principle of evil that had once preferred a robber and murderer to Christ, and the corrupt flesh to the spirit.

The religious implications of *The Jew of Malta* run right through the play. Most modern commentators tend to underrate them, but in an important essay, "The Theology of Marlowe's *The Jew of Malta,*" G. K. Hunter has shown just how far-reaching they are. Even the famous line in which Barabas celebrates his wealth, "Infinite riches in a little room," is a parody of a traditional Christian image, repeated by countless writers, contrasting the infinitude of Christ's power with the "little room" of the Virgin's womb. The cauldron into which Barabas falls had a long prehistory, too: it was a standard part of the iconography of Hell, a fit destination for a character who has many of the attributes of Antichrist.

How far Marlowe endorsed these theological underpinnings is an open question. Probably he felt divided about them, pulled this way and that. But there can be no doubt that he took them seriously, and that they form an essential part of the play's structure. In Shakespeare, by contrast, the religious elements are more diffuse. They are certainly present, but an essay entitled "The Theology of *The Merchant of Venice*" would sound much too diagrammatic and clear-cut.

There is at least one other major respect in which Marlowe and Shakespeare differ. In his essay on Marlowe, T. S. Eliot praises *The Jew of Malta* for its "terribly serious, even savage comic humor." Barabas is a "prodigious caricature"—and as such he represents "something which Shakespeare could not do, and which he did not want to do." This seems to me true, and its truth is reinforced when you juxtapose those passages where the two writers are superficially at their closest. "We Jews can fawn like spaniels," says Barabas—

I learned in Florence how to kiss my hand,
Heave up my shoulders when they call me dog,
And duck as low as any barefoot friar . . .

Compare and contrast Shylock, reminding Antonio of the insults he has endured:

Still have I borne it with a patient shrug,
For sufferance is the badge of all our tribe.
You call me misbeliever, cut-throat dog . . .

The gestures in Marlowe are theatrical and overdrawn: Barabas is mocking his situation, looking at himself from the outside. With Shylock, passion is uppermost, and every word carries its charge of feeling. Perhaps Marlowe's humor deserves to be called "terribly serious" in comparison with most other humor; but in comparison with Shakespeare, seriousness doesn't seem its most obvious quality.

A final word about caricature. That Marlowe was a master of the art is beyond dispute. Eliot quotes, among other things, the opening lines of the extraordinary speech in which Barabas regales his servant Ithamore with details of his criminal career:

As for myself, I walk abroad a-nights
And kill sick people groaning under walls:
Sometimes I go about and poison wells . . .

The unexpected touch of "groaning under walls," the clinching half-rhyme of "walls" and "wells"—this is powerful writing, and the whole speech is a virtuoso display. We aren't meant to take it literally: Barabas is sounding out Ithamore to see whether he will make a suitable accomplice, and he can't resist piling on the sinister absurdities.

Yet at least one detail ought to give us pause. When Marlowe worked in the reference to poisoning wells, he wasn't indulging in a flourish of his own, but drawing on a deep-rooted popular fantasy. The Jew as poisoner, often the Jewish physician as poisoner (and Barabas has "studied physic"), was a recurrent figure in the demonology of medieval Europe. During the Black Death, accusations of poisoning the water supply provoked massacres that cost innumerable Jewish lives: in many cases whole communities were wiped out. And the myth persisted into modern times, as part of the psychology and imagery of the more extreme varieties of anti-

Semitism. It provides a macabre link, indeed, between the last days of the two bloodiest tyrants of the twentieth century. Hitler ended the political testament that he dictated just before his death by enjoining his successors to maintain a merciless struggle against "the universal poisoner of all peoples, international Jewry." Stalin died convinced (or purporting to be convinced) that a group of Jewish doctors were planning to poison the Soviet leadership: the charge was dropped once he had gone, but had he lived there is no telling what fresh horrors it might have led to.

None of this means that we should not acknowledge the skill and dramatic force of *The Jew of Malta*—only that it is a play with which, if we have any sense of history at all, we can't expect to feel completely comfortable. And it is no bad thing to be reminded that caricature, so often celebrated as an end in itself, can be a problematic art. The best caricaturists do not always serve the best causes.

• 3 •

In the trial scene, tormented by the thought that Jessica has fled with Lorenzo, Shylock exclaims:

Would any of the stock of Barabas
Had been her husband, rather than a Christian.

Was Shakespeare recalling *The Jew of Malta* when he penned these lines? Quite possibly, but they might well have occurred to him even if Marlowe had never lived. Nobody in Elizabethan England needed to see a play to be reminded who Barabas was—the original Barabas, that is; and nobody needed to be told about Jews. Their image had been fixed by centuries of Christian teaching, and the broad presuppositions that went into the making of Shylock were far more important than any literary sources.

We start off with the assumption that Jews and Christians are implacably at odds. "How like a fawning publican he looks!" says Shylock when Antonio first enters—

I hate him for he is a Christian:
But more, for that in low simplicity

He lends out money gratis, and brings down
The rate of usance here with us in Venice.

"I hate him for he is a Christian"—the line could be made to sound almost perfunctory, a quick stock response before Shylock hurries on to the more personal issue of commercial antagonism. But that would be to miss its true resonance. For any Elizabethan audience, for any European audience at the time, it would have been a reminder that Jews were supposed to hate Christians by definition, with the same hatred that their ancestors had shown towards Christ. All Jews, on this view, bore responsibility for the original rejection of Christ's message, and for the Crucifixion.

There are many reminiscences of the New Testament in *The Merchant of Venice.* some are assigned to Shylock himself, and of these the most pointed is his reaction to Portia's speech about mercy. Deaf to her argument that without mercy none of us could hope for salvation, he returns to the attack:

My deeds upon my head! I crave the law . . .

According to St. Matthew, the crowd at the trial of Jesus cried out: "His blood be upon us, and on our children." In echoing their words, Shylock is renewing the ancestral curse.

Ultimately the degree of theological malice that was attributed to the Jews could admit of only one explanation. They were in league with the devil; indeed, they *were* the devil, in one of his guises. The first seeds of this belief had been planted by St. John, the most polemical of the four evangelists, when he reported Jesus as telling the Jews who rejected him : "You are of your father the devil." The Church Fathers and their successors took up the theme, and by the Middle Ages it had given rise to an enormous body of legend, superstition and calumny.

It is only against this background that the reference to Shylock as a devil can be fully understood. And not just the direct references (there are no less than nine of them in *The Merchant of Venice*), but the oblique ones, too. When Jessica says that "our house is hell," she may sound as though she is simply using a metaphor, but she is also reinforcing a view of her father that has already been put forward by characters as different as Antonio ("the devil can cite Scripture . . .") and the chattering servant Lancelot Gobbo: "Certainly the Jew is the very devil incarnation."

How much weight should we attach to such talk? Lancelot Gobbo is a clown; some of the remarks in the same vein made by other characters are not much more than routine jibes, and even the bitterest of them are only figures of speech. There is no suggestion that Shylock is *literally* a devil. He remains strictly human, first and last. But to his enemies, he is a human who still has a strong flavor of the devil about him; and to an Elizabethan audience, the fiery red wig that he almost certainly wore spelled out his ancestry even more insistently than anything that was actually said. It was the same kind of wig that had been worn by Marlowe's Barabas, and before that by both Judas and Satan in the old mystery plays.

The Jew of medieval myth was not just a devil in some abstract or generalized sense. His devilishness could take all too specific forms. He was a poisoner, as we have seen, and a sorcerer; he was accused of committing ritual murder, crucifying children and desecrating the Host.

None of these charges are alluded to in *The Merchant of Venice,* and in the half-romantic, half-naturalistic atmosphere of the play they would sound like grotesque anachronisms if they were. Yet once again, beneath the surface, the medieval legacy lingers on. In insisting on the terms of his bond, Shylock is proposing to commit ritual murder at one remove.

The origins of the pound of flesh story go back to antiquity, possibly to ancient India or Persia. In Western Europe the tale began to assume its modern form in the twelfth century, but in the earliest surviving versions there is no mention of Jews. It was only towards the end of the thirteenth century that a Jewish link was introduced, in a section of the anonymous Middle English poem *Cursor Mundi* ("The Course of the World"). This was also the first known appearance of the pound of flesh theme in English.

Cursor Mundi, which was probably written by a priest from

Northumbria, weaves together paraphrases of Scripture with the legend of the Holy Cross. In one of its episodes, set in Constantinople, a Christian craftsman working for "Queen Eline" (St. Helena, the mother of the emperor Constantine) borrows money from a Jew, and finds himself unable to pay it back. When the Jew goes to court to claim his pound of flesh, he is foiled in the usual way ("If you shed a drop of his blood . . ."). He curses the judges, and the Queen orders that his goods should be confiscated and his tongue cut out; but she relents after he promises to show her where the Cross is buried—"where your Lord's rood-tree lies."

There are two points of particular interest here. First, the poet sets up a connection, even if it is only an indirect one, between the pound of flesh and the Crucifixion. Secondly, he was writing against the background of Edward I's expulsion of the Jews in 1290. (In celebrating "Queen Eline" he may well have been paying tribute to Edward's mother, the strongly anti-Jewish Eleanor of Provence.) Shakespeare can hardly have been aware of it, but *The Merchant of Venice* picks up a thread that goes back across three centuries to the last days of medieval English Jewry.

In the later Middle Ages and the Renaissance the pound of flesh story gained in popularity, and so did the notion that the most appropriate candidate for the role of predator-creditor was a Jew. Versions with Jewish villains can be found in Italy (*Il Pecorone*), France, Germany, as far afield as Serbia, and new twists were still being added in Shakespeare's own time. In 1599, for instance, a play entitle *Moschus,* by an author who went under the name of Jacobus Francus, was performed at the University of Jena to celebrate the wedding of a lawyer and the daughter of a professor. Written in Latin, it features a student called Musophilus and a Shylock-figure called Rabbi Mosche (or Moschus) ben Jehuda. Musophilus falls into Moschus's clutches, but everything comes right for him after he reveals that one night, while taking shelter in a church, he saw a group of foreigners, Muschus among them, murder a child and drain off its blood.

In other words, he stumbled across a ritual murder. The

juxtaposition of themes in *Moschus* spells out what other versions of the story only hint at—that behind the usurer enforcing his bond there looms that ultimate bogeyman, the Jew intent on shedding Christian blood for its own sake. And that means that there is also, hovering in the background, an analogy with the sufferings of Christ Himself. At the most popular level, the ritual murder accusation belonged to the world of black magic: it was based on the belief that Jews, like witches, were desperate to obtain blood for supernatural purposes. But in its more "elevated" forms (which flourished in spite of being condemned by successive popes), the myth was closely associated with the Crucifixion. The commonest period for raising the alarm was around Easter.

An awareness of this tradition makes the flesh-bond in *The Merchant of Venice* seem marginally less disturbing. If Shakespeare had invented the whole business, you would feel that he was suffering from a nasty private phobia. As it is, he used material that came to hand, and he muted some of its uglier aspects.

Yet nothing can alter the fact that, seen through the eyes of the other characters, Shylock is a deeply threatening figure, and that the threat he poses is of a peculiarly primitive kind. He is intent on cutting, gouging and mutilating; he seeks to possess and devour. At a number of points, indeed, beginning with his first vow of revenge against Antonio—

I will feed fat the ancient grudge I bear him

there are hints, not perhaps of outright cannibalism, but of a cannibalistic impulse; and here too, though he probably arrived at it through the free play of imagination, Shakespeare comes close to a dark traditional prejudice—one of the darkest. Along with the other slanders they had to bear, Jews in the Middle Ages were not spared the accusation that they feasted on Christians when they could, literally ate them. It was one of the charges brought against the Jews of Paris and the Île de France, for example, when they were expelled by the young king Philip Augustus in 1182.

•

Such, then, were some of the materials out of which Shylock was fashioned—and few modern readers are likely to feel that they represent a very promising point of departure. Shakespeare would not have been Shakespeare if he had not moved on, if he had remained content with the stereotypes he inherited; but it was with stereotypes that he undoubtedly began.

CHAPTER TWO

Jews

· 1 ·

So far the Jews we have been considering have been fantasy figures, the product of somebody else's bad dream. But there were also real Jews, living in the real world.

Shakespeare was born at a time when the Jewish presence in western and central Europe was only a shadow of what it had been seventy or eighty years before. In the 1490s, the Jews had been expelled from Spain and Portugal; in the course of the sixteenth century they had been hammered by Reformation and Counter-Reformation alike. As a result, there was a major exodus eastwards, towards the Ottoman Empire and Poland and Lithuania. By 1570 most of the Jewish communities in the west had disappeared, and those that survived, in northern Italy and scattered parts of Germany, had suffered a sharp decline in numbers and influence.

In the 1570s, the tide began to turn. With the spread of mercantilist thinking, of policies designed to foster trade, the economic skills and international connections of the Jews came to seem too valuable an asset to cast aside. There was a revival of Jewish life in Italy; Jews were readmitted to German-speaking cities from which they had been expelled; new communities sprang up, pointing the way ahead. In the closing years of the sixteenth century—around the time that *The Merchant of Venice* was written—a group of refugees from Portugal established the first openly Jewish community in Amsterdam.

England remained on the outer edge of these developments. Officially there had been no Jews in the country for centuries. But a handful of Marranos, crypto-Jews from Spain and Portugal, made their way to London during the reign of Henry VIII, and a somewhat larger colony, numbering perhaps a hundred in all, established itself during the reign of Elizabeth. Its members played an important part in overseas trade; the most prominent of them, Hector Nunes, was also a physician, and—thanks to the foreign intelligence he was able to supply—an associate of Lord Burghley and Sir Francis Walsingham.

Outwardly the Elizabethan Marranos were Christians, but they retained many Jewish affiliations, and some of them may well have practiced Jewish ceremonies in private. Could Shakespeare have met them or observed them at close quarters? Yes—but there is absolutely nothing to show that he did.

There was one Marrano, however, whom he was bound to have known about. In 1593 the Queen's physician, the Portuguese-born Roderigo (or Ruy) Lopez, was accused of trying to poison her, together with the Portuguese Pretender, Don Antonio, at the instigation of the King of Spain. Although Lopez was an intriguer who had fished in dangerous political waters, the charge was fairly obviously trumped up: the Queen herself gave every sign of not believing in it. But Lopez had made some powerful enemies, including the Earl of Essex. At his trial both the prosecutor, Sir Edward Coke, and the judges laid special stress on his being a Jew—"worse than Judas himself," according to Coke. He was eventually convicted (on the basis of a confession extracted under threat of torture) and hung, drawn and quartered at Tyburn in June 1594. On the gallows he protested that he loved the Queen and

Antonio "as well as he loved Jesus Christ." The mob responded with laughs, jeers and cries of "He is a Jew!"

The case caused an immense sensation, and it is hard to believe that it didn't make a strong impression on Shakespeare. Stephen Dedalus in *Ulysses* was sure that it must have done:

> All events brought grist to his mill. Shylock chimes with the jewbaiting that followed the hanging and quartering of the queen's leech Lopez, his jew's heart being plucked forth while the sheeny was yet alive . . .

This seems to imply that Lopez's sufferings were transmuted by Shakespeare into Shylock's savage thoughts about Antonio ("I will have the heart of him if he forfeit"). It is a suggestive idea, but one that lies beyond the realm of proof or disproof; and any systematic attempt to equate Shylock and Lopez is bound to founder on the differences between them. Lopez—the Lopez portrayed by his enemies, the poisoner and conspirator—had far more in common with Barabas in *The Jew of Malta,* a play that was successfully revived while his trial was still in progress.

A number of commentators have argued that there are none the less two direct allusions to the Lopez affair in *The Merchant of Venice.* The first is Shakespeare's use of the name Antonio (but it is a common enough Italian name, and one that he seems to have been rather fond of—there are characters called Antonio in *The Two Gentlemen of Verona, Much Ado About Nothing, Twelfth Night* and *The Tempest*). The second, more interesting suggestion, is that there is a veiled reference to Lopez in Gratiano's tirade against Shylock in the trial scene:

> *Thy currish spirit*
> *Governed a wolf, who—hanged for human slaughter—*
> *Even from the gallows did his fell soul fleet,*
> *And whilst thou layest in thy unhallowed dam*
> *Infused itself in thee . . .*

"Lopez," it has been pointed out, recalls *lupus,* the Latin for "wolf." But the allusion, if there was one, would presumably have been lost on most of Shakespeare's audience; and human predators were often compared to wolves anyway. That doesn't mean, on the other hand, that memories of Lopez weren't still fresh at the time *The Merchant of Venice* was first performed, or that Gratiano's ferocity doesn't retain something of the mood that the case provoked. There must have been lots of Gratianos in the crowd that watched Lopez being dismembered and disembowelled on the scaffold.

After the Lopez affair the Marrano community in London went into decline, although it didn't finally disappear until 1609. In that year it was split in two by a quarrel. One faction denounced the other to the authorities as "Judaizers"; as a result of the investigation that followed, all Portuguese merchants suspected of being crypto-Jews were expelled from the country.

The Marranos were not the only Jews in Tudor London. A second group arrived during the reign of Henry VIII—musicians from Italy who had been recruited by royal command in order to raise the level of music at court. They and their families stayed on, and the most successful of them established important dynasties of performers and instrument makers. Unlike the Marranos, they were fairly quickly absorbed into English society. Most of their children married Christian partners; their descendants were unaffected by the expulsion of 1609. They remained aware of their origins, however, and in the view of one present-day historian, Roger Prior, it is likely that all the families concerned continued to think of themselves as in some sense Jewish "at least until 1600, and probably beyond."

Among the most prominent members of the group were the Bassano family, who came from Venice. The name, so close to Bassanio, suggests tantalizing Shakespearean possibilities; so does the fact that one of the family, Emilia Bassano—after her marriage, Emilia Lanier—has been identified by A. L. Rowse with the Dark Lady of the Sonnets. If the identification could be proved, it would set one thinking afresh about many aspects of Shakespeare's work, including (needless to say) his attitude towards Jews in *The Merchant of Venice.* But few fellow-scholars have been convinced by Dr.

Rowse's theory, and it remains no more than an interesting speculation.*

• 2 •

There had been a time, before the expulsion of 1290, when London had been open to Jews and Venice had been closed. For hundreds of years the Venetian authorities refused to countenance Jewish settlement, or even to permit Jewish merchandise to be carried on ships flying the Venetian flag. Individual Jews found their way into the city, however, and in the course of the fourteenth century their presence was formally if reluctantly recognized. Then, in 1397, they were forced to withdraw to the town of Mestre, on the mainland, and only allowed to transact their affairs in Venice for a few days at a time. (Mestre is the home of the moneylender in *Il Pecorone.*) On those occasions when they did return to the city, they were compelled to wear first, a circular yellow badge, and then, because they became adept at concealing it, a yellow hat.

It was not until the early sixteenth century that permanent settlement was resumed. In 1509 Jews were among the refugees who arrived in Venice from Mestre and other mainland cities in flight from the victorious armies of the League of Cambrai. On account of their economic usefulness the government allowed them to stay, but in the face of calls for their expulsion it decided to confine them to a specially designated part of the city. In 1516 the Venetian Senate passed a decree ordering them to move to an island known as the Ghetto Nuevo (the name means "new foundry"); in 1541 an adjoining island, the Ghetto Vecchio, or Old Ghetto, was assigned to Jews from the Levant.

Even then their position was precarious. In 1571, after the victory over the Turks at Lepanto, the Senate voted to expel all Jews

* *In 1611 Emilia Lanier published a poem about the life of Christ,* Salve Deus Rex Judaeorum *("Hail, God, King of the Jews")—a title which she claimed had come to her many years earlier in a dream. It is notable for its strong feminist sentiments, but almost wholly conventional in its account of the part played by the Jews in the Crucifixion—"The Jewish wolves, that did our Saviour bite."*

from the city. But the decree was never carried out, and by the end of the Turkish war, three years later, it had been effectively reversed. Jews from the Levant, who played an increasingly important part in Venice's Balkan trade, were encouraged to settle; so were Marranos. In 1550 there had been less than 1,000 Jews in the ghetto. By 1600 there were at least 2,500.

The ghetto system, which was subsequently adopted, along with the name "ghetto," by other Italian cities, remained in force until the era of the French Revolution. It had a clear purpose: to enable Jews to take part in economic life, while setting strict limits on their participation in social life. The Venice ghetto was surrounded by high walls; the gates, which were manned by Christian watchmen, were locked from sunset to dawn, and any Jew found outside after hours was subject to a heavy fine. In reality Shylock would no more have felt free to dine with Bassanio, as he does in the play, then Bassanio would have felt free to invite him.

The world inside the ghetto was a complicated one. It consisted of three separate communities or "nations," each with its own traditions and institutions, and its own subdivisions, too—the "German Nation," the "Levantine Nation" and the "Ponentine" or "Western Nation," made up of Spanish Jews and Marranos. In time the differences between the three began to fade, but at the end of the sixteenth century they were still sharply defined—and historically, as Cecil Roth pointed out, Shylock could only have been a member of the German Nation, the *Nazione Tedesca.* The Levantines and Westerners were merchants, specializing in foreign trade; the "Germans" were the only group in the ghetto permitted to practice moneylending.

To be a "German" didn't necessarily imply that one was an immigrant, or the child of immigrants. The German Nation was the oldest and most numerous of the three communities; many of its members belonged to families that had lived in Italy for generations. But there are two aspects of Shylock which suggest, perhaps inadvertently, that he or his family might be more recent arrivals. He doesn't have an Italianized name, and we know that he has had business dealings in Frankfurt: it was there that he paid 2,000 ducats for the diamond that Jessica steals from him.

This has some bearing on those modern productions in which Shylock is portrayed as a Jew of Eastern European origins, with a Yiddish accent. One's first reaction is that such an interpretation is hopelessly anachronistic and inauthentic; but it was at any rate the case that many members of the German Nation spoke Yiddish until well into the seventeenth century. On the other hand there is nothing in the play to suggest that Shylock does not speak the same flawless English as the other characters—that Shakespeare would certainly have been capable of fitting him out with a distinctive accent if he had wanted to. You only have to think of Dr. Caius the funny Frenchman in *The Merry Wives of Windsor,* or Fluellen the Welshman, Jamy the Scotsman and Macmorris the stage Irishman in *Henry V*.

In a sense all this is beside the point, since Shakespeare's knowledge of Jewish life in Venice was clearly very limited. It is true that in a number of respects the picture he draws coincides with actual conditions. He is right, for example, in his assumption that Shylock's legal status is that of an alien. (Until the end of the eighteenth century no Jew, however long his ancestors had lived in the city, could become a Venetian citizen.) But there are also mistakes, such as the notion that a Jew would have been allowed to have a Christian servant living in his house, in the way that Lancelot Gobbo does; and there is one omission that is enough in itself to imply large depths of ignorance elsewhere. Not only are we shown Shylock going to dine outside the ghetto; nowhere in the play is there any mention of the ghetto, or any indication that it ever existed.

A work of art must be taken on its own terms, and nobody needs to know much about Venice itself in order to appreciate Shakespeare's Venice. But if one stands back, it is hard not to sigh a little over the gulf between the world of Shylock and the real world of his Venetian coreligionists.

The ghetto was badly overcrowded. Living in it was both constricting and demeaning, as it was meant to be. Yet within its bounds there was an exceptionally high degree of social and cultural vitality. For the most part "culture" inevitably meant religion, whether it manifested itself in education or public festivals, ceremonial art or a multitude of charitable organizations. Religious learning flourished: sixteenth-century Venice was particularly famous as a center of Hebrew printing and publishing. But the community also produced doctors, poets, musicians and craftsmen, and humanists versed in Latin and Italian—for there were far more cultural contacts between Christians and Jews than those high walls might lead one to suppose. In 1558, for example, a play called *Esther* was performed in the ghetto. (The author, Salomon Usque, was a poet whose other literary activities included translating Petrarch into Spanish.) The following year it was performed again before an audience of Venetian nobility and gentry.

Anyone reading a history of the ghetto will encounter some remarkable personalities. But one figure stands out, partly for his gifts, partly because he has left a graphic account of his career. Leone da Modena (1571–1648) was a distinguished rabbi, although before he was ordained he earned his living in a wide variety of other ways—as a teacher, a letter-writer, a legal clerk, a proofreader, a composer of dedicatory poems. He was renowned both for his sermons and for the breadth of his learning, and many Christians consulted him or sought him out. Among those who did were a number of Englishmen. They included Sir Henry Wotton, the English ambassador to Venice, and it was at Wotton's request that in 1614 he agreed to write an account of Jewish religious practices for King James I. Subsequently published (in 1637) under the title *Historia de' riti hebraici,* it was to remain a standard work for generations.*

Modena is best known today for his autobiography, *The Life of Judah,* which only came to light in the nineteenth century. Written in Hebrew—Judah was one of his Hebrew names—it gives a fascinating account of a world saturated with religion, which still found room for astrology and alchemy; of an intensely Jewish

* *Wotton, a friend of John Donne and the subject of a memorable brief biography by Izaak Walton, also merits a passing mention in the annals of the Jacobean stage. In a letter written at the time he gives an account of the blaze that destroyed the Globe theater in 1613, after it had caught fire during a performance of* Henry VIII.

existence, which nonetheless remained open to other cultures. (A single symbolic instance: at the age of thirteen he wrote a poem which can be read so that it makes sense—the same kind of sense—in either Hebrew or Italian.) The picture of life that emerges from the book is richly detailed, and often admirable and animated. But it is far from idyllic. We learn a good deal about the author's disappointments, his quarrels, his poverty, his compulsive gambling, and we are given a brutal reminder that the ghetto had its seamy side—an account of how his youngest son was murdered by a gang of Jewish toughs with whom he had fallen out.

The Life of Judah is a long way from Shakespeare, but you can't help wishing that Shakespeare had been able to read it. Modena offers us a self-portrait which, as Natalie Zemon Davis has written, "Is discrepant from Shylock on almost very page: a Jew who chances his money with thriftless abandon, who cries for revenge against Jewish slayers of his son, who basks in Christian admiration, and who invokes against Christian scorn not merely a common humanity, as Shylock does, but an ancient lineage and learning."

There is one discrepancy that seems especially sad, a gap that divides Shylock not only from Modena, but from countless other Jews as well. One of the great positive values of *The Merchant of Venice* is music. It is the symbol of moral harmony: "the man that hath no music in himself" is dangerous. And Shylock, in his denunciation of the carnival, has marked himself down as just such a creature.

In reality, Jews not only had their own liturgical music; they also made an important contribution to the general musical life of the Renaissance. The court musicians who were imported by Henry VIII have already been mentioned, and they belonged to a well-established tradition.

In Venice itself, there were schools of music and dancing run by Jewish instructors as early as the 1440s, at a time when Jews were still officially barred from the city; and in due course the ghetto developed its own musical culture. It is true that the more rigidly orthodox rabbis condemned secular music as sinful, and stood firm against any changes being made in the traditional music of the liturgy. But they didn't necessarily get their way. Leone da Modena, for one, resisted. He had taught music himself, and his favorite son-in-law was a dancing master; he defended the introduction of choral singing in synagogues, and served as director of a musical academy set up by refugees from what had previously been (until its Jewish population was expelled) the foremost center of Jewish musical activity in Italy, Mantua.

In the end, the restrictions of ghetto existence took their toll almost everywhere. Jewish participation in secular culture was held back, and the promise of the Renaissance era had to wait until the nineteenth century for its fulfillment. It is only right to add that the ghetto also had its great strengths, both moral and intellectual; but that is a story that would take us too far from our subject.

• 3 •

Although Shylock is a figure rooted in Christian myth, many of his Jewish beliefs and practices are true to life. The first thing we learn about him in this respect—indeed, our first intimation that he is a Jew—is his strict adherence to dietary laws. When Bassanio asks him to dine, he doesn't merely refuse, he recoils:

> Yes, to smell pork, to eat of the habitation which your prophet the Nazarite conjured the devil into. I will buy with you, sell with you, talk with you, walk with you, and so following; but I will not eat with you, drink with you, nor pray with you.

It is unlikely, to say the least, that any Jew would have responded like this in reality. (He would certainly have been asking for trouble if he had.) It is equally unlikely that anyone who felt so vehemently on the subject would have changed his mind and accepted Bassanio's invitation shortly afterwards. Yet there is a core of psychological realism in the scene. Shakespeare conveys effectively enough that Shylock is in the grip of a fierce taboo, and that it is experienced by Bassanio and the other Christians as an act of rejection.

Shylock is also eager to score a point. "How can you deny that there is anything wrong with the flesh of a pig, if Jesus himself, with the whole of creation to choose from, elected to conjure the devils that he had cast out into the Gadarene swine?"

Possibly Shakespeare had picked up some notion of the Jew as disputant, dialectician, scrutinizer of texts. But it is the New Testament rather than the Old that he makes Shylock cite—both here and, even less plausibly, a moment later, when Antonio first appears. "How like a fawning publican he looks!"—the reference is to the parable in Luke which contrasts the Pharisee ("God, I thank thee that I am not as other men are") with the publican or tax-collector ("God be merciful to me a sinner"). Psychologically, the line carries a powerful charge. Shylock has every reason to mistrust Antonio, and in lampooning the idea of false humility, he is reasserting his own pride. Fawning was one of the things Jews were supposed to be good at: Barabas in *The Jew of Malta* has learned to fawn like a spaniel. Well, here is one Jew who isn't prepared to fawn—least of all now, when Bassanio is being friendly to him, when even Antonio shows signs of being civil. But he still uses New Testament allusion to underline his resolve.

As soon as he and Antonio clash, however, it is to the Old Testament that he turns. The question of the loan is raised; Antonio confirms that under normal circumstances he neither pays nor charges interest; Shylock counters with a story:

When Jacob grazed his uncle Laban's sheep—
This Jacob from our holy Abram was
(As his wise mother wrought in his behalf)
The third possessor; ay, he was the third—

Not surprisingly, Antonio interrupts: "And what of him, did he take interest?" It is bad enough to be side-tracked by an apparent digression; it is even worse when one digression leads on to another. But for Shylock, these are essential points. In justifying himself, he goes back to the beginning, to the patriarchs. He has just reflected, in an aside, on how Antonio "hates our sacred nation." Now, as though in direct response, he invokes "our holy Abram." And this pride in the original convenant between God and the Jews is matched by faith in its transmission. For if Abraham was the founding father, Jacob was the foremost example of the inheritor who passed the legacy on. Indeed, as Israel—the alternative name that

God conferred on him—he might almost be said to have founded the succession all over again.

But Antonio's question still stands. Did Jacob take interest? Shylock hems and haws—no, not exactly—and then, in a dozen lines or so, proceeds to explain what happened. Jacob had spent many years working for his uncle (and father-in-law) Laban. They agreed that as payment, before he returned home, he should receive all the lambs in Laban's flocks that were born spotted or speckled. Then he devised an artful plan, based on the belief that offspring are influenced by what the mother sees during conception. He took a number of twigs, peeled off their bark so that they were a mixture of dark and light, and planted them in sight of the ewes that were mating. In due course a large number of parti-colored lambs were born—"This was a way to thrive, and he was blest."

The speech in which Shylock unfolds this story has its own strange flower, at once exotic and deeply English. (You can almost hear a Warwickshire accent coming through.) It is also the most obviously biblical speech in the whole of Shakespeare: he follows the original account in Genesis as closely as on other occasions he followed Holinshed or North's translation of Plutarch. But Antonio is unmoved. In the first place, he insists that Jacob's scheme was a "venture"—a speculation. There was no guarantee that it was going to work: its success depended on divine favor. Secondly, he objects to the implied analogy between living creatures, rams and ewes, and dead metals, gold and silver. And finally, what bearing does the whole business have on the point at issue? "Was this inserted to make interest good?"

It is hard not to feel a certain sympathy. The curious thing is that, if Shylock was determined to cite Scripture, he need have looked no further than the fateful, much-invoked verse in Deuteronomy (xxiii. 20) which permits the charging of interest on loans to "strangers," or foreigners (though not on loans made to "brothers"). Instead, he launches into a story that has no obvious connection with usury, and that doesn't seem to offer much by way of a moral beyond the general lesson that you must make the most of your opportunities—*les affaires sont les affaires.*

The full biblical account of Jacob's dealings with Laban leaves a somewhat different impression of their relationship. Jacob had been amply provoked: Laban was a tough customer, who had cheated him out of the reward he had been promised for seven years' labor. Yet the picture that Shylock paints is true as far as it goes. The Jacob we encounter in Genesis is a visionary and a servant of the Lord, but he is also a schemer: he plans, perseveres, uses duplicity when it suits him. And Shylock goes out of his way to remind us of the most notorious of his stratagems. Inspired and guided by Rebecca, his "wise mother," he disguised himself as his brother Esau, tricked his father, Isaac, whose eyes had grown dim with age, and received the blessing that would otherwise have gone to Esau as the first-born. In this way he ensured that he was third in line from Abraham—"ay, he was the third." Shylock is emphatic; perhaps over-emphatic, as though he were quelling possible objections.

Even among the devout, the story of the stolen blessing has often proved a stumbling block. If we were reading about one of the exploits of Odysseus, say, we could rejoice in his guile and leave it at that. But from a patriarch, a party to the Covenant, we look for a bracing moral example, and what we are given instead is at best an unresolved conflict of ends and means. It was right for Jacob to receive the blessing. It was wrong of him to resort to sharp practice in order to make sure of it. Perhaps he should have simply trusted to fate. But he was still the right candidate: Esau—the wild, impulsive Esau—would have been a disaster.

For Shylock, there are no problems. He sees Jacob as a wholly exemplary figure, almost a guardian spirit: later in the play he reinforces his sense of kinship with him when he swears "by Jacob's staff." This was the staff that Jacob carried when he first set out alone across the Jordan to join Laban. It was an emblem of his endurance and his eventual prosperity.

Whether Shakespeare had his own misgivings about Jacob's career it is impossible to say.* Certainly he could have found res-

* *In Hebrew, as Esau emphasizes after he finds that he has been cheated, one of the meanings of "Jacob" is "supplanter." Ruskin thought that the adverse associations of the name lingered in Shakespeare's mind and surfaced again in the names of Iago and of Iachimo in* Cymbeline.

ervations expressed in the most respectable quarters. In the "Bishop's Bible," for example, which was the version of the Bible he probably knew best, the story of Isaac's blessing was accompanied by a disapproving marginal comment: "Jacob was not without fault, no might have tarried until God had changed his father's mind." Still, there were limits beyond which no Christian could go, or would have wanted to go, in criticizing a figure who had played such a decisive role in sacred history. Jacob was also the pilgrim who had wrestled with the angel, the same Jacob who had been entrusted with the promise of divine redemption. It was entirely natural for John Donne, for example, to invoke him at the most solemn moment of one of his most magnificent sermons: "They shall awake as Jacob did, and say as Jacob said, Surely the Lord is in this place, and this is no other but the house of God, and the gate of heaven."

Reverence for the Old Testament could of course coexist with hostile feelings toward Jews. We are meant to think of Shylock as misusing his biblical heritage—misappropriating it, even, since it now belongs to Christianity. Yet there is a degree of empathy with him as he makes his case, and a relative absence of caricature, that prevent the image of the moneylender and the image of the patriarch from being kept completely distinct.

This was ultimately to provide posterity with an opening for a more positive reading of the part, a revaluation. Jacob, whatever his imperfections, was a figure robed in grandeur; and the time would come, implausible though it might have seemed to an Elizabethan, when actors and commentators began to see some of that grandeur clinging to Shylock.

There are a number of other explicitly Jewish touches in the play. Shylock swears an oath "by our holy Sabbath." Recalling Genesis once again (on this occasion, the story of Ishmael), he refers to Lancelot Gobbo as "that fool of Hagar's offspring." At a crucial turn in the plot, he tells his countryman Tubal to meet him "at our synagogue"—a summons which sounds innocuous enough today, and can be made to sound deeply impressive, but one which would have carried inescapably sinister overtones for most members of the original audience.

When all the details have been added up, it is still possible to wonder whether they amount to more than external trappings. How far is Shylock "really" Jewish? A delicate question, to which any answer has to be subjective: but that doesn't mean that it isn't a question worth asking.

The most direct modern attempt to grapple with it that I know occurs in Harold Fisch's book *The Dual Image.* "It is often said," Fisch writes,

> that in Shylock, Shakespeare penetrated into the psychology of the Jew. There *is* something Jewish about him certainly, or shall we say something of the Jew of the *Galut* [the Hebrew term for the Diaspora], in his dark and gloomy resentments, his feverish care of his possessions, his sense of family (he prizes the jewel left him by his dead wife), his loyalty to his fellow Jews, his love of his daughter, his gestures, his faith in the absolute validity of the written bond (the stress on this is a master-stroke), his appeal to law as against sentiment.

One could argue about the details, but much of this seems to me true. It helps to explain, I think, why Jewish actors and audiences have so often been attracted by *The Merchant of Venice,* rather than angered or repelled. I am not sure, on the other hand, that the emphasis on "dark," "gloomy," "feverish" isn't excessive. Professor Fisch used to teach at Bar-Ilan University in Tel Aviv; to some extent he seems to me to be putting forward an excessively Israeli view of the Diaspora and its history.

Where I find myself in complete agreement with him is in his diagnosis of what is missing: "the whole region of Jewish spirituality." There is no hint in Shylock of an inner faith, or of religion as a way of life, as opposed to a set of rules. Not that Fisch complains. Given the circumstances under which Shakespeare was working—his limited knowledge of Jews, the built-in assumptions of his society—it could hardly have been otherwise, and the wonder is that he humanized his Jew as much as he did. But the fact remains that he also left out, in Fisch's phrase, "the tap-root of his historical existence." Shylock's stage-Judaism is a pseudoreligion, a fabrication: there is no true piety in it, and nothing to hold him back as he pursues his revenge.

CHAPTER THREE

Three Thousand Ducats

· 1 ·

Shylock reveals a great deal of himself with his opening words. "Three thousand ducats." The phrase can be spoken dryly or slyly or thoughtfully; it can be savored or rasped out. But however it is delivered, it identifies Shylock from the outset with the spirit of calculation—and money.

Money plays a pervasive role in *The Merchant of Venice.* The action of both the main plots in the play is set in motion by a group of people of whom, with the exception of Antonio, we know nothing: Bassanio's creditors. Bassanio assures Antonio that his "chief care" is to repay them. To achieve that end he hopes to marry an heiress, but first he needs a further loan to finance his wooing. Antonio, however, is unable to help him directly, as he has in the past, since his entire capital is currently locked up in a series of business ventures.

We are in a world where no one can have any doubts about the power of the purse. Yet Shylock stands alone. With Portia, Antonio, Bassanio, we are encouraged to think less in terms of money than of wealth—a positive good. Shylock, by contrast, embodies money-power in its most naked form. His profession is enough to establish his harsh nature, even before we see him in action: he may resent having the opprobrious word applied to him, but in the eyes of everyone else he is a usurer.

The Elizabethans, like their medieval predecessors, were brought up to think of lending money at interest—any interest—as a grievous sin. The whole weight of Christian teaching was against it, from the Gospels onwards: it was denounced by the Church Fathers, and inveighed against in innumerable sermons. Until the middle years of the sixteenth century it was also a criminal offense. It had been sanctioned for the first time between 1545 and 1552, but it was only in 1571 that the ban against it was finally lifted. And even then the act which legalized it contained a sop to traditional opinion, a section declaring that "all usury being forbidden by the law of God is sin and detestable."

There had always been a gulf between moral doctrine and economic reality. Men needed to raise money, and other men were willing to provide it—at a price. In the Middle Ages, as R. H. Tawney wrote, the whole mass of legislation and legal commentary on the subject of usury was "in itself a proof of the prevalence of lending and borrowing." With the economic expansion of the Tudor period, the demand for credit inevitably increased still further. There were as yet few professional moneylenders. Most loans were negotiated as a sideline by neighbors with capital to spare—farmers and yeomen in the countryside, shopkeepers and tradesmen in town. But if the system was haphazard, it was also on its way to becoming ubiquitous. By the latter part of the sixteenth century—to quote Tawney again—"agriculture, industry and foreign trade were largely dependent on credit."

The act of 1571 was designed to regulate an existing reality. It acknowledged the hard facts, and sought to soften them: the maximum permissible rate of interest was fixed at 10 percent. But old sentiments persisted, and denunciations of usury went on unabated. Everyone knew, for a start, that the new law was frequently broken. Lenders squeezed out a good deal more than 10 percent where they could; a poor man might easily find himself having to pay a local shark a penny a month—100 percent—for the loan of a shilling, or even a penny a week. But it was not just exorbitant rates of interest that preachers and moralists attacked. For two or three generations after 1571, until well past Shakespeare's time, they continued to condemn the taking of interest *per se,* in the old medieval manner. And though the term usury was often used loosely, to indicate any kind of extortion or one-sided bargain, the usage itself was significant. For the traditionally minded, money-lending at a profit remained the very type of exploitation.

Here, at least, there was no sharp break between the Catholic past and the Protestant present. Anglican writers against usury drew freely on the work of their pre-Reformation predecessors—men like Miles Mosse, for instance, whose *Arraignment and Conviction of Usury* (1595) was dedicated, by permission, to the Archbishop of Canterbury. Among the learned, religious objections were backed up by appeals to classical antiquity—to Plato and Plutarch, Cato and Seneca; above all to Aristotle, who had argued that there was something unnatural about the idea of inorganic matter like money reproducing itself.

When did friendship take
A breed of barren metal for a friend?

A breed of barren metal: Antonio, remonstrating with Shylock, makes the traditional Aristotelian assumption. And as for popular opinion, which did not need to cite the philosophers, it remained as hostile to usury as ever.

If anything, the hostility intensified as the sixteenth century wore on. Moneylenders were roughly handled by moralists, satirists and pamphleteers, in terms that varied little from writer to writer. They were also familiar figures on the stage. Jonson and the other Elizabethan and Jacobean dramatists created a whole swarm of them—Gripe, Hornet, Bloodhound, Lucre; Moth Interest, Perfidious Oldcraft, Sir Tyrant Thrift. Their names proclaimed their nature.

In many respects Shylock conforms to the conventional type.

He is old, as usurers were generally assumed to be. He pretends that he has to raise the money for his loan to Antonio from a friend—a standard trick. Like other stage usurers, he keeps his servant short of food. And although his cruelty raises its own particular frisson, it deserves to be put in perspective. Most moneylenders in Elizabethan literature were thoroughly sadistic. They were shown rejoicing at the thought of debtors wasting away in jail; it was a common saying that they were ready to make dice of their victims' bones.

There were other conventions that Shakespeare rejected, traditions which would have pushed his portrait much further in the direction of unqualified caricature if he had made use of them. Shylock is one of the very few stage usurers who isn't described as physically repellent, for example. Nor is he plagued by those supposedly characteristic diseases of usury, dropsy and gout. He is frugal in his habits, but apart from his treatment of Lancelot Gobbo the impression he gives is one of sobriety rather than stinginess. We never see him gloating over his gold, or worshipping the goddess Pecunia—indeed, we never see him practicing his everyday trade. The truth is that usury is only one aspect of his character, and in the end not the one that interested Shakespeare most. He is driven by resentment and a perverted sense of justice rather than greed.

At the same time the money theme keeps reverberating through the play. In the midst of his rage, after Jessica has eloped, Shylock still finds time to recall that his hatred of Antonio has a sound commercial rationale: "Were he out of Venice, I can make what merchandise I will." And in the scene where he accompanies Antonio on his way to prison, he exults not only in the ruin of an enemy, but also in the showing-up of an economic fallacy: "This is the fool that lent out money gratis." The clash between the two men may ultimately be one of beliefs and world views, but economic conflict remains an essential part of it.

• 2 •

The most solid money in the play is Portia's. It is old money, clean money: she knows nothing of bargaining or trading or "well-won thrift." True, somebody's thrift must have amassed the family fortune in the first place—her "ever-virtuous" father, perhaps, or, more probably, one of his less virtuous forebears. But that was a long time ago. What is important about the money now is that it sustains Belmont and all that Belmont stands for.

"In Belmont is a lady richly left . . ." Enumerating Portia's virtues in the opening scene, Bassanio goes straight to the point. She is wealthy. But anyone who supposes that we are meant to mark him down as a narrow-eyed opportunist simply isn't hearing the music of Shakespeare's lines. She is also fair,

and, fairer, than that word,
Of wondrous virtues . . .

If this is rhetoric, it is rhetoric that carries conviction. Wealth wouldn't have been enough in itself to make Portia what she is, but it is indissolubly bound up with her other attractions. She positively glows with it:

her sunny locks
Hang on her temples like a golden fleece . . .

It is part of her natural coloring.

Her first appearance, in the scene that follows, bring us firmly back to earth. "By my troth, Nerissa, my little body is aweary of this great world." Hard on the heels of Bassanio's poetry, we find ourselves confronted by some unsentimental prose. Portia chafes under the tyrannous conditions that her father's will has imposed on her; she compiles a scathing catalogue of her unsuitable suitors; she quickly establishes that she can be warn, cool, hard, soft, witty, imperious. In other words, she is a living woman rather than a fixed icon—a woman capable of development and change.

One element remains constant, however. She is the only major figure in the play for whom money is no problem, and it gives her a confidence and spaciousness that none of the other characters enjoy. At every stage she speaks with the accents of privilege—enlightened privilege, but privilege all the same.

From such a position, Shylock's bond at first seems the mere buzzing of an insect, easily brushed aside. By the standards of Belmont, three thousand ducats is a minor consideration:

What, no more?
Pay him six thousand, and deface the bond.
Double six thousand, and then treble that . . .

But Shylock is implacable, and Portia soon learns that if she wants to save Antonio, money isn't enough: she has to give of herself.

Her other great act of giving is the speech with which she accepts Bassanio after he has chosen the right casket. She pledges herself to him as a wife; and that means—such was the law at that time, and for hundreds of years afterwards—that she makes her property over to him as well:

But now I was the lord
Of this fair mansion, master of my servants,
Queen o'er myself; and even now, but now,
This house, these servants, and this same myself
Are yours, my lord's.

In real life, we might tremble a little at the thought of her fortune falling into the hands of such a proven profligate. But the fairytale conventions of the story don't allow for the possibility that things could end badly. Belmont's future, like the lovers' happiness, is secure.

Socially, too, Bassanio makes an appropriate consort for Portia. He is "a scholar and a soldier"; he has strong aristocratic connections (he first came to Belmont in the company of the Marquis of Montferrat), and it seems entirely natural for Portia, when she accepts him, to address him as "Lord Bassanio." Nor would the Elizabethans have found anything incongruous in the idea of an aristocrat or near-aristocrat living on borrowed money, as he has been doing for a long time when we first meet him. Far from it. Maintaining an estate, and the style of life that went with it, could be a ruinous business, and many of the most famous courtiers of the age were heavily in debt—Sir Philip Sidney, for example. The Earl of Southampton, Shakespeare's patron, was forced to mortgage every scrap of land he owned; the Earl of Leicester owed over £60,000 at the time of his death, the equivalent of many millions in modern terms.*

If Bassanio were pitted directly against Shylock, the play would be a simple clash between two opposing worlds: Belmont (to which Bassanio belongs in spirit, even before he meets Portia) versus the Rialto. But what Shakespeare wrote was more complicated, and much more interesting. As the kinsman and friend of Antonio, Bassanio also has his inescapable links with the Venetian money-world, and it is Antonio who is Shylock's principal antagonist. There is a contrast in the play between Belmont and Venice, and a much sharper contrast within Venice itself, between two versions of capitalism.

The commonest mistake that people make about *The Merchant of Venice* is to suppose that the title refers to Shylock rather than Antonio. This is partly a tribute to the fact that Shylock is the more memorable character, but it is also a sign of how thoroughly Antonio has thrown off any taint of the countinghouse. He is a friend, a generous benefactor, a melancholic, a potential martyr. By comparison, his trading activities can easily be made to seem a mere sideshow, not much more than a plot mechanism for putting him at Shylock's mercy.

Yet a merchant is what he is, on the grand scale. The scope of his activities sets him apart from "petty traffickers"; his ships are on their way home

> *From Tripolis, from Mexico and England,*
> *From Lisbon, Barbary and India. . . .*

Technically speaking, "Mexico" is a mistake on Shakespeare's part, since Venice was excluded from the markets of Spanish America. This means that Antonio's ventures are even more far-flung than the

* *Exact figures are impossible to work out. Shylock's loan of three thousand ducats was worth around £700 in Elizabethan money: a good round sum, which would run into six figures today, although Shakespeare scaled it down from his original. In* Il Pecorone *the merchant borrows ten thousand ducats.*

most successful Venetian merchant's would have been in reality. And there are no half-measures about them: he has invested in them up to the hilt, with every ducat he has.

He is also a kind of one-man charitable foundation, lending out money gratis, and delivering debtors from Shylock's grasp. These are good deeds, but they are only possible because he can afford them: they are what he chooses to do with the money he has already made. Like any merchant, his first aim has to be to show a profit.

On the subject of profit, however, he is strangely silent. It is hard to picture him driving a bargain, or calculating a rate of return. He prefers to talk about friendship, and he leaves it to Shylock to remind us that very little business in the Rialto is conducted in the spirit of pure loving-kindness. The mainspring of a mercantile society is the hope of gain.

Between them, Antonio and Shylock represent two extreme versions of Economic Man, one benevolent, the other malign. Jekyll-Antonio embodies the fantasy that you can enjoy the benefits of economic enterprise, and confer them on your society, without being competitive and self-assertive. Hyde-Shylock is the capitalist as total predator, conferring good on no one except himself. They are twin aspects of the same phenomenon; and a tremendous amount of the play's energy is spent keeping them apart.

• 3 •

Critics sometimes complain that too much has been made of Shylock's Jewishness; that he is a usurer first, a Jew second. It is unlikely, however, that many members of an Elizabethan audience would have thought the distinction worth making. "Jew" and "usurer" were virtually synonymous.

European Jews had been forced to adopt moneylending as their principal means of support in the early Middle Ages, as trade and other occupations became closed to them. Here, if nowhere else, they enjoyed an economic freedom that was denied to their Christian neighbors. In a society where the lending of money at interest was generally forbidden, they were the one licensed source of credit. A dubious privilege: it left them in a more precarious situation than ever, and even though those Jews who argued in favor of charging interest to "strangers" could always cite Deuteronomy, many Rabbinical authorities were strongly opposed to the practice. In the eleventh century, at a time when the shift towards usury was still in its early stages, the great Talmudic commentator Rashi warned that "he who loans money at interest to a foreigner will be destroyed." But there was no holding out against economic pressures, and by the end of the following century Jews were far more closely identified with moneylending than with any other activity.

In practice, as has already been seen, the Church's ban on usury was repeatedly circumvented. Christians lent money and charged interest throughout the Middle Ages, often on a large scale. The most celebrated instances were the groups of Italian financiers, the Lombards and Cahorsins, who operated in many different parts of Europe. They were unpopular, and sometimes suffered expulsion. But the Jews were unique in the degree of hatred that they attracted. The worst thing you could say about a Christian usurer was that he was as bad as a Jew, or perhaps even worse. In Germany, Christian moneylenders were denounced as *Christen-Juden,* "Christian Jews." In those countries which had expelled the Jews, the equation of Jew and usurer survived long after they were gone. *"Juif"* was a term commonly applied to a rapacious French moneylender—to Harpagon in Molière's *L'Avare,* for instance—at a time when very few Frenchmen had ever set eyes on a Jew. And in England, where memories of a Jewish presence were even more remote, the Jewish moneylender remained a constant point of reference. Thomas Dekker, in his pamphlet *The Seven Deadly Sins of London* (1606), could speak of brokers who "shave poor men by most Jewish interest." The preacher Henry Smith began his *Examination of Usury* (1591) by pointing out to his readers (did they really need reminding?) that "there be no such usurers on earth as the Jews." Bacon, in his essay *Of Usury* (1625), cited as one of the "witty invectives" that had been made against usurers the suggestion that "they should have orange-tawny bonnets, because they do Judaize."

Such was the tradition that Shylock was born into. In many respects he is bound to strike us as a medieval figure, still walking the same narrow groove marked out by his moneylending ancestors. Antonio, by contrast, seems a man of the future—if we are to judge him by his business activities, that is. His reach extends to the Indies and the New World.

From another point of view, however, the two men's roles are reversed. Antonio embodies the medieval morality of friendship; Shylock represents the challenge of unrestrained bargaining and calculation. Seen in this light, Antonio is the traditionalist and Shylock the innovator.

Eventually the innovators triumphed, on paper as well as in practice. It was not until the 1640s and 1650s that the modern doctrine of interest acquired intellectual respectability; but Bacon, in the essay which has just been quoted, had already pointed the way. Distancing himself from the invectives, the proposed to talk about usury "usefully." It had many drawbacks and "discommodities," some of which he duly listed, but it also had undeniable advantages. It enabled young merchants to start up in trade; it saved men who had got into difficulties from being force to sell their land or their goods. Above all (and here his tone became unusually brisk) it tallied with the facts of human nature:

> It is a vanity to conceive, that there would be ordinary borrowing without profit; and it is impossible to conceive the number of inconveniences that will ensue, if borrowing be cramped. Therefore, to speak of the abolishing of usury is idle. All states have ever had it, in one kind of rate, or other. So as that opinion must be sent to Utopia.

A detached view of moneylending didn't necessarily imply a lack of prejudice against Jews. But it might; and in Bacon's case it looks as though it did. As a young lawyer he had attended the trial of Dr. Lopez and drafted an official memorandum affirming the physician's "detestable treason." But by the time he wrote his utopian tract *The New Atlantis* (around 1624, a year or two before his death), he had shifted towards a position that could fairly be described as philosemitic. There are Jews as well as Christians on his imaginary island, practicing their religion openly, and living amicably with their neighbors. It is one of them, a merchant called Joabin, who takes him to meet the father of "Salomon's House," the secluded scientific institute that was to serve, thirty-five years later, as an inspiration for the founding of the Royal Society. Joabin goes a little too far, we are told, in claiming that the original inhabitants of the island were descended from Abraham, and that Moses himself ordained their laws "by a secret cabala." But "setting aside these Jewish dreams, the man was a wise man and learned, and of great policy."

The American historian Lewis Feuer has suggested, with some plausibility, that if Joabin had a prototype, it can only have been the Jewish mining engineer Joachim Gaunse. Certainly it is hard to think of anyone else in Elizabethan England who would fit the role. Gaunse's background was very different from that of the Spanish and Portuguese Jews who had settled in London. Unlike them, he had had a traditional Jewish upbringing, and never made any pretense of being a Christian. Born in Prague, he became a metallurgist (after originally studying the Talmud), and arrived in England in 1581 to advise on the smelting of copper. He introduced striking improvements in the copper mines at Keswick, in present-day Cumbria; he was also, in the words of his fellow-investigator Thomas Harriot, the "mineral man" on the Roanoke expedition to Virginia in 1585–1586, entrusted with the responsibility of prospecting for mineral deposits. These activities brought him into contact with a number of leading Elizabethans, including Burghley—and quite possibly with Burghley's nephew, Bacon, who took a strong interest in mining.

In 1589, while he was visiting Bristol, his career was cut short. He was drawn into a dispute with a local clergyman, in the course of which he denied that Jesus was the son of God. Hauled before the magistrates, he explained that he had been raised as a Jew, and reaffirmed that he was unable to accept the central tenets of Christianity. A problematic case, which didn't fall under the usual laws against heresy. The Bristol authorities decided to send him to London, to be examined by the Privy Council—at which point he disappears from history. It seems likely that any charges against him were dropped, on condition that he leave the country.

In spite of its abrupt termination, Gaunse's career was a portent. He was an early example of a Jew who found social acceptance on the neutral ground of science and technology. And it was a nascent industrial capitalism which gave him his opportunities. The Company of the Mines Royal, which employed him, was the first company formed in England (in 1568) for the purposes of manufacture, as opposed to trading.

We are a world away from Shylock. Impossible to imagine *him* conducting experiments in Cumbria or prospecting in Virginia. Yet in one respect he is a portent too. For all the prejudice he arouses, he anticipates the extent to which capitalism was to override national distinctions. A cosmopolitan economy, he assumes, depends on foreigners enjoying the same legal rights as natives; and Antonio agrees with him:

The duke cannot deny the course of law:
For the commodity that strangers have
With us in Venice, if it be denied,
Will much impeach the justice of the state,
Since that the trade and profit of the city
Consisteth of all nations.

Shylock undoes himself by pursuing his mad revenge. But there is nothing in the play to suggest that if he had stuck to the rules, he couldn't have gone on as before, an unloved but legitimate participant in the city's prosperity. The business of Venice was business.

• 4 •

The scattered references to usurers in Shakespeare's other plays are as hostile as those in *The Merchant of Venice.* In *Romeo and Juliet,* for example, usury is decried (in passing) by Friar Lawrence. In *King Lear,* "the usurer hangs the cozener"—the thief, serving as magistrate, passes judgment on the cheat.

So much for Shakespeare the playwright. When we turn to Shakespeare the man of affairs, we are confronted by a rather different picture.

The story of the Shakespeare family is one of a rise in economic status over three generations, interrupted and then resumed. Richard Shakespeare, the poet's grandfather, was a tenant-farmer at Snittersfield, a village some three miles northeast of Stratford. He seems to have made a comfortable living—when he died, in 1561, his goods were valued at the respectable sum of £38; but the little world of Snittersfield was too small to accommodate the ambitions of his son John, the poet's father. Around 1550 John Shakespeare moved to Stratford, where he set up in business as a glover, prospered, purchased property, and married a wife who brought him a substantial dowry. In 1568 the Stratford council chose him as its bailiff, the town's highest elective office. (There was no mayor.) Then, around 1576, things began to go wrong. He ran into financial difficulties and became embroiled in legal actions; eventually he was deprived of his alderman's gown for failing to attend council meetings. But he never became poor. At the time of his death, in 1601, he still owned the large double house where his children were born.

To describe him as a glover, and leave it at that, conveys far too narrow an idea of his activities. He also made and sold all kinds of other leather goods; he dealt in wool; he invested in land. And, on the side, he was a moneylender: at one stage he found himself taken to court and accused of charging twice the legal rate of interest on loans of £100 and £80—hefty sums, at a time when a schoolmaster was regarded as doing well if he earned £20 a year.

Did William Shakespeare follow his father's example and lend out money "on conditions"? He is known to have gone to law to recover debts on at least three separate occasions: in 1600, in order to get back £7 that he had lent to a man in London eight years before; in 1604, on account of the unpaid balance of a loan that he had made to an apothecary in Stratford—some £2.5s., including damages; and in 1608, when he demanded the return of £6 (plus damages) from another Warwickshire man. Not that there was anything unusual for the period about his persistence in pursuing these claims: As S. Schoenbaum points out (in *William Shakespeare: A Documentary Life*), "in an age without credit cards, overdrafts or collection agencies," he was following the normal course. Nor is there anything to show that he charged interest on any of these loans. Like Antonio, he may have made them gratis.

But then again he may not. The one surviving letter addressed to him was written by his "loving good friend" Richard Quiney in 1598. Quiney, a Stratford neighbor who was in London at the time, requested a loan of £30. Two further letters with a bearing on this transaction have survived, both addressed to Quiney—one from his father, Adrian Quiney, the other from Abraham Sturley, a business associate of the Quineys and a former bailiff of Stratford. Whether Quiney got his money is unknown (although whatever the outcome, it doesn't seem to have affected his friendship with Shakespeare—his son Thomas married Judith Shakespeare, the poet's daughter, in 1616). It is equally uncertain whether he expected to pay interest. In the past, writers tended to assume that the question didn't arise, that Shakespeare simply did what he could to help out. But E. A. J. Honigmann, in his book *Shakespeare's Impact on His Contemporaries,* has recently cast a colder eye on the Quiney correspondence. All three letters contain phrases which imply that there was likely to be bargaining over the terms of the loan, and it is significant that when Sturley heard that the money might in fact be forthcoming, he remained wary. It was a possibility, he told Richard Quiney, "which I shall like of as I shall hear when, and where, and how; and, I pray, let not go that occasion if it may sort to any indifferent conditions"—i.e., fair conditions, with the obvious implication that they might not turn out to be as fair as he and the Quineys hoped.

There are a number of other reasons, in Honigmann's view, for believing that Shakespeare was no stranger to the idea of charging interest. The company he kept, or sometimes kept, is one pointer. In 1596, for example, he was co-defendant in a legal action with Francis Langley, the owner of the Swan Theatre on Bankside, and a notorious moneylender. His friends in Stratford included another large-scale moneylender, John Combe, whose loans (at the legal rate of 10 percent) were reputed to have made him the wealthiest man in the town. When he died in 1614 he left Shakespeare £5 in his will.

The evidence Honigmann has assembled falls some way short on conclusive proof. But he makes out a strong case, and one which is consistent with everything else that is known about Shakespeare's financial dealings. Many writers have been indifferent to money, but he was not one of them. His theatrical earnings are thought to have averaged at least £200 a year (in addition to being paid for his plays, he was a leading shareholder in the Globe Theatre, and later the Blackfriars). By his mid-thirties he was able to buy the second largest house in Stratford, and he went on to make substantial investment in the neighborhood: his purchases included 120 acres of farmland just outside the town, acquired for £320 in 1602, and a half-interest in the tithes of three nearby hamlets, acquired for £440 in 1605. In 1613 he paid £140 for a house in the Blackfriars district of London—possibly with an eye to using it himself, but quite possibly, in Schoenbaum's words, as "a real-estate investment pure and simple." He traded in malt; he drew up an elaborate and hard-headed will. At one level, in short, his career was that of a tough and successful businessman.

The Merchant of Venice has a closer bearing on his role as a man of affairs than anything else he wrote. To suggest that he identified himself with Shylock would be absurd; but I don't think that it would be too much to claim that he understood the usurer from the inside, that he sensed an affinity with him even while rejecting it. Stephen Dedalus in *Ulysses* put it best: "He drew Shylock out of his own long pocket."

The question of whether or not he charged interest seems to me a secondary consideration. If he was inconsistent, if he didn't practice what he preached, his entire society was engaged in a similar piece of double-think. But there is a more fundamental conflict discernible in the play. Property is desirable, but the means by which property is acquired are problematic; and if the problem is "solved" by the means being idealized (in the person of Antonio), it is at the cost of their also being demonized (in the person of Shylock).

For some recent commentators such a conflict doesn't exist—not as a moral conflict, at least. Private property, they maintain, is bad; Shakespeare, though he sometimes transcended it, was the servant-spokesman-beneficiary of a vicious socioeconomic system. An extreme statement of this position can be found in Edward Bond's play *Bingo* (1976), in which the poet, living in retirement in Stratford, acknowledges that he has done nothing to change the world and commits suicide. Bond doesn't mince his words: in his preface to the play he claims that Shakespeare the property-owner was "closer to Goneril than Lear." (He means the Lear who denounces authority, the Lear who loses his mind during the storm.)

To argue the full case against views like these would take a book in itself—a book about human nature, power, freedom, economic progress. That being so, I shall simply register my flat disagreement, with the one additional observation that the whole Elizabethan theater was itself the product of an expanding economy.* In the words of John Maynard Keynes, "we were just in a financial position to afford Shakespeare at the moment when he presented himself!"

The moral conflict remained, however. Whether Shakespeare felt any qualms about his own business dealings, we shall never know. But in his writing, there is a clear discontinuity between Venice and Belmont. A competitive world, a harmonious world: how do you get from one to the other?

* *And a credit economy. James Burbage, for example, built the first permanent London playhouse, the Theatre (opened in 1576), "with many hundred pounds taken up at interest."*

CHAPTER FOUR

"Shylock Is My Name"

Shylock would not have held the stage for four hundred years if he were a mere stereotype. His greatness is to be himself, to transcend the roles of representative Jew and conventional usurer. He is Shylock, with his own private history, his own vivid individuality.

His first distinguishing mark is his name. It is a name that is not found anywhere else, and scholars have searched assiduously for its possible origin. In the eighteenth century there was excitement over the discovery of a reference in a Jacobean pamphlet to "certain prophecies of a Jew called Caleb Shillocke." Later scholars have canvassed the claims of Shelah, an ancestor of Abraham (Genesis 10.24), "shallach," the Hebrew word for a cormorant, and "shullock," a dialect word meaning "to idle about, to slouch." But neither these nor any of the other suggestions that have been made have won much support: if there was an outside source, it remains a mystery.

There can be no doubt, however, that Shakespeare knew what

he was doing when he declined to settle for either a common biblical name (as he so easily might have done), or a baldly allegorical one. A Shylock who was called Moses or Isaac would not have been at all the same thing; neither would a Shylock called Lucre or Mammon. And the name is not only distinctive, it feels right. It is the right name for the man who locks up his money and tells his daughter to lock up his doors.

A name is a precious possession. Like other possessions, it can be taken away. Shylock is "Shylock" to his face, but behind his back he is almost always referred to as "the Jew"; and as the final confrontation approaches, even such minimal signs of respect as he has been shown are dropped. Antonio, while he is being hauled off to jail, can still attempt to plead with him man to man: "Hear me yet, good Shylock." But after that, it is open war. In the trial scene, the other characters, beginning with the Duke himself, repeatedly address him as "Jew," or speak of him as "the Jew" in his presence. They are not only closing ranks against him; they are also letting him know that his personal identity is of no account.

He is undeterred. When Portia, in the guise of Dr. Balthazar, puts her first question to him—"Is your name Shylock?"—he replies with a ringing affirmation: "Shylock is my name." And however hard his enemies try to strip him of his right to be himself, they cannot succeed. His image has become far too clearly established in our minds.

How well we get to know him! He is present in only five of the play's twenty scenes, and for the purpose of the plot, it would have been enough for him to be mean and vengeful—which he is. But his is also remarkable for pride, energy, quickness in argument. He has an abrasive sense of humor and a large capacity for being hurt.

Character means more than a list of attributes, however. It means a distinctive aura, a unique flavor. As G. K. Chesterton once said, we can talk for hours about a person's identity, and still jump on hearing his voice. With Shylock, we can hear the voice.

His language is concentrated and terse. He does not waste words, any more than he wastes ducats, and he prefers short words to long ones. Could anything be more tight-packed, for example, than his comment after he has learned that Lancelot Gobbo is planning to leave him? "Drones hive not with me"—the concision of the phrase perfectly matches the sentiment. And though he can be exultant, and even exalted ("An oath, an oath, I have an oath in heaven!"), his style is much plainer than that of the other characters. He fights shy of decorative effects and rhetorical tropes; he interrupts himself; his lines are punctuated by questions and exclamations.

There are other speech habits that set him apart. Otto Jespersen, in *Growth and Structure of the English Language,* singles him out in order to illustrate Shakespeare's skill at endowing a character with linguistic idiosyncrasies. Some of these are biblical (words such as *synagogue* and *Nazirite* are not found elsewhere in Shakespeare). Others are simply unusual: the plural *moneys* is a famous example, so successful that it has sometimes persuaded later generations, quite wrongly, that it is a Jewish idiom. *Equal* (for "exact") and *estimable* (for "valuable") are no less odd, while Shylock alone in Shakespeare uses the noun *misbeliever* and the verb to *bane.* His syntax is often irregular, too. He talks of *trifling* time, and says that he has no mind *of* feasting forth. (Elsewhere it is always *mind to.*) "I have counted some forty such deviations from Shakespeare's ordinary usage," Jespersen concludes, "and cannot dismiss the thought that he made Shylock's language peculiar on purpose, just as he makes Caliban, and the witches in *Macbeth,* use certain words and expressions in order to stamp them as beings of no common sort."

An even more marked characteristic of Shylock's speech is the extent to which he uses prose. Stylistically, as Brian Vickers has pointed out (in *The Artistry of Shakespeare's Prose*), this represents a major innovation. Where Shakespearean prose had previously been the province of comic characters, Shylock employs it for wholly serious purposes. And the prose style tells us a great deal about the man.

Its most obvious features—to cite Brian Vickers again—are repetition and parallelism. The habit of sounding the same note two or three times over establishes itself in his opening lines, when he quizzes Bassanio about the ducats. A moment later, he draws up his first list of parallels ("ships are but boards, sailors but men, there be land-rats and water-rates, water-thieves and land-thieves . . ."). A moment after that, he demonstrates his taste for antithesis as he defines the social boundary between Jew and Gentile: "I will buy with you, sell with you, talk with you, walk with you, and so following; but I will not eat with you, drink with you, nor pray with you." When Antonio appears, he switches to verse; but in the street scene in Act III, at the heart of the play, he reverts both to prose, and to his compulsive verbal pattern-making. There are staccato repetitions ("good news, good news: ha ha! heard in Genoa!") and symmetrical constructions ("the thief gone with so much, and so much to find the thief"). The catalogue of his grievances against Antonio ("He hath disgraced me, and hindered me half a million . . .") divides the items into pairs, with Point A systematically balanced against Point B.

These speech habits bear an obvious relation to Shylock's business habits—to the world of ledgers, double-entry book-keeping, profit and loss. He is a man with a need to tabulate and enumerate, to keep a tight grip on reality and underline what he means. But there is nothing prosy about his prose. Much of the time, it is white-hot with emotion, and it provides the medium for his most famous outburst. Antonio has disgraced him and scorned him—

> and what's his reason? I am a Jew. Hath not a Jew eyes? Hath not a Jew hands, organs, dimensions, senses, affections, passion? Fed with the same food, hurt with the same weapons, subject to the same diseases, healed by the same means, warmed and cooled by the same winter and summer as a Christian is? If you prick us, do we not bleed? if you tickle us, do we not laugh? if you poison us, do we not die? And if you wrong us, shall we not revenge?

No amount of familiarity can rob these lines of their power. Where else, in Shakespeare's time, can you find such sentiments? Where else, in later times, can you find them expressed with such eloquence? Yet critics have never been slow to point out that the passage culminates in a threat, that Shylock is invoking his humanity in order to justify an inhuman purpose.

It would plainly be wrong to suppose that "Hath not a Jew?" somehow excuses everything else that he does. The real question is deciding what we are to make of the lines themselves. Are they merely sophistical, the calculated pleading of a clever advocate? I think not. They are wrenched from Shylock; they have the stamp of anger and spontaneity. And the fact that they are in prose only heightens the impression. You feel that if Shakespeare had really wanted Shylock to indulge in some specious rhetoric, it is far more likely that he would have made him resort to verse.

At the end of the speech, Shylock abandons the high moral ground. So in a sense, does Shakespeare. He introduces Tubal, who proceeds to play on Shylock mercilessly, alternating the bad news about Jessica with the good news about Antonio. It is an ugly device—one Jew, a supposed friend, goading another, out of what looks like pure malice. The effect is ugly, too. Shylock is driven further along the road to revenge. When he summons Tubal to meet him "at our synagogue," it is in order to take his irreversible oath.

Yet nothing that happens in the rest of the play cancels out "Hath not a Jew?" The words have been spoken; the stereotype will never be the same again.

CHAPTER FIVE

Wife and Daughter

Shylock's wife is no longer living, and we only get to hear of her once—after Tubal brings word from Genoa that Jessica has traded one of the rings she has stolen for a monkey:

> Thou torturest me, Tubal. It was my turquoise, I had it of Leah when I was a bachelor. I would not have given it for a wilderness of monkeys.

"It was my turquoise, I had it of Leah when I was a bachelor." A single sentence, but one of those Shakespearean sentences that go a mile deep. It is of the same order as Lady Macbeth's explanation, out of the blue, for her inability to kill Duncan: "Had he not resembled my father as he slept, I had done't."

The name Leah links Shylock more firmly than ever with the story of Jacob. Leah was Jacob's first wife, and the mother of seven of his children. She was also the daughter of Laban, who had tricked Jacob into marrying her after he had toiled for seven years for the love of her younger sister Rachel. (He had to labor for another seven before Rachel could become his second wife.) Possibly Shakespeare chose the name because it did not have particularly romantic associations. But marriages can be strong without being romantic, and even those for whom Shylock can do nothing right have stopped short at ridiculing him in his role of husband.

The fact that the stolen ring was a turquoise gives it added significance, since turquoises were widely believed to have magical properties. They were said to change color, in order to warn those who wore them of impending danger; they were also supposed "to reconcile man and wife." An appropriate stone for a keepsake—and if the ring was dear to Shylock while Leah was alive, it must have been doubly precious now she was dead. He dealt in jewels, but this one was not for sale at any price.

Disposing of the ring was heartless. It is as though Jessica were trying to undo her parents' entire marriage at a stroke. Exchanging it for a monkey added whimsical insult to injury. To the Elizabethans, monkeys symbolized lechery (Othello's "goats and monkeys") and mockery; for a man like Shylock, the mere idea of acquiring such a pet must have seemed unbearably frivolous. He gives vent to his outrage in his unforgettable, quasi-biblical phrase, "a wilderness of monkeys"—"a find Hebraism," Hazlitt called it.*

Something can be said in Jessica's defense. She had just made her escape from an environment where she felt stifled. She was young, in love, swept up in the great adventure of her life. Perhaps the business with the ring was no more than a moment's thoughtlessness.

But does she really need defending, anyway? If we accept the traditional reading of the play, we rejoice in her progress: at worst, the business with the ring is a mere blip. She is the ogre's beautiful daughter, who makes her escape from his castle, and it is the clearest proof of her goodness that she is as different from him as possible. She is "a gentle, and no Jew."

* *Shakespeare has used a similar phrase before: in* Timon of Athens *(c. 1589) a character describes Rome as "a wilderness of tigers." It is the context that gives Shylock's words their biblical coloring.*

For an example of the depths that an ungentle Jewess could stoop to, we might consider the ballads inspired by the death of "little Hugh of Lincoln" in 1255, and by the accusations of ritual murder which followed. The affair, which cost eighteen Jews their lives, remained a vivid popular memory for hundreds of years, and the folklore which sprang up around it included the belief that the boy had been lured to his death by a "Jew's daughter." In one version of the story, from Scotland, he is described as accidentally throwing his ball through a window, and trying to get it back:

> *"Throw down the ba, ye Jew's daughter,*
> *Throw down the ba to me!"*
>
> *"Never a bit," says the Jew's daughter,*
> *"Till up to me come ye."*

Eventually the woman comes down to the garden and entices the boy into the house with "an apple red and green"; once they are inside, she duly slaughters him.

The Jewess as temptress and potential murderess—given the way that Jewish women were portrayed, such an image is not to be wondered at. What is surprising, on the other hand, is how early a rival legend emerged. Stories about the love of a Christian youth for a Jewess can be found in collections of preachers' tales, the so-called *exempla,* from the thirteenth century onwards, and the young women in them, who often end up being converted to Christianity, tend to be shown in a fairly favorable light.* Abigail, in *The Jew of Malta,* belongs to this tradition: she starts out as her father's accomplice, but after he has betrayed her Christian lover she repents and retires to a nunnery (where Barabas has her poisoned). Finally, with Jessica, the bad Jew's good daughter attains classic perfection.

The history of the type, with all its variants, constitutes a curious chapter in Western culture, extending to the nineteenth

* *An American scholar, Beatrice Brown, has drawn attention to one* exemplum, *from a collection compiled by a Dominican friar in the thirteenth century, that has some striking parallels with* The Merchant of Venice: *a Christian lover, a fair Jewess, a rich old father. The lover is a spendthrift, and the daughter encourages him to steal her father's money.*

century and even beyond. In the 1820s Chateaubriand, inspired by the example of Rebecca in *Ivanhoe,* wrote an essay, *Walter Scott et les Juives,*" in which he puzzled over the question of why "the women of the Jewish race are more beautiful than the men." The answer he came up with was that Christ had been denied and crucified by the men of Judea alone, while the women "believed in him, loved him, followed him, comforted him in his afflictions." Few people can have been satisfied with such an explanation, even at the time, and today any attempts to account for the myth of the bad father/good daughter are likely to be resolutely psychological. But theology played its part, too: Leslie Fiedler is surely right when he argues that the myth had its origins in the "dogmatic compromise by which Christianity managed to make the New Testament its Scripture without surrendering the Old." The Jews were so near and yet so far. They were the people whom God had chosen, and the people who had chosen to murder His son; and to sharpen the paradox, Christ had been born to a Jewish mother when he assumed earthly form—a mother who in Christian eyes, was both Jewish and profoundly non-Jewish. What more natural than to think of the salvageable, redeemable part of Judaism as being embodied in a woman rather than a man?

The transition from the old order to the new is also hinted at in Jessica's name. Its origins are unknown, but it carries distinct overtones (or so I would judge) of Jesse, the father of David and ancestor of Jesus. Isaiah's prophecy that "there shall come forth a rod out of the stem of Jesse" was assumed by Christians to foretell the coming of Christ; a "Jesse," a tree displaying Christ's genealogy, was a familiar form of decoration in churches.

Allegorical readings of Shakespeare should not be pressed too hard, however. His characters can seldom be reduced to a formula, and whatever point he started out from in depicting her, in practice Jessica is individualized and semi-realistic. Her initial plight, for instance, is far less extreme than it would be in a folktale. She is not so much afraid of her father as ashamed of him, and the domestic hell of which she complains turns out to be mainly a matter of "tediousness."

Nor is her elopement an unqualified idyll. She has misgivings about how much Lorenzo really loves her, misgivings which his hurried reassurances are not quite enough to set at rest; and if she is uncertain about him, we cannot help feeling a little uncertain about *her.* When she momentarily holds back from the light, is she being coquettish, or genuinely modest? When she returns to the house to "gild herself" with more ducats, is she anxious to make herself more attractive to Lorenzo, more of a prize? Or is she simply a greedy child, her face smeared with stolen jam?

Comparable doubts hang about her in the later scenes. It has been pointed out by more than one critic, for instance, that she is not made especially welcome at Belmont. Portia in particular scarcely addresses a word to her, in spite of which she can't get over how wonderful she is. Possibly the speech in which she sings her praises ("the poor rude world/Hath not her fellow") should be thought of as an impersonal, choruslike comment; but if it is meant to be spoken in character, it suggests an almost abject willingness to please. Again, when she is in company at Belmont she is generally silent. Perhaps this doesn't signify; but it is hard to escape the impression that she feels excluded.

It is when she is alone with Lorenzo that she comes to life again, especially in the superb exchange at the beginning of Act V. "In such a night . . ." Lorenzo is reminded of Troilus; Jessica counters with Thisbe. He talks of Dido, "with a willow in her hand"; she conjures up a picture of Medea. Legendary lovers—but none of them were happy; two of them, Troilus and Dido, were betrayed; and Jessica goes on to tell Lorenzo that the vows he has sworn to her were insincere.

One should not make too much of this. The prevailing note is still one of romance. Jessica's teasing show of scepticism does not disrupt the essential mood, and neither does Lorenzo's reply:

In such a night
Did pretty Jessica (like a little shrew)
Slander her love, and he forgave it her.

"Little shrew," in the context, is a term of endearment—it is on a par with the pet monkey; and Jessica's final retort, before the lovers are interrupted, makes it clear how far they have been playing a game: "I would out-night you, did nobody come."

Still, there can be no denying that the game has an edge to it. There are undertones of regret, of a recognition that life will always have hurtful possibilities; and Jessica's comment when the lovers are alone again, preparing to welcome back Portia, suggests a more settled vein of sadness. "I am never merry when I hear sweet music." It is the last line she speaks in the play, although the final scene still has well over two hundred lines to run.

The one thing about her that is not in doubt is that Shylock loves her. Even the cry that amuses his enemies so much—"O my ducats! O my daughter!"—implies that if he did not love her more than his ducats, at least he did not love her less. We should remember, too, that we never hear the cry ourselves. It occurs in the account of his distress that Solanio gives to Salerio, an account which shows every sign of being a highly colored comic turn. Solanio also expects us to believe that "the dog Jew" cried out "O my daughter! Fled with a Christian! O my Christian ducats!," and that he raised an unintended laugh by bewailing the loss of "two rich and precious stones" ("stones" being Elizabethan slang for testicles).

Shylock himself, when we see him again, makes a somewhat different impression. His reply, when Solanio begins with a needling question, "What news among the merchants?," is, "You knew, none so well, none so well as you, of my daughter's flight." His response to a smutty attempt to distort the meaning of "flesh" is to insist that "my daughter is my flesh and blood." His first thoughts are about Jessica, not about the ducats, and it takes Tubal's reappearance to make him revert to his financial loss—although as soon as he does, he works himself into a deadly rage:

> A diamond gone cost me two thousand ducats . . . Two thousand ducats in that, and other precious, precious jewels. I would my daughter were dead at my foot, and the jewels in her ear: would she were hearsed at my foot, and the ducats in her coffin.

A terrible curse—but it *is* a curse, and not an expression of greed. On the contrary, the jewels and ducats are to be buried along with the girl who took them. In his self-punishing, self-pitying fury, Shylock calls down destruction on everything that he has lost.

An Elizabethan audience probably laughed at all this, but that does not mean that *we* have to. Nor need we feel obliged to applaud when Jessica—breaking her silence for once—intervenes in the discussion at Belmont to report on what she knows about her father's state of mind:

> *When I was with him, I have heard him swear*
> *To Tubal and to Chus, his countrymen,*
> *That he would rather have Antonio's flesh*
> *Than twenty times the value of the sum*
> *That he did owe him; and I know, my lord,*
> *If law, authority and power deny not,*
> *It will go hard with poor Antonio.*

Rather pointedly, nobody takes her up on this. (The next remark is addressed by Portia to Bassanio.) But then she is not really telling those present anything that they do not already know. They have just had a graphic account from Salerio of how "keen and greedy" Shylock is to enforce the full terms of the bond: he "plies the Duke at morning and at night," and he would not accept belated payment of the money even if it were available. Jessica may believe that she still has a duty to underline the seriousness of the situation, but she is also plainly anxious to distance herself as far as possible from her father and "his countrymen" (*"his"* countrymen—they are no longer hers).

After this, she never refers to him again. Presumably she is glad to hear about his forcible conversion, but her reaction lies beyond the confines of the play; and if she ever thinks of him with pity or regret, she does not give any sign of it. Effectively, her emotional bond with him is broken.

Yet worse parents than Shylock have retained a hold over their children's affections. In Philip Massinger's *A New Way to Pay Old Debts* (c. 1625), a play which bears certain surface resemblances to *The*

Merchant of Venice, the central character is a cruel extortioner, Sir Giles Overreach. He has a daughter, Margaret, whom he treats as a pawn in his schemes, and who runs away with her lover. Eventually, after he has been outwitted by some of his potential victims, he goes mad; and in spite of all the grounds she has for hating him, Margaret feels a stab of pity. "Oh, my dear father!", she cries, as she sees him led away to Bedlam.

From Jessica, however, there is nothing.

CHAPTER SIX

"I Stand for Judgment"

· 1 ·

Shylock is hot for revenge, but in his own mind what he seeks is no more than justice. "I stand for judgment. Answer: shall I have it?"

The Merchant of Venice is the most legalistic of Shakespeare's plays, and it has attracted an enormous amount of legal discussion. In a survey published in 1972, O. Hood Phillips examined over fifty studies by lawyers, jurists and legal historians; others have appeared since. Yet a layman may well wonder—initially, at least—how much point there is in applying professional expertise to a case which is so far removed from anything than can ever have taken place in an actual courtroom.

Considerable energy has been devoted, for example, to the question of Portia's exact status during the proceedings: does she take part in them as a judge, or a defending counsel, or an expert referee (*amicus curiae*)? By ordinary standards, however, she is plainly disqualified from performing any kind of judicial role, since the defendant—Antonio—is a close friend of her husband. (That she appears in disguise, under an assumed name, only makes matters worse.) Again, it is interesting to learn that the relatively subordinate role of the Duke matches the limited judicial powers enjoyed by a real Venetian Doge. But *this* duke is chiefly remarkable for his lack of impartiality. He opens the proceedings by commiserating with Antonio; he denounces the suit before Shylock has had a chance to speak.

The case itself has some equally unsatisfactory features. Antonio makes no attempt to plead fraudulent misrepresentation, even though Shylock had assured him that the bond was only a "merry" one. Nothing in the bond specifies that the pound of flesh should be cut off by Shylock himself: on the contrary, the practice in civilized countries, as one authority puts it, has always been for mandates of the court to be carried out by officers of the court. And, more irregular still, the whole nature of the proceedings changes in mid-course. A civil action is suddenly transformed into a criminal case, and the court, without in any way reconstituting itself, delivers a verdict and passes sentence.

The "quibble" by which Portia saves the day for Antonio does admittedly raise an important point of principle. If one has the right to something, are there any circumstances under which one does not have the right to what necessarily accompanies it? This is not an issue which would be very rewarding to debate in this particular context, however. The terms of the bond are too extreme, the gap between the rightful claim (the repayment of a debt) and the concomitant circumstance (the taking of a life) is too great. For perhaps the only legal point that needs to be made, if we judge *Shylock* v. *Antonio* as though it were a real case, is that the bond was null and void to start with. In the words of the nineteenth-century German jurist Rudolf von Ihering, its provisions were *contra bonos mores,* contrary to good morals: no civilized authority would have countenanced them for a moment.

Ihering did not feel that this in any way diminished the play's value. "The poet," he wrote, "is of course free to make his own jurisprudence, and we do not regret that Shakespeare has done it here, or rather that he has kept the old story unchanged." Another eminent jurist, Sir Frederick Pollock, reached the same conclusion. He believed that Shakespeare must have known that the procedures in the trial scene were absurd, but that if he had been challenged he would have said: "I am a maker of plays, not of law books; I wanted a good scene, not justice."

All of which seems fairly obvious. Law makes good theater, but only when it is heightened, simplified, speeded up, bent to the dramatist's purpose. Law is one thing, literature is another. And yet the legal interest of *The Merchant of Venice* does not end with its failure to conform to the standards of a legal textbook. At its own imaginative level it confronts one of the great central issues of law—equity, the attempt to keep law true to its underlying principles. Shylock abuses the letter of the law, Portia reasserts its spirit.

Much of the legal discussion of the play in recent years has centered on the question of how far its handling of the conflict between strict justice and equity reflects the actual state of affairs in the Elizabethan courts. According to one group of commentators, Portia embodies the legal philosophy of the court of Chancery, "the court of conscience," as opposed to that of the common law courts, where statutes were rigorously enforced. The most stimulating exponent of this view, to a layman, is W. Nicholas Knight in his article "William Lambarde, *The Merchant of Venice* and Equity" (1974)—partly, it is true, on account of Knight's excursions into biography and social history. The article traces some of the possible connections between Shakespeare and William Lambarde, a Master of Chancery and legal scholar who once described Chancery as "the Gate of Mercy."* It also lends new interest to the long legal battle between Shakespeare's parents and their nephew, John Lambert.

In 1578 John and Mary Shakespeare borrowed £40 from Edmund Lambert, who was married to Mary's sister. As security they mortgaged a house and some land which Mary had inherited. The loan was not repaid, and Edmund retained possession of the prop-

* *It was in conversation with Lambarde that Queen Elizabeth made her one recorded reference to Shakespeare, shortly after the Earl of Essex's abortive uprising: "I am Richard II, know ye not that? . . . This tragedy was played forty times in open streets and houses."*

erty, which was duly inherited by his son John. In 1587 the Shakespeares brought an unsuccessful action against John in the court of Queen's Bench, claiming that they had been promised an extra £20 in return for outright ownership of the property. In 1597 they sued him again, in Chancery: on this occasion they alleged that they had offered to pay back his father the £40, but that the offer had not been made within the time specified in the original agreement—in this respect it resembled the offer to repay Shylock his ducats—and that the Shakespeares had therefore forfeited their right to the property. The case dragged on for at least two years, with the court appointing a commission to examine witnesses. The terms under which the dispute was settled are unknown, but the property remained in John Lambert's hands.

Nicholas Knight underlines the significance of the episode. At the age of fourteen William Shakespeare had seen an estate which he was one day due to inherit temporarily made over to an uncle. At the age of thirty-five or so he had to reconcile himself to the fact that the same estate was irrevocably lost. Who can doubt that the affair rankled, or that between 1597 and 1599—around the time he wrote *The Merchant of Venice*—he was much preoccupied in his own life with the question of loans, binding agreements and forfeitures? But Knight goes further. Even though the Shakespeares did not get any joy out of their Chancery suit, he believes that it helped to make their son especially receptive to arguments for the supremacy of equity over common law:

> In *The Merchant of Venice,* William Shakespeare is not just dramatizing a generalized court scene and sentimentalizing about mercy; rather he is presenting Chancery procedure and arguing that it be used precisely along its theoretical lines of a superior court with its accompanying appellate function and humane spirit . . .

Another legal historian, E. F. J. Tucker, strongly dissents. In practice, he argues, Chancery judgments were not especially swayed by notions of equity; at the same time, "the judicial problems arising from a strict interpretation of the letter of the law were perfectly well understood by common lawyers." And as for the idea that Shakespeare was presenting and advocating Chancery procedure "along its theoretical lines," it was hard to see what that meant in terms of what actually took place on the stage:

> In the trial scene, one finds no allusions to written pleadings; there are no answers, demurrers, rejoinders, surrejoinders, and surely no commissions of *dedimus potestatem* in any formal or technical sense. Is Portia supposed to be the Chancellor (she is referred to several times as a judge), a Master of Chancery, a Six-Clerk, or what?

A non-lawyer naturally quails in the face of such specialized considerations; but fortunately the issue is not one on which it is necessary to take sides. The wisest general study of law in *The Merchant of Venice* can be found in a book by an American judge, Richard Posner's *Law and Literature;* and according to Posner, the whole debate over the relation between the trial scene and the sixteenth-century court of Chancery is sterile, since "the concept of equity—as a more flexible, moralistic system of jurisprudence than rule-bound 'law'—is not tied to a specific court system."

Shakespeare did not need to be told that manmade laws can be imperfect, both in substance and in execution. "The world is still deceived with ornament," says Bassanio, just before he makes his choice among the caskets, and the first example he gives comes from the courtroom:

> *In law, what plea so tainted and corrupt,*
> *But being seasoned with a gracious voice,*
> *Obscures the show of evil?*

This would be an odd point to make if we were meant to look at it in the light of what is still to come in the play, since in the trial scene it is Portia who speaks with a gracious voice. But it is a general observation. There are more ways than one of abusing a legal system, and Shylock shows how it can be done without resorting to fine words. He makes no attempt to appear gracious during the trial—far from it. It is enough for him that he has the law on his side.

When Portia appears in court, disguised as Dr. Balthasar, the grounds on which she urges Shylock to waive his claims are purely moral. Mercy, the key word in her appeal, is not the same thing as equity, and whatever else it may be the "quality of mercy" speech does not constitute a legal argument. Yet it is still possible for Richard Posner to write that in this scene she "personified the spirit of equity—the prudent recognition that strict rules of law, however necessary to a well-ordered society, must be applied with sensitivity and tact, so that the spirit of the law is not sacrificed unnecessarily to the letter."

The important thing is that she makes the speech *in the role of a lawyer,* not that of a detached moralist or outside observer. She is dressed like a lawyer, she takes part in the rituals of the court, she comes armed with the authority of the learned Dr. Bellario of Padua. What we are presented with is a spectacle which presupposes—never mind the exact details—that humanity and moderation have a place within the legal system.

After Shylock has rejected a final plea for mercy, Bassanio asks Portia-alias-Balthasar whether she cannot override the formal demands of the law: "To do a great right, do a little wrong." But she assures him that it is impossible:

> *It cannot be; there is no power in Venice*
> *Can alter a decree established.*
> *'Twill be recorded for a precedent,*
> *And many an error by the same example*
> *Will rush into the state: it cannot be.*

On the face of it, this is putting as strict a construction on the law as Shylock does. But Portia has two tricks up her sleeve. First, the stipulation about not shedding blood, which destroys Shylock's claim to the pound of flesh; second, the law designed to prevent aliens seeking the life of a citizen, which leaves him completely at the mercy of the state. She could of course have saved everyone a lot of trouble by disclosing her plan of campaign at the outset, but that would have put paid to Shakespeare's dramatic design. It is only after the claims of mercy have been exhausted that she is ready to fall back on the claims of strict liability; and when she does, she demonstrates that if she has to, she can beat Shylock at his own game. The bond becomes a weapon in her hands.

We are meant to admire her resourcefulness. We are also meant to find, in the happy outcome of the action-cum-trial, a vindication of the law itself. For abuses of the law are no argument in Shakespeare's eyes against the rule of law—something to which, as he makes clear again and again, he was profoundly attached. The remedy for misapplied law in *The Merchant of Venice* is well-applied law, and Antonio is finally saved, not by an angel or a miracle, but by a woman who combines the roles of wise jurist and smart advocate.

• 2 •

Shylock's role in the trial scene is a simple one. His behavior has become rigid and predictable: all that he has to do, to advance the drama, is to keep insisting on the legality of his claim. But in the first half of the scene, before Portia arrives, he makes two speeches which nobody could have predicted, one as extraordinary as the other. Neither is strictly necessary to the action; both serve to deepen our sense of his personality.

When the Duke opens the proceedings by telling him that in spite of his apparent cruelty, everyone expects him to show "human gentleness and love," he replies that he has sworn an oath to have the precise forfeit that is due under the terms of his bond. Then he forestalls the obvious question:

You'll ask me why I rather choose to have
A weight of carrion flesh than to receive
Three thousand ducats. I'll not answer that—
But say it is my humor: is it answered?
What if my house be troubled by a rat,
And I be pleased to give ten thousand ducats
To have it baned? What, are you answered yet?

Some men there are love not a gaping pig;
Some that are mad if they behold a cat;
And others when the bagpipe sings i'the nose
Cannot contain their urine: for affection
Masters oft passion, sways it to be mood
Of what it likes or loathes. Now for your answer:
As there is no firm reason to be rendered
Why he cannot abide a gaping pig,
Why he a harmless necessary cat,
Why he a wollen bagpipe, but of force
Must yield to such inevitable shame
As to offend, himself being offended:
So I can give no reason, nor I will not,
More than a lodged hate and a certain loathing
I bear Antonio, that I follow thus
A losing suit against him. Are you answered?

Shylock has already told us, in the first act, his conscious reasons for hating Antonio—because he is a Christian, and because he brings down the rates of interest in Venice. We have also seen Antonio treating him, as he always has, in a manner that is bound to incur his resentment. True, these are not reasons that would do him much good if he brought them up in court; but then why raise the question of motive at all? At most he might have said something to the effect that "a bond is a bond—and in addition, Antonio has never shown me any kindness. Why should I be expected to show him kindness now?"

At one level the speech that he *does* find himself making is utterly unrealistic: no one, even allowing for theatrical artifice, could possibly argue a courtroom case in such terms. But it also has a startling psychological urgency. It lays bare the innermost pressures which are driving Shylock on; indeed, it is hard to believe that it did not simply "come" to Shakespeare, straight from his own unconscious.

Rats inspire horror not so much because they bite and gnaw—lots of animals do that—but because they get inside the house.

While the idea is particularly disgusting to Shylock, who keeps his house tightly locked against the outside world, the fear of rats is common enough for him to instance it as a universal symbol of revulsion. After that, however, he goes on to cite three altogether more specialized phobias, although it is still possible to see a link between the rat and the first two of them, the pig and the cat. The pig is a *gaping* pig, served up at a table with fruit in its mouth: it both eats (like a rat) and gets eaten—though not by Shylock, to whom its flesh is profoundly unclean. The cat, too, eats and bites, and in Shylock's fantasy it is assimilated to the rodents that it devours. Up to this point, there is a loose logic in the progression of images. But the shift to the bagpipe is far more surreal. It takes us beyond the animal world; and unlike the other phobic objects, which arouse generalized loathing, bagpipe music produces a specific reaction—an infantile loss of self-control.*

The speech, as much as any in Shakespeare, invites Freudian attentions, and it has been analyzed at length by a psychoanalytic critic, Robert Fliess. According to Fliess (the son of Freud's sometime close friend, Wilhelm Fliess), Shylock's murderous impulses "have all the infantile violence of the child-in-us, and he justifies them in terms of grisly childhood fantasies that themselves would provoke a wild reaction on an infant's part." A house is a common symbol for the body, and the image of the "rat gnawing at a hole down in the bowels of the house" (an image which Fliess connects with fantasies about feces) "is enough to provoke a whole wave of emotions surging up from the unconscious." The cat—"soft, furry, feminine"—suggests the female genitals, as an anxious small boy might imagine them; "the projecting bagpipe" (later described as "woollen") is its masculine counterpart. In their different ways, the animals introduce the idea of "unrestrained oral behavior"; bagpipes introduce the idea of "unrestrained wetting"; and "all rep-

* *The association between bagpipes and urinating was not a purely private crotchet. The Arden edition cites a parallel passage in Ben Jonson's* Everyman in his Humour, *and there are further background details in the New Cambridge edition.*

resent to Shylock a justification of his own moral incontinency."*

"This is no answer, thou unfeeling man," exclaims Bassanio, when Shylock has finished. In a sense, "unfeeling" is the wrong word; Shylock might well have retorted that his feelings were his answer. But he has an intellect as well as passions, and a minute later, under further pressure from the Duke, he switches from unashamed irrationality to cold logic:

> *What judgment shall I dread, doing no wrong?*
> *You have among you many a purchased slave,*
> *Which, like your asses and your dogs and mules,*
> *You use in abject and in slavish parts*
> *Because you bought them. Shall I say to you,*
> *"Let them be free! Marry them to your heirs!*
> *Why sweat they under burdens? Let their beds*
> *Be made as soft as yours, and let their palates*
> *Be seasoned with such viands"? You will answer,*
> *"The slaves are ours." So do I answer you.*
> *The pound of flesh which I demand of him*
> *Is dearly bought; 'tis mine, and I will have it.*

This is not an argument against slavery. On the contrary, Shylock is using slavery as a precedent to justify his own claim. In a slave-owning society, why shouldn't he have the right to purchase a life himself? Yet we cannot help reflecting that the comparison cuts both ways. If demanding a pound of flesh is no worse than keeping a slave, keeping a slave is no better than demanding a pound of flesh. And if it is enough for Shylock that slavery is a precedent, he chooses to present his case in such a way that we are left wondering whether it is a very good precedent. He could, after all, have confined himself to saying that slavery was a respectable institution, which all law-abiding Venetians took for granted. Instead, he stresses its dehumanizing aspects, where he doesn't have to, and he raises the possibility of emancipation, without equating it with anarchy.

* *Quotations in this paragraph come from the summary of Fliess's argument in Norman Holland's* Psychoanalysis and Shakespeare.

A remarkable speech, given that virtually no voices were raised against the principle of slavery either at the time or for long afterwards.* It may not be the produce of a warm heart, but at least it testified to Shylock's reasoning powers and his detached realism.

• 3 •

Whatever refinements Shakespeare introduces, Shylock still pursues the same unswerving course. Law, judgment, the bond—these are his reiterated cries. The bond in particular takes on an almost magical quality. It is indestructible: "Till thou canst rail the seal from off my bond," he tells Gratiano, in one of his most powerful images, "Thou but offend'st thy lungs to speak so loud."

Behind his obduracy lies the notion of grim Old Testament justice, as opposed to New Testament forgiveness. In Christian eyes, Jews were doubly inflexible. Their lives were governed by rigid rules, and they refused to acknowledge that their laws had been superseded by the coming of Jesus. They had also been responsible for bringing Jesus to trial. Memories of that trial are at work in the ordeal of Antonio; in addition, a number of scholars have argued that there are echoes of the medieval legend of the "Processus Belial," which would make Shylock's conduct more devilish still. G. W. Keeton gives a brief account of the legend's essential features:

> The Devil makes his appearance before God, in the court of Heaven, and demands that mankind, which has belonged to him since the Fall, should be delivered up to him. God therefore sets a day for the trial of this plea, and when the proceedings are opened He asks if there is anyone who will appear on behalf of mankind. The Virgin Mary agrees to act for the defense, and the proceedings are opened with the Devil's plea that he stands

** The historian David Brion Davis points out, for instance, that "no protest against the traditional theory [of slavery] emerged from the great seventeenth-century authorities on law, or from such philosophers and men-of-letters as Descartes, Malebranche, Spinoza, Pascal, Bayle or Fontenelle."*

> for strict justice, which the court must grant, and in accordance with which, mankind must suffer damnation. The Virgin Mary, in reply, pleads for mercy, arguing that mercy is as much an attribute of God as justice. The Devil, feeling that the case is going against him, produces scales, and purposes that the portion of mankind which is due to him should be weighed out and delivered, if strict justice is denied and he is not to have the whole of mankind. In the end he is driven out of court in disgrace and mankind is saved.

Shylock as the Devil (or Belial), Portia as the Virgin, Antonio as a reminder that, without divine grace, even the best of mankind stand in peril . . . The parallels are close enough to make it likely that Shakespeare was familiar with the Processus Belial story in one form or other.

But the Shylock we see on stage during the trial scene is not the Devil. He is a flesh-and-blood human being—a human being, moreover, who is completely friendless and isolated. "We all expect a gentle answer, Jew," the Duke tells him, and "all" deserves nearly as much emphasis of "gentle" and "Jew." Everyone's voice is raised against him; he is reviled, heckled, heaped with sin like a scapegoat.

There is in fact a paradox at the heart of the scene. At one level, until Portia turns the tables, it is like a bad dream, in which a solitary malevolent figure holds an entire society to ransom. Formally, this part of the scene corresponds to the civil action Shylock v. Antonio, and tidy-minded critics are correct in pointing out that "trial scene" is a misnomer. But in another sense it is the right term, since at its deepest emotional level the entire scene consists of a trial—the trial of Shylock. Every point he urges in his ostensible role of plaintiff is also a further piece of evidence against him in his true role of defendant, and every insult hurled at him from the well of the court is an assault by the prosecution.

Not only do we know from the start that it is Shylock who is on trial; we also know (as even the play's first audience must have) that in the end he is going to be crushed. To that extent the trial is a show trial, in a manner which uncomfortably undercuts Portia's lesson in equity; and our sense of Shylock's isolation is deepened still further by the fact that when he is convicted, it is under a law specifically directed against aliens—as though the attempted murder of a Venetian was not just as much of a crime when the perpetrator was a fellow citizen.

The penalties that the law prescribes are twofold. First, the offender's goods are to be confiscated and divided equally between his intended victim and the state; secondly, his life "lies in the mercy of the Duke only, 'gainst all other voice." Shylock stands in immediate danger of being sentenced to death, and Portia orders him to his knees: "Down, therefore, and beg mercy of the Duke." Compelling him to beg, rather than asking him if he has anything to say, is not an especially merciful gesture in itself, but then it is not meant to be. It is a punishment for his failure to recognize the very principle of mercy earlier in the scene, when it was still in his power to dispense it.

The Duke's first act of clemency is to spare him this particular humiliation:

That thou shalt see the difference of our spirit,
I pardon thee thy life before thou ask it.

We may wince a little at the note of self-congratulation, but the great thing is that Shylock's life is spared: the potential death sentence is not even commuted to a lesser penalty. The act of confiscation still applies, however, and for Shylock it amounts to a second death sentence:

Nay, take my life and all, pardon not that:
You take my house when you do take the prop
That doth sustain my house; you take my life
When you do take the means whereby I live.

It is possible, I suppose, to interpret this as first and foremost a mark of ingratitude (and it is true that Shylock nowhere thanks the Duke). But most of us are more likely to find his words impressive in their bitter realism; and anyone tempted to accuse him of being unduly materialistic at this point should remember that Antonio comes close to making the same equation in Act V, when Portia tells him that his ships are safe after all: "Sweet lady, you have given me life and living."

The Duke himself shows no sign of being put out. Instead, he leaves the question of whether to render further mercy in the hands of Antonio, and Antonio responds by asking the state to forego its share of Shylock's estate. As for the other half, which is now his by right, he will administer it and hand it over to Lorenzo and Jessica after Shylock's death, although Shylock will enjoy the income from it as long as he lives.

If Antonio had stopped there, it would be hard even for those critics who dismiss the Christians in the play as hypocrites to deny that Shylock is treated with considerable generosity. He will still be a rich man, in full possession of half his capital and receiving the income from the other half; and all this is being granted to him at a time when Antonio himself, as far as he knows, is still penniless. There are two further stipulations, however:

Two things provided more: that for this favor
He presently become a Christian;
The other, that he do record a gift,
Here in the court, of all he dies possessed
Unto his son Lorenzo and his daughter.

"Art thou contented, Jew," Portia asks, and Shylock answers laconically, "I am content"—although it is obvious he is no such thing.

Are *we* content? It is painful for Shylock to be reminded of Jessica, and painful for him to hear Lorenzo referred to as his son, but within the fairy-tale terms of the play the stipulation that he leave them his money after his death—he has no other heirs—is surely not unreasonable. No, what sticks in the throat, and what has made generations of readers and playgoers uncomfortable, is the demand that he "presently become a Christian."

From Antonio's point of view, he is conferring an inestimable boon: baptism offers Shylock his one chance of redemption. From

Shylock's point of view, however, unless he accedes willingly, it is a form of soul-murder: he is being ripped away from what matters to him most. And in judging how much spiritual weight to attach to his conversion, we must consider the circumstances under which it takes place. It is imposed on him pretty much as though it were a punishment. It is to take effect "presently," straight away: there is to be no time allowed for preparation or instruction. No one treats it as an occasion for rejoicing. No one even mentions it, once he has consented—apart from Gratiano, who sees him off the stage with a final jibe:

In christening shalt thou have two godfathers:
Had I been judge, thou shouldst have had ten more—

in other words, a full jury—

To bring thee to the gallows, not to the font.

As for Shakespeare's own attitude, we shall never know what it was, but two somewhat contradictory points are worth bearing in mind. First, the enforced conversion seems to have been a Shakespearean addition to the story: no hint of it can be found in *Il Pecorone* or any of the other probable sources. Secondly, there are the last words we hear Shylock speak, after Portia has ordered the clerk to draw up his deed of gift to Lorenzo and Jessica:

I pray you give me leave to go from hence:
I am not well. Send the deed after me
And I will sign it.

I am not well. For those to whom Shylock is a tragic or partly tragic figure, the words have a supreme rightness. For those to whom he is an unqualified villain, they simply signal that he had been bruised by his defeat. But either way they are the words of a man who is sick at heart, not the words of a man who believes that he has been set on the path to salvation.

CHAPTER SEVEN

Christians

· I ·

One reason why Shylock's enforced baptism is disconcerting is that it is contrary to predominant Christian tradition. This is not to underestimate the enormous role played by forcible conversion in European Jewish history, both in the Middle Ages and in succeeding centuries. Countless Jews were coerced into Christianity; countless others suffered martyrdom rather than submit. But however frequent the exceptions, the rule was one of reluctant toleration. At the end of the sixth century Pope Gregory the Great established the principle that Jews were not to be baptized by force. In the thirteenth century St. Thomas Aquinas reaffirmed it on the grounds that true belief had to be voluntary.

That still left scope for debating exactly what constituted "force." Some argued that the prohibition only applied to outright physical violence: near-violence (the threat of mass-expulsion, for example) was permitted. Others were prepared to exert varying degrees of social or economic pressure. Still others hoped to convince the Jews of the truth of the Gospels by simple persuasion.

There were a whole range of attitudes available—and the treatment meted out to Shylock belongs at the harsh end of the spectrum. He is a convicted criminal, at the mercy of the court. The Duke makes it clear that if he refused to become a Christian, he will once again be liable to lose his life:

He shall do this, or else I do recant
The pardon that I late pronounced here.

What makes the episode all the more jarring is that it is out of key with so much that has gone before, or that is still to come. If *The Merchant of Venice* were a severely religious play, we might at least feel that Shakespeare was being fairly consistent. But it is a comedy, and one in which most of the characters are thoroughly worldly. In their different styles Venice and Belmont are both dedicated to pleasure, and the fact that life in Venice is also subject to the hazards of business only serves as a further unspiritual distraction. In the opening scene, Salerio—an average Venetian gadabout—tries to imagine what he would feel if his fortunes were entirely at the mercy of the wind and waves, like Antonio's:

Should I go to church
And see the holy edifice of stone
And not bethink me straight of dangerous rocks,
Which touching but my gentle vessel's side
Would scatter all her spices on the stream,
Enrobe the roaring waters with my silks,
And (in a word) but even now worth this,
And now worth nothing?

This is admittedly playful, a conceit embroidered for its own sake; even so, the striking thing is that the imagined shipwreck is so much more vivid than the real church. And any attempt to interpret the play as a Christian allegory has to take account of Salerio—just as it has to take account of Portia's satirical description of her suitors, and a great deal of gallantry and raillery, and the fact that the proceedings close, not on a note of high solemnity, but with Gratiano cracking a joke about Nerissa's "ring." (Her vulva, as the New Cambridge edition usefully explains).

Systematic allegory is not Shakespeare's way, however. His themes rise out of the story or the dramatic situation with which he is dealing. Sometimes they are sustained, sometimes they disappear and reappear, sometimes they fade away. In *The Merchant of Venice,* the religious element is far from pervasive; at the same time it is unmistakable, and it manifests itself most strongly in two of the central characters, Antonio and Portia.

In the opening scenes we learn about Antonio's melancholy, his opulence, his generosity and his capacity for friendship. Only Shylock alludes directly to his being a Christian (as a reason for hating him), and it is only in connection with Shylock that he alludes directly to Christianity himself ("The Hebrew will turn Christian; he grows kind"). His selflessness, however, especially in lending money without interest, is plainly understood to be a Christian virtue. He represents an attempt to resolve—or deny—the tension between Christian ideals of renunciation and the pursuit of worldly wealth.

In signing the bond, he goes further: even though the prospect seems remote, he shows himself ready in principle to lay down his life for the sake of a friend. The supreme model for such a sacrifice was Christ, offering himself as "ransom" for the salvation of mankind; and when Antonio finds that Shylock is in earnest, that the bond means what it says, he prepares to follow Christ's example. In a culture soaked in Christianity, it would surely have been hard for any audience, watching his plight, not to be reminded of the Man of Sorrows. His good deeds are rewarded with suffering; he is brought from prison, and led like a lamb towards the slaughter.*

Not that there is anything mystical about the trial scene. However much Antonio attempts to pattern himself on Christ, he

* *A minor Jacobean poet, Joseph Fletcher, confirmed the analogy, in a back-to-front way, in his poem* Christ's Bloody Sweat *(1613)—assuming that it was* The Merchant of Venice *he was thinking of, which seems likely. "The Cross his stage was," he wrote of Christ.*

remains a mortal man, the same Antonio. "I do oppose my patience to his fury," he tells the Duke, has he prepares to confront Shylock in court; but when it comes to it, he cannot refrain from venting his feelings in a bitter speech about the uselessness of trying to soften the hardest thing imaginable, Shylock's "Jewish heart." It is curious, too, how little his thoughts are turned towards Heaven. We are no doubt meant to admire this fortitude, but there is nothing Christ-like, or even overtly Christian, about the speech with which he resigns himself to what looks like his fate. He is thinking exclusively of Bassanio, and—with a tremor of self-pity—of Bassanio's bride:

Tell her the process of Antonio's end
Say how I loved you, speak me fair in death,
And when the tale is told, bid her be judge
Whether Bassanio had not once a love.

Resignation, when it is expressed in terms like these, leaves us feeling uncomfortable; and the play itself celebrates a more active virtue. The trial scene belongs, not to Antonio, but to Portia—the decisive, energetic Portia, who carries the fight into the enemy's camp, and who probably thinks of Antonio (though she doesn't say so) as a defeatist rather than a saint.

Portia is a complex character. She is at once a goddess and an heiress, a dutiful daughter and a woman of the world. She is also, when the need arises, an Iron Lady, and if all we knew of *The Merchant of Venice* were a précis of the plot, we might well conclude that her conduct at the trial is distinguished mainly by its toughness. She is fair-minded enough to give Shylock a chance to relent, but she is all the time laying a trap for him.

What makes the essential difference, in seeing or reading the play, is her response when he asks "on what compulsion" he must be merciful:

The quality of mercy is not strained,
It droppeth as the gentle rain from heaven
Upon the place beneath. It is twice blessed:

It blesseth him that gives and him that takes.
'Tis mightiest in the mightiest, it becomes
The throned monarch better than his crown.
His sceptre shows the force of temporal power,
The attribute to awe and majesty,
Wherein doth sit the dread and fear of kings;
But mercy is above this sceptred sway.
It is enthroned in the hearts of kings,
It is an attribute to God himself,
And earthly power doth them show likest God's
When mercy seasons justice.

Many modern commentators hurry past this speech. It is too famous. Its sentiments are too obvious. Once Portia's virtues have been called into question, it is tempting to dismiss it as a sham, and you end up with Leslie Fiedler talking of its "saccharine banalities." Yet is it a noble piece of writing. Its "banalities" are among the great commonplaces of many different cultures, and if Portia, in her cat-and-mouse treatment of Shylock, does not entirely live up to them, the speech itself still stands as the expression of a permanent ideal. Shylock's faults do not make nonsense of "Hath not a Jew?" Why should Portia's faults make nonsense of "The quality of mercy"?

Elsewhere, the imagery and atmosphere associated with her are largely those of love, music and classical mythology. Here, the emphasis is squarely on religion:

We do pray for mercy,
And that same prayer doth teach us all to render
The deeds of mercy.

Addressing her fellow-Christians, whether in the court or in the audience, she reminds them of the Lord's Prayer. Addressing Shylock, she speaks the language of universal prayer.

But religion serves to divide as well as to unite, and the one sentence that she directs at Shylock alone strikes a more confrontational note:

Therefore, Jew,
Though justice be thy plea, consider this:
That in the course of justice none of us
Should see salvation.

Shylock *may* get the message, but Portia reminds us that he is unlikely to, because he is a Jew—"Jew" signalling here a diseased moral condition, just as it does in Antonio's reference to Shylock's Jewish heart.

Needless to say, the notion that Judaism has an inadequate grasp of the concept of mercy is a travesty—as much of a travesty as it would be to suppose that Christianity has an inadequate grasp of the concept of justice. The word for mercy, *rachamim,* carries tremendous resonance in the Hebrew liturgy (it is related to *rechem,* the word for a womb), and endless exhortations to deal mercifully can be found in the writings of the Rabbis. To prove the point, indeed, we need look no further than the opening lines of "The quality of mercy" itself. If they have a single source, it is generally agreed to be a passage from Ben Sira, the Jewish sage who lived in Jerusalem around 200 B.C., and whose teachings appear in the Apocrypha under the title Ecclesiasticus.* There are further reminiscences of the same work later in the speech, and of the Psalms; but then the Golden Rule ("Love thy neighbor . . .") goes back to Leviticus, and the Lord's Prayer itself has its origins in traditional Jewish sources.

One brief digression seems in order.

The preconceptions of *The Merchant of Venice* are Christian preconceptions. In the real world there were also Jewish preconceptions: during the Middle Ages, and, in most cases, down to the era of enlightenment or beyond, both communities remained fully embedded in their own codes and convictions. For Christians, the Jews

* *"Oh how fair a thing is mercy in the time of anguish and trouble! It is like a cloud of rain, that cometh in a time of drought." Shakespeare echoed the Apocrypha on numerous occasions (Shylock's "A Daniel came to judgment" is another instance); he also gave both his daughters names which can be found in its pages—Susanna and Judith.*

were primarily defined as the people who had rejected Christ. For the Jews, Christians—like all non-Jews—were defined by their refusal to accept the Holy Law, the *Torah.* The result, as Jacob Katz sums it up in his study of medieval and postmedieval Jewish-Gentile relations, *Exclusiveness and Tolerance,* was that "a more or less abstract, stereotyped notion of the Gentile" was "part and parcel of the Jewish conception of the Gentile world—much as an even more rigid stereotype of the Jews was perpetuated in the mind of the Gentile."

None of this has any direct bearing on Shakespeare's play. But it is worth remembering, in case our revulsion from the prejudice to which the play bears witness tempts us to cast the real-life equivalents of Shylock wholly in the role of passive (and pallid) victims. The facts were more complicated, and it takes the unravellings of an exemplary historian like Katz to do them justice.

• 2 •

One of the key words in the play is "gentle." It signifies a whole range of virtues, from good breeding to compassion; it is applied, in various forms, to Portia, Antonio, Bassanio, Lorenzo, Gratiano and "Dr. Balthazar." It also serves to set Shylock still further apart, since there is a running pun on "gentle" and "gentile." Antonio, under the impression that his old enemy has mellowed, addresses him as "Gentle Jew."Lorenzo reflects that if "the Jew her father" ever gets to Heaven, it will be for "his gentle daughter's sake." And when the Duke exhorts Shylock to show mercy, he is in effect asking him to be something which he is not: "We all expect a *gentile* answer, Jew."

The gulf between Shylock and the other characters is as much cultural as religious. They are divided from him by tastes, preferences, habits of speech, habits of mind. Jessica laments that she is ashamed to be her father's child—

But though I am a daughter to his blood,
I am not to his manners

Manners, rather than religious doctrines, are what she chafes at.

There is no suggestion that Shylock is boorish or brutish. He has his own rough dignity; his shrewdness preserves him from obvious *faux pas.* But ease, grace, attractiveness—those are the province of his enemies. Nothing in his world, for example, corresponds to Portia's assumption that conviviality is a good thing in itself, her description of friends as "companions/That do converse and waste the time together." Shakespeare's editors hasten to reassure us that "waste" is being used here in the neutral and now archiac sense of "spend," but if Shylock could have overheard the speech, he would undoubtedly have taken the word in its purely modern sense. And perhaps there is a hint of wastefulness in Portia's own use of it, an aristocratic pride in being lavish with time, as opposed to merely doling it out. It is a sentiment of which Yeats would have approved: "Only the wasteful virtues earn the sun."

We should not take the professions of the "gentle" characters entirely at face value. They can be decidedly businesslike when it comes to pursuing their own interests; there are tensions between them; even if we set aside their treatment of Shylock, they are far from flawless. But that does not mean that we are supposed to "see through" them, or identify them with their limitations. They partly embody the ideas which at other times they fail to live up to: Shakespeare offers us a mixture of realism and romance.

It is worth recalling at this point that when he set about adapting the story in *Il Pecorone,* almost the first thing he must have decided was to raise its tone. In the original, the lady is a witchlike creature who sleeps with her suitors and ruins them: the Bassanio-figure only succeeds in outwitting her because a servant tips him off. At Belmont, they order things differently. It is also worth bearing in mind that if he had wanted to portray a corrupt society, Venice—the Venice of legend—would have suited his purpose well. Along with its splendors, the city had a reputation among Englishmen for immorality and dark deeds. It was the home of Iago and Volpone, and the original home of Vittoria Corombona, the "White Devil"; one Jacobean dramatist, John Day, described it as "the best flesh-shambles in Italy." But none of this gets into *The Merchant of*

Venice. The city as it appears there is a coarser place than Belmont, but its leading citizens—those of them we meet—all prove themselves worthy of Belmont.

The highest values of the play are love and friendship (though if they are in conflict, it is friendship that must yield), and, higher still, the idea of universal harmony which Lorenzo expounds to Jessica:

> *How sweet the moonlight sleeps upon this bank!*
> *Here will we sit, and let the sounds of music*
> *Creep in our ears; soft stillness and the night*
> *Become the touches of sweet harmony.*
> *Sit, Jessica. Look how the floor of heaven*
> *Is thick inlaid with patens of bright gold.*
> *There's not the smallest orb which thou behold'st*
> *But in his motion like an angel sings,*
> *Still choiring to the young-eyed cherubins.*
> *Such harmony is in immortal souls,*
> *But whilst this muddy vesture of decay*
> *Doth grossly close it in, we cannot hear it.*

The first part of Act V (which is where these lines come from) has served as a potent inspiration for composers. Berlioz drew on the words of "In such a night" for the ravishing love-duet between Dido and Aeneas in *The Trojans* ("O nuit d'ivresse"). The sequence beginning with "How sweet the moonlight" provided Vaughan Williams with his text in *Serenade to Music.* And it is not hard to see why: music permeates this entire section of the play. But Lorenzo, in explaining its spell, moves beyond the harmonies we can hear to the heavenly order of which they supply an intimation. The speech is the most purely religious utterance in the play.

It is at this point that Jessica says that she is "never merry" when she hears sweet music. Lorenzo, taking "never merry" to mean nothing worse than "subdued" or "calm," tells her, approvingly, "The reason is, your spirits are attentive," and embarks on a second speech in which he praises the benign influence of music, its therapeutic, heart-easing qualities. By contrast, the man without music in his soul is "fit for treasons, stratagems and spoils." "Let no such man be trusted"—and there is only one man in *The Merchant of Venice* whom the description plainly fits, the man who ordered his daughter to ignore the "vile" music of the carnival.

Many critics find these last remarks hard to swallow. Who is Lorenzo to start preaching? He has persuaded Jessica to commit domestic treason; they have both practiced stratagems; their pockets are lined with spoils. For that matter, we are just about to see the acting out of a fresh subterfuge, one that has been set in motion by the Lady of Belmont herself. No sooner has Lorenzo finished speaking than Portia and Nerissa return from Venice. They have tricked Bassanio and Gratiano out of the rings which they gave them as keepsakes; now they claim them back, and there are hard words. In the end, the ruse is revealed, and amity is restored. But the men have been given a warning, as Portia intended, and so has the audience: even in Arcadia, jealousy and betrayal are lurking possibilities.

How much all this is meant to color our response to Lorenzo's remarks is another matter. My own view is that Shakespeare did not feel the irony of "treasons, stratagems and spoils" very strongly. He knew, of course, that men and women seldom live up to their best selves for long (Lorenzo himself says as much), and that golden moods are soon broken. But that only made him value the best selves and golden moods all the more. Nor are we meant to feel that Lorenzo and Jessica's misdemeanors are remotely in the same class as the murder which Shylock was plotting. Indeed, if we follow the lead of the other characters, we are meant to condone them. When Antonio, at the end of the trial, sets out the terms on which he is prepared to "render mercy" to Shylock, he refers to Lorenzo, quite unblushingly, as "the gentleman/ That lately stole his daughter." Shylock being Shylock, the theft is no crime.

And Lorenzo is still a gentleman. So are his friends: the gentlemanly ethos prevails. Apart from Antonio, the Christian characters are gentlemen first and Christians second; and even Antonio—when Bassanio wants to commend him to Portia—is described in strictly pagan terms, as

one in whom
The ancient Roman honor more appears
Than any that draws breath in Italy.

Shylock, by contrast, is the complete outsider. Antonio may insist on him becoming a Christian, but it would appear hopeless to demand that he become a gentleman. If he were baptized ten times over, he would still be out of place at Belmont.

As it is, he is only referred to twice in the last act (and in neither case by name.) Once near the beginning, when Lorenzo risks a provocative pun:

In such a night
Did Jessica steal from the wealthy Jew . . .

Once near the end, when Nerissa hands Lorenzo the deed of gift from "the rich Jew," and he is almost overcome with gratitude:

Fair ladies, you drop manna in the way
Of starved people.

The image, in context, is an extraordinary one. Manna was what fed the Children of Israel in the wilderness. Shylock, like the Jewish God, is providing his daughter and son-in-law with miraculous sustenance—although this time the credit has to go to the Christians who have extracted it from him.

The revels can now proceed. As far as the other characters are concerned, Shylock has been consigned to oblivion; at any rate, if they have any further thoughts about him, they keep them to themselves. For practical purposes, he has been banished. He no longer exists.

PART TWO

Interpretations

(1600–1939)

CHAPTER EIGHT

From Comical to Tragical

• I •

Very little is known about the early stage history of *The Merchant of Venice.* Possibly the part of Shylock was created by Richard Burbage, possibly (though it seems less likely) by the low-comedy actor Will Kempe. By 1600, according to the title page of the First Quarto, the play had already been acted "divers times" by the Lord Chamberlain's Servants. In February 1605, on Shrove Tuesday, it was performed at Whitehall by the King's Servants, in the presence of James I; it must have been a success, since they were ordered to perform it again two days later. But beyond this, no details of early performances have survived—nothing at all from the entire period between 1605 and 1642, when the theaters were closed down.

Nor have any comments on the play survived from the same period. The one passing allusion that has been preserved, in a character sketch written in 1617, manages to mix up Shakespeare and Marlowe. The essayist Geffray Mynshull, who was in prison for debt at the time, imagined himself addressing a creditor: "If with the Jew of Malta, instead of coin, thou requirest a pound of flesh next to thy neighbor's heart, wilt thou cut him in pieces?"

Meanwhile playwrights continued to assume that Jews made good dramatic copy. There are Jewish references and Jewish characters in Webster, Marston, Fletcher and most of the other Jacobeans. The characters are needless to say villains, usually usurers; and in at least one instance, the borrowings from *The Merchant of Venice* are unmistakable.

The Travels of the Three English Brothers (1607), was the joint handiwork of John Day, William Rowley and George Wilkins. It was based on fact—on the wide-ranging, much-publicized adventures of the brothers Thomas, Anthony and Robert Sherley, all of whom were very much alive at the time. At one stage in the story Anthony, on his way home from Persia, finds himself in Venice, where he falls into the clutches of Zariph, a Jewish moneylender. He pleads for time to settle his debt, but Zariph has other ideas:

> *Now by my soul 'twould my spirits much refresh*
> *To taste a banquet all of Christian's flesh . . .*
>
> *A hundred thousand ducats! Sweet remembrance.*
> *I'll read it again: a hundred thousand ducats!*
> *Sweeter still: who owes it? A Christian,*
> *Canaan's brood. Honey to my joyful soul:*
> *If this sum fail (my bond unsatisfied)*
> *He's in the Jew's mercy; mercy! Ha, ha!*

—and a good deal more in the same vein. In a subsequent scene, Zariph has his victim arrested, and stands by gloating while he is tortured.

The rest of the play is not quite as grim as this miserable stuff suggests. Between the two scenes in which Zariph appears there is a remarkable little episode in which Anthony Sherley meets Will Kempe, who is travelling in Italy: Kempe's plans to present a harlequinade are interrupted when Zariph shows up with a warrant for Sherley's arrest. By 1607 the real Kempe had either retired or died, and in any case he had belonged to a different theatrical company from the one for which Day, Rowley and Wilkins wrote. This meant that he had to be played by somebody else—surely the earliest example of an actor appearing as a character in a play and being impersonated by another actor. If Kempe had taken part in the original production of *The Merchant of Venice,* as he probably had (if not as Shylock, then perhaps as Lancelot Gobbo), it can only have added to the piquancy.

None of this stops the Zariph scenes from being thoroughly nasty. Doubly nasty, for a reason that was first pointed out by John Day's nineteenth-century editor, A. H. Bullen. There is no historical foundation for Zariph—and no mention in *The Three English Brothers* of another episode which the playwrights must have come across in the pamphlet from which they drew most of their facts. During his imprisonment in Constantinople, Sir Thomas Sherley, the eldest of the brothers, was befriended and given help by a Jewish merchant.

Scattered references to Jews continued to crop up in the plays of the Caroline period. There may not have been any Jews living in England, but the dramatists, equating Jewishness with a moral condition, were liable to speak as though there were. "Your English Jews," exclaims a character in Thomas Heywood's *A Challenge for Beauty* (1636), "they'll buy and sell their fathers, prostrate their wives, and make money of their own children." Venice was not forgotten, either. On the eve of the Civil War, in 1639, the poet James Shirley produced a play called *The Gentleman of Venice,* in which there is a certain amount of standard talk about moneylenders and "Jew tricks"—a last echo from Shylock's Rialto.

Then came the great hiatus. The theaters were closed down, by order of the Long Parliament; when they reopened, in 1660, it was in a different world. "The old plays," John Evelyn noted in his Diary in 1661, "begin to disgust this refined age" (he had just seen a production of *Hamlet*), and for a brief period it looked as though Shakespeare might be permanently set aside. However, the threatened eclipse never took place. His plays went on being performed—

mostly, it is true, in badly mangled versions—and his unique status among English writers began to be more clearly recognized. By 1675, Dryden could talk of "Shakespeare's sacred name." But *The Merchant of Venice* was not one of the works that was revived. There were no Restoration Shylocks; the stage history of the play for the rest of the seventeenth century is a complete blank.

If theatergoers were denied a chance to see it, it was of course still available to readers. It had been reissued in quarto editions in 1637 and 1652; it was included, along with Shakespeare's other works, in the Third Folio of 1663 and the Fourth Folio of 1685. But the Folios were cumbersome and expensive, and only reached a very restricted readership. When George Granville's adaptation, *The Jew of Venice,* was first performed in 1701, few members of the audience can have known the Shakespearean original.

The Jew of Venice was a success. It held the stage for forty years; it brought Shylock, Portia and the rest back into repertoire, after a fashion. But what a fashion! Granville chopped, changed, mutilated, tacked on new material. His alterations killed most of the poetry; his additions, where they were not merely trite, introduced a note of awesome vulgarity.

The chief victim in this last respect was Shylock. When Granville's Jew proposes his "merry bond" to Antonio, he is merry indeed:

Let me see. What think you of your nose,
Or of an eye, or of—a pound of flesh
To be cut off, and taken from what part
Of your body I shall think fit to name.
Thou art too portly. Christian!
Too much pampered.

When he dines with Bassanio, and the other guests drink to Friendship, to Love and to Woman ("the Sex in general"), he counters with a toast of his own:

My Money is my mistress! Here's to
Interest upon Interest

And when Portia springs her big surprise and warns him about the consequences of shedding Antonio's blood, his response is monosyllabic: "Humph."

This is not a Shylock who was likely to inspire much fear. He is primarily a figure of fun, and his antics, divorced from any serious purpose on the author's part, belong in the never-never world of pantomime.

The prologue had promised something rather different:

Tonight we punish a stock-jobbing Jew.
A piece of justice, terrible and strange,
Which, if pursued, would make a thin Exchange.

The play was going to be a satire, by the sound of it—and one with a highly up-to-date theme. Stock-jobbers were still a novelty. They had only emerged as a professional group in the previous decade, and as yet nobody had a good word for them. A parliamentary committee, reporting in 1697, condemned their practices as "pernicious"; they were formally excluded from the precincts of the Royal Exchange. But in the new commercial world that had opened up after the Revolution of 1688–1689, the services they performed were indispensable. They simply moved their operations to the coffeehouses and the warren of lanes around 'Change Alley, where they continued to flourish; and there were certainly Jews among them. What proportion, it is impossible to say, but the Royal Exchange (where "broker" meant a dealer in commodities rather than shares) may provide a clue. There, Jewish representation was limited by a law enacted in 1697 to just under 10 percent—twelve brokers out of 124.

If Granville had in fact turned Shylock into a jobber, *The Jew of Venice* would have been even more grotesque than it is, but at least it would have gained in interest as a historical document. Instead, he was content to make him a clown: in the original production, at the Lincoln's Inn Fields Theatre, the part was duly assigned to Thomas Doggett, the leading comic actor of the day. Doggett specialized in playing old men and characters from low life. One of his contemporaries described him as "very aspectabund" (expressive), "wearing a farce in his face," and, improbable though it may seem today, when you read the text he had to work with, his Shylock plainly succeeded in making audiences laugh.* Other actors starred in the role, too. In the 1730s the play was staged in the newly built theater in Covent Garden; on one occasion it was performed at Southwark Fair.

For a modern reader who comes to it from the masterworks of eighteenth-century literature, the most surprising thing about it is the identity of the author. George Granville was a Tory politician, raised to the peerage in 1711 as the first Lord Lansdowne; he was also the friend and early patron of Alexander Pope. Pope dedicated *Windsor Forest* to him, and in the *Epistle to Dr. Arbuthnot* he gave him his lasting epithet—"Granville the polite." Politeness is hardly the most conspicuous feature of *The Jew of Venice;* the only conclusion to be drawn is that the refined and coarse elements in Augustan culture often coexisted quite comfortably.

Not everyone was willing to think of Shylock as a buffoon. In 1709, in the first critical edition of Shakespeare, Nicholas Rowe offered a much darker view of *The Merchant of Venice.*

> . . . though we have seen that play received and acted as a comedy, and the part of the Jew performed by an excellent comedian, yet I cannot but think it was designed tragically by the author. There appears in it such a deadly spirit of revenge, such a savage fierceness and fellness, and such a bloody designation of cruelty and mischief, as cannot agree either with the style or characters of comedy.

Savage fierceness, a deadly spirit of revenge . . . This was the Shylock that eighteenth-century playgoers eventually came to know; but another thirty-odd years were to go by before he made his first appearance on stage.

* *In private life Doggett had a reputation, appropriately enough, for shrewdness and tight-fistedness. When he died, in 1721, he left a sum of money to provide the prizes for an annual boat race between Thames watermen—the celebrated Doggett's coat and badge.*

• 2 •

In 1741 the actor Charles Macklin persuaded the management at Drury Lane to put on a production of *The Merchant of Venice*—Shakespeare's play rather than Granville's. Macklin himself took the part of Shylock, and from the outset he was determined to get away from the comic interpretation, to stint nothing of the character's ferocity. His colleagues, however, were uneasy about the whole enterprise; one or two of them, including the redoubtable James Quin, who was to play Antonio, were actively hostile. Under the circumstances, Macklin judged it best to keep his plans to himself. At rehearsals, he ran through his lines without giving any real indication of how he proposed to deliver them when the time came.

Meanwhile he applied himself to mastering the part on his own terms. If he made notes, they have not survived, but it is clear that one of the things he was anxious to achieve was at least some degree of historical authenticity. He went to the trouble of finding out that Jews in Venice had worn red hats, for example, and according to an account published in the 1750s, in a periodical called the *Connoisseur,* he pursued his researches closer to home: "He made daily visits to the center of business, the 'Change and the adjacent coffee-houses, that by a frequent intercourse and conversation with 'the unforeskinned race' he might habituate himself to their air and deportment." Aiming at a loftier perspective, he also read Josephus's *Jewish Antiquities,* and—presumably—reflected on the Jewish role in history. There is a suggestive entry in his dairy:

> Jews, their history. An instance of human incertainty—from the Creation to the Flood—in Egypt leaving it—robbing their masters, mutinying—Jericho—wilderness—murder of the Innocents—captivity—lion's den—Shadrach, Meshach, Abednigo, Babel. Go thro' the history of it—act the great characters.

Few actors before or since can have prepared themselves for a role more single-mindedly.

At the time, he was already in his forties. An Irishman from

County Donegal—his original name was McLaughlin—he had joined a strolling company in Bristol at the age of seventeen or eighteen, and spent the next fifteen years touring the West of England. During the same period he had also acquired the reputation of being "a great fives player, a great bruiser, a hard drinker and a general lover." In 1733 he had joined the Drury Lane company, and after seven years, playing everything from the First Witch in *Macbeth* to Peachum in *The Beggar's Opera,* he was a familiar figure to regular playgoers. But he was not yet identified with a major role, not yet a star. With *The Merchant of Venice,* he must have sensed that his hour had finally come.

The play opened on 14 February 1741. Before the curtain rose, there was an uncomfortable atmosphere backstage. The other actors were already blaming Macklin for the failure that they foresaw; and initially, as though to bear them out, the audience was cool. When Macklin made his first entry, he did not get the round of applause that he would normally have expected. But he soon won the house over. By the time he reached the scene with Tubal, there were prolonged ovations, and by the end of the evening the seal had been set on one of the great triumphs of the eighteenth-century stage. "By God, sir," he reportedly told one of his early biographers, "though I was not worth fifty pounds in the world at that time, yet, let me tell you, I *was Charles the Great* for that night."

His achievement was all the more remarkable in that it owed nothing to the rest of the production. The trial scene in particular must have been strangely incoherent: while Shylock stood urging his claim, Kitty Clive, as Portia, was putting on a light-hearted comic turn, complete with imitations of well-known lawyers of the day. But even this could not blunt Macklin's enormous impact.

The Shylock he portrayed was unyieldingly malignant. It was a harsh performance, and it could be highly disturbing: "there was such an iron-visaged look, such a relentless, savage cast of manners, that the audience seemed to shrink from the character." One playgoer who testified to Macklin's power in the part was George II. The King visited Drury Lane soon after the play opened, and he was so overwrought by the experience that he could not sleep afterwards.

Subsequently, when Sir Robert Walpole remarked during an audience that he wished there was some way of frightening the House of Commons, he was able to make a helpful suggestion: "Vat you tink of sending dem to see dat Irishman play Shylock?"

Macklin went on to do other things, but Shylock was to remain his most famous role. Indeed, it became one of the fixed points of the Georgian theater. Zoffany commemorated it in two separate paintings—one of the trial scene, one of the scene with Tubal. In 1747, when David Garrick began his long reign as co-manager of Drury Lane, the Macklin *Merchant of Venice* was the play with which he chose to open. And Macklin continued to appear in the part twenty, thirty, forty years after that. In his late eighties, in spite of lapses of memory and increasing deafness, he was still showing the old fire. But eventually time caught up with him. At a performance in May 1789, shortly before his ninetieth birthday, his memory gave out completely; he apologized, his understudy took over, and he retired from the stage forever.*

Of the accounts of his Shylock that have been handed down, the most interesting was written by the German scientist and aphorist Georg Christoph Lichtenberg. Lichtenberg went to see him perform during a visit to London in 1775. "You know," he told the German friend to whom he wrote, "the announcement of Macklin as Shylock sounds as attractive on the playbill as Garrick in *Hamlet*." He had heard a good deal about him, and he was not disappointed:

> Shylock is not one of your petty cheats, who can spend an hour talking about the excellence of a cheap watch-chain. He is slow, calm in his impenetrable cunning, and when he has the law on his side unflinching, to the very limit of malice.
>
> Picture to yourself a rather stout man with a coarse sallow face, a nose by no means lacking in any one of the three dimensions, a long double chin; as for his mouth, Nature's knife seems to have slipped when she carved it

* *He lived on until 1797, dying in povety. His name is preserved in Macklin Street—a turning of Drury Lane, a few hundred yards up from Kean Street and Kemble Street.*

> and slit him open on one side all the way up to the ear. He wears a long black gown, long wide trousers, and a red three-cornered hat . . .
>
> The first words he utters when he comes on are spoken slowly and deliberately: "Three thousand ducats." The two *th* sounds and the two *s* sounds, especially the *s* after the *t,* which Macklin lisps voluptuously, as though he were savoring the ducats and all that they can buy—these sounds make an impression which nothing can efface. Three such words, spoken in this way at the very outset, reveal his entire character.
>
> In the scene in which he first misses his daughter, he appears hatless, with his hair all flying or standing on end, as though it had been lifted up by a breeze from the gallows. Both hands are clenched, his gestures are quick and convulsive. It is fearful to see such uncontrolled emotion being shown by a man who up to now has been a calm and determined villain . . .

Another memorable account was written many years later by John Boaden in the course of his biography of the actor John Philip Kemble. In the trial scene, he wrote, Macklin

> "stood like a TOWER," as Milton has it. He was "not bound to *please*" anybody by his pleading; he claimed a right, grounded upon LAW, and thought himself as firm as the Rialto. To this remark it may be said,"You are here describing Shylock." True; I am describing Macklin.

Inevitably there were some dissenting voices. The poet Charles Churchill, in his satire *The Rosciad* (1763), summed up Macklin's acting as "hard, affected and constrained." The actor John Bernard recalled him as having been "as rough and husky as a coconut, with a barking or grunting delivery more peculiar than pleasing." But even the unflattering accounts could not help conveying an effect of power. Under Macklin's shaggy brows, Bernard said, his eyes burned bright, "like a tiger peeping out of the bush."

In the right part, Macklin's rugged looks were of course a major asset. "If God writes a legible hand," his old enemy James Quin once remarked of him, "that fellow is a villain." So why not play a villain? He had an intimidating reputation, too. In 1735 he had stood trial for murder, after killing a fellow-actor during a backstage dispute over a wig. The jury, accepting that he had been badly provoked, returned a verdict of manslaughter; and in the often turbulent world of the eighteenth-century theater, the incident was not quite as exceptional as it may sound. Quin had also killed a man in a quarrel; so had another leading actor of the period, Lacy Ryan. Still, Macklin was an unmistakably rough customer. When the time came to play Shylock, both temperament and appearance stood him in good stead.

As for his attempts to learn more about the Jews, everything suggests that they were simply a means of feeling his way into the part: after that, he lost interest. He did return to a Jewish theme later in his career, however. In *Love a la Mode,* a comedy which he wrote in 1759, four suitors pay court to a young heiress: an Irishman, a sporting squire, a Scotsman, and a Beau Mordecai—a Jew who (according to the heroine) "in spite of nature and education, sets up for a wit, a gentleman and a man of taste." A descendant of Shylock, you might say, vainly trying to pass himself off as a Bassanio. In fact Mordecai is far more polite than his rivals, and no more mercenary than at least two of them. (Only the Irishman turns out to love the girl for her own sake rather than for her money.) But in a play where a great deal of abuse is flung around, he naturally comes in for his fair share of it. The Scots suitor, Sir Archy MacSarcasm, makes him a particular target, railing at him as a baboon, a reptile, a "bonny Eesraelite."

A hit when it was first produced, *Love a la Mode* remained a favorite with audiences for over fifty years. Macklin himself who was notorious for his dislike of Scotsmen, frequently took the part of Sir Archy: generally, as on the opening night, in a double bill with *The Merchant of Venice.* First he would play Shylock; then he would switch around and enjoy himself jeering at "Eesraelites"—and at Englishmen and Irishmen too.

•

For most eighteenth-century playgoers, a degree of hostility towards Jews was something to be taken for granted. In that respect Macklin's Shylock did not give them anything very new to think about. But there was at least one observer, a product of the Enlightenment, to whom its impact suggested how easily, even among the enlightened, ancient fears and hatreds could be brought back to life. "It cannot be denied," wrote Lichtenberg, "that the sight of this Jew is enough to awaken at once, in the best-regulated mind, all the prejudices of childhood against the race to which he belongs."

Some twenty years after Macklin's death, the novelist Maria Edgeworth went a step further, and tried to imagine, briefly, the effect that his performance might have had on a Jew.

Harrington, published in 1817, was one of Maria Edgeworth's last novels. There had been Jewish characters in half a dozen of her previous stories—all of them unpleasant, some with distinct Shylockian traits, some even worse—and in 1816 a Jewish admirer, a Miss Mordechai, had written to her from Richmond, Virginia, to protest. The letter moved her; she became convinced that she had been guilty of unthinking prejudice; she resolved (as her correspondent had requested) to make amends. Hence *Harrington.*

The best thing in the book is the opening. We are in London, in the mid-eighteenth century. It is twilight; six-year-old Harrington, tired and overexcited, looks down from the balcony of his house and sees a man with a white beard and a bag over one shoulder, making his way slowly along the street crying, "Old clothes! Old clothes!" Then his nurse tells him that it is time to go to bed. He kicks and frets, and she warns him that if he does not do as he is told, "I'll call to Simon the Jew there, and he shall come and carry you away in his great bag." In the days that follow the mere mention of "Simon the Jew" is enough to subdue the child; and as the threat begins to lose its potency, the nurse reinforces it with stories about Jews stealing children and doing away with them at midnight feasts. The "prejudices of childhood" of which Lichtenberg spoke are vividly implanted.

As Harrington grows up, the fear fades, but the aversion remains. Both his father and his schoolfriend, young Lord Mowbray, confirm him in his anti-Semitic opinions. Gradually, however, as he comes to know one or two not unsympathetic Jews—first while he is at school, then during his time in Cambridge—his feelings soften; and he has already shed much of his prejudice by the time Mowbray (now a man about town) offers to introduce him to "the most celebrated Jew in England." Eagerly accepting the invitation, he is taken round to a lodging house in the theater district, where he meets none other than Macklin. Mowbray coaxes the actor into giving an account of his first appearance as Shylock, nearly thirty years before; Harrington, deeply impressed, is determined to see him play the part as soon as possible.

The great day comes. Harrington finds Macklin even more powerful than he had expected, but he is also distracted by a fuss in the adjoining box. A party of rich City folk are embarrassed because they had not realized that the play was going to be *The Merchant of Venice.* If they had, they would have chosen another evening, since they have a Jewish guest with them: Berenice Montenero, the daughter of a wealthy banker. At first Harrington cannot see her clearly, but as soon as he catches a full view of her face—"a countenance of great sensibility, painfully, proudly repressed"—his pleasure in the play is over. At every exclamation against Shylock, and still more at every hostile reflection on Jews in general, all he can think of is the pain she must be feeling. He even begins to see some passages in the play in a new light: "No power of imagination could make me pity Shylock, but I felt the force of some of his appeals to justice." Berenice, for her part, tries not to draw attention to herself, but in the end she comes close to fainting and is forced to leave the theater. Harrington, this being the kind of novel it is, has already begun to fall in love with her.

The next day he calls on her father. It is obvious at a glance that Mr. Montenero is a gentleman, and, contrary to Harrington's expectations, he is completely candid about the reason for his daughter's distress. She had been upset at seeing Shylock the Jew held up for execration by "the genius of the greatest poet that ever wrote," abetted by the talents (or so he has been told) of an exceptionally fine actor. All this he explains in a foreign accent; but "to an Englishman," Maria Edgeworth adds, "what accent that conveys the praise of Shakespeare can fail to be agreeable?" It is honest praise, too, transparently sincere.

Mr. Montenero is not always as indulgent towards works of art. Later in the story he buys a painting at Christie's, the portrait of a medieval Jew having his teeth torn out by order of the reigning King John or King Richard. At a dinner party the following day he cuts the picture up in the presence of his guests and throws the pieces on the fire, explaining to his daughter as he does that his whole aim in acquiring it was to destroy it— "to destroy it, my dear, as I would, were it in my power, every record of cruelty and intolerance." For Shakespeare, on the other hand, he is willing to make large allowances.

Harrington was written as an act of reparation, and the author's good intentions are more in evidence in its pages than her artistic skills. The plot creaks; every incident is there to make a didactic point; the character of Berenice is a mere blur. But the book still has its interest, both social and psychological, and no one who stops to consider the great sludgelike weight of prejudice against which Maria Edgeworth was contending will be disposed to undervalue what she was trying to do. (Mr. Montenero is in fact the first full-length portrait of a sympathetic Jew in English fiction.)

Lord Mowbray, incidentally, turns out to be a thoroughgoing scoundrel. But he is right about one thing. In the 1760s and 1770s, the period during which most of the novel takes place, Charles Macklin (*né* McLaughlin) of Donegal was undoubtedly "the most celebrated Jew in England."

• 3 •

Macklin's success ensured that *The Merchant of Venice* was never again absent for long from the stage. The play became a firm favorite not only at Drury Lane, but at the other major London theaters, Covent Garden and the Haymarket; travelling companies took it to the provinces; by 1752, when William Hallam's company performed it in Williamsburg, Virginia, it had reached America.

Eighteenth-century productions were frequently embellished with songs, dances and other diversions. Lorenzo, for example, was given a serenade to sing under Jessica's balcony, just before she eloped; the action in one production at Drury Lane was punctuated first by a pierrot's dance, then by a pastoral dialogue, then by a hornpipe. Entire scenes could be dropped, too, especially from the casket story, and on occasion the whole of Act V was dispensed with. The effect of these cuts was to concentrate attention more than ever on Shylock, to make him the unquestioned center of dramatic interest. But Portia also became established as a major test for leading actresses. Most of them attempted the part, and after Kitty Clive there was no more larking around. It was as Portia that the twenty-year-old Sarah Siddons made her debut in London, in 1775. She failed, and fled back to the provinces; but after her triumphant return six years later it became one of her regular roles.

In spite of Macklin's predominance, Shylock was far from being his exclusive preserve. Garrick (with whom his relations were often stormy) steered clear of the part, but at least a dozen other Shylocks appeared on the London stage during his time. Shepherd, Roscoe, Lalauze . . . Today most of them are the merest shadows, barely that: such is the eventual fate of all but the greatest actors. But one name flares briefly into life. John Henderson won immediate acclaim when he played Shylock at the Haymarket in 1777—his first appearance in London. Even Macklin praised him, and although the manager of the Haymarket, George Colman, complained that his costume looked as though it had been hired from a pawnbroker, he also said that in the scene with Tubal he acted with an intensity that reminded him of Lear, "a mad king in a storm." Henderson repeated his success in other Shakespearean roles, and if he had lived, he could easily have gone on playing them into the era of Edmund Kean. He would be much better remembered if he had; but he died in 1785, at the age of thirty-eight.

The previous year John Philip Kemble had played Shylock for the first time, at Drury Lane. It was a role in which he was often to appear, generally with Sarah Siddons—his sister—as Portia, but it was not one of his more memorable efforts. This is hardly surprising: there was little obvious affinity between the demands of the part and the elevated neo-classical style for which Kemble was famous. (Hazlitt, who disapproved, once described him as "an icicle on the bust of Tragedy.") When he took over the management of Covent Garden in 1803, and staged his own production of *The Merchant of Venice,* he cast himself, more plausibly, as Antonio. His Shylock was an actor who was already well known in the part at the same theater, George Frederick Cooke.

Cooke was as tough, heavy-drinking character who had put in more than twenty years as a strolling player before he got his chance in London. The main qualities he brought to Shylock are apparent from the account of him that Leigh Hunt gives in his *Autobiography:*

> Cooke, a square-faced, hook-nosed, wide-mouthed, malignantly smiling man, was intelligent and peremptory, and a hard hitter: he seized and strongly kept your attention; but he was never pleasant . . . He loved too fondly his own caustic and rascally words; so that his voice, which was otherwise harsh, was in the habit of melting and dying away inwardly in secret satisfaction. He limited every character to its worst qualities; and had no idealism, no affections, no verse.

In retrospect he was often compared unfavorably with Kean, but Kean himself admired him to the point of idolatry. He saw him as a predecessor, and felt a kinship with him, in his bohemian ways, that he could never feel with the gentlemanly Kemble.

Although he did not have the field completely to himself, any more than Macklin had done, Cooke was undoubtedly the leading Skylock of his day. Over the years, however, his drinking got worse. He was often drunk on stage, often so drunk that he did not even show up at the theater, and in 1809, having exhausted most of his credit with London audiences, he decided to accept an invitation to appear in New York. As the first established star of the English stage to visit America, he proved a major attraction. His sins were overlooked; his performances were extolled—and one of the parts that he played was naturally Shylock.

Thomas Abthorpe Cooper, the New York actor-manager who was responsible for bringing him over, had frequently played Shylock himself. By this time *The Merchant of Venice* was a familiar play to American audiences. It had received its first performance in Philadelphia in 1766, followed by one in New York two years later, and once the American theater had been set up on a regular basis, in the 1790s, it became a standard item in the repertoire. But Cooke offered something new. American playgoers thrilled to his sarcasm, his harsh exultant laughter, his rage, his rapid shifts of mood. They applauded him when they first saw him, in 1810, and again in 1811; but by September of that year he was dead. His drinking had remained as reckless in New York as it had been in London: friends testified that he had no difficulty putting away three bottles of port in an evening. (Did he ever smile to himself, one wonders, when he came to the line where Shylock speaks of his "sober house"?)

Eight years later Edmund Kean visited America for the first time. One of the last things he did before returning home was to arrange for Cooke's remains to be shifted to a new site in the church where he was buried, St. Paul's in lower Manhattan, so that a monument could be erected in his honor. During the reburial he managed to abstract one of the toe bones; he took it back to England, and on his return he compelled the other actors at Drury Lane to kneel down and pay homage to it. After that he kept it permanently displayed on his mantelpiece, as a kind of sacred relic, until Mrs. Kean threw it away in disgust.

However much they may have differed from him (and from one another) in details of emphasis and technique, the actors who followed Macklin in playing Shylock remained faithful to his general conception of the character. The Shylock they portrayed was wolfish, cunning, eaten up with hatred; and nobody doubted that this was the correct reading of the part. The common view was summed up in the jingle about Macklin's performance, allegedly composed by Alexander Pope, which everyone who writes about the stage history of *The Merchant of Venice* is doomed to quote sooner or later:

This is the Jew
That Shakespeare drew.

Eighteenth-century criticism of the play, such as it was, told the same story. At one point, it is true, Dr. Johnson was moved to agree with Shylock—in his comment on the passage in the trial scene about the Venetians keeping slaves. The Jew's argument, he wrote, seemed to him conclusive: "I see not how Venetians or Englishmen, while they practice the purchase and sale of slaves, can much enforce or demand the law of 'doing to others as we would that they should do to us.' " Johnson, who once proposed a toast "to the next insurrection of the Negroes in the West Indies," was not going to let slip a chance of expressing his abhorrence of slavery. But that was in passing, In other comments he made it clear that, like everyone else, he regarded Shylock as an object of detestation.

At the very end of the century, one curious voice was raised against the general verdict. In 1796 a "society of gentlemen" in Exeter published an anonymous collection of essays which included three papers on Shakespeare—the work, as it soon became known, of a local clergyman and antiquary named Richard Hole. In one of his essays, Hole undertook a plea in mitigation on behalf of Iago; in another, he presented "An Apology for the Character and Conduct of Shylock." His main points are that Shylock's faults are the result of the ill treatment he has received, that he never knowingly violates the law, and that he is ultimately defeated by mere quibbles; but the best part of the argument takes the form of an imaginary theater review. We are asked to look ahead to a remote future, in which the Jews are once again living in Palestine. A Jewish adaptation of *The Merchant of Venice* has just been performed, and the next morning a notice appears in the *Jerusalem Daily Advertiser:*

> On the fourth day of the first week in the month of Nisan was represented the tragedy of "Shylock," written by Nathan Ben Boaz. The plot is borrowed from an old

> British bard, who flourished about the beginning of the 17th century of their era; and who composed it under the influence of the spirit of inveterate malice against our nation for which, in that and many preceding ages, the Europeans were notorious . . .

The critic proceeds to describe the action from Shylock's point of view, down to his enforced conversion. ("At the inhuman proposal not an eye was to be seen unmoistened with tears in our theater.") The most shocking thing, he adds, is that even two hundred years later no one seems to have objected to the original play's violations of natural justice:

> On examining Shakespeare's numerous commentators, and other records of the times, it appears that no censure was ever cast, no unfavorable sentiment entertained of the unjust judge, the injurious merchant, the undutiful daughter and prodigal lover. What an idea does this give of the English nation when such sentiments could be applauded!

Most commentators have assumed that Hole was being ironical. There is, after all, the companion piece on Iago. But his irony when he writes about Shylock is so fine as to be barely visible: the essay is more like a game of let's pretend, and one which anticipates future developments to an almost uncanny degree. In the nineteenth century apologists for Shylock would advance very similar arguments in earnest. In the twentieth century there would indeed be productions of *The Merchant of Venice* in a Jewish state, with Hebrew newspapers to review them, while the adaptation by "Ben Boaz" foreshadows later attempts to recast the story of Shylock and tack on a new ending. In the words of the *Jerusalem Daily Advertiser,* "the sudden yet natural death of the benevolent Merchant is well imagined. The turbulent frenzy of the judge, brought on by his corrupt decision, and the tender melancholy of the daughter, who bewails her misconduct too late, are equally affecting."

Meanwhile, in the real world, on the real stage, the old Shylock went about his familiar business. Looking back in 1817, Hazlitt drew a composite portrait of the character as actors since Macklin had presented him:

> . . . a decrepit old man, bent with age and ugly with mental deformity, grinning with deadly malice, with the venom of his heart, congealed in the expression of his countenance, sullen, morose, gloomy, inflexible, brooding over one idea, that of his hatred, and fixed on one unalterable purpose, that of his revenge.

This was the Shylock to whom three generations of playgoers had grown accustomed—the Shylock that Hazlitt himself had been expecting to see, when he went to Drury Lane on 26 January 1814, and found himself confronted instead with the impassioned acting of Kean.

CHAPTER NINE

Romantics and Revisionists

· 1 ·

Kean was five feet, four inches tall. Force of character in an actor can always overcome lack of inches: Kean could comfort himself with the precedent of Garrick, another short man, and eventually he was to achieve what was probably his greatest success as Othello, a character whom no one has ever thought of as diminutive. But when he was first given the chance of appearing at a big London theater, he could hardly help being aware that his height was a potential handicap. It was this more than anything else that made him opt for the role of Shylock, and insist on sticking to it when the management started having second thoughts—"The Jew, or nothing!"

His exact date of birth is uncertain, but he was probably twenty-three at the time. The illegitimate son of an alcoholic father whom he had never known and a wayward minor actress, he had had a disordered childhood, much of it spent fending for himself in fairgrounds and on the fringes of the theatrical world. Then, around the age of fifteen, he had begun work as a strolling player. The setbacks and privations he suffered in the years that followed were no worse than those that had been endured by Henderson, Cooke and countless others in the same profession, but he felt them more keenly than most. As Giles Playfair has written, "a stroller needed to be either very tough or very philosophic, whereas Edmund was proud, sensitive and extravagantly impatient." He also had a wretched private life. He was constantly at odds with his wife, and only two months before he made his Drury Lane debut his elder son, the darling of his heart, had died at the age of four.

The Drury Lane management first got to hear of him from a theater-lover called Joseph Drury, who had seen him acting at a small theater in Devon. Drury, a former headmaster of Harrow, was a man with influential connections, but even so his friends at Drury Lane might well have hesitated to follow up his recommendation in more flourishing times. The theater was going through a difficult period, however, and badly in need of fresh talent. The manager went down to the West Country to see for himself, and in due course—not without some intervening complications—Kean was engaged.

His first night as Shylock was to become one of the great theatrical legends of the century. The weather was dismal, with snow and slush everywhere. His parting words to his wife, as he trudged off to Drury Lane, were, "I wish I was going to be shot." At the theater, the stage manager was suspicious—during the one rehearsal that had taken place, he had caught a whiff of "innovations"—and most of the other actors kept their distance. (Shades of Macklin's first night!) When the curtain rose, those spectators who had shown up were surrounded by a sea of empty places. Kean made his entrance. He leaned on his cane and looked askance at Bassanio—and even before he spoke, Dr. Drury, who was watching from the wings, knew that everything was going to be all right. A few moments later there was a burst of applause for his reply to Bassanio's assurance about the bond ("I *will* be assured"); then more applause; by the end of the evening, such concentrated and vehement applause that it sounded as though the house, far from being three-quarters empty, was packed from top to bottom. When Kean got back to his lodgings, his first words to his wife were: "Mary, you shall ride in a carriage yet, and Charley"—his surviving son—"shall go to Eton."

There were only two reviewers present in the theater that night. One was the critic of the *Morning Post,* who praised him, without going overboard, for his artistry and intelligence. The other was Hazlitt, who began his notice for the *Morning Chronicle* the next day with a bold unqualified claim. It had been many years, he wrote, since an actor had appeared at all equal to Kean "for voice, eye, action and expression." Returning to report on the second performance, six days later, he went even further: "His style of acting is, if we may use the expression, more significant, more pregnant with meaning, more varied and alive in every part, than any we have almost ever witnessed." By now most of the other London critics were also present, and they were unanimous in their praise. Ten days later Kean scored an even bigger triumph when he made his first appearance as Richard III; two weeks after that the Drury Lane management doubled his salary to £16 a week, and added a bonus of a hundred guineas. These were substantial sums for the time, but modest in comparison with the £10,000 a year that he would soon be earning—and spending.*

Many accounts of Kean's Shylock have been preserved. Some confine themselves to excited superlatives; others go into a good deal of detail. Spectators thrilled equally to the sudden musical charm of his voice when he addressed Jessica, to his chuckle when he said "I cannot find it in the bond," to the look of withering contempt that he shot at Gratiano before his final exit. One piece of business in the scene with Tubal made an impression on the journalist W. J. Fox that he could still recall thirty years later:

> At the exclamation, "I would my daughter were dead at my foot, and the jewels in her ear! would she were hearsed at my foot, and the ducats in her coffin!" he started back, as with a revulsion of paternal feeling from

**One of his purchases, in the early years of his glory, was a black stallion which he named Shylock. (He also had a spaniel called Portia.)*

> the horrible image his avarice had conjured up, and borrowing a negative from the next inquiry ("no news of them?") gasped an agonizing "No, no, no."

In the trial scene he was praised both for the deadly gleam in his eye, and for his dignity in defeat.

It was the intensity of his acting that impressed audiences most—the sense of total involvement, the suggestion (though in fact every move was carefully worked out in advance) of impulsiveness and spontaneity. Coleridge said that watching him was "like reading Shakespeare by flashes of lightning." His other admirers included Byron, Shelley, Keats: he might not have thought in such terms himself, but he was the actor that a romantic age had been looking for. And his romanticism made him to some extent "of the devil's party." It enabled him to discern a damaged greatness in Richard III, Macbeth, even in Shylock.

His Shylock was still a villain. It was still possible for *The Times,* in its original review, to praise him for his portrayal of "the sordid and malignant Jew." But "sordid" was a stock epithet, applied by force of habit. Both critics and ordinary playgoers increasingly agreed that his great achievement was to raise Shylock above sordidness, to endow him with a large measure of dignity and humanity.

Nothing signalled his intention more clearly than his decision to play the part wearing a black wig and beard. For the first time, the traditional red wig was abandoned, and with it went the most obvious link with the play's medieval origins. Whatever his faults, Shylock was no longer automatically identified as a kinsman of Judas. The New Testament clouds hanging over him thinned out; and as they did, he was allowed to assume a degree of Old Testament grandeur. Kean's Victorian biographer F. W. Hawkins quotes one reaction to the Jacob and Laban speech from an unnamed spectator who was present on the first night:

> Shylock is in Venice with his money bags, his daughter, and his injuries; but his thoughts take wing to the East; his voice swells and deepens at the mention of his sacred

> tribe and ancient law, and he dwells with joy on any digression to distant times and places, as a relief to his rooted and vindictive purposes.

Douglas Jerrold, more succinctly, said that Kean impressed the audience at such moments "like a chapter of Genesis."

How much any of this weighed with Kean himself is uncertain. He was an actor, on the lookout for dramatic opportunities: religious and social questions were of little if any account to him. But it is interesting to note that when he appeared in *The Jew of Malta,* in 1818, he gave Barabas such humanizing touches as he could. (A number of lines derogatory to Jews were also removed from the text.) This was the first production of the play since the seventeenth century. In spite of the praise Kean received for his performance, it failed to attract the public, and the next revival did not take place until 1922.*

The Jew of Malta was only a minor episode in Kean's career. *The Merchant of Venice* remained one of its cornerstones. It was the play with which he chose to reestablish himself in 1827, for example, when he returned from his long second stay in America. On that occasion, according to *The Times,* he was not only received with acclaim while he was on stage: "during the whole of the fifth act, in which Shylock does not appear, the cries for 'Kean' were incessant." He enjoyed many similar triumphs in the role, and he returned to it again and again.

In time, it is true, dissipation and ill health took their toll. There was one evening when he was so exhausted by the Tubal scene that he could not leave the stage without help: he was forced to change the line "Go, Tubal, and meet me at our synagogue" to "Lead me to our synagogue." But as late as March 1833, at the opening of his final season, he was able to recover much of his old form. The Shylock that he gave on that occasion, which was en-

**Matters were not helped by the fact that it was boycotted by Jewish playgoers, a small but conspicuous section of the London theater-going public. They refused to be placated by a prologue assuring them that no offense was intended to Jews in general, and they are said to have been incensed that the first performance coincided with Passover.*

thusiastically received, was also the last performance of any role that he completed. Four days later he collapsed halfway through a performance of *Othello.* He lingered on for two months after that, but he was plainly a dying man.

Even in his prime there were spectators he failed to carry along with him. Carlyle, who saw him as Shylock in the 1820s, thought that "he exaggerated everything, and was like a wild beast." An extreme reaction, no doubt, but not one that can be wholly disregarded. If we could watch Kean acting today, we would probably be startled, possibly dismayed, at how close he came to outright melodrama. Yet the weight of evidence in his favor is overwhelming. Hazlitt and his other admirers had seen plenty of acting that was melodramatic and nothing else. They knew the difference.

Perhaps the most balanced verdict was the one delivered a generation later by George Henry Lewes in his book *On Actors and the Art of Acting.* Lewes, the outstanding theater critic of the early Victorian period, was only sixteen when Kean died, but he had often seen him perform (he came from a theatrical background), and he trusted his boyish impressions. Indeed, he had already been mature enough at the time to recognize that the actor had serious limitations. He could be wildly uneven; he was often tricky or flashy. But Lewes remained convinced that at his best he had never been surpassed. Among his major roles, he ranked Shylock second only to Othello, and he thought that he had been at his greatest in Shylock's greatest speech: "Anything more impressive than the passionate recrimination and wild justice of argument in his 'Hath not a Jew eyes?' has never been seen on our stage."

• 2 •

It was a happy turn of events that Hazlitt should have begun his career as a theater critic only a month or two before Kean began *his* career at Drury Lane. The new reviewer proved to be the newly promoted actor's most formidable champion; the actor provided the reviewer with what he would otherwise have lacked, a subject that called on him to exert his full powers.

Left *Charles Macklin, by Johann Zoffany (1767–8)*

Below *Edmund Kean (1827)*

Henry Irving (1879)

Edwin Booth (1870)

Set for Charles Kean's production, (1858)

Above The Ingoldsby Legends — *illustration by George Cruikshank (1840)*
Right *Ludwig Devrient playing Shylock in Weimar — a sketch by Thackeray (1831)*
Below The Merchant of Venice, *a drawing by Sir John Gilbert (1864)*

Left *John Gielgud, with Peggy Ashcroft as Portia (1938)*
Below *Laurence Olivier, with Jeremy Brett as Bassanio (1970)*

Left *Ludwig Devrient, with Lebrun as Gratiano (c. 1820)*
Below left *Firmin Gémier (1917)*
Below right *Jacob Adler (1901)*

Left *Ellen Terry as Portia (1879)*
Below *'Jessica and her Daughters', illustration by Arthur Szyk to Ludwig Lewisohn,* The Last Days of Shylock *(1931)*

Set by Theodore Komisarjevsky and Lesley Blanch for Komisarjevsky's production (1932)

A Japanese Merchant of Venice, *Tokyo (1966)*

Left *Werner Krauss (1943)*

Below *Among the ruins — Felix Bressart and Tom Dugan in Ernest Lubitsch's* To Be or Not To Be *(1942)*

Hazlitt's most extended consideration of Shakespeare can be found in his book *Characters of Shakespear's Plays* (1817). In the chapter on *The Merchant of Venice* he once again praises Kean for breaking through the crust of theatrical convention, although he also suggests that some contemporary playgoers—the more thoughtful ones—had already been edging away from the traditional view of the play on their own initiative: "In proportion as Shylock has ceased to be a popular bugbear, 'baited with the rabble's curse', he becomes a half-favorite with the philosophical part of the audience, who are disposed to think that Jewish revenge is at least as good as Christian injuries." Hazlitt's own account of the moneylender is the first sustained statement of the case for the defense, and one of the best. He not only sympathizes with him in his embattled isolation, and pities him in his downfall; he sees a touch of "fine Hebraism" in his language, and admires him for his energy and acuteness. "That he has but one idea, is not true; he has more ideas than any other person in the piece."

Coming to the rescue of Shylock inevitably meant entering some heavy reservations about Antonio: the persecutor and the victim changed places. But Hazlitt went further. He was ready to admit that he was no great admirer of Portia: there was "a certain degree of pedantry and affectation about her, which is very unusual in Shakespeare's women"—though perhaps it was "a proper qualification for the office of a 'civil doctor,' which she undertakes and executes so successfully." As for the speech about mercy, "it is very well; but there are a thousand finer ones in Shakespeare."

Of all Shakespeare's qualities, the one Hazlitt admired most was his ability to enter into his characters' feelings: "He was nothing in himself, but he was all that others were, or that they could become." Shylock was a striking example of dramatic empathy in action. But in taking up his cause, Hazlitt was also moved by broader historical issues:

> There is a strong, quick and deep sense of justice mixed up with the bitterness and gall of his resentment. The constant apprehension of being burnt alive, plundered,

> banished, reviled and trampled on, might be supposed to sour the most forbearing nature, and to take something from that "milk of human kindness" with which his persecutors contemplated his indignities.

That Shylock is not actually threatened with being put to death in the play itself seems a pedantic objection. Where else would the kind of hatred directed against him lead, if it were pushed far enough? Hazlitt wrote about *The Merchant of Venice* with a full sense of the history that lay behind it, and in the same spirit with which he customarily attacked radical and religious bigotry. One of his last essays, published in 1831, was a vigorous plea for Jews to be given the various civil rights (most conspicuously, the right to sit in Parliament) that were still withheld from them. Jewish emancipation, he wrote, was "but a natural step in the progress of civilization."

The mellowing of attitudes towards Shylock was inseparable from the growth of nineteenth-century liberalism. Hazlitt was a man of the left; so was Leigh Hunt, whose weekly paper the *Examiner* rivalled Hazlitt in the enthusiasm with which it greeted Kean's debut. Hunt himself was in prison at the time—he had been convicted of libelling the Prince Regent—and the review was written by his assistant, Thomas Barnes*; but two years later he took the opportunity to endorse Hazlitt's account of Shylock in an editorial note on the newly published *Characters of Shakespear's Plays.* He had one observation of his own to add. Shakespeare, he believed, had endowed both his Christians and his Jew with virtues, and at the same time set out to show that both sides were bound fast by their preconceptions: "We suspect that the main feeling he had in writing the play was to give a kindly lecture to the egoism of sects and opinions." His review of the Kean production of *The Jew of Malta,* the following year, painted a similar picture of Shakespeare (in contrast to Marlowe) soaring above the inherited hatreds of his age, rescuing Shylock from the land of monsters and "clothing his dry bones and his vizard face with flesh and blood."

**Subsequently a celebrated editor of* The Times.

From this time on it became commonplace to look at Shylock in the light of the whole long history of relations between Christians and Jews. In his life of Kean (1835), for example, the actor's first biographer, Barry Cornwall, broke off at the end of his account of the Drury Lane *Merchant of Venice* and spent several pages deploring the maltreatment of a people "on whom the world had been spitting its scorn for nearly two thousand years." A little later, in 1838, Charles Armitage Brown—Keats's friend, the owner of the house where the "Ode to a Nightingale" was written—published a study of Shakespeare in which he argued that *The Merchant of Venice* ought to be seen as a plea for tolerance:

> Representing the persecutor [Antonio], on all other points truly estimable, and the persecuted in no degree estimable, yet entirely unanswerable in his defense, puts personal merit out of the question, and places the argument on the broadest principle.

And in the same year the poet Thomas Campbell, in his popular edition of Shakespeare, praised the way in which the playwright had set Shylock's behavior in an intelligible context: "In fact Shakespeare, whilst he lends himself to the prejudices of Christians against Jews, draws so philosophical a picture of the energetic Jewish character, that he traces the blame of its faults to the iniquity of the Christian world." Campbell's literary judgment was in line with his social and political views. He was well known in his day as a champion of oppressed nationalities (the Poles in particular); he was also closely associated with the Jewish financier and philanthropist Isaac Lyon Goldsmid in setting up the first nonsectarian university institution in England, University College, London.*

By mid-century the idea of an impressive, half-sympathetic Shylock was well established. How far or how fast it penetrated down to ordinary readers and playgoers is hard to say. Most of them were probably untouched by it: a villain was a villain, and the

**It was Goldsmid who had first suggested to Hazlitt the idea of writing a paper on Jewish emancipation.*

traditional image of the cruel usurer still prevailed. But among critics, at least, it was the revisionist view that was making the running.

• 3 •

As long as Kean played the part, his was the only Shylock that really counted. There were other Shylocks on offer, of course. They included, by way of curiosity, the earliest instance of the part being performed by a Jewish actor—a Mr. Sherenbeck of Rochester, who took the role at Covent Garden in July 1817. The other novel aspect of this production was that Sherenbeck adopted a lisp, which for some unknown reason had become a regular feature of stage-Jewish dialect. The result, to judge from the comments of the magazine the *Theatrical Inquisitor,* had little to recommend it: "The equipment of this Jew in the dialect of his tribe seemed equally absurd and ineffective. His enunciation was painfully correct and divested of every claim to professional merit." Poor Sherenbeck! His was not a glorious career. But if he has been forgotten, so have the more substantial Shylocks among his contemporaries.

The one exception is William Charles Macready (1793–1873). Macready came from a theatrical background—his father, a well-known actor-manager, had once played Gratiano to Macklin's Shylock—but he originally planned to become a lawyer. It was only after the family got into financial difficulties, while he was still at school, that he turned to the stage himself. He was a reluctant actor, forever standing on his dignity, convinced that the theater was not quite a profession for gentlemen. But he had great theatrical gifts—almost, you might say, in spite of himself. He was also highly intelligent, unusually forceful, endowed with a true Victorian earnestness. By dint of hard work and hard thought he turned himself into the most considerable English actor between Kean and Irving.

You can get some idea of how he worried at a part from the entries he made in his diary while he was playing Shylock in 1839. He had first appeared in the role in 1823, but sixteen years later he could still confess that he did not feel at home in it: "I have not got the key to the character," he wrote during rehearsals, "and must sternly and resolutely take the part in hand." Before the first night he was in "a very nervous and wandering state of mind," and after it he was dejected: in his own eyes his performance had been an utter failure. Then he gradually got a grip on things, and three weeks later he decided that he had "acted Shylock very fairly, better, I think, than on any previous occasion." (At the end of the same evening, when he got home, he was further cheered to find a parcel containing a presentation copy of *Nicholas Nickleby*. Dickens had dedicated the novel to him—"What a dear fellow he is!")

Historically Macready's importance lay as much in his work as a manager-cum-director as in his acting. His watchword was unity; his aim was to get away from the haphazard practices that had served the theater up till then, to achieve a harmony in which all the elements in a production, visual no less than verbal, blended together. Plays were no longer to be treated as star vehicles: every scene was to be given its due weight, and secondary parts were to be cast with as much care as leading roles.

As far as *The Merchant of Venice* was concerned, this meant making Shylock less dominant. When Macready chose the play for the opening production of his management of Drury Lane in 1841, the *Theatrical Journal* welcomed the restoration of balance. In the past, its critic wrote:

> It was a Jew wheedling, a Jew storming, a Jew affronting the whole state of Venice, but a Jew always triumphing some way or other, even to the last look at Gratiano. But here, though the actor of Shylock might still tower over the rest, as by the writer's intention it was fit he should, there were matters to preclude the absorption of interest in him. There was the gay Christian world as well as the dark Jewish; there was the power and majesty of Venice to hold in awe and suspense even the terrors of the bond.

In spite of the acclaim which greeted this production, Shylock was never one of Macready's favorite roles. When he played it, he looked picturesque, as he usually did. (He wore a short beard, flowing locks, a rich medieval-type gown.) That he was conscientious, goes without saying: before his entrance in the Tubal scene, for instance, he used to stand in the wings and work himself up, shaking a ladder fixed to a wall and muttering curses with a fury that made the stagehands gather round and stare. Yet somehow the inner life of the character eluded him. G. H. Lewes thought that his mistake was to drop the malignity of the part, while at the same time failing to allow for any tenderness or family affections. The result was an essentially petty Shylock: "abject, sordid, irritable, argumentative."

Lewes himself had had dreams of becoming an actor. In 1849, at the age of thirty-two, he finally took the plunge, and persuaded the management of the Theatre Royal, Manchester, to let him appear first as Shylock, then in his own play *The Noble Heart.* He was already widely known as a man of learning, the author of a bulky *Biographical History of Philosophy,* and the reviewers were respectful. If the *Manchester Guardian* felt that his Shylock was too mild-tempered, it put its complaints almost apologetically, while another local critic, Mrs. Carlyle's great friend Geraldine Jewsbury, managed to summon up some positive enthusiasm: "Mr. Lewes never for one instant allowed the audience to lose the impression that he was a noble nature driven to outlawry by MEN." By the sound of it, his interpretation of the part was the most sympathetic that had yet been attempted. But it is also clear, reading between the lines of the reviews, that he lacked the natural gifts that were needed to put his conception across. There was no further demand for his acting, and he devoted himself instead to journalism, to natural history, to writing the life of Goethe. Ultimately he was to win his most lasting fame as the companion of George Eliot.

The actor who played Bassanio to Lewes's Shylock (and who resented him, as a mere jumped-up amateur) was Barry Sullivan—already well known in his native Ireland, but then only at the beginning of his English career. Sullivan was a "big" actor in the traditional mold: vehement, resonant, energetic. He would probably be better remembered today if he had not spent most of his career in the provinces.* Bernard Shaw, who had idolized him ever since he first saw him in Dublin as a boy, thought that he was far more effective than Irving; in the fullest and finest of the many tributes he paid to his memory—an article written in 1947, when he was ninety-one—Shaw placed him firmly in the line of Burbage, Betterton and Kean. And while the plays that he was most widely associated with were *Hamlet* and *Richard III,* one of Sullivan's stock parts (predictably enough for a Shakespearean of his generation) was Shylock.

Another leading actor of the period who starred in the same role was Samuel Phelps, famous for raising the level of Shakespeare productions during his twenty years at Sadler's Wells. Yet another was Charles Kean. "Charlie" had indeed gone to Eton, as his father had promised, but had eventually found his way on to the boards. His heyday was as an actor-manager in the 1850s. He specialized in lavish productions, with historically accurate costume and decor, and few of them were more opulent than the *Merchant of Venice* that he presented at the Princess's Theater in 1858. The costumes, as he proudly let the world know, were "chiefly selected from a work by Caesar Vecellio, entitled *Dagli Habiti Antichi e Moderni di Venetia,* 1850, as well as from other sources found in the British Museum". The Rialto was thronged with exotic and picturesque figures, among them a small girl carrying a basket of doves—ten-year-old Ellen Terry, the envy (as she recalled in her memoirs) of the other children in the cast. A single ingenious set served for the Venetian scenes in Act II, including a bridge under which gondolas could pass and repass. There were something like a hundred colorfully outfitted extras in the trial scene—judges, senators, heralds, miscellaneous retainers.

This was allowing the production values that Macready had

**This should not necessarily be construed as settling for second-best. Sullivan was partly attracted by the money. When he died in 1891 he left £100,000—a reminder of the size of the audience that the provincial theater catered for in the nineteenth century. A reminder, too, that there was relatively more demand for Shakespeare in the provinces than in the West End.*

advocated to get out of hand. The effects were gorgeous, but they constantly threatened to swamp the poetry and the drama. And while an actor of the first rank might have been able to redress the balance, Charles Kean lacked the fire and genius of his father. "There are no tears in his pathos," wrote Lewes; "there is no terror in his wrath." He was also handicapped by occasional lurches into the blocked-nose enunciation that used to be known as a "pudding-voice": he would find himself talking about "de prop dat both sustain my house," or "de beans whereby I live."

Macready was a great actor but not a great Shylock. Barry Sullivan pitched his appeal at a relatively unsophisticated level (and it seems likely that Shaw—relying largely on boyhood impressions, and always ready to score off Irving—exaggerated his stature). Whatever their virtues, none of the other British actors who played Shylock in the period between Edmund Kean and Irving created a lasting impression.

To find an actor who did, one has to turn to America.

• 4 •

It would have been hard to be a playgoer in nineteenth-century America without seeing a performance of *The Merchant of Venice* sooner or later. There were over a hundred productions in New York City alone in the course of the century. The celebrated Edwin Forrest appeared as Shylock, though it was not one of his favorite parts, as a matter of course; a New York production with James Wallack enjoyed what was at the time (1858) a longer run than any previous Shakespearean production on the American stage. And if the cities had their stars, rural America had its barnstormers. Strolling troupes took the play, along with *Hamlet, Macbeth* and the rest, to the remotest and most recently opened-up parts of the country—travelling by wagon, raft, flatboat, river steamer, performing in improvised theaters wherever they could. The humorist "Sam Slick," writing in the 1850s, gave an account of a typical backwoods production that he had once seen:

> There was an old Jew in it, and there was a fellow run away with his daughter and his money puss, and if ever there was a critter ravin, tarrin mad it was old mister Shylock . . . I never see such work as he made on it, a-runnin up and down the floor, and a-pulling at his wig and frothin at the mouth like a hoss with the blind staggers.

The most notable American Shylock in the first half of the century was Junius Brutus Booth. According to his reverential (though not always dependable) biographer Thomas R. Gould, who had often seen him act, Booth's performance produced an effect of patriarchal grandeur. He discerned in Shylock "the representative Hebrew," and his interpretation brought out, from behind the character's obvious vices, "a reserved force, as if there centered in him the might of a people whom neither time, nor scorn, nor political oppression could subdue."

Booth, who was born in London, had begun his acting career in 1813. Some three years later, at the age of twenty, he made his debut in Covent Garden, playing Richard III. The management pushed him forward as the rival and equal of Kean; taking up the challenge, Kean invited him to play Iago at Drury Lane, and gave a performance that decisively put paid to his pretensions. ("That night," Booth told a friend long afterwards, "Kean's Othello smothered Desdemona, and my Iago too.") In 1821 Booth abandoned his family and made a hurried departure for America, accompanied by a Covent Garden flower-girl whom he eventually married. The couple had ten children. The fourth of their six sons, Edwin, grew up to be an actor whose fame far outshone his father's; their fifth son, John Wilkes Booth, fired the shot that killed Abraham Lincoln.

Junius Booth's first professional appearance in America was in Richmond, Virginia. Then came New York; then he settled into a routine of touring the country, travelling deep into the South and West, returning home between tours to the Gothic manor house that he built for himself near Baltimore. He was unpredictable, full of odd fancies, addicted to the bottle; a friend of the Texan hero

Sam Houston and of Davy Crockett; a Rosicrucian who was also attracted at various times to Judaism, Hinduism and Islam; a man, as Van Wyck Brooks wrote, who might have stepped out of the pages of Poe. He also suffered from periodic bouts of madness, which his children used to refer to as "Father's calamity."

One of his convictions was that he was of partly Jewish descent. No evidence for this has come to light, however, and it seems even less likely when we learn that he also believed that the name "Booth" was connected with "Beth," the Hebrew word for a house. Everything suggests that the idea was a complete fantasy—though who is to say that it did not lend his portrayal of Shylock added power?

Edwin Booth was only nineteen when his father died, in 1852. He had already had a good deal of theatrical experience, but it was not until 1857 that he established himself as one of the leading players of the day, with appearances in Boston and New York. Before that he had spent four arduous and adventurous years touring in California, with forays to Australia and the Pacific islands. In 1861 he acted in England; between 1863 and 1867 he presented a series of memorable seasons at the Winter Garden Theatre in New York; in 1869, after the Winter Garden had burned down, he opened his own theater, Booth's, but in 1874 he went bankrupt and was forced to relinquish control. The remainder of his career was taken up with tours, including a second visit to England in 1880–1881 and a third in 1882. (He also toured Germany, where he was greatly admired.) He retired in 1891 and died two years later.

He had grown up in an atmosphere saturated in Shakespeare, and the best-known Shakespearean characters—Shylock among them—must have been familiar presences to him from early childhood. At the age of twelve he got into trouble when he staged a juvenile production of *Richard III* in a cellar and surreptitiously cut up the "Jewish gaberdine" that his father wore in *The Merchant of Venice*: he wanted to use the spangles on it as decorations for his suit of homemade armor. In later life, in the course of his professional career, he often donned a Jewish gaberdine himself. He first played Shylock at Sydney in 1854, at the start of his Australian tour; it was also the part in which he made his first appearance in England, at the Haymarket in London in 1861. The English critics were fairly cool towards him—cooler than English audiences—but they were probably right: he had not yet achieved complete mastery of the role. That was to come with his performance at the Winter Garden in January 1867.

The Winter Garden production was one of the most sumptuous that New York had ever seen. There were beautifully designed and executed sets (all destined to be destroyed in the fire that swept the theater only a few weeks after the play opened). San Marco served as a backdrop in the street scene; the walls of the senate chamber were hung with Tintorettos. Visually, no doubt, the effects were comparable to those of Charles Kean's production in London nine years before, but on this occasion the pageantry was not allowed to overshadow the central performance. Almost everyone who saw Booth play Shylock in his prime agreed that he brought a mesmerizing quality to the part. There were moments when, to one spectator, he seemed "nothing but a pair of eyes, large, dark, awful, and bright—above all, bright, and seeming to give out light."

His conception of the character, once it had crystallized, was a simple one. He saw Shylock as a man driven by personal hatred and greed. Any considerations of racial or religious animosity were secondary: there was no reason not to believe the moneylender when he said that Antonio's chief offense in his eyes was bringing down the rate of interest "here with us in Venice." Nor was there anything in Shylock's behavior to inspire pity, still less awe or veneration. His grief at the loss of Leah's ring? It would be more accurate to call it chagrin: it was the financial loss that moved him, not the sentimental associations. His thirst for revenge? Pure narrow-minded malice. "I believe you hold a different estimate of the character, as many do," Booth wrote to his friend William Winter in 1884, "but I have searched in vain for the slightest hint of anything resembling dignity or worthiness in the part."

Winter, the theater critic of the *New York Tribune* (a post he held for no less than forty-four years, from 1865 to 1909), had in fact initially urged Booth to present "a majestic Hebrew of the old Bible." At the stage, he tells us, his own views were colored by those of Victor Hugo and the German author Ludwig Börne. (Shylock had his advocates among Continental writers as well as among Anglo-Saxons.) But in time he was completely won over by Booth's interpretation. It had been derived, he came to believe, "exclusively from Shakespeare, and it was correct." This was the Jew that Shakespeare drew.

Simplicity of outline did not preclude scrupulous attention to detail. Booth was also a friend of the American Shakespeare scholar Horace Howard Furness, and the notes he contributed to Furness's Variorum edition of *The Merchant of Venice* (1888) demonstrate how carefully he worked out individual bits of business. In Shylock's first scene, for example, when he says "Cursed by my tribe," "this is said in a lower tone, almost growled *sotto voce.*" When he tells Antonio "You called me dog," he speaks "sarcastically—with a pause and a gulp before 'dog' " ("as Kean is said to have uttered it"). When Antonio and Bassanio leave the stage at the end of the scene, he overhears Antonio's complacent comments and grins; then, "moving slowly up the stage, he turns as they exeunt, and looks after them with intense hatred."

William Winter thought that there were moments of pathos in Booth's performance, but that they were involuntary, the unintended by-product of the actor's innate sensibility and melodious voice: they did not seriously modify the overall impression of evil. Certainly Booth's final estimate of the character was unsparing. In a long letter which he wrote to Furness, and which Furness reprinted in the Variorum edition, he admitted that he had once tried to view Shylock in the light of "the venerable Hebrew, the Martyr, the Avenger."* But the more he had reflected, the more fantastic such an idea had come to seem. There were no redeeming features, and he ended up by denying Shylock even the right to be considered a human being:

**Possibly under the influence of his father, although he later convinced himself that Junius—and indeed Edmund Kean—had been content to follow the Macklin tradition.*

> If we side with him in his self-defense, 'tis because we have charity, which he had not; if we pity him under the burthen of his merited punishment 'tis because we are human, which he is not—except in shape, and even that, I think, should indicate the crookedness of his nature.

"We are human, which he is not . . ." There is nothing, as far as I know, to suggest that Booth was anti-Semitic. (Nothing, that is, beyond a tendency to fall back on the old familiar stereotypes when the occasion arose: he had no problem, any more than most of his contemporaries would have had, about describing Shylock's refusal to be fobbed off with money in the trial scene as "an un-Jewlike action.") If he had been asked whether he thought that he might be in danger of fanning the flames of prejudice with such a harsh portrayal, he would probably have replied that *The Merchant of Venice* was a play, not a contribution to the history of the Jews; that if Shylock was non-human, it was because he was an ogre in a romance. But his performances did not take place in a social and historical vacuum. It was possible to admire their artistry, and still feel troubled about the inartistic real-life conclusions that some people might draw from them. One famous American who was uneasy was William Cullen Bryant. In 1867 Bryant was in his seventies, with his career as a poet of any interest long behind him. But he was still a powerful voice in New York journalism, and after seeing *The Merchant of Venice* at the Winter Garden he was moved to publish an article under the heading "Shylock Not a Jew." Shylock as played by Booth, he insisted, was "not a Jew, but a fiend . . . Revenge is not a characteristic of the Jew." When it came to the question of Jews and money, on the other hand, Bryant himself revealed some distinctly ambivalent feelings. "It is true," he wrote,

> that money-changers once spat on in the ghetto are now hugged in the palace. Rothschilds and Goulds, Belmonts and Benjamins are found in the ante-chambers of princes and presidents. But we fear that it is not so much that the prejudice against the Jews has ceased but that the

> love of money has increased—not that the Jews have become as Christians, but that the Christians have become as Jews.*

This was an old notion brought up to date: Christians who succumbed to the love of money were *Christen-Juden.* But Bryant was also the heir to a quite different tradition. There had been a strong Hebraic strain in the religion of his New England forebears. It was still something he shared with them, in a looser form, and by the end of the article he had worked his way round from denigrating the Jews as the servants of Mammon to glorifying them as the servants of God. He complained that Booth had failed "to do justice to the grandeurs of the Jewish race;" he extolled "the wonderful working of the soul of the Hebrew . . . which gave mankind its noblest religion, its noblest laws and some of its noblest poesy."

When Booth returned to England in 1880 and in 1882, he scored notable successes in *King Lear* and in a production of *Othello* in which he and Henry Irving alternated in the leading parts. He also offered English audiences a more mature version of Shylock than the one they had seen twenty years before; but here he was much less successful. The Shylock of the hour—the Shylock of the century, many admirers would have said—was Irving's. In comparison, Booth's reading of the part seemed bleak and old-fashioned.

**Jay Gould was not Jewish, though his enemies often said that he was. As a fervent supporter of Lincoln, Bryant detested the former Confederate statesman Judah Benjamin.*

CHAPTER TEN

Henry Irving

· 1 ·

Henry Irving was forty when he took over the management of the Lyceum in 1878. It was in the same theater, in 1871, that he had graduated from admired leading man to popular idol with his legendary performance as the guilt-racked burgomaster in Leopold Lewis's melodrama *The Bells.* Now at last, seven years later, he was in full command, with an entire company at his disposal.

The main attractions of his first season as manager were *Hamlet* and Bulwer-Lytton's *The Lady of Lyons,* an old-fashioned romance chosen partly for the opportunities it offered his leading lady, Ellen Terry. The second season opened according to plan in September 1879 with an even more venerable piece, a gloomy affair called *The Iron Chest,* which had been a favorite of Kean's; but after less than a fortnight Irving startled his assistants by announcing that he wanted to drop it and put on *The Merchant of Venice* instead. Preparations for the new production, including the painting of elaborate scenery, were completed in just over three weeks; it opened on 1 November 1879.

The play was one that he already knew well. Two of his early parts, while he was serving his apprenticeship in Scotland and the North, were Salerio and Bassanio: he had been the Bassanio to Edwin Booth's Shylock when Booth visited Manchester in 1861. But until now, the play itself had never held much appeal for him. What had changed his mind, he told friends, were the North African Jews he had encountered that summer, when he had been a guest on a Mediterranean yachting cruise. In particular he had been struck by a Jewish merchant whom he had seen going about his business in Tunis, at one moment calm and self-possessed, then in a helpless rage over a dispute about money, then fawning, then "expressing real gratitude for a trifling money courtsey:"

> He was never undignified until he tore at his hair and flung himself down, and then he was picturesque; he was old, but erect, even stately, and full of resource. As he walked beside his team of mules he carried himself with the lofty air of a king.

The combination of qualities gave Irving his first clue as to how Shylock might be reinterpreted. By the time he got back to London, the idea of presenting *The Merchant of Venice* in a new light was simmering away in his mind.

There was a great deal in the part for him to seize on. Like Shylock, he was a man with an inner devil. *Le diable au corps,* Edward Gordon Craig called it: it drew him to sinister roles, and it was the source of his most powerful theatrical effects. Unlike Shylock, he had his devil under complete control. Off stage, he was courteous, even-tempered, a master of sardonic reserve. "I suppose" (to quote Gordon Craig again) "he was the coolest actor possessing *le diable au corps* that ever came upon this earth." He understood both Shylock's self-restraint, and what it would have been like to have such self-restraint break down; he must also have seen an opening in the role for his subtly sarcastic humor, his sense of the exotic, his ability to strike a chill. But all these qualities would have been consistent with playing Shylock as an out-and-out villain. Irving's most important decision was to portray him as a victim, even in his villainy. "The tendency of the play," he wrote shortly after the Lyceum production opened, "is undoubtedly to show that 'the worst passions of human nature are nurtured by undeserved persecution and obloquy.' " Five years later, in 1884, he went further: "I look upon Shylock as the type of a persecuted race; almost the only gentleman in the play, and the most ill-used." To anyone who had read Hazlitt, or a score of critics since Hazlitt, such a view would have been familiar. In the theater, it was still a novelty, though one for which Irving judged that audiences were now ready.

His reception offered resounding proof that he was right. There were a few dissenting voices (and later there would be more), but the most influential reviewers of the day were united in their praise. Famous personages came to the Lyceum and paid tribute to his performance ("his best, I think," said Gladstone). Most important of all, the public were enthralled. The production ran without a break for seven months—a triumphant refutation of West End managers who claimed that "Shakespeare spelled ruin"—and from then on the play remained a permanent part of Irving's repertoire. He is said to have played Shylock over a thousand times; it was the part he chose for his last appearance at the Lyceum in 1902, and the part he had been due to play the night after he collapsed and died in Bradford in 1905.

Almost everyone, even those who took issue with his reading of the role, agreed on the dignity with which he infused it. This was a Shylock who was sometimes hateful, but never contemptible. He was spare and gaunt, with worn features and a stoop (though when his pride was roused, he drew himself up), and with a wispy gray beard that still had a few streaks of black. The "Levantine" costume that set him apart was neat and becoming: a dark brown robe and tunic, a richly striped sash, a glint of gold earrings, a black cap with a yellow bar ("the badge of all my tribe"). He began quietly and reflectively, and the stages by which he was drawn into his scheme of revenge were carefully marked out. At first, despite flashes of anger, he was predominantly calm, urbane, even gay. When he finally broke into a frenzy, in the street scene, it was all the more frightening, although it was the way in which he subsided into pathos ("no tears but o' my shedding!") that impressed audiences most. And by the time the trial scene came, he had completely recovered himself. There were no histrionics, no heavy show of whetting the knife. His eyes were quick and watchful, but for much of the scene he barely moved. When he listened to the Duke's opening plea, he had what the *Saturday Review* described as "the horrible stillness and fascination of the rattlesnake." Another critic, Clement Scott, thought that "even Portia seemed to shudder under his icy gaze."

His fixity of purpose was so dreadful, and so sustained, that it seems reasonable to ask how anyone could have thought that this was a positively sympathetic reading of the part. He had had bitter provocations—but surely the memory of them must have paled as he urged home his cruel design. Irving underlined his cruelty, too, by restoring the short scene with the jailer, which previous productions had usually cut: Shylock at his most exultantly vindictive.

Yet at the same time he never lost the air of grandeur with which Irving had invested him. In his memoirs, the artist W. Graham Robertson recalled being taken to see the play at the Lyceum as a boy. He had fallen in love with Portia (or rather with Ellen Terry, who was playing her) on the spot, but he had to admit that even she could not prevent Irving from dominating the trial scene, to the point where he threw it off balance: "How small and mean sounded her quibbling tricky speeches when addressed to a being who united the soul of Savonarola and the bearing of Charles the First, with just a touch of Lord Beaconsfield that made for mystery." Soul, bearing, mystery—Irving's triumph was partly the triumph of personal magnetism over plot line.

This would not have been enough in itself, however, to keep audiences on Shylock's side. The actor's masterstroke was to put the maximum emphasis on the image of a man going down to defeat—and to put it there twice. The two incidents in the production which excited the most comment were Shylock's return to his house after Jessica has eloped, and his reaction to the final sentence of the court. One was an Irving invention, the other an Irving elaboration.

The elopement scene in his production closed in a whirl of music, lights and color, with Jessica and Lorenzo caught up in a crowd of masquers as it swept across the stage. The curtain dropped briefly; when it rose, in the words of Ellen Terry, "the stage was empty, desolate, with no light but a pale moon, and all sounds of life at a great distance—and then over the bridge came the weary figure of the Jew." He was bearing a lantern, returning (though he did not realize it yet) to a deserted house. Then the curtain fell again, without a word having been spoken. In later performances Irving extended the scene by having Shylock knock at the door, but either way the effect was piercing. For absolute pathos, Ellen Terry wrote, nothing she had ever seen in a theater could compare with it.

To others, Irving's supreme moment was his final exit, after the trial. When he heard that he was compelled to become a Christian, he looked over his shoulder, stared at Antonio, turned back, raised his eyes and murmured a few indistinct words. His lips moved, but he seemed distracted, and his gaze grew dull. Leaving the court, he summoned up enough energy to cast a searching look at Gratiano; then he took three slow steps towards the door,* stumbled (as though he were about to have a fit), recovered himself, and left the room with a sigh. A knot of Jewish onlookers stole out after him, followed at a distance by a much larger group of Christians; there was a pause, and some sharp yells were heard from outside. The mob was baying for blood.

Irving's approach drew a deep response from his audience. Many of them went halfway to meet him. They saw the production, whether consciously or not, as an act of reparation for past injustices towards Jews, and they gave Shylock the full benefit of biblical associations. Of Renaissance associations, too. One of the most impassioned of the original reviews, an unsigned article in the *Spectator,* began by stressing that, as Irving played him, he was a

**According to Irving's grandson and biographer, Laurence Irving, the actor had "a mystical belief in threefold action." During the trial, when Bassanio offered him money, he tapped the bags three times with his dagger before rejecting them.*

natural aristocrat: "Here is an usurer indeed, but no more like the customary modern rendering of that extortionate lender of whom Bassanio borrowed 'monies' than the Merchants *dei Medici* were like pawnbrokers down Whitechapel way." Then, as the reviewer warmed to his subject, the image of patrician gave way to that of patriarch. Shylock in the later scenes seemed to him so impressive and austere, so much a figure from another, older world, that it was hard to think of him spending his days as a mere trader on the Rialto. The Christian characters, by comparison, were shallow and frivolous. Even Antonio came across as a relatively commonplace type, who "had 'plunged' like any London City man in the pre-'depression' times." And as for the trial scene, it showed a Shylock who was solemn, terrible, perhaps something more: "There was a moment when, as he stood with folded arms and bent head, the very image of exhaustion, a victim, entirely convinced of the justice of his cause, he looked like a Spanish painter's Ecce Homo." The moment soon passed; the next words spoken were "My deeds upon my head! I crave the law." But while it lasted, there had been (in the reviewer's eyes, at least) a remarkable reversal of values. For just an instant, it was Shylock who had been seen as the Christ-figure rather than Antonio.

To mark the play's hundredth performance, Irving gave an elaborate dinner at the Lyceum. At eleven o'clock the curtain fell on the garden at Belmont; within fifty minutes a scarlet and white pavilion had been put up in its place, tables had been spread, the first of 350 guests were beginning to arrive. It was a full Victorian turnout—earls, M.P.s, judges, generals, admirals, miscellaneous ornaments of society, crimson carpets, champagne, a boys' choir singing the National Anthem, 350 presentation copies of *The Merchant of Venice* bound in white parchment and lettered in gold. For Irving, who had left school at the age of thirteen and started life as an office boy, it was a huge personal triumph.

There was one unexpected twist. An elderly peer, Lord Houghton,* had agreed to toast the health of Irving and the Lyceum (he

**The former Richard Monckton Milnes—man of letters, minor politician, man of the world.*

had been asked at the suggestion of one of Irving's friends), but for whatever reason much of his speech turned out to be flippant in tone and lukewarm in its praise. The theatrical guests present found his remarks about their profession horribly patronizing, and he did little better with his comments on the production they had all supposedly gathered to celebrate. He was reminded, he said, of those historians who took it on themselves to redeem the reputations of Nero, Richard III, Robespierre and all the other "great villains of the world." What audiences were flocking to see at the Lyceum struck him as being a rehabilitation of much the same kind:

> For the old Jew, Shylock, who was regarded usually as a ferocious monster, whose sole desire was to avenge himself in the most brutal manner on the Christians of his neighborhood, had become a gentleman of the Hebrew persuasion, with the manners of Rothschild, and not more ferocious than became an ordinary merchant of the period, afflicted with a stupid, foolish servant and a wilful, pernicious daughter.

He could quite imagine that "if Mr. Irving chose to personate Iago, it would be on the same principles as a very honest man, only devoted to the object of watching over Othello's wife."

Irving, like everyone else, was taken by surprise, but his impromptu reply was perfectly judged. He spoke for half an hour, defusing the situation with good humor, standing his ground with tact, returning banter for banter. He warned Lord Houghton that he was considering putting on a new play called "The After-Life of Shylock," which was calculated to arouse even more compassion for the old man—in the final scene he would be shown visiting Belmont as a pedlar, with a sack of lemons on his back. On the other hand he hoped everyone would agree that this was not the right time or place for a detailed discussion of *The Merchant of Venice*: they were not at a Shakespeare debating society, and the hour was late. He and his company were simply grateful that they had been able to carry on the play for as long as they had—"a result which he did not think could have been attained if Shylock had been the Whitechapel old gentleman which he has been sometimes represented. This latter appeared to be the ideal of the character in the mind of my Lord Houghton, but it was certainly not his own conception."

The implication was clear. People who did not know better might cling to their outworn notions, but Irving's improved model had the endorsement of the intelligent public.

• 2 •

In Ellen Terry, Irving had what none of the great Shylocks before him had had—a great Portia. The reviews rang with her praises; she received more letters about her performance (or so she reckoned, looking back in her memoirs) than about all her other parts put together.

She had already made a powerful impression in the same role four years before, in a production presented by the Bancrofts— the actor-manager Squire Bancroft and his wife, Marie Wilton—at the little Prince of Wales's Theatre off Tottenham Court Road. Up until then the Bancrofts had been chiefly associated with domestic "cup and saucer" comedies; *The Merchant of Venice* represented a new departure for them, and one over which they took a great deal of trouble. Their principal scene painter and his assistant were sent to Italy to study Venetian settings at first hand; Ellen Terry's companion, the architect E. W. Godwin, was appointed consultant on costumes and decor. Unfortunately, however, the actor who played Shylock, Charles Coghlan, let them down. According to Squire Bancroft, his performance was "very clever, very natural, exactly the Jew you might meet in Whitechapel, but it was grey instead of being lurid, and quite ineffective." Ellen Terry's verdict was less restrained: it was not even a bad performance, "it was *nothing.*" With a hole like this at its center, the production was beyond repair, and it closed after only three weeks. Yet during the same brief period, Ellen Terry established herself for the first time as an undoubted star. The enthusiasm of the reviewers confirmed what she had experienced during her performance, the sense of an audience not merely pleased, but enthralled:

> I knew that I had "got them" at the moment when I spoke the speech beginning, "You see me, Lord Bassanio, where I stand."
>
> "What can this be?" I thought. "*Quite* this thing has never come to me before! *This is different* . . ."
>
> Elation, triumph, being lifted on high by a single stroke of the mighty wing of glory—call it by any name, think of it as you like—it was as Portia that I had my first and last sense of it.

A group of admirers offered to keep the performances going by subscription. The proposal came to nothing, however, and the general public stayed away. But if audiences were sparse, they also included writers, artists, leading spirits of the new aesthetic movement. Ellen Terry herself, in a china-blue and white brocade dress, with a single crimson rose at her breast, was an aesthete's dream.

At the Lyceum she cast the same spell on a wider scale. This time she brought the Shakespearean image to life more literally, in a dress of shimmering gold—brocaded again, but looking when she moved in it "as though it were made of gossamer." She herself felt that her whole performance was more supple than it had been at the Prince of Wales's, and there was general praise for her lightness and tenderness. A few critics complained that she was unduly forward in her dealings with Bassanio—Henry James found her insufficiently the great lady, "too free and familiar, too osculatory." But it was the learned and pugnacious Shakespeare scholar F. J. Furnivall who voiced the majority view: "Your whole conception and acting of the character are so true to Shakespeare's lines, that one longs he could be here to see you. A lady gracious and graceful, handsome, witty, loving and wise, you are his Portia to the life."

Although he made a number of cuts, Irving gave Portia something like her true weight in the text he used. Above all, he retained the frequently deleted fifth act. His production was one that closed, not with Gratiano's final jeer, but with moonlight at Belmont. At least, it did for the greater part of the run. Then, in May 1880, Act

V was dropped to make room for a sentimental one-act trifle called *Iolanthe*—no connection with Gilbert and Sullivan—which was put on for Ellen Terry's benefit. The tireless Furnivall sent Irving an indignant letter ("*Et tu, Brute*"), and helped to drum up a public protest; but according to Alan Hughes, the foremost contemporary authority on Irving's Shakespeare productions, "the popular myth that Irving usually played *The Merchant* without Act V is a calumny." Apart from the two months or so when *Iolanthe* was substituted, "the play was usually presented intact."

A romantic, open-hearted, grave-and-gay Portia was very much in line with Victorian tastes. Few critics had followed Hazlitt in expressing reservations about her; the common nineteenth-century view was closer to that of Mrs. Jameson, the author of a widely read study of Shakespeare's heroines (first published in 1832), who had extolled her as combining "all the noblest and most lovable qualities that ever met together in a woman." Ellen Terry's Portia was more amorous, and more humorous, than such a description suggests, less of a stained-glass paragon. But nobility was still one of her key attributes—seen at its most stirring, inevitably, in the speech on mercy. In one of the lectures on Shakespeare that she used to give in the latter part of her career, Ellen Terry called the speech "a noble kinsman to the Lord's Prayer."

There was a problem, however. In productions which portrayed Shylock as an out-and-out villain, a noble Portia shone all the more brightly by contrast. But Irving's Shylock was a man who had been wronged, and a man who suffered—which made Portia one of his oppressors, or at the very least aligned her with them.

Both Irving and Ellen Terry, as Alan Hughes has pointed out, were well aware of the inconsistency. For Irving, the outcome of the trial was morally askew: "The Duke and Portia preach to Shylock of mercy, but when the day goes against him they do not practice what they preach." Ellen Terry praised the speech on mercy, but in the manuscript notes for her lectures she made it clear that she was unhappy about the way Portia used it to ensnare Shylock. The same notes reveal that she also had mixed feelings about Bassanio. In the published text of the lectures, she praised him as a loyal friend, and suggested that the fact that Portia was in love with him was commendation enough. In the manuscript she had taken a cooler view, summing him up as "a bit of a loafer, a well-dressed handsome youth of good birth who lives on his charm."

Little if any of this was reflected in what took place on stage. Shylock was a tragic figure, Portia was admirable; the contradictions were allowed to stand, and most members of the audience, or so it would seem, barely noticed them—though if Irving had been challenged, he would probably have replied that he was simply being faithful to the contradictions of the play itself.

• 3 •

In November 1879 the *Theatre,* a magazine which Irving owned, published an article on *The Merchant of Venice* by a theatrical journalist called Frederick Hawkins. Timed to coincide with the Lyceum production, it argued fervently that in essence the play was a plea for toleration: "the sympathy enjoyed by Shylock is designedly aroused in the interest of the great but downtrodden race he represents." Shakespeare, Hawkins reasoned, would never have taken part in "an outburst of vulgar envy and fanaticism," and in those passages where he appeared to be endorsing popular prejudices, it was necessary to read between the lines. In any case, "he more than counteracted with one hand what he seemed to do with the other."

The following month, the magazine published a symposium on Hawkins's views. Irving, writing under the pseudonym "An Actor," was naturally in broad agreement: both sides in the play, he conceded, were guilty of intolerance, but Shylock was less to blame than his enemies. Another contributor, Israel Davis, an Anglo-Jewish *littérateur* (and part proprietor of the *Jewish Chronicle*), put the same case rather more cautiously. Shakespeare, he reminded readers, was too much an artist to have written a play with a set moral purpose. Nonetheless a moral suggested itself, one of which the playwright can hardly have been unaware—that "if the Jew had been treated in a better way, he would have been a better man."

And this was no small thing: "It was a greater step for Shakespeare, in the sixteenth century, to create the Shylock of *The Merchant of Venice* than for George Eliot, in our own times, to imagine the Mordecai of *Daniel Deronda.*"

The other contributors expressed varying degrees of scepticism, with the strongest note of dissent coming from a distinguished literary scholar, James Spedding.* Spedding, who was in his seventies, confessed that he had "an old man's difficulty in accepting these new discoveries of profound moral and political designs underlying Shakespeare's choice and treatment of his subjects." As far as he was concerned, the playwright was primarily a man of business, whose first task had been to provide "plays which would draw." In the case of *The Merchant of Venice*, that meant welding the disparate elements of the plot into an acceptable romantic comedy. But supposing,

> instead of looking about for a story to "please" the Globe audience, he had been in search of a subject under cover of which he might steal into their minds "a more tolerant feeling towards the Hebrew race," I cannot think he would have selected for his hero a rich Jewish merchant plotting the murder of a Christian rival by means of a fraudulent contract . . . It seems to be possible for a skillful actor to work on the feelings of a modern Christian audience so far as to make a man engaged in such a business an object of respectful sympathy. But can anybody believe that, in times when this would have been much more difficult, Shakespeare would have *chosen* such a case as a favorable one to suggest toleration to a public prejudiced against Jews?

Irving never lacked for powerful critics. And where Spedding confined himself to arguing against the general notion of his Shylock,

**A lifelong friend of Tennyson; best-known for his monumental edition of the works of Francis Bacon. In a private comment four years earlier he had described Irving's Hamlet as "simply hideous—a monster."*

a greater figure, Henry James, took issue with his actual performance.

James had already written coolly about Irving on a number of previous occasions, and when he reported on *The Merchant of Venice* for the readers of *Scribner's Monthly,* he saw no reason to change his mind. "Of his Shylock last winter," he told them,

> it was often said that it presents his faults in their mildest and his merits in their highest form. In this there is possibly a great deal of truth; his representation of the rapacious and rancorous Jew has many points of interest. He looks the part to a charm, or rather we should say, to a repulsion, and he might be painted as he stands. His conception of it is a sentimental one, and he has endeavored to give us a sympathetic and, above all, a pathetic Shylock.

Was this a legitimate enterprise? James declined to say. His attention "was fixed primarily on the superficial execution of the thing," and here he found much to disconcert him:

> The actor struck us as rigid and frigid, and above all as painfully behind the stroke of the clock. The deep-welling malignity, the grotesque horror, the red-hot excitement of the long-baffled, sore-hearted member of a despised trade, who has been all his life at a disadvantage, and who at last finds his hour and catches his opportunity—these elements had dropped out. Mr. Irving's Shylock is neither excited nor exciting, and many of the admirable speeches, on his lips, lack much of their incision; notably the outbreak of passion and propsective revenge after he finds that Antonio has become forfeit, and that his daughter has fled from him, carrying off her dowry. The great speech, with its grim refrain: "Let him look to his bond!" rising each time to an intenser pitch and culminating in a pregnant menace, this superb opportunity is missed; the actor, instead of being "hissing

> hot," as we have heard Edmund Kean described at the same moment, draws the scene out and blunts all its points.

In spite of James's disclaimer, this is something more than a discussion of technicalities, of "the superficial execution of the thing." Irving had provoked him into a fierce evocation of the traditional Shylock—malignant, rapacious, vengeful, sore-hearted, red-hot. The traditional Shylock and, he plainly implied, the true Shylock: it is clear that he did not really countenance the idea of a sympathetic Shylock at all. Nor does he seem to have found anything troubling about the element of racial and religious conflict in the play—though it is curious to see him side-step the issue by referring to Shylock as a member of a despised trade rather than a despised race (which is what you would expect). Hath not a usurer eyes?

Another famous literary figure who disagreed with Irving's interpretation was Bernard Shaw. In June 1880, when he was an unknown twenty-three-year-old, Shaw sent an unsolicited review of the Lyceum *The Merchant of Venice* to John Morley, who had just been appointed editor of the *Pall Mall Gazette*. Morley turned it down, and Shaw forgot about it; but fifteen or sixteen years later, during his great days as a theater critic, he returned to the subject more than once.

The long campaign which he waged against Irving was fought on different levels—personal, social, artistic. He was animated by a mixture of malice, rivalry and an honorable determination to carve out a space for the kind of plays he wanted to write himself. But even at his most ill-natured, he never attempted to deny the actor's extraordinary magnetism. "He was utterly unlike anyone else," he once wrote; "he could give importance and a noble melancholy to any sort of drivel that was put into his mouth; and it was this melancholy, bound up with an impish humor, which forced the spectator to single him out as a leading figure with an inevitability that I never saw again in any other actor until it rose from Irving's grave in the person of Charlie Chaplin."

At the same time Shaw thought that it was nonsensical to talk of Irving "interpreting" his roles. It would be truer to say that he superimposed himself on them: the only characters that the mature Irving played were characters of his own devising. How much better, if he had been an author himself! But having failed to master that "supplementary trade," he was compelled to use other men's plays as his raw material:

> His first success in this sort of adaptation was with *The Merchant of Venice.* There was no question then of a good Shylock or a bad Shylock: he was simply not Shylock at all; and when his own creation came into conflict with Shakespear's, as it did quite openly in the trial scene, he simply played in flat contradiction of the lines, and positively acted Shakespear off the stage.

His portrait of Shylock as "a martyred saint" was a remarkable piece of work, in its way. It was also completely unwarranted.

With critics like James and Shaw in the audience, Irving had some formidable opponents ranged against him. But James's article, after its first appearance in *Scribner's,* was to remain buried for seventy years, and Shaw's hour had not yet come. For the moment Irving's version of Shylock was the one that counted, and it continued to exercise a potent influence until well into the twentieth century.

• 4 •

How far did Irving himself believe that what he was offering audiences was the "real" Shylock, or the best possible Shylock? According to Ellen Terry, he "played Shylock for sympathy and told me himself (smiling) he *ought* to play him as a ferocity."

Was it primarily a case, then, of tailoring the part to his physical and vocal limitations? At least one fellow-member of the original Lyceum cast—Jack Barnes, who played Bassanio—felt that it was. Looking back more than forty years later, Barnes wrote that "from observation at rehearsal I think he 'shot' for Shakespeare's Shylock, and finding at least two of the scenes were beyond his powers, he developed a Shylock he *could* compass."

Two points are worth making. First, Irving may or may not have come to the conclusion that "a ferocity" was beyond him. But it was certainly well within his range (as he showed at many points in his original performance) to portray a Shylock who was sinister, vengeful, malicious. That he nonetheless played the part as sympathetically as he did represented a positive act of choice, not something that was forced on him. Secondly, it is generally agreed that his interpretation grew less sympathetic over the years; but no one has ever suggested, as far as I know, that there was a corresponding loss of power, or that in presenting a harsher Shylock he was straining his resources.

Where there *are* conflicting reports is on the question of exactly how harsh his portrayal eventually became. The most extreme view of the case was that taken by William Winter, who knew him well, and who had often seen him act both in London and during his visits to America. "When Irving first acted Shylock he manifested a poetically humanitarian ideal of the part," Winter wrote. But "as time passed a radical change in the personation was little by little effected, till at last, without entire abandonment of a purpose and power to awaken sympathy, it became the true Shylock of Shakespeare—hard, merciless, inexorable, terrible."

As against this, there are many accounts of him playing Shylock in his later years which stress the grandeur and pathos that he continued to bring to the part. A. B. Walkley, a fine critic, took it for granted, in *Playhouse Impressions* (1892), that his interpretation was still "idealized"—as of course did Shaw, writing at roughly the same time. (Unlike Shaw, however, Walkley approved.) The poet Humbert Wolfe, who saw him act the part in 1900, was struck by the element of "unbending arrogance" in his performance, but also by the way in which he conveyed "the blackest despair of the crucified heart." Watching him return home and beat on the door after Jessica had fled, Wolfe (who was only a schoolboy at the time) found himself thinking of David's lament over Absalom—"Absalom, Absalom, my son."

A particularly interesting reaction was that of Eliza Aria, the Jewish journalist who became Irving's *chère amie* during the last seven or eight years of his life. In her autobiography, *My Sentimental Self,* she records that on the first occasion she met him, at a dinner party in 1897, she began by being virtually tongue-tied, but that things improved a little when "in the name of all the Jews, I ventured to thank him for his representation of Shylock." Mrs. Aria, as anyone who reads *My Sentimental Self* will discover, was a fairly frivolous woman, who carefully cultivated the light touch; but she took pride in her Jewish origins, and there is no reason to suppose she did not mean exactly what she said.*

It seems unlikely, on the other hand, that Irving himself ever gave much thought to the Jews, or at any rate to real Jews, as opposed to stage Jews.** He was an actor; he was drawn to the role of Shylock strictly for the dramatic opportunities it offered—not least the opportunity of playing against the grain, looking for neglected virtues and redeeming features. True, his observations during his Mediterranean cruise had given him a living social context within which his imagination could get to work. But the result was still, historically considered, exotic to the point of unreality—an amalgam of Biblical, Sephardic, Italianate and vaguely Oriental, refracted through a Victorian lens.

This exoticism made it easier for audiences to accept a Shylock who was also imposing and austere. The alternative, down-market reading of the character was most readily summed up—by the *Spectator* critic, by Squire Bancroft, by Irving himself—as "Whitechapel"; and in the popular mind "Whitechapel" conjured up a picture, or caricature, of everyday Jews: shopkeepers, small businessmen, tailors, pawnbrokers (the *Spectator*'s example), street

**She was a member of the Frankau family—sister of Julia Frankau, who wrote novels under the name "Frank Danby," aunt of another novelist, Gilbert Frankau, and of the comedian Ronald Frankau and great-aunt of the novelist Pamela Frankau. Of her husband, who left her and took off for South Africa, little is recorded apart from his first remark to her after they had been married and were driving away from the synagogue: "I wonder what has won the Lincoln Handicap."*

***It is curious to recall in this context that his most famous non-Shakespearean role, Mathias in* The Bells, *was that of a man racked with guilt at having murdered a Jew.* The Bells *was based on Erckmann-Chatrian's story* Le juif polonais—le juif *being the victim.*

traders. It also meant, increasingly, Jews from Eastern Europe. By 1879 the old Jewish settlement in the East End had been reinforced for some years by a flow of immigrants from Tsarist Russia, though it was as nothing compared to the influx that began after the pogroms of 1881 and the savage anti-Jewish laws enacted by the Russian Government in 1882. The quarter of a century during which Irving played Shylock coincided with the peak period of Jewish immigration (by chance, the year in which he died, 1905, also saw the passage of the restrictive Aliens Bill), and with the growth of a teeming, energetic, mainly Yiddish-speaking community in the East End—the community that Israel Zangwill portrayed in *Children of the Ghetto.* It was all a long way away from the Venetian fantasy-world of the Lyceum.

Yet it would be implausible to suppose that there was no connection whatever between Irving's *The Merchant of Venice* and either his own or his contemporaries' attitude towards Jews in general. At the very least, he instinctively distanced himself from the prejudices of the past: in the view of A. B. Walkley, his Shylock was "the Jew idealised in the light of the modern Occidental reaction against the *Judenhetze.*" He also assumed, rightly, that most members of his audience would go along with him. And what was important about his production, in this respect, was precisely what it took for granted. It was not conceived in a spirit of propaganda, and it would not have worked if it had been. But it did reflect an underlying commitment to toleration, and it was the product of a society in which—formally, at least—the ideals of liberalism had prevailed.

• 5 •

In the course of one of Irving's American tours, an unkind journalist published what he claimed was an accurate transcription of the way the actor delivered Shylock's speech to Antonio:

Wa thane, ett no eperes
Ah! um! yo ned m'elp
Ough! ough! Gaw too thane! Ha! um!
Yo com'n say
Ah! Shilok, um! ouch! we wade hev moanies!

Ellen Terry protested that this was a cheap form of wit—spoken words could almost always be made to look ridiculous when they were set down in phonetic spelling. But she did not positively deny that the squib bore *some* relation to what Irving sounded like.

It is entirely possible that if we were spirited back in time and given a chance to watch him act, we would be more struck by the oddities of his diction than by anything else. But in reality, of course, we can never hope to judge the acting of the past (or the past before there were films and recordings) except at second hand. Would we have found Irving's voice mannered and unpleasant, as many contemporaries did? Would we have found it beguiling and expressive, appropriate to the kinds of parts he favored in its very strangeness? We shall never know.

Let us suppose, however, that we succumbed to his spell; more particularly, to the spell of his *Merchant of Venice*. That might still leave us with divided feelings. A great theatrical experience, yes; but might we not conclude, even so, that what we had been watching was something different from Shakespeare, and something less than Shakespeare?

There are Shakespearean productions which debase the text, or travesty the text, or set out to demonstrate originality at the expense of the text. We have had no shortage of such productions in recent years; indeed, in one's darker moments they have come to seem the norm. Verse effects are sacrificed to gimmicky stage effects; plots are wrenched out of their settings and distorted by false analogies; there is a heavy-handed effort to impose a "relevance" that directors are unable to find in the play itself.

Whatever its innovations, Irving's *Merchant* was plainly not a production of this kind, but one which kept within the spirit of the play—provided we accept that "the spirit of the play" can cover a number of possibilities, and that to emphasize some of them inevitably means understating others. There is no one definitive Shylock, any more than there is a definitive Hamlet or Macbeth. The most we can ask is that an actor exploit opportunities with which Shakespeare has presented him, rather than opportunities that he has invented for himself; and if the favorable accounts of his performance are to be trusted, this is what Irving did. The aspects of the character that he chose to stress were only part of the story (and he never pretended otherwise). But they were aspects that were already there, in the text, waiting to be brought out.

If we were still to feel that his reinterpretation went too far, two extenuating factors would surely weigh with us. First, he was a pioneer, presenting a view of the case which no English actor, certainly no actor of comparable rank, had presented before. Secondly, he was right to recognize something disturbing in the traditional way of playing Shylock—more disturbing than his hostile critics were willing to concede.

Many of those who saw him act when they were young lived long enough to learn of Nazism and its consequences, and some of them must have felt that, in however horrible a fashion, he had been vindicated. One such veteran was the educationist and man of letters George Sampson (1873–1950). Sampson, who is best remembered as the author of *The Concise Cambridge History of English Literature,* was not the man to lightly endorse anything that could be construed as a betrayal or perversion of Shakespeare. Nonetheless he had no hesitation in affirming that "Irving's Shylock is implicit in the play." In an essay published when he was in his seventies, in 1947, he recalled his pleasure in the actor's performance, and made it clear that he had come to find it even more persuasive over the years:

> When I saw the play as a boy I had no feelings about Jews, for I had never met any. Now I think the plot worthy of Hitler—the plot, I say, not the play. In considering *The Merchant of Venice*, we must distinguish sharply between the plot and the play. It was Shakespeare himself who lifted Shylock above the plot; and Irving played the Jew that Shakespeare drew.

Like the interpretation which inspired it, this is a verdict that can be argued over forever; but whether or not we agree with it, it is one that we can hardly fail to respect.

CHAPTER ELEVEN

Stage and Study

· I ·

None of Irving's immediate successors made the same impact when they played Shylock; none of them had anything like the same influence. But *The Merchant of Venice* remained as popular as ever.

Of the big Edwardian productions, the most spectacular was the one staged by Herbert Beerbohm Tree in 1908. Spectacle was Tree's stock in trade. He represented the culmination (or the gorgeous decadence) of the scenic tradition inaugurated by Charles Kean, and his Shakespeare productions at Her Majesty's from 1898 onwards were famous for lavish pictorial effects—a Roman Forum designed in consultation with Sir Lawrence Alma-Tadema; the battlements of Flint Castle; a wood near Athens complete with real rabbits; Falstaff and his followers riding down a sunlit Windsor street. Naturally he was not going to let slip similar opportunities in *The Merchant of Venice*. His production opened with the Doge's procession. Portia's early suitors took their leave in an elaborate dumb-show. Shylock's house stood on one side of a lovingly reconstructed ghetto, with a synagogue facing it, and lines of washing suspended from the tenements in between.

Tree's own performance was broadly in line with Irving's but cruder and more garish. He appeared in most of his scenes with a ragged, toothless, squalid-looking Tubal hanging around him like a familiar spirit. In Act I, as Antonio and Bassanio left the stage, he aimed a large gobbet of saliva at their backs. (According to Hesketh Pearson, who was in the cast, "the effect was more humorous than venomous.") He borrowed the business about Shylock returning to his empty house, and spoiled it; instead of simply knocking, he pushed the door open, rushed around the rooms (which were visible through the windows) shouting Jessica's name, and re-emerged sobbing hysterically as he set off in search of her.

He also differed from Irving in the emphasis he put on Jewish, quasi-Jewish, or pseudo-Jewish effects. Audiences were left in no doubt that this was a Shylock whose life was dominated by his religion. In the earlier part of the play, he was shown making his way to synagogue, leaning on Jessica's arm; and when the time came to lament her treachery, he sat on the ground like Job, tearing his robes and strewing ashes on his head. For Tree's wife, as she recalled in the memoir she wrote after his death, this last scene was one of the high points of the production. Another was "the beautiful Jewish hymn that was lifted up, sonorously and religiously, against the light music of the revellers."

Many of Tree's contemporaries assumed that he was Jewish or partly Jewish himself. There is no evidence that he was—his father, Julius Beerbohm, was descended from an old German family with military and court connections; but he can only have encouraged the belief with his predilection for Jewish parts. Financially, the most successful of all his roles was Svengali in *Trilby*—hirsute hypnotist, musician of genius, eternal alien, latter-day variant of the Wandering Jew. If anything, Tree's Svengali was more "Hebraic" than George du Maurier's: in a scene he tacked on to the dramatized version which had no equivalent in the novel, Svengali was made to recite the opening verse of the most ancient of Jewish prayers, the

Shema. Another of his virtuoso roles was Isidore Izard, a millionaire of the South African, Barney Barnato type in an adaptation of Octave Mirbeau's *Les Affaires sont les Affaires.* Yet another, in which he first appeared two years before *The Merchant of Venice*, was Fagin—a sly, scuttling, crooning, reptilian Fagin. A dangerous character; but then his Shylock, for all the touches of nobility, was designed to be dangerous too.

Tree's brilliant half brother Max Beerbohm had a theory of his own about the staging of *The Merchant of Venice*, and a very odd one. During his years as a theater critic, Beerbohm wrote about the play on several occasions. His general approach was always the same: apart from Shylock it was a tedious piece of work, and even Shylock was an uncomfortable composite, half bogeyman (Shakespeare held back by his sources) and half fine figure (Shakespeare managing to break free from them). Luckily however, changing historical circumstances now allowed us to get much closer to the Jew Shakespeare wanted to draw, rather than the one he was forced to draw to please the groundlings:

> Among the Elizabethans, who thought the Jews merely absurd and remote monsters, the part of Shylock was played in a spirit of grotesque farce. In later times, when the Jews began to make their power definitely felt in England, and were feared and hated as a coming terror, Shylock became a melodramatic villain. Nowadays, when we all have a very great admiration and sympathy for the Jews (the admiration which is always given to people who have us in their power), Shylock has become a romantically pathetic hero.

This is a curious passage. Whatever prejudices eighteenth-century playgoers held against Jews, there is nothing to suggest that they thought of them as "a coming terror"; and as for "people who have us in their power" . . . If one did not know whom one was reading, one might have taken a guess that it was Hilaire Belloc, or someone of that stripe. Yet Beerbohm also made it clear that he was on Shylock's side. Elsewhere he summed up the play—the part of it he valued—as a "study of racial strength against contempt and persecution."

One "romantically pathetic" stage Shylock that he praised was Franck Benson's, which he saw in London in 1901. By that time Benson and his company had already been travelling up and down the provinces for nearly twenty years, establishing themselves as the mainstay of Shakespeare production in the country. Ardent, athletic, high-spirited, with a strong tinge of public school and Oxford about them, they were generally not at all to Beerbohm's taste: he once wrote a memorable essay describing a Benson production in terms of a cricket match. ("Speech after speech was sent spinning across the boundary, and one was constantly inclined to shout 'Well *played* sir! Well played *indeed!*' ") But when it came to *The Merchant of Venice*, he was prepared to relent. He commended Benson, who had begun his professional career working under Irving at the Lyceum, for maintaining the Irving tradition, and for showing "much more of imagination, and much less of angularity, than is his wont." Another admirer spoke of the actor's "Major Prophet" manner in the role, an effect accentuated by his bearing and his height.

Benson played a leading part in the movement to set up the Oxford University Dramatic Society, which was founded in 1884. The undergraduate who actually got the society going, Arthur Bourchier, later became a well-known actor-manager himself: his productions included a big West End *The Merchant of Venice* in 1905. In 1911 he was invited back to Oxford by the Vice-Chancellor to lecture on the drama. It was a very Establishment occasion ("we welcome an old friend, and we welcome a successful friend"), in the course of which Bourchier took the opportunity to plead for the establishment of a National Theatre. He also spoke about Shakespeare, and about Shylock, the "Hath not a Jew?" speech, he reminded his audience, "was written at a time when Jews were not allowed to settle in England—written three hundred years before the recent massacres of Jews in Russia." (This was the epoch of the Kishinev pogrom and the savageries of the "Black Hundreds.") That Shakespeare had been able to put such words into Shylock's mouth, living when he did, showed both the range of his sympathy and the keenness of his insight into human nature—and Bourchier went on to draw a comparison with Queen Margaret in *Henry VI,* another character maddened by "senseless slights and undeserved wrongs." Bourchier's own portrayal of Shylock six years earlier has been less sympathetic than this suggests: J. C. Trewin, a dependable historian, describes him as playing "a revengeful and uncomplicated usurer."

Matheson Lang's Shylock at the St. James's Theatre in 1915 had rather more depth. Early in the run, Lang was visited in his dressing room by Israel Zangwill, whom he had never met before. The writer sat himself down and proceeded to talk excitedly about how he thought the part ought to be played—with less cringing in the early scenes, and with a greater display of intellectual strength and self-sufficiency. "This reading greatly intrigued me," Lang recalled, "and I resolved immediately to act upon it." He felt sure that the changes he made were very much for the better; Zangwill in turn, perhaps not surprisingly, decided that in its improved version Lang's Shylock was the most sympathetic he had seen*. . . .

Many other leading actors of that era played Shylock in the course of their careers—Johnston Forbes-Robertson and Oscar Asche, to cite only two of the names at which hearts once beat faster. But a comprehensive survey of their work is a task for specialists, and specialists alone. A non-specialist, faced with old theater programs, dusty memoirs and fading or forgotten legends, is likely to be left reflecting yet again on the impermanence of the actor's art. "Into the night go one and all."

The same considerations naturally apply when we turn to the American theater. In the generation before the First World War *The Merchant of Venice* was at least as popular in America as it was in Britain, possibly even more popular. But we must limit ourselves to one or more of the more prominent names.

The English-born actor Richard Mansfield, who is best-known today for having introduced American audiences to Shaw, first

**While it may not be strictly relevant, I cannot resist quoting Beerbohm Tree's description of Zangwill: "his face shining like Moses, his teeth like the Ten Commandments, all broken."*

played Shylock in New York in 1893. To begin with, he tried to out-Irving Irving, searching for every redeeming feature in the character that he could find. (William Winter believed that he had one eye on the "Hebrew" section of his audience.) Later, he shifted the emphasis from exacerbated sensibility to pure malice. But in neither case did he aim much beyond the picturesque. Anticipating Harley Granville Barker, he decided that the play was "a fairy tale"; lacking Barker's judgment and taste, he indulged in all kinds of fanciful tricks. When he came to the line "To bait fish withal," for instance, he pointed towards the canal. In the trial scene, he found himself surrounded by Jewish supporters who had pressed forward to inspect the ducats that he had been offered. And the biggest stunt of all was reserved for last. At the end of the trial, to quote Winter's account, "he made Shylock place the point of his curved knife inside his dress, at the throat, intimating the purpose or act of suicide, and he spoke the words "I am not well" in a weak, thin voice, as though to signify that the Jew was bleeding to death." He had in fact been anticipated in the particular piece of business by an aspiring American actor called James Owen O'Connor, who had had Shylock commit suicide in court when he played the part in New York in 1888. O'Connor himself later died in a mental hospital.

Augustin Daly staged a sumptuous *Merchant of Venice* in New York in 1898, with the celebrated Ada Rehan as Portia and the relatively unknown Sidney Herbert as Shylock. It was well received, but achieved only a short run—the moral being, in the view of Daly's biographer, that "the public wanted a star in the role of the Jew."

The American actor who proved the biggest draw as Shylock in the early years of the twentieth century was just such a figure. Edward Hugh Sothern was already a celebrated leading man when he teamed up with Julia Marlowe on the first of their Shakespeare tours, in 1904, although until then he had specialized in romantic dramas and light comedies: the role that made him famous was Rudolph Rassendyll in *The Prisoner of Zenda* (1895). His partnership with Julia Marlowe quickly became a major theatrical legend, and they remained together, devoting themselves principally to Shakespeare, for the rest of their careers. *The Merchant of Venice* was one of their regular offerings: they first toured in it in 1905, took it to New York in 1907, and were still appearing in it in the 1920s.

Sothern's Shylock was a severe-looking figure, dressed in black, with his face made up to resemble Michelangelo's Moses. There was nothing particularly Michelangelesque about his performance, however. He overacted shamelessly: in the trial scene, for instance, he not only praised Portia—"A Daniel come to judgment!"—but knelt down and kissed the hem of her robe at the same time, and when he was told that he had to become a Christian, he tried to bolt from the court. (The guards turned him back). It is clear, as Toby Lelyveld says, that he saw the play "neither as tragic nor as comic. It was pure melodrama."

His interpretation also hardened as he grew older. Initially, critics found humanizing touches in it, or complained of its contradictions—now light, now dark; but by 1921 the *New York Times* could write that "Mr. Southern's Shylock is a cruel Shylock, untouched by any consideration save his revenge." In effect, he had followed the course marked out by Richard Mansfield and (to a much lesser degree, and at a much higher level) by Irving. "Good and bad" Shylocks sometimes shed their virtues; "bad" Shylocks never seem to have mellowed.

• 2 •

One theatrical enterprise stood quite apart from the world of stars, actor-managers and West End or Broadway plush. For over fifty years, in the face of innumerable discouragements, William Poel (1852–1934) fought a single-minded campaign for "authentic" Shakespearean productions—productions which were faithful to Shakespeare's text and to Elizabethan stage conventions. Almost everything about the established manner of presenting Shakespeare seemed to him misconceived: the elaborate sets (and the long intervals that were needed while they were changed), the emphasis on star parts, the arbitrary cuts, the slow pace of the verse, the accumulated theatrical fuss and bother of two centuries. Salvation, he argued, lay in a return to speed, simplicity, fluidity, a bare platform stage, and respect for what the words actually said. In 1894, after a number of earlier experiments and "directed dramatic readings," he founded the Elizabethan Stage Society in order to put his principles into practice. Most of the Society's productions were staged in lecture halls or borrowed premises rather than regular theaters; the actors, who were almost always amateurs, performed in Elizabethan costume; the accompanying music was either Elizabethan or specially composed in the Elizabethan style.

The Merchant of Venice was the first play Poel ever saw. He was twenty at the time, and working as a clerk for a building contractor, when his father took him to a production, with John Ryder, a veteran of the Macready era, as Shylock. His interest in the theater dated from that occasion, and possibly also his sense that the theater needed to be reformed. After reading the play when he got home, he was struck (so he said) by how widely the performance he had seen departed from what the playwright had written. He did not specify what the differences were, but six years later, in 1878, he went to hear a reading of the play given by an actress called Miss Glyn, and noted approvingly that her conception of Shylock accorded with his own: "not feeble and sympathetic but vigorous and implacable, the most impenetrable cur that ever lived."

By this time he had become a professional actor himself. After touring in the provinces, he went on to spend two years as manager of the Royal Victoria Coffee Hall (the future Old Vic), and six months as stage manager with Frank Benson. But it was an Elizabethan-style *Hamlet* which he staged in April 1881—a single matinée, using the First Folio text—that marked out the course he was eventually to follow. In 1887 he took a further step forward when he accepted an invitation to become "instructor" for the Shakespeare Reading Society, a group founded by students at University College, London. There was nothing casual about the Society's readings: Poel could spend up to three months rehearsing a single recital, preparing the ground for his later work with the Elizabethan Stage Society as he did. The first reading he directed, in 1887, was *The Merchant of Venice*.

In the course of the same year he delivered two lectures on the play. The first, to the Church and Stage Guild, created a small rumpus. While he was outlining his ideas, the chairman who was a fervent admirer of Irving, stood up and protested; when he continued, undeterred, the chairman left the meeting. The second paper, which he read to the New Shakespeare Society, was built around the assumption that Shylock is an unqualified villain to start with, and a figure of fun to end with. The purpose of the first scene in which he appears is to show him directly plotting to take Antonio's life. In the trial scene, the biter is bit, and everyone else, including the audience, is meant to feel relieved and gratified. Certainly there was nothing to shed tears over. Citing the original version of the story in *Il Pecorone,* Poel argued that at the conclusion Shylock ought to rush off the stage in a mad rage (though his biographer, Robert Speaight, rightly wonders how he managed to square this with "I pray you give me leave to go from hence; I am not well").

It was inevitable that the Elizabethan Stage Society would get around to the play sooner or later. The Society's production was in fact its twelfth. (It had begun with *Twelfth Night* in 1895.) Three performances were presented at St. George's Hall, Langham Place, in November-December 1898, with a professional actress, Eleanor Calhoun, playing Portia—Poel's revival of Elizabethan practices did not extend as far as using boy actors in women's parts—and Poel himself playing Shylock. Miss Calhoun wore a dress taken from a portrait of Elizabeth I; Poel wore a red wig and a big false nose, indulged in a good deal of clowning, and followed his own prescription by rushing off at the end in a fury, pursued by hoots of laughter.

As though to compensate for the loss of seriousness in scenes where audiences had come to expect it, Poel tried to heighten the solemnity elsewhere. In the casket scenes, for example, as Robert Speaight explains, "the religious character of Portia's obligation to respect the terms of her father's will was underlined by the introduction of a priest and four acolytes, who stood by while the suitors were making up their mind." There is nothing about this in the text: it was quite as much of an innovation, in its way, as any of Irving's.

The production had its admirers—Frederic Harrison the Positivist and George Wyndham the Tory politician were among those who wrote to Poel telling him how much they approved; but most members of the audience, even if they sympathized with his aims, seem to have felt that a ludicrous Shylock simply did not work. Nor did he fare any better when he revived the production in 1907. He remained impenitent, however, and in an article written in 1909 he covered much of the old ground. *The Merchant of Venice* is a romantic comedy; for the purpose of having a villain, the dramatist thrusts into it a malicious usurer, of a type going back to the old Latin comedy; Shylock is meant to be laughed at and defeated "not primarily because he is a Jew"—religious differences are at most a side issue—"but because he is a curmudgeon." Later still, in an article published in 1912, Poel amused himself by rewriting the title page of the first quarto in the light of current opinion: "The tragicall Historie of the Jewe in Venice, with the extreame injustice of Portia towards the sayd Jewe in denying him the right to cut a just pound of the Merchant's flesh, together with the obtayning of the rich heiress by the prodigal Bassanio."

It seems appropriate that Poel should be represented in the National Portrait Gallery by a painting of him in the role of Father Keegan, the exalted visionary priest in *John Bull's Other Island.* (It was a part he played on various occasions from 1906 onwards, initially at Shaw's own suggestion.) He was a dedicated man, often ridiculed, who fought long and hard for the things he believed in. Some of his productions, most notably his 1901 *Everyman,* were outstanding achievements and even his lesser work helped pave the way for a much better understanding of Shakespeare's dramatic workmanship. But he could also be simplistic and wrong-headed, and in the case of *The Merchant of Venice* you feel that he was essentially over-reacting. Irving's interpretation of Shylock seemed to him so wrong that its opposite had to be right: he could not allow for the possibility that there might be a middle way. The theater-going public needed to be reminded that Shakespeare was an Elizabethan—and nothing but an Elizabethan. But if he had been just "an Elizabethan," would he still have been Shakespeare?

• 3 •

In the course of the nineteenth century, English literature became an instrument of education, and by 1900 most books on Shakespeare were being written by academics. The newly installed professors saw themselves as guardians of tradition: there were as yet no exciting "revaluations," no attempts to dislodge established names. But what did tradition mean in the case of Shylock? Not, on the whole, an attempt to recapture the Elizabethan Shylock, the villain in the red wig, but a continuation of the more sympathetic approach that had taken root during the romantic period. Most of the founding fathers of "Eng. Lit." were closer in spirit to Irving than to Poel.

A. C. Bradley, for example, never wrote at length about *The Merchant of Venice*, but a passing comment in *Shakespearean Tragedy* makes it pretty clear what line he would have taken if he had. "One reason why the end of *The Merchant of Venice* fails to satisfy us," he observed, "is that Shylock is a tragic character, and that we cannot believe in his accepting his defeat and the conditions imposed on him." George Saintsbury was convinced that "Shylock has the best of the argument." For Walter Raleigh, he was an outstanding example of Shakespeare's habit of creating characters that "engage the interest of the audience beyond what is required (almost beyond what is permitted) by the story." The story had called for a monster, but Shakespeare had given us a man:

> Antonio and Bassanio are pale shadows compared with this gaunt, tragic figure, whose love of his race is as deep as life; who pleads the cause of a common humanity against the cruelties of prejudice; whose very hatred has in it something of the nobility of patriotic passion; whose heart is stirred with tender memories even in the midst of his lament over the stolen ducats; who, in the end, is dismissed, unprotesting, to insult and oblivion.

Not everyone took such a charitable view. Stopford Brooke, in his book *On Ten Plays of Shakespeare* (1905), piled on the hostile adjectives. Shylock was "mean, mercenary, ungenerous, ignoble in thought and deed, consumed with evil passions"; he was "the darkness to Antonio's light." Moreover, he was not just Shylock, but

> the personification, in Shakespeare's intention, of the evil side of the Jewish nation. And, in Shakespeare's mind, the evil side was rooted in money. It was in the carelessness and contempt of gain for gain's sake that Antonio found the greatness of his character. It was in the sordid care for money that Shylock lost his soul.

Brooke was a clergyman (and an early Fabian); the preaching style died hard with him. But even he had to admit that there might be some excuse for Shylock's hatred: "in an odd recess of our nature, it is possible to give it some faint sympathy."

There were other critics who reminded their readers not to lose sight of Shylock's villainies—but much less forcibly, with much more emphasis on the ambivalent feelings he aroused. "Shakespeare, the man, shared the prejudices of his public," wrote C. H. Herford in a widely used textbook; "the poet and artist rose instinctively and unconsciously above them. He entered into the situation and into the soul of Shylock with an intensity of imaginative understanding which the after world has excusably mistaken for sympathy." The American critic Brander Matthews, who held the chair of dramatic literature at Columbia, went further. Shakespeare "builded better than he knew," and however much the Elizabethans may have execrated Shylock, or laughed at him, "to us in the twentieth century he is a supremely pathetic figure."

F. S. Boas, by contrast, was on guard against pathos—in principle, that is. In *Shakespeare and His Predecessors,* which was first published in 1896, and which was still in print in the 1940s, Boas expressed horror at Shylock's conduct where he thought horror was due, and cautioned his readers against supposing that Shakespeare meant to arouse pity for him in the episodes where he was discomfited. Yet a feeling of regret hovers over Boas's pages when he writes about *The Merchant of Venice*, a regret stirred not so much by Shylock's fictional fate as by the play's broader historical significance:

> It must assuredly be counted part of the tragic inheritance of the Hebrew race that it should have attracted Shakespeare's gaze at the moment of its deepest degradation, when for it alone the Renaissance was in no sense "a new birth," and when Luther himself had only sought to rivet faster its chains.

Regarded in this light, Shakespeare's "almost superhuman plastic power" only made matters worse. It meant that "for the majority of modern readers Shylock, a product of the dramatic imagination, has supplanted the great historical figures of law-givers and prophets as the type of the sons of Israel."

The strength of feeling here must surely be related to the fact that Boas was Jewish himself. His father, who originally came from Lubeck, had been one of the founders of the small Jewish community in Belfast; and though he severed his own links with Judaism, he plainly retained some sense of affiliation to the Jewish past. It shows itself at several points in his discussion of Shylock, above all when he comes to "Hath not a Jew?" This "magnificent outburst," he writes, "is wrung forth not only by the taunts of Antonio, but

> By the torture, prolonged from age to age,
> By the infamy, Israel's heritage,
> By the ghetto's plague, by the garb's disgrace,
> By the badge of shame, by the felon's place,
> By the branding-tool, the bloody whip,
> And the summons to Christian fellowship."

The lines are from Browning's *Holy-Cross Day.* They are more effective when they are read in context, near the end of that ultra-vigorous, far from lachrymose poem; but they make their point well enough even in isolation.

It was another scholar of Jewish origin who first put forward the case for a connection between *The Merchant of Venice* and the Lopez affair: Sidney Lee, or (as someone does not fail to point out in the Library scene in *Ulysses*) "Mr. Simon Lazarus, as some aver his name is."* Lee developed his argument in an article published in 1880, while he was still an undergraduate at Oxford; it was the first step in a career which was to lead to the editorship of the *Dictionary of National Biography,* a knighthood, a leading position among the Shakespeareans of his time. His *Life of William Shakespeare* long held the field as the standard work on the subject. In the first edition (1898) he stuck to biographical data, but in the expanded edition of 1915 he allowed himself the luxury of a few critical opinions—among them, a comparison between *The Merchant of Venice* and *The Jew of Malta.* Barabas, he concluded, typified " a savage greed of gold." Shakespeare's Jew, in spite of his mercenary instinct, was "a penetrating and tolerant interpretation of racial characteristics which are degraded by an antipathetic environment."

Lee, as this may suggest, was not a very exciting writer.** Sir Arthur Quiller-Couch gave his readers and lecture audiences a much more enjoyable time. He spoke his mind, and in the case of *The Merchant of Venice* that mainly meant explaining why the play had never been one of his favorites. He conceded that it has some magical things in it, especially in the fifth act, and he admired its stagecraft. But most of the characters remained irredeemably unsympathetic. Antonio was a merely static figure; the other Venetians were either "wasters" or "rotters," and it was poor workmanship on Shakespeare's part to make "a predatory young gentleman" like Bassanio double as a high-sounding moralist. Quiller-Couch quoted his soliloquy while choosing the lead casket—

**Lee's original name was in fact* Solomon Lazarus. *Is "Simon" a genuine mistake, or some kind of complicated cross-reference to Stephen Dedalus's father, Simon Dedalus? With Joyce you can never be sure.*

***He did however pen one immortal sentence (first pointed out by Harold Nicolson), in his official life of Edward VII: "The king had a splendid appetite at all times, and never toyed with his food."*

The world is still deceived with ornament

and added that he felt moved to interrupt: "Yes, yes—and what about you, my little fellow? What has altered you, that you, of all men, start talking as though you addressed a Young Man's Christian Association?"

As for Shylock, he had been "over-philosophized." He was cruel and crafty, just such a villain as Elizabethan audiences loved to hate. Yet one had to admit that it was impossible to condemn him out of hand. Shakespeare's imagination was so large and so catholic that it could not help entering into his point of view, any more than it could help entering into the point of view of Caliban. And if he was heartless, his heartlessness was matched by that of his supposedly merciful adversaries, never more so than when they compelled him to turn Christian: "Being such Christians as the whole gang were, they might have spared him *that* ignominy!"

Quiller-Couch, who was nearly fifty when he first became a don in 1912, retained much of the free and easy style of the man of letters that he had been up till then. The ascendancy of the professional academic was not yet complete: when the editors of the Home University Library wanted to commission a volume of Shakespeare in 1910, for instance, they asked John Masefield. The book Masefield wrote for them was simple, heartfelt and idiosyncratic. The chief point he makes about Shylock is that he is "a man of intellect born into a despised race"; his tragedy is that "the generous Gentiles about him can be generous to everything except intellect and Jewish blood." However plausible this may sound at first, it will not stand up to serious examination. The most you can say is that Shylock's keen intelligence makes him a potential intellectual, perhaps the ancestor of future intellectuals. But there are no grounds within the play itself for arguing that he sets more store on intellect than such cultivated characters as Antonio, Bassanio and Lorenzo.

The non-academic and unacademic Shakespeare commentator who made the greatest noise during these years was Frank Harris. One of the unexpected things about *The Man Shakespeare* (1909), Harris's attempt to reconstruct the poet's life from his work, is how little space he devotes to Shylock, as opposed to Antonio. The moneylender is accorded a few paragraphs; the merchant gets a chapter to himself. But then Harris believed that Antonio was a Shakespearean self-portrait. "Here for the first time we discover Shakespeare in direct relations with real life"—"real life," in this context, meaning the world of money-making and practical affairs. Antonio had other Shakespearean traits as well: the melancholy resignation that had already found expression in the character of Richard II, for example. But above all he embodied Shakespeare's disdain for money. This made him a walking paradox, since he was also a successful merchant; but Shakespeare identified with him so uncritically that he could not see the contradiction.

The other side of the coin—appropriate metaphor—was Shakespeare's detestation of Shylock. For anyone who doubted that he really did hate him, Harris urged a number of points. He had gone out of his way to make Shylock a bad father, for instance, whereas the family affection of Jews was proverbial. (With good reason: "the pressure from the outside, Herbert Spencer would say, tends to bring about cohesion among the members of the despised caste.") The clinging evidence of his hatred, however, was Gratiano's jibe about the gallows and the font: "A brutal insult from a gallant gentleman to the broken Jew: it is the only time in all Shakespeare when a beaten and broken man is so insulted."

Harris's contention that Shakespeare himself was indifferent to money has won few converts: the facts, where they can be ascertained, suggest otherwise. But he does deserve credit for insisting that Antonio, so often dismissed as two-dimensional or colorless, is an important character—and an interesting one.

• 4 •

In the years just before the First World War a new critical presence came looming out of the West. Elmer Edgar Stoll (1874–1959), who taught at the University of Minnesota, did not become well known in England until the 1920s, but he had begun staking out his position a good deal earlier, with essays on Shakespeare's ghosts (1907), on

Shylock (1911) and on Shakespeare's criminals (1912). That position can best be summed up as a tough-minded historicism, a firm conviction that an author can only be properly understood in the context of his own times. In the case of Shakespeare, that meant entering into Elizabethan attitudes and beliefs; it meant accepting that his art had been shaped by theatrical conventions and the expectations of his audience. Unfortunately most nineteenth-century criticism had gone astray, wandering off into a maze of subjective or anachronistic fantasy, and it was time to get back to the facts. In many respects Stoll can be seen as the academic equivalent of Poel.

He was a more intimidating figure, however. "The hardest-boiled of the hard-boiled," was Logan Pearsall Smith's way of describing him; and though Smith joked nervously in his little book *On Reading Shakespeare* about "Professor Elmer Edgar Stoll, Ph.D., of Minneapolis on the Mississippi River," it is obvious from other references in the book that he was rather in awe of him. So were many of his contemporaries: indeed, no one who had previously felt comfortable with impressionistic criticism, or with the free-ranging character studies of A. C. Bradley, could fail to be discomposed (to quote Logan Pearsall Smith again) by this "altogether awkward customer," this "fierce eagle in the fluttered dovecotes," this "wolf in the quiet fold of literary professors."

Then, gradually, the challenge was absorbed. Younger critics rejected the idea of identifying the meaning of a literary work with its author's intentions (even assuming we could be certain what those intentions were). They were equally impatient with the notion that a play could only be judged in terms that would have been acceptable to its original audience; it was absurd, wrote W. K. Wimsatt, to suppose that "all critical insights about Shakespeare stopped shortly after the time of Shakespeare."

Something remained of Stoll's case, even so—enough to ensure him a regular place in the surveys and anthologies of Shakespeare criticism. But as time passed, he acquired the reputation of being too rigid to repay extended attention; and a brief summary of his essay on Shylock might well seem to confirm such a view. In its revised version, the essay runs to over eighty pages, but the main points it makes are fairly simple ones. First, we are told, the comments of the other characters provide a clear indication of what we are meant to think of Shylock; so do his own avowals, and a whole battery of dramatic devices. Second, the treatment he receives as a Jew is entirely consistent with the general attitude towards Jews at that time. Third, usurers in Elizabethan plays were villains by definition. Finally, he is a comic character, and comic in a rugged traditional mode that allows no room for pathos.

None of this, recounted in bare outline, sounds particularly exciting or particularly new. But the effect of reading Stoll himself is rather different. He is a learned writer, at home in the dramatic literature of half a dozen languages, but a lively writer, too—ranging among the moderns (Anatole France, H. G. Wells, the moderns of 1911) as readily as he cites a parallel from Plautus or Lope da Vega, expressing himself trenchantly, worrying away at the evidence with lawyerlike tenacity. And he has the strength that comes from feeling completely sure of himself. Other critics before and since have argued the case for a purely villainous, purely "Elizabethan" Shylock, but no one else has done so with such consistency and force.

He was equally sceptical of attempts to discern a modern, post-Elizabethan outlook in Shakespeare's other plays, and there is no question of his having singled Shylock out for special treatment: he argued just as strenuously for an Elizabethan Falstaff and an Elizabethan Hamlet. But there *was* something special about Shylock, even so. Stoll's concerns may have been those of a detached scholar, but near the end of his essay he felt impelled to acknowledge, if only in passing, that *The Merchant of Venice* touched on prejudices that were still current. Having reiterated that Shakespeare's contemporaries had laughed and shuddered at Shylock, and that we should try to do the same, he added a qualification— "except at popular performances, where racial antipathy is rather to be allayed than fomented."

This raises some interesting questions. Is the implication that popular audiences ought to be fobbed off with a harmless, noninflammatory Shylock? And what exactly does a "popular" performance mean in this context? One would like to know, but Stoll does not supply any answers. He is too intent on reassuring us that we have nothing to lose, artistically, by exchanging the idealized Shylock of the nineteenth century for Shakespeare's Shylock. On the contrary (and this is his final message), such an exchange will bring its own reward: "That Hebraic and picturesque figure"—the authentic Shylock—"will be remembered long after he has retreated from the warm circle of our sentiments." He will be "visited again and again, by an exhilarating sally of the imagination, in the midst of the harsh and sturdy life to which he belongs."

CHAPTER TWELVE

Between the Wars

· 1 ·

Writing in 1936, John Middleton Murry bracketed *The Merchant of Venice* with *Hamlet* as the two most enduringly popular works in the Shakespeare canon. Theater critics in the Twenties and Thirties sometimes announced that they were tired of the play, but they were in a minority: it continued to attract producers and audiences alike. Between 1918 and 1939 there were nine separate productions in Stratford-upon-Avon, ten in the West End of London and ten at the Old Vic.

The first Shylock to create a stir on the London stage in the years following the First World War, Maurice Moscovitch, was Jewish—unmistakably so. So, by chance, was the most widely publicized American Shylock of the same period, David Warfield.

Moscovitch (1871–1940) was born in Odessa. He emigrated to America while he was still in his teens, took a job in a button-factory, and got his start in the New York Yiddish theater working under its most celebrated star, Jacob Adler. Subsequently he became an actor-manager himself, touring in most of the countries where there were Yiddish-speaking communities, from Rumania to Brazil. He enjoyed a particular success in London, where from 1909 he appeared regularly at the Pavilion Theatre in Whitechapel. In time his fame spread beyond the East End, and in 1919 the Irish-born manager J. B. Fagan, who had taken a lease on the Court Theatre in Sloane Square, invited him to play Shylock—his first part in English.

Six foot tall, lean and hungry-looking, in his early days he had generally found himself cast as a thief or small-time villain. When he was at last able to choose his roles, he naturally took more commanding ones, but also broadened his repertoire to include Yiddish versions of work by Ibsen, Gorky and other European masters. For his farewell performance at the Pavilion in 1913, for example, he selected Strindberg's *The Father*—a much bolder choice than any West End star would have made at the time. He also played Shylock in Yiddish, but it was not one of his successes. According to the theatrical historian M. J. Landa, the audience at the Pavilion found the piece absurd, and could not understand why it was so highly thought of. During the trial scene they burst into laughter.

No such fiasco awaited him at the Court. Fagan's production ran for nine months, and it was Moscovitch's performance that drew the crowds. In other respects the occasion was generally agreed to be a routine affair: Desmond MacCarthy spoke of "the tame, histrionic conventions of the stock Shakespearean touring company." But in MacCarthy's view that only made Moscovitch's achievement stand out all the more sharply. In the first place he was impressed by the actor's authenticity:

> For deprecating movements of the hands, shrugs, dubious slantings of the head, agitated shakings of the wrists, for a certain pervasive subserviency of manner, for effusiveness in cajolery, for homely expansiveness in joy, for childish abandonment to weeping (poor miserable puckered face!), for gusto in *schadenfreude,* his Shylock is perfect.

But such skills were only part of the story. If they had been all that Moscovitch had to offer, MacCarthy went on, "what I have said would be consistent with his having played Shylock as a little Yiddish pawnbroker" (that pawnbroker again!). In the event, there was also a dark dignity in his passion that was "Rembrandtesque."

Possibly MacCarthy was getting carried away and claiming too much. Other critics were struck by the deliberate *absence* of dignity in Moscovitch's performance, by such cold, businesslike details as the way in which he took off his rings and turned up his sleeves while preparing to cut the pound of flesh. On one point, however, everyone was agreed: the keynote of his interpretation was unyielding hatred. Pity for such a Shylock, wrote W. A. Darlington, would have been utterly out of place. "You might equally well pity a Bengal tiger in mid-spring."

It seems hard to believe anyone could have gone much further than this, but during the last two weeks of the run Moscovitch was replaced by a Shylock who was by all accounts even fiercer—and, in the context, even more exotic. Louis Bouwmeester was a seventy-four-year-old tragedian from the Netherlands who performed in Dutch, while everyone else in the play continued to speak English.* Such was the force of his personality, however, or of his *grand guignol* techniques, that the audience was transfixed. According to Reginald Denham, who was in the cast, his Shylock was "a fiend incarnate." In the trial scene, he flourished "an evil little knife" and fingered the scales "in a peculiarly sickening way"; then, as he was moved towards Antonio, he was seized with a paroxysm of excitement. ("It was like watching a maniac shaken by some profane orgasm.") Just the kind of thing, Denham surmised, that the Elizabethans would have revelled in.

Where London was invited to contemplate cruelty, New York was offered pathos. David Warfield's Shylock, a big draw on Broadway during the season of 1922–1923, went further than any previous interpretation in portraying the moneylender as a sad-eyed victim.

**Bouwmeester's son stood in the wings and waved a handkerchief whenever it was another actor's turn to speak.*

Warfield, whose original name was Wohlfelt, was born in San Francisco in 1866. As a young man he became a member of the Weber and Fields vaudeville team, specializing in dialect humor—Irish, German and Jewish, but Jewish in particular. Irving Howe, in *World of Our Fathers,* has given a finely judged account of the way in which the American popular arts of that era "came to serve as a sort of abrasive welcoming committee for the immigrants." The humor was rough, but seldom vicious, and when Jewish vaudevillians took over the stereotypes that had already been established by non-Jewish performers, they naturally tended to give them a more genial cast. One typical Warfield sketch featured Sigmund Cohenski, a self-made American Jewish millionaire vacationing in Paris:

> FIFI: You might bring me a demi-tasse.
> COHENSKI: Bring me the same, and a cup of coffee.

Pleasing though such material was, it could not ultimately satisfy Warfield's ambitions. He aspired to wring his audiences' hearts as well as to make them laugh; he began appearing in sentimental dramas, with considerable success, and took to expounding the principles of his art with self-important solemnity. Irving Howe quotes from an article he wrote about his "studies of the Hebrew race": "The expression of the eyes is pleading, fearful, intelligent and gentle . . . the favorite tone is a piano and often a pianissimo." As Howe remarks, "Weber and Fields, brought up on the raucous streets of the East Side, no doubt had some pungent reflections about their former partner."

The Merchant of Venice represented the furthest flight of Warfield's post-vaudeville career. The production itself, which was staged by David Belaso, was elaborate, ornate, rich in Renaissance detail; and there at the center, dwarfed by the palatial sets, was a forlorn "little man," weighed down with anxieties, pummelled by circumstance—a "little man" even when family tragedy finally drove him to seek a bizarre revenge.

Although audiences turned up out of curiosity, Warfield did not receive the acclaim for which he had been hoping, and the relative failure of the production is said to have hastened his retirement. Toby Lelyveld has forcefully summed up the case against it in *Shylock on the Stage.* The text was mangled. Scenes were wantonly rearranged. There were too many gimmicks—Shylock's first scene, for instance, was introduced by a cantor reciting prayers in Hebrew. Above all, the practical effect of Warfield's playing, whatever he intended, was to rob his part of significance: the nonentity he portrayed aroused very few feelings one way or the other.

It is worth setting alongside this indictment the testimony of Stark Young, the most gifted American theater critic of the time. Young, who was not an easy man to please, found a good deal to commend in Warfield's performance, considered in isolation. It had humanity, he wrote, and infinite pathos; it moved him "as I have been sometimes when I saw some old, ragged father on the East Side who stood on the corner peddling to the people he despised in his heart trifles that he scorned and who had in his eyes so much goodness, unapproachable fanaticism, patience, tragic silence and distress." Yet the final result was all wrong. Shakespeare's Shylock stirred the imagination with his elemental force. By contrast, Warfield was tame, and his tameness created an imbalance that was more distressing than the traditional conception he was trying to avoid. When the part was played in this way, what happened to Shylock in the trial scene came to seem "not a legal but a kind of natural justice":

> Biologically, even, it seemed right and necessary that such a creature—no matter what his wrongs may have been—should be defeated. On the side of the Venetian gentlemen, these senators, these lovers and friends, there was gorgeous vitality, beauty, open love and the desire for happiness, there was generosity, brave passions and prodigal, abounding life. They might be cruel but they were no more cruel after all than the animal world, no crueller than nature. But this creature that they destroyed so gaily, as birds kill one of their kind sometimes—it was not wholly his fault, but the fact remained that he had no dignity, no taste, no style, no health, no

> beauty, no volume of creative life; he had only pitiful defeat, thwarted mind and purpose, sick wrongs and dumb, profound, unwholesome intensity.

Shakespeare had intended something very different—"a fight between powers, not a humiliation of humanity."

A number of older American actors continued to present traditional Shylocks between the wars: Walter Hampden, for example, and Otis Skinner. But none of them aroused as much interest as the English actor George Arliss, who came to New York to play the part in 1928. Arliss was already well known to cinema audiences for his performance in *The Green Goddess* and the silent version of *Disraeli* (1921), but his reputation was still primarily that of a stage actor, with a particular flair for courtly and patrician roles. (Shaw thought he would have been perfect as King Magnus in *The Apple Cart.*) As Shylock he was steely, sardonic, well spoken, well mannered: a villain, but with an outward demeanor that might have been inspired by Irving's description of the character as "the only gentleman in the play." One New York paper headed its review "Shylock Goes Slumming."

It was while touring with the production in Los Angeles that Arliss was approached by Jack Warner and Darryl F. Zanuck, who came to the theater, went to his hotel afterwards, and offered to sign him up for a remake (in sound) of *Disraeli.* This marked the beginning of his true Hollywood career. The second *Disraeli* won him an Oscar, and he scored an equal success several years later in *The House of Rothschild.* On the strength of his roles in these two films it was widely assumed—mistakenly—that he was Jewish himself, and the rumor would no doubt have gained even more credence if he had achieved his ambition of appearing in a film of *The Merchant of Venice.* "I have always believed," he wrote of the play in his memoirs,

> that it would make a magnificent movie. It would be an expensive production, and could not be done as I should like to see it unless both the American and the English markets were open to it. Unfortunately the Jews don't

> like it, and as they are great supporters of the cinema and the theater in the United States, the American producer doesn't care to hurt their feelings—or his own.

He added that he could not understand Jewish objections. If anything it was Gentiles who had a right to complain, since "a greater collection of dishonorable cads than Antonio and his set it would be difficult to find." Shylock was palpably their superior.

The idea of filming *The Merchant of Venice* was in fact far from being a novelty. No less than seven different versions had been made in the early days of the silent cinema: one apiece in Italy, France, Germany and England, three in the United States. But by the era of the talkies—even assuming Arliss had been able to win a producer around to his own view of the play—the subject matter was too sensitive for Hollywood to handle.*

Arliss had originally hoped that the New York production could be restaged in London, but after Warner Brothers wooed him away the plan was abandoned. Meanwhile, however, English playgoers had had no shortage of other Shylocks to ponder. There was Hay Petrie, for instance—better known until then for his Shakespearean clowns—who played the part at the Old Vic in 1924. Petrie's Shylock was not so much a "little man" as a subsidiary character: shrewd enough in his honor, with touches of dignity and pathos, but never allowed to dominate the rest of the play. James Agate described him as "a *Shylock,* Potash's neighbor, the wealthy relative of the stallholders in the New Cut near by, the tree whose sprigs enliven our West End on Saturday nights, the friend whose interest may be purchased.** The following year Baliol Holloway turned in a solid traditional performance at the same theater, though he was overshadowed by Edith Evans's Portia. And in 1927

**Three of the silent versions were of some interest. In 1916 a British company filmed Matheson Lang's stage production, with the actor who played Antonio—had someone been reading Frank Harris?—got up to look like Shakespeare. For the 1913 French version, see* *below, p. 249; for the 1923 German version, see p. 243.*

***Potash, as in the long-running comedy* Potash and Perlmutter. *"The New Cut near by"—i.e., near the Old Vic.*

Lewis Casson, at the Lyric, Hammersmith, underlined both the villainy and what one might call the pawnbrokerishness. As the critic of the *Evening News* reported, under the headline "Best Shylock Since Irving," "he spoke in the accent of the Jews of the modern East London ghetto. He pronounced 'well' as 'vell' and 'was' as 'vas'." More generally, he saw the character, in his own words, as "a mean little miser with some glimmerings of good in him." When St. John Ervine, in an otherwise favorable review, complained that his performance lacked "magnificence," that it failed to suggest "the courageous abandon of a man whose life is filled with despair," he replied that he simply could not find the qualities Ervine had asked for in the text.

However much these Shylocks differed from one another, they all bore a discernible relation to what Shakespeare had written. At the Cambridge Festival Theatre production in 1926, on the other hand, audiences were given a taste of what a director could do when he set out to be original at all costs. Shylock made one of his entrances grinding away at a barrel organ; as soon as Portia launched into "The quality of mercy," the Duke started playing with a yo-yo. The director responsible, Terence Gray, dreamed up many similar gimmicks during the years in which he ran the Festival Theatre (1926–1933)—a *Twelfth Night,* for instance, with Sir Toby Belch and Sir Andrew Aguecheek waltzing around on roller skates. Gray is a forgotten figure today; but his work was a portent.

So, on a much bigger scale, was the *The Merchant of Venice* staged at Stratford-upon-Avon in 1932 by Theodore Komisarjevsky. This was the first of the guest productions by the Russian director which were one of the features of Stratford in the 1930s. Its novelties included a prologue of cavorting pierrots, a Prince of Morocco in blackface (looking not unlike Al Jolson), and a trial presided over by a drowsy, half-senile Duke, with senators poking their heads through holes in a painted cloth. Lancelot Gobbo wove in and out of the action like the Vice in a medieval morality; Portia appeared in court wearing enormous horn-rimmed glasses; Antonio, in a grotesquely large ruff and flame-colored tights, was portrayed (in the words of one reviewer) as "a depraved exquisite."

Komisarjevsky saw himself as a revolutionary twice over. He believed that the old actor-manager tradition was incurably "bourgeois" and individualistic in its values; his mission was to replace it with fluid, irreverent productions governed by the guiding hand of the director rather than the vanity of the leading player. He also thought of the theater as a vehicle for social criticism. In *The Merchant,* that meant lampooning the Christians as representatives of a decadent ruling class— "dissipated, fast, bright young people," he announced, "like the crowd we have in London today." They were also guilty of rank racial prejudice; but recognizing this did not entail drumming up any extra sympathy for Shylock. On the contrary, Komisarjevsky condemned attempts to endow the money-lender with tragic stature, *à la* Irving, as bourgeois pathos at its most bogus. What was needed, what he proposed to offer, was a modern equivalent of the Elizabethan Shylock—a "twisting, comic devil," arrayed in brightly colored clothes like a sinister Pantaloon. The actor who took the part, Randle Ayrton, was initially unhappy with this interpretation: he diluted the caricature a little, and retained some of the sombre touches that audiences had come to expect. But for the most part he went along with Komisarjevsky's wishes, and the predominant note of his performance was malice. The critic of the *Observer* summed it up as the portrait of "a wicked old scamp, a scamp with drollery inherent, but meriting all the punishment that comes his way."

Dissipated young capitalists pitted against an Elizabethan ogre—if the production was something of a muddle, so was the political thinking which lay behind it. Komisarjevsky's views on politics in the 1930s boiled down to the conviction that democracy was a plutocratic sham, and that any revolution which put paid to it was better than none. In his little book *The Theatre and a Changing Civilization* (1935), he wrote that "the political doctrines of Mussolini, Lenin, Stalin and Hitler are the only ones in our time that have genuinely idealistic foundations." And given their idealism, the excesses that such doctrines gave rise to—liquidating opponents, say, or rounding up Jews—had to be forgiven. They were a regrettable necessity, a price that was worth paying for the sake of social progress.

Perhaps we should not take this unpleasant stuff too seriously. Komisarjevsky was primarily a showman, and it is unlikely that many of those who went to see his production were looking for political enlightenment. They went to be amused by his iconoclasm and diverted by his tricks. At *The Merchant of Venice*, for example, they were intrigued by the stylized modernistic sets—semi-cubist palaces, slanting towers, broken perspectives, bridges at impossible angles, "all bathed alternately in a crimson or pea-green glow." At a time when the doublet-and-hose tradition was still largely unchalleneged, innovations like these seemed a refreshing change. The public were enthusiastic—there was a revival the following year—and even hostile critics were generally prepared to grant that Komisarjevsky (who had made his name in Britain directing Chekhov) had abundant theatrical flair.

Still, the underlying implications were clear. Shakespeare stood badly in need of jazzing up; a director was free to impose his own whims in the name of reinterpretation. The result was in most respects an imposition on Shakespeare, a substitute for Shakespeare—and the forerunner of countless other productions undertaken in the same spirit. Komisarjevsky himself, who died in 1954, was still at it twenty years later: in the *Cymbeline* which he staged at Montreal in 1950, for instance, Cloten was made to serenade Imogen with a song from *The Wizard of Oz*.

There were three other noteworthy productions of *The Merchant of Venice* in 1932. By a piquant historical overlap, Stratford played host that summer not only to Komisarjevsky but also to F. R. Benson—Sir Frank Benson since 1916—who chose Shylock for his farewell appearance: the supporting cast consisted of former members of his company, among them Cedric Hardwicke as Tubal and Robert Donat as Lorenzo. At the Old Vic, John Gielgud made his first foray into directing Shakespeare with a production distinguished by bold colors and extensive use of music and dancing: he had a competent conventional Shylock in Malcolm Keen (even if Keen slightly spoiled things on the first night by saying "If you tickle us, do we not bleed?"). Finally, Ernest Milton, an actor venturing into the uncertain world of management, put on the play at the St. James's Theatre.

Milton (1890–1974) was an American of part Jewish, part Italian extraction, who had first come to England in 1914 to appear in *Potash and Perlmutter.* He stayed on, established himself as a leading player at the Old Vic, and achieved a number of striking successes in the West End—in *Rope,* in Pirandello's *Henry IV,* as the wealthy Jewish houseguest who breaks the unwritten rules in Galsworthy's *Loyalties.* But he never obtained the final accolades that he thought his due, that would have set him incontrovertibly in the front rank of his profession, and disappointment embittered an already difficult nature. Alec Guinness has given a memorable account of him in his autobiography—of his tantrums and manias, his extravagant reactions and melodramatic hatreds. But Guinness adds that his Hamlet was "the most thrilling performance I have ever seen."

Such a man was well equipped to play Shylock, and despite a few patches of overacting it was widely agreed that he gave an outstanding performance. "Proud and inflammably racial," were J. C. Trewin's words for it. *The Times* praised him for the way in which he showed the iron slowly entering Shylock's soul. When he realized that Jessica had gone, he dropped his lamp: the paper compared the effect to that of "a thunderclap on a summer's evening." And Graham Robertson—the same Graham Robertson who had thrilled to Irving in the same role over fifty years before—decided that this new Shylock was finer still. "Of course," he wrote to a friend, "the blessed memory of Irving's crucified saint remains with me quite undisturbed—but it wasn't Shylock." Milton, by contrast, "gave no fantastic reading, performed no tricks;" he played the part "straight and with wonderful effect."

The production had other things to recommend it, too: an unusually good supporting cast, handsome sets by E. McKnight Kauffer. A few weeks earlier Milton's first managerial effort at the St. James's, *Othello,* had failed disastrously; now he might reasonably have supposed that his luck had turned. But if he did, he was soon disillusioned. In spite of favorable notices *The Merchant of Venice* played to half-empty houses, and within three weeks it was forced to close.

• 2 •

The 1920s were strangely bare of critical writing about *The Merchant of Venice*, but two studies that are still worth reading were published in the early years of the following decade. Harley Granville-Barker devoted a chapter to the play in the second series of his *Prefaces to Shakespeare* (1930); G. Wilson Knight turned his attention to it in the course of *The Shakespearean Tempest* (1932).

Granville-Barker's essay opens with a bold clearing of the decks:

> *The Merchant of Venice* is a fairy tale. There is no more reality in Shylock's bond and The Lord of Belmont's will than in Jack and the Beanstalk.

This is picturesquely put. It has often been cited, and cited as though it represented Granville-Barker's last word on the subject as well as his first. For the rest, it is assumed, he was concerned with stagecraft, which was his speciality; with the means by which the fairy tale was given effective dramatic shape.

Certainly he brought to his criticism immense practical experience of the theater, as actor, playwright and director. The *Prefaces to Shakespeare* bear the stamp of that experience; it would be very odd if they did not. But they are far from being the mere production manuals they are sometimes made to sound. By the time he wrote them, Barker was as much a man of letters as a man of the theater—he had retired from active theater work in 1914; and in any case, he would never have supposed at any stage of his career that questions of technique could be divorced from questions of meaning. His interests ranged freely over poetry, character, moral import. Among the commentators who preceded him, there was no one he admired more than the notoriously non-theatrical A. C. Bradley.

As for *The Merchant of Venice*, he may have begun by proclaiming its simplicity, but he was soon adding an important qualification. A fairy tale, yes, but also a play that moved on two different levels, a fairy tale in which "unlikelihood of plot" was partly counterbalanced or redeemed by "veracity of character". Without such veracity, the play would have never worked in the theater; nor would it have provided adequate scope for Shakespeare's powers.

Admittedly he was only thinking of the major characters when he wrote this. The role of the minor characters, he argued, was largely limited to fulfilling their allotted parts in the plot. But Shylock, Portia and Bassanio were three-dimensional human beings—Shylock above all. The man was real, even though his story was fabulous.

Much of Barker's commentary is devoted to underscoring this reality, and pointing out the turns of thought and phrase that help to create it. The dryness of Shylock's opening lines, for instance (made all the drier by the contrast with the echo of Portia's laughter from the previous scene); the parting with Jessica—"that constant calling her by name, which tells us of the lonely man!" If we were in any danger of forgetting how vivid a personality Shylock has, we are forcefully reminded.

But what of his Jewishness, which also makes it impossible for us to think of him in purely fairy-tale terms? Here Barker betrays a certain degree of discomfort. Shylock, he writes,

> is no more a mere means to exemplifying the Semitic problem than is Othello for the raising of the color question. "I am a Jew." "Haply, for I am black . . ." Here we have—and in Shylock's case far more acutely and completely—the *circumstances* of the dramatic conflict; but at the heart of it are men; and we may surmise, indeed, that from a maturer Shakespeare we would have had, as with Othello, rather more of the man, and so rather less of the alien and his griefs.

This seems unlikely. Othello is a military hero, an honored public servant, and a Christian—an outsider, but far less of one than Shylock can ever hope to be. And though Barker himself is inclined to play down the strictly Jewish aspects of Shylock's story, every so often he makes a comment which not only brings them home sharply, but suggests that he found them somewhat troubling. In the

"Signior Antonio" speech, for instance ("you call me misbeliever, cut-throat dog"), he visualizes Antonio and Bassanio as seeing nothing in Shylock's accusations but "the Ghetto denizen," and hearing only "the bondman's whine." Wherease "to us," he adds, "there is now all Jewry crouched and threatening there, an ageless force behind it." To *us,* let it be noted: the issue is still a living one.

Wilson Knight, in *The Shakespearian Tempest,* has much less to say about the characters of the play. He is preoccupied with symbols; he explores the central contrast (as he sees it) between images of tempest and images of music. Viewed in this context, Shylock is not so much a flesh-and-blood individual as a "tragedy-force," a storm disrupting the play's harmonies.

But Knight did not leave it at that. There are many comments on *The Merchant of Venice* scattered around his later writings; and in 1963, in the revised edition of his book *Shakespearian Production,* he published some powerful reflections devoted purely to Shylock. (They were partly inspired by his having acted the part in a production at Leeds University a few years earlier). By this time he had come to see the character as one of the two major precursors of the great tragic characters, the other being Falstaff. In both of them, "greater powers are felt bursting the bounds of an otherwise normal drama." He was equally concerned that readers should not overlook Shylock's "compacted force": much of his account dwells on the extra charge of meaning carried by individual lines or phrases, on what he called their "radiations." But beyond the details, he offers a new reading of the entire role—in its later stages, at least.

Shylock, he contends, is not someone "to whom implacability comes easily." When he confronts Antonio on the way to jail, for instance, the language he uses is that of a man fighting down his better tendencies; when he keeps repeating "I'll have my bond," he is stiffening his resolve, giving himself over ("not without an effort") to a demonic power. True, he cannot bring himself to acknowledge that the course he has embarked on is evil; but he does recognize that it is profoundly ugly. The repellent imagery of the speech with which he justifies himself in the trial scene—"carrion-flesh," "rat," "gaping pig," "urine"—is proof enough of that.

Knight also makes a larger, vaguer claim. Shylock, he argues, is a tragic hero *manqué*. He defies the values of his society, but he is never allowed to transcend them; in the end he is forced to endure "a maximum of external humiliation." Subsequently, however, Shakespeare went on to create a series of tragedies in which Shylock's "inward soul-worth" was given positive poetic form, embodied in heroes whose submission to demoniac powers, unlike his own, was "an accepted element in a purposive scheme." Such heroes may be defeated, but they are never humiliated: "In them the Dionysian principle takes over, at least for a while, and has its fling . . ."

We are in deep waters. Few people will want to venture out as far as this; yet if we accept that Shylock has a tragic (as opposed to a merely pathetic) quality, it is hard not to feel that Knight is pointing to connections that actually exist. The hand that created Shylock was also the hand that created Macbeth's black desires and Lear's ungovernable rages. And Knight goes further, arguing that there is an affinity between Shylock and the most misanthropic of Shakespeare's heroes:

> In the later scenes of *Timon of Athens,* Timon as denunciatory prophet might well be called "hebraic"; he is also, like Shylock, an outcast; and yet both are finally sued to in vain for favor, as was Sophocles' Oedipus, by the community that had scorned them.

There are also obvious differences between the two men, but they are not what Knight is interested in:

> It would be to lay too limited an emphasis on the fictional surfaces to fail to see in these dramas signs of poetic genius taking a mighty pleasure in putting the community in its place.

We may well feel that this is carrying speculation as far as it can reasonably go. In the play, after all, the community puts Shylock in *his* place. But the suggestion, like so many of Wilson Knight's, reverberates: we turn back to Shylock in the trial scene—

If you deny me, fie upon your law!

—and we hear an even keener note of exultation and scorn than we did before.

• 3 •

The year 1933 was one of the great black dividing lines of history. For no one was this more obviously or more tragically the case than for the Jews of Europe; and even though hardly anyone at the time could foresee what Hitler's coming to power would ultimately entail, it was clear from the start that something deeply horrible was under way, something for which there was no real parallel in modern times. Anti-Semitism of the most vicious kind had become the official policy of one of the most advanced nations in the world.

In retrospect, responses to Hitler during the 1930s are bound to seem slow and inadequate (as indeed most of them were), and it would be absurd to single out the theater in this regard, let alone the Shakespearean theater. Ideally, it is true, one might have hoped for a shift of emphasis in productions of *The Merchant of Venice*, an oblique recognition that contemporary events had given the play frightening new overtones. But while such a thing was always possible, it was never very likely; and in the event, it was not to be.

The most notable production of the late 1930s was John Gielgud's at the Queen's Theatre in 1938. Six years earlier, at the Old Vic, Gielgud had confined himself to directing the play; now he played Shylock as well. But the predominant note was still light and lyrical. Pastel shades, Canaletto perspectives, an opulent Venice, an enchanted Belmont—the impression playgoers were meant to come away with was one of gallantry and romance.

Standing out against such a background, Shylock seemed more of an intrusive presence than ever. This was the effect that Granville-Barker had recommended, in a letter to Gielgud that previous year in which he had emphasized that the moneylender was above all a "sordid little *outsider*"; and this was how Gielgud played him. For Audrey Williamson, looking back in *Theatre of Two Decades* (1951), his interpretation had been a narrow one—without pride, with "hardly a hint of the swell of passion"—and the Jew he had portrayed had been "a dingy, rancorous, fawning creature of the ghetto, greyly redolent of the slum and the usurer's attic." The anonymous reviewer in the *New Statesman,* writing at the time, was more enthusiastic. He praised Gielgud for successfully combining "the squalor of a Transylvanian usurer" (why Transylvanian?) with "the ardor of an Old Testament prophet"—though once again, the squalor seems to have been uppermost:

> When he stropped his knife upon his shoe, we were appalled, not by fear for Antonio, but by the sight of hatred turned to madness. His appearance throughout was extraordinary—gummy, blinking eyes, that suggested some nasty creature of the dark, and loquacious hands with as many inflections as his voice.

"What if my house be troubled with a rat . . . ?" The nasty, dingy creature plainly had to be expelled before romance could reign unchallenged.

And was there simply no connection between this theatrical apparition and the stories of persecution that were filling the papers—the reports coming out of Austria, for example, where the *Anschluss* had taken place only a few weeks before the production opened? Unlike some of his colleagues (the critic of *The Times,* for instance), the *New Statesman* reviewer refused to push the question to one side. "At a time," he wrote, "when Jews are being driven to mass-suicide by unsurpassed brutalities, the spectacle of Shylock's baiting becomes almost unbearable." Yet it was also to Gielgud's credit, he added, that the actor had been "most careful not to sentimentalize the part." In the end the play had to be allowed to stand by itself, free from the shadow of contemporary events.

A reader would have found nothing to contradict such a view in the best-known general study of Shakespeare to appear in the 1930s, Middleton Murry's *Shakespeare* (1936). For Murry, *The Merchant of Venice* existed on two levels. Shakespeare had humanized the melodrama that he started out with, endowing his characters—Shylock above all—with sentiments and thoughts which were often incompatible with the actions required of them by the plot. At the same time, the old melodramatic groundplan remained. Whatever wrongs Shylock may have suffered, he was guilty; whatever wrongs his opponents had committed, they were essentially innocent. In effect, he was a member of a different species. But Murry saw no reason to relate his separate moral status to his role as Jew, still less to the resurgent reality of anti-Semitism in Germany and beyond.

To have made too much of contemporary parallels, to have pressed them too hard, would admittedly have been to destroy the play. But not to mention them at all—in 1936, a year after the Nuremberg laws had been enacted—was a bit eerie. At least two academic writers of the period, H. B. Charlton and John Dover Wilson, showed themselves more sensitive in this respect.

The chapter on *The Merchant of Venice*, in Charlton's *Shakespearian Comedy* (1938) contains what is probably the fullest defense of Shylock ever undertaken by a reputable scholar—the general line being that the play was marked by a continual clash between "the proposals of Shakespeare's deliberate will and the disposals of his creative imagination." Since Charlton believed that it was a critic's duty to try to see a work *sub specie aeternitatis,* undistorted as far as possible by contemporary bias, he was worried that he might be accused of writing propaganda. His book, he pointed out, was based on lectures that he had been giving for many years (he taught at the University of Manchester); his interpretation of Shylock dated back to a time when Hitler had barely been heard of outside Germany, and in committing it to print he had been anxious to guard against "modifications directly due to today's affairs." But once the subject had been raised, he felt dutybound to make it clear where he stood: the Nazi persecution of the Jews was "an entirely indefensible exhibition of those animal passions which it has been the trend of civilization to subdue."

Dover Wilson's *The Merchant of Venice in 1937* also had its origins in a lecture—one of a series, delivered in 1938, which many years later the author worked up into a book, *Shakespeare's Happy Comedies.* Dover Wilson subscribed to the view that Shylock was both a villain, "a terrible old man," and very much a fellow human being, "one of ourselves," and he felt sure that in humanizing him, Shakespeare had known what he was doing:

> Shylock may have taken him to some extent by surprise, but Shylock was the child of *his* imagination and *his* intellect, and it seems to me absurd to suppose that the sympathies of such a father can have been wholly on the side of the spitting Antonio.

In arguing his case, Dover Wilson inevitably covered some familiar ground, but he also pointed to an important piece of evidence which no one had cited before. It is generally agreed by modern scholars that one of the scenes in the manuscript-play *Sir Thomas More* (probably written around 1594–1595) is the work of Shakespeare—the episode based on the May Day riots of 1517, during which the London apprentices rose against the aliens living in the city, sacked their houses, and (in Dover Wilson's words) "generally behaved very much as the Nazis behaved in the streets of the cities in Germany." In the play the disturbances are quelled by Thomas More, who was sheriff of London at the time. Addressing the rioters, he partly invokes Tudor commonplaces about authority and obedience, and partly, more interestingly from Dover Wilson's point of view, appeals to their compassion and good sense. Imagine, he tells them,

> *Imagine that you see the wretched strangers,*
> *Their babies at their backs, and their poor luggage,*
> *Plodding to the ports and coasts for transportation.*

If this were to happen, he continues, all you would have done would have been to have set an example to other ruffians, who would "shark on you" in turn. As it is, you are rebels, and if you persist the King is bound to punish you. And suppose he is lenient, and does no worse than banish you—

> *What country by the nature of your error*
> *Should give you harbor? . . .*
> *Would you be pleased*
> *To find a nation of such barbarous temper*
> *That breaking out in hideous violence*
> *Would not afford you an abode on earth,*

Whet their detested knives against your throats,
Spurn you like dogs, and like as if that God
Owned not nor made not you, nor that the elements
Were not all appropriate to your comforts,
But chartered unto them. What would you think
To be thus used? This is the strangers' case . . .

As Dover Wilson pointed out, "Spurn you like dogs" is virtually the same phrase that Shylock uses, while the lines about the elements are very close in spirit to "Hath not a Jew?" ("warmed and cooled by the same winter and summer as a Christian is"). In spite of this, More's speech, remarkable enough in itself, doesn't positively *prove* anything about *The Merchant of Venice*. But what can hardly be denied is that the man who wrote it was capable of sympathizing to an exceptional degree with the plight of the despised and persecuted stranger.

For Dover Wilson, when it came to Shylock, the events shaking contemporary Europe were unignorable.* For Mark Van Doren, in *Shakespeare* (1939), they were no more part of the story than any other events extraneous to the plays themselves. Van Doren, a celebrated teacher at Columbia University for some forty years, aimed at a timeless approach in his study. Shakespeare seemed to him "the kind of story-teller who can be judged by the most general standards we have"; each play was a world in itself, to be understood and enjoyed on its own terms.

In *The Merchant of Venice*, the leading theme was love. With one obvious exception, love was the natural language of the principal characters: "love, and its elder brother generosity." The exception, however, was a figure so alien, so hostile and so forceful that he threatened to tear apart the play's "web of magic happiness." For him alone there could be no generosity:

> Where Shakespeare's sympathies lay it has long since been useless to inquire. His gentlemen within the code

**Having originally been invited to deliver his 1938 lectures at the University of Liverpool, he repeated them later the same year in Edinburgh, as public lectures in aid of academic refugees from the Continent. They succeeded in raising £150.*

> are as harsh to Shylock as Shylock is to them; however much love they have, they cannot love him. Nor has Shakespeare made the last inch of him lovely. He would seem in fact to have attempted a monster, one whose question whether a Jew hath eyes, hands, organs, dimensions, senses, affections and passions would reveal its rhetorical form, the answer being no.

True, even a critic who endorsed this harshness had to concede that the attempt had failed. It was not in Shakespeare's nature to deal in monsters, and in the event he had made Shylock a man—but a man "thrust into a world bound not to endure him":

> In such a world he necessarily looks and sounds ugly. In another universe his voice might have its properties and uses. Here it can issue as nothing but a snarl, an animal cry sounding outrageously among the flute and recorder voices of persons whose very names, unlike his own, are flowing musical phrases.

Van Doren was enlightened, humane, something of a *beau ideal* among the American men of letters of his time. He had no particular axe to grind, and in describing *The Merchant of Venice* he was simply setting down his honest response to the play as he found it. Yet to write in such a way at such a time was surely rather chilling. The year, it is worth repeating, was 1939; the last restraints on Nazi terror were about to be removed. If Van Doren's reading of *The Merchant* was correct, how was it possible for him not to sound at least a passing note of regret? (Regret, incidentally, which it was much easier for a critic to express than for a theatrical production to imply.) For Shylock did not "just happen" to be a Jew; nor, indeed, was he just a character in Shakespeare. In the course of 350 years he had also acquired a permanent place in world mythology.

Van Doren would no doubt have retorted such matters were not his concern—not, at least, while he was pursuing his task as a critic. His goal was to see the work as it really was, and in a world where literature can easily be crushed by politics or ideology, such detachment has a great deal to recommend it. Generally speaking, that is. But there are also times (and this was one of them) when single-mindedness in a critic becomes indistinguishable from a failure of imagination.

PART THREE

A Citizen of the World

CHAPTER THIRTEEN

A Legend and Its Legacy

• 1 •

In the extent of his fame Shylock belongs with Don Quixote, Tartuffe, Sherlock Holmes, Robinson Crusoe. He is a familiar figure to millions who have never read *The Merchant of Venice*, or even seen it acted; he has served as an inspiration for hundreds of writers, and a point of reference for innumerable publicists. There are times when one might wish it were otherwise, but he is immortal.

Absent from the post-Commonwealth stage until 1700, he took longer to establish himself in the public mind than Hamlet, Falstaff and some of the other great Shakespearean characters. But by the early eighteenth century he had become a byword—sufficiently so for Alexander Pope to cite him as the very type of transparent infamy. In the first of his *Moral Essays,* the *Epistle to Lord Cobham* (1733), Pope reflects that there are some men who are unable to conceal their true natures, however hard they try—

And every child hates Shylock, though his soul
Still sits at squat, and peeps not from its hole.

The brilliantly horrid image contains a reminiscence of Satan in *Paradise Lost*—

him there they found
Squat like a toad, close at the ear of Eve.

It also foreshadows the Jew in Eliot's *Gerontion,* the landlord of the decayed house who "squats on the window sill."

For the Georgians, allusions to *The Merchant of Venice* were common currency. During the clamor raised against the Jewish Naturalization Act of 1753, for instance, the weekly paper the *Gray's Inn Journal* lampooned the prime minister responsible for the Act, Henry Pelham, under the guise of "Launcelot Gobbo"—a servant of the Jews, as it were. Later, after the Act had been repealed, the same paper joined in the campaign to unseat William Calvery, an M.P. who had been one of Pelham's principal supporters in pushing the original bill through the Commons. Among other stunts, it published an account of a supposed meeting of grateful "stock-jobbers, children of Israel, & C." who had pledged themselves to work for Calvert's reelection. Those taking part were said to have included "Melchizidec Mammon" and "Josephus Shylock."

As for the Jewish characters in eighteenth-century plays and novels, they remain predictably true to form. Most of them are brokers or moneylenders; almost all of them are cunning and avaricious. But if they are descendants of Shylock, it is at a considerable remove. Their knives have been sheathed; they are primarily figures of fun, held up to scorn for their low tricks and uncouth manners.

It was this kind of contemporary caricature that Richard Cumberland set out to redress in his once-celebrated play *The Jew* (1794). Yet Cumberland was well aware (as who could fail to be?) of the grim original looming in the background. Some ten years earlier, in a series of essays, he had invented a character called Abraham Abrahams, a "friendly Israelite." Abrahams was a devoted theatergoer, but he complained equally of the rough handling he got whenever a rowdy in the audience spotted that he was Jewish, and of the treatment meted out to Jews on the stage itself:

> I observe with much concern that your great writers of plays take delight in hanging us up to public ridicule and

> contempt on all occasions: if ever they are in search of a rogue, an usurer, or a buffoon, they are sure to make a Jew serve the turn: I verily believe the odious character of Shylock has brought little less persecution upon us poor scattered sons of Abraham, than the Inquisition itself.

In the 1770s Cumberland had scored a hit with comedies in which he reversed the normally unflattering images of the stage Scotsman and the stage Irishman. In his philosemitic essays of the 1780s he virtually pledged himself to perform the same service for the Jews.

Sheva, the hero of *The Jew,* is an elderly moneylender living in Georgian London. To outward appearances he is a classic miser—in good traditional fashion, he even keeps his servant hungry; but it turns out that he is secretly dispensing charity on a lavish scale. By the end all is revealed, and one of his Christian beneficiaries salutes him as "the widow's friend, the orphan's father, the poor man's protector, the universal philanthropist."

Swinging from one extreme to the other, Cumberland does not even attempt to explain why Sheva should keep up pretenses in the way he does. The result is an impossible hybrid—in the words of the nineteenth-century Jewish historian James Picciotto, a character who is "a Harpagon in appearance and manners, a Cheeryble in feeling." But at the time, audiences who had been reared on the conventions of sentimental comedy found the mixture easy enough to swallow. The play enjoyed a resounding success; it was translated into German and French; Sheva remained a favorite part with comic actors for at least thirty years. And Cumberland was praised, as he would have wished, for counteracting the influence of his greatest predecessor. As one reviewer put it, he had made the Jew "act like a *Christian,* in opposition to Shakespeare's Shylock."

Among all the tributes he received, the Jews themselves remained silent. So at least he reports in his memoirs, with a good deal of acerbity. This is regrettable, but also perhaps intelligible: certainly it was something that Sir Walter Scott had no difficulty understanding. "We cannot be surprised," he wrote in his account of Cumberland in *Lives of the Novelists,* "that the people in question felt a portrait in which they were made ludicrous as well as interesting to be something between an affront and a compliment. Few of the better class of the Jewish persuasion would, we believe, be disposed to admit Sheva as a fitting representative of his tribe."

Scott made his own attempt to transcend traditional Jewish stereotypes in *Ivanhoe* (1819). Like Cumberland, only rather more obviously, he built on Shakespearean foundations. The chapter in *Ivanhoe* in which we first meet the moneylender Isaac of York is headed by a quotation from *The Merchant of Venice* ("Hath not a Jew eyes?"). Isaac formerly had a wife, now dead, called Rachel (which is as close as you can get to Leah). He has a daughter, Rebecca, his one remaining child. The chapter in which money is wrung from him under threat of torture, and in which he also learns that Rebecca has been abducted, is ushered in by another Shakespearean quotation (inevitably, "My daughter! O my ducats!"). There are further echoes of Shylock in his thoughts and his turns of phrase. But all these resemblances only go so far. *Ivanhoe* is set in the early Middle Ages; the whole framework of the story is very different from Shakespeare's, and so is the spirit in which the Jewish characters are presented.

With Rebecca, at least, Scott succeeded in establishing a strong positive image. From the very first, it was generally acknowledged that she, rather than the colorless Lady Rowena, is the true heroine of the novel. "Divine Rebecca," Francis Jeffrey called her, writing in the *Edinburgh Review* in 1820. She is courageous, gifted, high-principled and (of course) surpassingly beautiful; she also remains unswervingly loyal to her religion. When she is in prison, falsely condemned as a sorceress, she recites a hymn which Scott pieced together out of the Psalms—

When Israel of the Lord beloved,
Out of the house of bondage came . . .

—and which he interrupts his narrative to print in full. All in all, she is an opera heroine rather than a credible human being; but throughout the nineteenth century, and well into the twentieth, the formula worked.

Her father presents more of a problem. At one level he is a living argument for toleration: Scott leaves us in no doubt that he would have been a much more attractive figure if his character had not been distorted by oppression and insecurity. At another level, we have to take him as we find him—as devious, cringing, avaricious. Even in his moments of torment, the old half-comic, half-sordid stereotype is never very far away.

Yet we gradually learn to overcome our initial revulsion. He has his generous and even heroic impulses: when he purchases his freedom from the rapacious Norman baron Front-de-Boeuf, for instance, he tries his best to ensure that the Saxons who have been taken prisoner are released at the same time. And whatever his other faults, there is nothing sinister or vindictive about him. Front-de-Boeuf's castle is a symbol of oppression; Isaac's home is a safe haven where the injured Ivanhoe can be nursed back to health. Above all—and this is enough in itself to differentiate him sharply from Shylock—father and daughter are bound fast by mutual devotion. If Isaac is good enough for the divine Rebecca, he ought to be good enough for us.

Scott's own day-to-day attitude towards Jews was one of tolerance tempered by distance (or perhaps the other way round). He summed up his views in a letter he wrote to a friend after reading *Harrington:*

> I think Miss Edgeworth's last work delightful, though Jews will always be to me Jews. One does not naturally or easily combine with their habits and pursuits any great liberality of principle, although certainly it may and I believe does exist in many individual instances. They are money-makers and money-brokers by profession and it is a trade which narrows the mind.

Such a passage may help to explain some of the limitations of the Jewish episodes in *Ivanhoe,* but it also heightens one's admiration for what Scott achieved. Given the date at which they were written, and the assumptions tugging him the other way, they represent a triumph of large-mindedness.

There is an unhappy footnote. In the 1820s, when Scott's finances came crashing about him, his most exorbitant creditors were William Abud & Son, a firm of London gold refiners who had bought up some of his bills. The Abud's were Jews, or generally assumed to be, and Scott allowed himself a wintry joke in his journal about "Ehud, or Ahab, or whatever name he delights in." He also spoke about the Abuds being determined to have their pound of flesh: the Shylock image was always there, waiting to be reactivated. But he did not go further than that; and considering that the firm was subjecting him to a form of legal blackmail, and threatening him with imprisonment, we may well judge that his reaction was rather mild.

Among writers who had been raised on both the Old Testament and the New, a certain ambivalence towards Jews remained hard to avoid. If it is readily discernible in Scott, it assumed an even more obvious form in his near contemporary, Byron. Most of the poems in Byron's *Hebrew Melodies* (1815) were written at the suggestion of the Jewish composer Isaac Nathan, who set them to music.* Most of them are biblical or quasi-biblical in inspiration: they evoke a Holy Land where "the blue wave rolls nightly on deep Galilee," and the sorrows of the Children of Israel in their dispersion—

Tribes of the wandering foot and weary breast,
How shall ye flee away and be at rest!

Rebecca's hymn from *Ivanhoe* would not have been out of place among them. But when the poet turned back to the contemporary world, another set of images took over. Most of the references to Jews in his satires and letters have a rough edge, and in the harshest

**The two men remained on friendly terms. There is a charming letter from Byron acknowledging the symbolic gift that Nathan sent him just before he left England for good—some "motsos" (as both men spelled it), unleavened bread of the kind eaten at Passover to commemorate the exodus from Egypt.*

passage of all, the familiar Shylockian imagery wells up yet again.

The Merchant of Venice was a play that meant a great deal to him. He frequently quoted from it; its associations haunted him while he was in Venice, and Wilson Knight has argued that he also felt a double involvement with Shylock—first on account of his own love of what he once described as "ambrosial cash," secondly because he found it easy to identify with the Jew as Outsider. In particular, Knight quotes from a letter he wrote to his publisher in 1819, echoing Shylock's words to Bassanio as he rubbed in his refusal to cultivate the favor of a public that he had come to despise.

> I know the precise worth of popular applause, for few Scribblers have had more of it; and if I chose to swerve into their paths, I could retain it, or resume it, or increase it. But I neither love ye, nor fear ye; and though I buy with ye and sell with ye, I will neither eat with ye, drink with ye, nor pray with ye.

Byron was a complicated man; the cross-currents that Knight claimed to detect may well have been present. But when it came to his poetry, his use of Shylock was quite unambiguous.

In the twelfth canto of *Don Juan,* written in 1822, there is a well-known reference to the power wielded by bankers in post-Napoleonic Europe. "Who hold the balance of the world?"—"Jew Rothschild and his fellow Christian Baring." After completing the canto, Byron interrupted his labors on *Don Juan* to write *The Age of Bronze,* a satire inspired by the maneuverings of the Great Powers at the Congress of Verona (November 1822). Here, the bankers are identified exclusively with Jews:

> *How rich is Britain! not indeed in mines,*
> *Or peace or plenty, corn or oil, or wines,*
> *No land of Canaan, full of milk and honey,*
> *Nor (save in paper shekels) ready money:*
> *But let us not to own the truth refuse,*
> *Was ever Christian land so rich in Jews?*
> *Those parted with their teeth to good King John,*

And now, ye kings! they kindly draw your own:
All states, all things, all sovereigns they control,
And waft loan "from Indus to the pole."

Pursuing his theme through Russia, Spain and Latin America, Byron finally pictures the vultures descending on Verona:

Oh, holy Abraham! dost though see the sight?
Thy followers mingling with these royal swine,
Who spit not "on their Jewish gaberdine,"
But honor them as portion of the show . . .
On Shylock's shore behold them stand afresh,
To cut from nations' hearts their "pound of flesh."

That a handful of Jewish bankers had come to acquire enormous influence during this period is indisputable. For the great majority of Jews, however—even in Western Europe—it was another story. The years following the fall of Napoleon saw them deprived of many of the rights that they had gained since the French Revolution, and nowhere was this more the case (though one would never guess it from *The Age of Bronze*) than in Italy. In varying degrees the old restrictions and disabilities were reimposed throughout the peninsula.

As a liberal, Byron might have been expected to seize on this as further evidence with which to damn the forces of reaction. But he had hit on something that excited him far more: a new myth, the transformation of Shylock from shabby money grubber to uncrowned king of the modern world.

• 2 •

How far can a stereotype be transformed and yet remain the same?

In his admirable study *From Shylock to Svengali,* Edgar Rosenberg suggests that sooner or later any inquiry into the portrayal of Jews in English literature is bound to reach an impasse:

> At the heart of the problem is Shylock, and the Shylock myth is not a continuous fact of literature, capable of

> evolving new and complex configurations and relationships, but a stable one, which different generations do not so much reinterpret for themselves as rehabilitate. Every so often Shylock is patched up, moved up or down the economic ladder, invested with aberrant religious motives or divested of his religion, and sent into the world as Rachub, Fagin, Nucingen, Levy.* The essential Shylock has always a knife and has always the money-bags; he is always funny, and always horrible.

There are also the Good Jews, Sheva and his successors. But Sheva, Rosenberg writes, "has only Shylock to fall back on. The impulse behind his conception was a desire to rationalize Shylock out of the world by providing the anti-Shylock; and such a figure lends, as it were, an existence at second hand. The two types are two sides of the same myth."

All this seems to me true—but it is also the view of a scholar, patiently analyzing his chosen material. The casual reader, coming unprepared upon this or that variant of the myth, is more likely to be struck by the energy with which it kept renewing itself, and by the number of different shapes which it was able to assume. Nor is the invocation of Shylock something that has to be taken literally. "Shylock myth" and "Shylock figure" are useful bits of shorthand, and an acknowledgment of Shylock's preeminence in this particular rogue's gallery; but the stereotype existed before him, and it would have gone on flourishing without him.

Take Fagin, for example. He inhabits a very different world from Shylock, and insofar as the two men resemble each other—in their rapacity and cruelty—it is because they both derive from a common ancestor: the demonic deicidal Jew of the Middle Ages. Fagin is in fact a good deal closer to the medieval model. He is a creature of darkness, a bogeyman, a grinning devil; and he would surely have been the same in every aspect if *The Merchant of Venice* had never been written.

**Rachub in Maria Edgeworth's* Murad the Unlucky, *the Baron de Nucingen in Balzac, Baron Levy in Bulwer-Lytton's* My Novel.

Unflattering references to Jews abound in Dickens (in the earlier stages of his career, at least), but there is no evidence that Shylock had any particular hold over his imagination. The vision that he conjures up in his account of his first visit to Venice is purely picturesque: "In the errant fancy of my dream, I saw old Shylock passing to and fro upon a bridge, all built upon with shops and humming with the tongues of men." At the same time, when he decided to make amends for Fagin in *Our Mutual Friend* (1864–1865), it was the Shylock image that he set out to reverse. Riah, the careworn old Jew in the later novel, is a wholly innocent scapegoat: the world takes him for a usurer, whereas in reality he is an involuntary front man for his non-Jewish employer, the odious Fledgeby. Unfortunately he is also a completely unconvincing character. Dickens is so intent on emphasizing his meekness, his kindness, his noble nature, that he fails to endow him with any real life. But at least we have no trouble believing in Fledgeby, or in the jeering farewell with which he sends Riah off on his errands: "Toddle, Judah."*

When a Jew in a Victorian novel was a moneylender, a comparison with Shylock can never have been very far from the surface, in either the author's or the reader's mind. With characters who operated on a larger scale—bankers, financiers, the kind of men you might expect to meet in a respectable drawing room—the potential parallel was more remote. But it was always there, ready for use, if a writer chose.

One novel in which it is pressed into service is Trollope's *The Prime Minister* (1876). This is a book in which politics play a less prominent role than the title suggests; much of it is devoted to a domestic theme, the story of Emily Wharton and her disastrous marriage to Ferdinand Lopez. On the face of it, Lopez has his

**A more effective act of reparation on Dickens's part was his revision of the text of* Oliver Twist *in 1867, cutting out most of the repeated references to Fagin as "the Jew" and replacing them with either "Fagin" or the pronoun "he." The title of the condemned-cell chapter, for instance, was changed to "Fagin's Last Night Alive;" in all previous editions it had been "The Jew's Last Night Alive."*

attractions. He is handsome, intelligent, winning enough in his ways to arouse the friendly interest of the Duchess of Omnium. When he turns out to be a scoundrel, however, we cannot complain that we have not been given (in Trollopean terms) fair warning, since he is also an interloper, a man from nowhere. His father, about whom nothing else seems to be known, was Portuguese. He went to a good English school (although there is some question about who paid the bills), studied at a German university and started life in London working in a stockbroker's office. Beyond that, however, his antecedents are a mystery, and Emily Wharton's family, who are bitterly opposed to the match, quickly decide that he must be a Jew. At first, her father merely fancies that he can detect "Jewish signs" in his features, but before long, admittedly in a moment of extreme anger, he is describing him as "a greasy Jew adventurer out of the gutter." Religion certainly does not come into the picture—Lopez is a member of the Church of England; nor are we ever given definite evidence about his ancestry, one way or the other. Trollope makes it quite clear that the Whartons are in the grip of prejudice. But it is a prejudice, he implies, which points in the right direction.

There is one scene which comes close to clinching the matter—the exchange between Lopez and his disreputable associate, Sexty Parker, after Lopez has refused the offer of a drink:

> "You'd better get somebody else to be jolly with. To tell you the truth, Sexty, I suit you better at business than at this sort of thing. I'm like Shylock, you know."
>
> "I don't know about Shylock, but I'm blessed if I think you suit me well at anything. I'm putting up with a deal of ill usage, and when I try to be happy, you won't drink, and you tell me about Shylock. He was a Jew, wasn't he?"
>
> "That is the general idea."
>
> "Then you ain't very much like him, for they're a sort of people that always have money about 'em."
>
> "How do you suppose he made his money to begin with? What an ass you are!"

Who can doubt that we have tracked down Lopez's ultimate ancestor? He as good as tells us so himself; and the admission reinforces the irony of the terms in which, in the very same chapter, he writes to Emily's father:

> You have asked for a schedule of my affairs, and I have found it quite impossible to give it. As it was with the merchants whom Shakespeare and the other dramatists described—so it is with me. My caravels are out at sea, and will not always come home in time.

A descendant of Shylock appropriating the language of Antonio—it is all of a piece with Lopez's other masquerades. For the most disturbing thing about him, in Trollope's eyes, is that he is a stranger who has got into the club; that until he emerges in his true colors, the world is prepared to take him for a gentleman. With Shylock himself, you at least knew where you stood from the very beginning.

One measure of the popularity of *The Merchant of Venice* is the number of skits and burlesques that it inspired. The best-known English specimen, in its day, was Francis Talfourd's *Shylock, or The Merchant of Venice Preserved,* first produced in London in 1853, with Frederick Robson in the title role, and frequently revived.* Talfourd's writing was chiefly notable for its manic Early Victorian punning; it is perhaps enough to record that he described the piece as "a Jerusalem hearty-joke." In New York, his nearest equivalent was John Brougham, whose *Much Ado About A Merchant of Venice,* first produced in 1868, continued to attract audiences into the 1890s, in large part because it was spiced with topical jokes about Wall Street. And there were many other low-comedy versions of the play, some of them cropping up in unlikely places. *The Merry Merchant of Venice*, for example, was a piece of Anglo-Indian fun published in Allahabad

**Robson was one of the great popular entertainers of his time, especially famous for his rendering of the tragi-comic cockney ballad* "Villikins and his Dinah." *There is an admiring account of him in Henry James's* A Small Boy and Others.

Talfourd was the son of Thomas Noon Talfourd—celebrated lawyer, litterateur, dedicatee of The Pickwick Papers.

in 1895. Shylock figured in it as a pawnbroker and old-clothes dealer; Jessica was "Miss Shylock," who, not receiving enough to dress from dear pa, runs an ice-cream cart on her own account.

It would take a stout heart to plough through this mass of ancient mirth, but one nineteenth-century burlesque stands apart by virtue of quality. In 1842 the Rev. Richard Harris Barham published the second series of *The Ingoldsby Legends,* including "The Merchant of Venice: A Legend of Italy":

I believe there are few
But have heard of a Jew,
Named Shylock, of Venice, as arrant a "screw"
In money transactions, as ever you knew . . .

There are two aspects of Barham which distinguish his work at its best. In Edmund Wilson's words, "he was gifted with some special genius which makes his meters and rhyming as catching as music, so that they run in your head after reading"; and in his mastery of the macabre, he exercises a spell "which is half-diabolical." In "The Merchant of Venice," which is one of his lesser pieces, the diabolical touch is lacking. But the verse rattles along with its usual dexterity, and the satire is brisk and amusing.

The Shylock of the poem, it is true, is a wholly conventional figure, straight out of the comic papers. He addresses everyone as "ma tear;" he wears three hats perched one on top of the other, which is how old-clothes men were customarily portrayed by caricaturists of the time. But the main thrust of the comedy is directed elsewhere, at Bassanio and Antonio.

Bassanio is introduced as "a Lord of the Tomnoddy school." He is a wastrel and a fool, but not so foolish that he does not know a good thing when he sees one. His solicitor has already ascertained that, in addition to Portia's vast estates,

Her strong iron box
Seems bursting its locks,
It's suffered so with shares in "Grand Junctions" and "Docks,"
Not to speak of the money she's got in the Stocks,

French, Dutch, and Brazilian,
Columbian and Chilean,
In English Exchequer-bills full half a million . . .

And much more besides. Naturally, as Bassanio tells Antonio, a prize of such magnitude has attracted all sorts of suitors.

Yet Portia—she's named from that daughter of Cato's—
Is not to be snapped up like little potatoes,

and if his dear old friend will only stump up three thousand to subsidize his wooing, he is confident of success:

I have not a doubt
I shall rout every lout
Ere you'll whisper Jack Robinson—cut them all out—
Surmount every barrier,
Carry her, marry her!
Then hey! my old Tony, when once fairly noosed,
For her Three-and-a-half per Cents—New and Reduced!

Antonio, for his part, is far from being the sombre figure that he is in Shakespeare. He is a seasoned man of the world, "sly, caustic and dry;" and the epilogue to the poem shows him in an even less expected light. A manuscript which Barham claims to have consulted reveals what happened to him after his troubles with Shylock were over:

Antonio, whose piety caused, as we've seen
Him to spit upon every old Jew's gaberdine
And whose goodness to paint
All colors were faint
Acquired the well-merited prefix of "Saint."
And the Doge, his admirer, of honor the fount,
Having given him a patent, and made him a Count,
He went over to England, got naturalized there,
And espoused a rich heiress in Hanover Square.

A fine cynical conclusion; and if Antonio's saintliness is not to be taken very seriously, neither is Shylock's villainy.

•

Most Early Victorian humorous writing about Jews was more unpleasant: the "hearty-joke" had a way of turning into the straightforward racist taunt. In its early years, for example, *Punch* (founded in 1841) poked fun at Jews in scores of sketches and drawings. They were generally crude, often ill-natured; and even when the paper was in a serious mood, it could not resist backing up justified social criticism with an additional appeal to prejudice. One of its favorite targets was the big clothing establishment of Moses & Co., of Tower Hill, and some of its angriest rhetoric was provoked by a prosecution which the firm brought against one of its women employees:

> What is the cannibal to such money-spinning knaves? The savage *slays* his victim before he commences his revolting feast, the slopseller refines upon such cruelty, and banquets day by day on some throbbing nerve or wasting muscle—"the pound of flesh nearest the heart" . . .

The woman being prosecuted was a widow with two small children, who had been reduced by near-starvation (she was paid seven shillings a week) into temporarily pawning some of the clothes she was working on. The case should never have been brought, and as individuals Moses and his colleagues deserved to be pilloried every bit as much as they were. But the pound of flesh reference is ugly, too—though it is only fair to add that on this particular occasion *Punch* took its cue from *The Times,* which had already compared Moses to Shylock in a leading article.

The Shylock parallel also had its uses in politics. When Disraeli stood as parliamentary candidate for Taunton in 1835, an anonymous broadside circulating in the town compared his conduct in a quarrel in which he was engaged at the time to that of "the cruel, revengeful, bloodthirsty Jew in *The Merchant of Venice*." When David Salomons, a professing Jew, was elected M.P. for Greenwich in 1851, and while the courts were debating whether or not he could take his seat, fictitious theater bills appeared in the constituency advertising a new production called *Shylock!* The leading role, they announced, was to be played by "Ikey Salomons"; the show was to include a scene in which Shylock, having spent his "monish" too freely and suffered a setback, confided to a friend, "Never mind, my poy, I'll Jew 'em yet."

One must keep the jibes in proportion. Salomons had, after all, been elected; he was forced to stand down, but in 1859, after the last legal obstacles to Jews sitting in Parliament had been removed, he was voted in again. And Disraeli went on to triumphs which nobody needs to be told about. *Punch,* which had savaged him when he was young, could still invoke a distant memory of Shylock in 1875, during his second term as prime minister, but it was in a purely playful fashion. A Tenniel cartoon of that year showed Hartington, the Liberal leader, reminding him that his government existed "only on sufferance," and a genial Disraeli tapping the ash from his cigar and replying: "Sufferance, my dear Hartington!—"Sufferance is the badge of all our tribe"!

Disraeli was unique, but his career fitted into a broader pattern of Jewish emancipation and acculturation. (The French statesman Guizot once told him: "I think that your being leader of the Tory party is the greatest triumph that liberalism has ever achieved.") Whatever tensions remained, the granting of full civil rights, in Britain as in other Western countries, became an accomplished fact: even Emily Wharton's irate father in *The Prime Minister* makes it clear that he has no objection to the admission of Jews into Parliament, "and even" (he is a lawyer) "to the Bench." Shylock, in short, might live on as a memory, but the circumstances that had produced him were a thing of the past.

One place where he was no longer to be found was on his old home ground. In 1866, in his book *Venetian Life,* the American novelist William Dean Howells reported back to his readers that

> Shylock is dead; that if he lived, Antonio would hardly spit upon his gorgeous pantaloons or his Parisian coat, as he met him on the Rialto; that he would far rather call out to him, *"Ciò Shylock! Bon dì! Go piaser vederla"* ("Shylock, old fellow, good-day. Glad to see you"); that if Shylock by any chance entrapped Antonio into a foolish

> promise to pay him a pound of flesh on certain conditions, the honest commissary of police before whom they brought their affair would dismiss them both to the madhouse at San Servolo.

Shylock was dead; and not only in Venice, but among enlightened men and women everywhere.

Meanwhile Shakespeare's play lived on. Indeed, it was almost impossible to escape it: if you did not see it in the theater, you were increasingly likely to encounter it at school. "Over *The Merchant of Venice,*" Peter Fleming once wrote,

> more heavily than over any other play of Shakespeare's, hangs the shadow of the classroom; of the classroom, not the study. The scholars have not made Venice their battleground. It is not Professor Robertson in a rage, but Smith Minor in a beard, who has stamped the play on our memory.

The scholars may have been more disputatious than Fleming suggests, but it is certainly true that *The Merchant of Venice* was a favorite choice once schools (or those schools with the necessary resources) began staging Shakespeare as a matter of course.* It was the first play to be produced at Winchester, for example, when a college Shakespeare Society was set up in the 1860s. And then, looming far larger than the joys of acting, there were essays, homework, examinations. For *The Merchant* was also a perennial "set book," in America no less than in Britain. Between 1886 and 1900, for instance, it was one of the two most widely studied literary works in American high schools. (The other was *Julius Caesar.*)

Schoolroom, theater and passing reference all pushed Shylock further than ever into popular awareness, and as they did the name began to be used as a word in its own right. The verbal and adjectival forms followed; by the end of the nineteenth century, "to Shylock,"

**School productions were still a comparative rarity in the first half of the nineteenth century, although the youthful Disraeli appeared in one—playing Gratiano!*

"Shylockian" and "Shylocky" had all found their way into the dictionary. But it was "Shylock" as a synonym for extortioner or usurer that enjoyed the widest currency.

It still does, although a difference has opened up between British and American usage. In Britain, the term has always tended to be used as a colorful analogy, a comparison which still keeps the original Shylock in view. In America, on the other hand, it has become far more of a free-floating common noun—a development signalled by the fact that in the 1920s, if not earlier, it began to be spelled with a small "s." (The only other Shakespearean character who has had a similar privilege conferred on him is Romeo.) Both noun and verb are also a good deal more deeply entrenched in American slang than they are in Britain. It is hard to imagine a contemporary British crime writer using the term quite as naturally and unselfconsciously as K. C. Constantine does, for example, in *The Big Fix* (1975), an American detective story set in a small town in Pennsylvania: "Everyone who wins gets paid, and no more than five per-cent on the shylocking to the losers."

One feature all the popular usages have in common. There is nothing ambiguous about them, no hint of complexity; they all identify Shylock firmly with hard-heartedness and greed.

• 3 •

By the beginning of the twentieth century, it had become quite common to hold two views of Shylock simultaneously: bad and not-so-bad, black and gray. No one could avoid the harsh traditional view—it was written into the language; but among the better educated, the half-sympathetic Henry Irving view was almost equally familiar. In his memoirs the actor Basil Rathbone describes how, as a schoolboy, he won a prize for an essay on "Was Shylock the Villain of a Melodrama or the Hero of a Tragedy?" This was at a conventional public school, Repton, around 1908. There was nothing revolutionary about setting such a question.

Among writers, the old stereotype still found abundant expression. In 1899, for example, an aspiring author (he was only seventeen at the time) wrote an account of a painting called "Ecce Homo," by the Hungarian artist Michael Munkacsy. One of the figures in the picture was "a well clad Jew"—

> a rich man, with that horrible cast of countenance, so common among the sweaters of modern Israel. I mean, the face whose line runs over the full forehead to the crest of the nose and then recedes in a similar curve back to the chin, which, in this instance, is covered with a wispish, tapering beard. The upper lip is raised out of position, disclosing two long, white teeth, while the whole lower lip is trapped. This is the creature's snarl of malice. An arm is stretched forth in derision, the fine, snowy linen falling back upon the forearm.

This is the "eternal Jew," essentially the same whether he is mocking Christ, or lording it over a sweatshop, or preparing to take his revenge on Antonia. The description holds no surprises in itself; what is interesting about it is that it is the work of a writer—James Joyce—who went on to create the most celebrated sympathetic portrait of a Jew in modern literature. It is what had to be overcome before Leopold Bloom could be called into being.

Joyce may have rejected the stereotype, but other writers were only too willing to perpetuate it. What a fine array of unpleasing Jews confront us in the literature of the first half of the twentieth century! Sir Reuben Lichtenstein, who becomes master of the great country house in H. G. Wells's *Tono-Bungay;* I. Z. Barnett, the German-Jewish financier who spreads out his tentacles in the novels of Hilaire Belloc; the international conspirators in *The Thirty-Nine Steps;* Meyer Wolfsheim, the man who fixed the World Series, in *The Great Gatsby;* sundry disagreeable characters in the early Graham Greene . . . The list goes on and on; but even a few names are enough to suggest that the stereotype permitted a great deal of flexibility. It would be truer, in fact, to speak of a cluster of stereotypes. The Jew could be cast according to taste as plutocrat, Bolshevik, parasite, huckster, gangster, destructive intellectual, moral degenerate, barbarian at the gate; and whatever he was charged with was made to seem all the more sinister by virtue of the Jewishness. "A useful tribe," wrote Wyndham Lewis in 1954, having recanted his former anti-Semitism. "They take the rap for everything."

Amid all this profusion, to speak of a "Shylock figure" is more than ever to use a mere shorthand label. Shylock himself has receded further into the background; for the most part he simply serves as a reminder of where his modern literary descendants have come from, and of what they once were. In Wyndham Lewis's massive satire *The Apes of God* (1930), we even have a hyper-sophisticated Jew, golden-haired Archie Margolin, who enjoys playing up his "Shylocky" East End origins for the benefit of an aristocratic friend. The scene is a mansion in Mayfair, and the principal form his teasing takes is dwelling on the fact (if it is a fact) that he once helped his elder brother Isidore hawk cheap goods around Mayfair basements and back doors, peddling "tin wrist-watches and plate, in plush cases—suitable for skivvies." The rigmarole is extended over several pages, with Archie flashing "his cheapest mass-production grin, for the part of the sham-Yid," and launching into a sing-song denunciation of Isidore's sharp practices:

> "It's too true Dick, he's what you'd call *awful* Dick, is my brother Isidore, he's a proper old shark!"
>
> "A shark?"
>
> "He sells tin watches to poor kids, the old Skylark—I mean Shylock—that aren't worth no not sixpence, for half a quid. He's some lad is Isidore not half! No. *I couldn't recommend him!*"

The joke, you cannot help feeling, is on Archie no less than Dick. In choosing this clever means of dissociating himself from the old Skylark or Shylock, he is reaffirming his links with him as well.

One established author of the interwar years who wrote about Shylock directly was St. John Ervine. Ervine's play *The Lady of Belmont* (published in 1923, produced in the West End in 1927) presents us with the characters of *The Merchant of Venice* ten years on. Jessica has grown tired of Lorenzo. Bassanio, an incurable philanderer, is planning to have an affair with her. He has also run through most of Portia's money, and she has no illusions left about him. Antonio has become an elderly bore, forever harking back to the story of the pound of flesh. When Shylock unexpectedly shows up—he has been taken ill on the road near Belmont—everyone except Portia wants to get rid of him, and the familiar anti-Jewish jibes start flying around. But he is not the Shylock he once was. At heart he may still be a Jew, secretly practicing his old religion, but he has turned the Christianity that was imposed on him to advantage. He is now a senator, a friend of the Duke, a merchant who is twice as wealthy as he was before. He has also grown wiser and more mellow. The play closes with Portia—the only other character we can respect—asking him, "And you forgive all that we have done to you?" Yes, he replies, "I must forgive. We must all forgive, because we have so much to be forgiven."

The Lady of Belmont is workmanlike and well intentioned, but it lacks the creative spark. Five minutes after you have finished reading it, it floats out of your mind. By contrast, T. S. Eliot's "Burbank with a Baedeker: Bleistein with a Cigar" is the vehicle for some unapologetically ugly feelings—but only a master could have written it. It is the cadences, the images, the dreamlike compressed drama that return to haunt you, not just the nastiness.

"Burbank" is set in Venice. One of the two central characters in it is a Jew. It is shot through with literary allusions and concealed quotations: *Antony and Cleopatra, Othello,* Théophile Gautier, Robert Browning, Henry James, a swarm of others. Given all this, Shylock at first seems conspicuous by his absence. He is in fact an important presence on the edge of the poem; and that he should not be more than that is in itself interesting and revealing.

The poem (which was written in 1918 or 1919) consists of three movements. In the first of them, the idealistic American tourist Burbank arrives in Venice and meets the Princess Volupine: "They were together, and he fell." Whether this means that he allowed himself to be bewitched by a worthless woman, or that he suffered a sexual fiasco, the experience was plainly not a very satisfactory one. In the third movement, the Princess extends her favors to the cosmopolitan and (by the sound of it) disgustingly rich Sir Ferdinand Klein, who is a much more suitable partner, while Burbank is left pottering among the relics of Venice's former glories. The story can be read in several ways—as a tale of high ideals and low realities, for example, or as a fable of American innocence and European decadence—but the general progression seems clear. In between, however, there looms up, unexplained, the cartoon figure of Bleistein:

But this or such was Bleistein's way
A saggy bending of the knees,
And elbows, with the palms turned out,
Chicago Semite Viennese.

A lustreless protrusive eye
Stares from the protozoic slime
At a perspective of Canaletto,

The smoky candle end of time
Declines. On the Rialto once.
The rats are underneath the piles.
The Jew is underneath the lot.
Money in furs. The boatman smiles . . .

And so back to Princess Volupine, and on to Sir Ferdinand.

Bleistein is a mere animal, incapable of appreciating the true achievements of European civilization. But why should he irrupt into the poem at this particular point? It can only be in contrast with what has just been disclosed, or at any rate heavily hinted at—the sad story of Burbank's failure with the Princess. Bleistein is Bleistein Erect: the big coarse uncomplicated brute, equipped with a phallic cigar, and the *ur*-version of the more polished (though scarcely less Jewish) Sir Ferdinand Klein. The hatred he attracts is a hatred born of frustration.

Just how deep the rage could run can be seen in "Dirge," a poem which Eliot wrote in 1921 but wisely decided not to publish. "Full fathom five thy Bleistein lies," it begins. Now that crabs have eaten away the lids, his eyes are more protrusive than ever ("Graves' disease in a dead jew's eyes!"), while his Jewish nose has undergone exquisite mutilation:

> *That is lace that was his nose*
> *See upon his back he lies*
> *(Bones peep through the ragged toes)*
> *With a stare of dull surprise . . .*

In "Burbank with a Baedeker," the horrors are hinted at more laconically. The piles on which Venice is built are infested with rats; the Jew (the representative, collective Jew) lurks lower still. Exactly who is thinking these thoughts is never specified; they simply drift past, without anyone having to take responsibility for them. Nor is there any way of telling whether it is Bleistein, or a fictitious narrator, or the poet himself who has been reminded of what happened "on the Rialto once." The one thing we can be sure of is that, without being a direct quotation, the reference points straight to Shylock.

Bleistein is one of Shylock's descendants. He has moved on, through Vienna, and who knows where else; his latest base of operations is Chicago, his latest speculation (or perhaps he is only speculating about a speculation) is in furs. But the ancient clash on the Rialto still reverberates. Something of Shylock lives on.

Shakespeare's objections to Shylock were primarily moral, however, and based on his behavior. Eliot's objections to Bleistein are primarily aesthetic, and based on his demeanor. True, the man carries an inescapable taint of Mammon with him, but his financial activities are less important to the poet than the supposed threat that he presents to civilized values. For Ezra Pound, whose anti-Semitism was entwined with economic theories, he would have been a symbol of Usura.* For Eliot, he is a symptom of disinte-

**Pound had relatively little interest in Shakespeare, but he makes an oblique reference to* The Merchant of Venice *in the Cantos:*

> *The Bard of Avon mentioned the subject,*
> *Dante mentioned the subject*

—the subject in question being usury. He also quotes "Or is your gold ewes and rams?" in his 1944 pamphlet Gold and Work.

gration and cultural decline (as in Ferdinand Klein—the pun is present in the poem). And he is much too lumpishly materialistic for the question of his religion ever to arise. If he were capable of thought, he might well be one of the free-thinking Jews whose excessive numbers Eliot was to deplore in *After Strange Gods.*

All this makes him a very different proposition from Shylock. But there is an even stronger reason why it would have been a mistake to have allowed memories of *The Merchant of Venice* to obtrude more than they do. In his essay on Marlowe, Eliot praises the portrait of Barabas as a "prodigious caricature," and then adds: "It is something which Shakespeare could not do, and which he did not want to do." In the course of his essay on Ben Johnson, he distinguishes "Barabas from Shylock, Epicure Mammon from Falstaff, Faustus from—if you will—Macbeth." His own practice, in early poems like "Burbank," favored the hard, external, Jonsonian-Marlovian method. But that did not prevent him from recognizing that Shakespeare's characters owe their greatness to "a more complex tissue of feelings and desires." Shylock has an inner life. Bleistein has none. Within the confines of the poem, he can be reduced to the image of a bulging, lusterless, less-than-human eye, staring out from the slime; but when Shylock asks "Hath not a Jew eyes?", he is answering the caricature in advance—answering it, and putting it to shame.

Meanwhile the double tradition of Shylock persisted. The idea that he might have his sympathetic side had become a commonplace, but not so commonplace that each generation did not have to discover it for itself.

In Philip Larkin's novel *Jill* (1946), a freshman called John Kemp comes up to Oxford in the autumn of 1940. On his first evening in college he casts an eye over his roommate's belongings:

> On the top of the books lay a squash racquet in a press, and there were also five or six notebooks, stamped "Lamprey College" in thick Gothic letters, one of which John opened, his eye catching the words:

> *Thus we see that in creating the character of Shylock, Shakespeare's original intention was deflected, and instead of a comic moneylender, he produced a figure of tragic significance.*
>
> The awareness that he himself had written something very like that gave John a strange thrill, part rivalry and part kinship, with a dash of disappointment that something he had in the past prided himself on knowing should be the common property of any stranger.

Did John Kemp subsequently find his view of the play being challenged by a tough-minded tutor? It is entirely possible; Larkin does not say. But at least no one was going to accuse him of being merely eccentric. He was treading a well-trodden road.

CHAPTER FOURTEEN

Other Voices, Other Cultures

· 1 ·

The first country outside the English-speaking world where Shylock became widely known was Germany. English theatrical troupes—often augmented by local players—performed in the various German states and principalities throughout the seventeenth century, and "Jew of Venice" plays, as we have seen, frequently featured in their repertoire. Most of these pieces must have borne some relation to Shakespeare, but they were primitive, rough-and-tumble affairs. It was not until 1777, when Friedrich Ludwig Schröder staged the play in Hamburg, that German audiences were given a chance to see *The Merchant of Venice* in an adaptation that did it justice.

By this time the Shakespeare-worship for which Germany was to be famous had already taken root. The founder of the cult (though he was more temperate than some of his successors) was Gotthold Ephraim Lessing, who repeatedly championed Shakespeare in his critical writings, and whose last play, *Nathan the Wise* (1779), was composed in blank verse inspired by Shakespeare's example. Set in Jerusalem at the time of the Crusades, *Nathan the Wise* is dedicated to the proposition that all religions reflect the same central truth. It owes nothing to *The Merchant of Venice*, but Nathan himself, a virtuous and tolerant Jewish trader, quickly came to be seen as the symbolic obverse of Shylock. The first English translation (1781), by Rudolf Erich Raspe,* carried a preface in which Raspe cited Shakespeare's play as a major source of prejudice against Jews; and many subsequent writers have spoken of Nathan and Shylock in the same breath, as though one offset the other. The comparison is unfair to Lessing—his didacticism, however deeply felt, cannot compete with Shakespeare's poetic power. But *Nathan the Wise* is not just a repository of noble sentiments. It has its own eloquence, and it has continued to be performed in Germany down to the present day. In the years before Hitler the title role was often played by actors who have excelled as Shylock—Albert Basserman, for example.

The German passion for Shakespeare produced its most notable monument in the verse translation of the plays begun by August Wilhelm Schlegel in 1797 and later continued by Ludwig Tieck and others. Schlegel, who was also the most influential German Shakespeare critic of his generation, set exceptionally high store by *The Merchant of Venice*. In his *Lectures on Dramatic Art and Literature* (1809–1811) he ranked it among Shakespeare's "most perfect works," and singled out Shylock as one of the poet's "inconceivable masterpieces of characterization." What he particularly admired was the subtlety with which the moneylender's Jewishness was delineated.

> It is easy for the poet and the player to exhibit a caricature of national sentiments, modes of speaking, and gestures. Shylock, however, is anything but a common Jew; he possesses a very determinate and original individuality, and yet we perceive a light touch of Jewishness in everything which he says and does. We imagine we

**Better known as the author of* The Travels of Baron Munchausen.

> hear a sprinkling of the Jewish pronunciation in the mere written words, as we sometimes still find it in the higher classes, notwithstanding their social refinement. In tranquil situations what is foreign to European blood and Christian sentiments is less perceivable, but in passion the national stamp appears more strongly marked.

These words were not written in a vacuum. Like many leading German intellectuals of his generation, Schlegel had a first-hand acquaintance with Jews—Jews who could meet him on his own ground—which no English or French writer of the period could have matched. He frequented the salons of gifted Jewish hostesses in Berlin; his brother Friedrich married one of the daughters of Moses Mendelssohn, the Jewish philosopher on whom Lessing had modelled Nathan the Wise. It seems unlikely that he did not cast at least a glance at the Jews in his own circle (most of whom eventually converted to Christianity) when he wrote about "the higher classes" and "social refinement." But of course in Shylock's case Jewishness was more than a question of tone and accent. Inaugurating an approach which many later critics were to follow, Schlegel saw him as above all the personification of Jewish legalism:

> The letter of the law is Shylock's idol . . . He insists on severe and inflexible justice, and it at last recoils on his own head. Here he becomes a symbol of the general history of his unfortunate nation.

Heinrich Heine, who had attended Schlegel's lectures when he was a student at the University of Bonn, was to arrive at a very different verdict, discussed in the next chapter. For the most part, however, Schlegel's successors accepted his general interpretation. Their own contribution consisted principally of a series of attempts to read *The Merchant of Venice* in the light of a single "leading idea." Hermann Ulrici, in *Shakespeare's Dramatic Art* (1839), saw all the main elements in the play as variations on the legal maxim *summum jus, summa injuria*—to exercise your rights immoderately is to commit a great wrong. For G. G. Gervinus, in his *Shakespeare Commentaries*

(1849), the theme that bound the action together was "the relation of man to property, to money." Both men were ponderous writers, quite without sparkle. (In his essay *Shakespeare the Individual* Walter Bagehot held "the learned and illegible Dr. Ulrici" up to ridicule as an archetypal solemn owl.) But they deserve credit for trying to move beyond mere piecemeal appreciation, and, in the case of Gervinus, for rather more than that. A good deal of modern criticism has been devoted to refining and elaborating the view which he was the first to put forward.

For the academic commentators, Shylock was almost always an unalloyed villain. It was in the theater that Germans were given a chance to consider his depths and complexities, to look at him in the round.

The part was popular with actors from the days of Friedrich Schröder onwards. Schröder himself aimed at a Macklin-like malignity. August Iffland, the leading player of the next generation, put the emphasis on greed, nervousness, and a delicate mimicry of Jewish or supposedly Jewish mannerisms. (To heighten the effect, he wore a fur-trimmed blue coat, a caftan and red stockings.) Then came the far more tormented performances of Ludwig Devrient. Devrient (1784–1832), who made his name in Breslau and came to Berlin at Iffland's invitation, was the greatest of German romantic actors. It is not only the fact that the two men were contemporaries—they died within a year of each other, both in their forties—that makes him remind one of Kean. In private life he was an alcoholic; on stage he was unbridled, tempestuous, over the top. His finest Shakespearean role was generally agreed to be Lear, but in the later years of his career it proved too much for him: by the end of a performance he would be in a state of collapse. Shylock, however, was a less demanding role, and one that he continued to play to the very last. He invested the character with dignity, and even nobility; he showed him in the grip of overpowering forces, born of long humiliation, which eventually dragged him to his ruin. At the same time there was something in his interpretation which transcended common-sense psychology, a suggestion of the uncanny and the bizarre which had its roots deep in his own temperament. "In principle," wrote the theatrical historian Karl Mantzius, "he had no intention whatever of forsaking the firm ground of reality . . . It was only that he ordinarily saw human beings in a glaring, fantastic light."

Karl Seydelmann (1793–1843) gave a more measured account of the role. He began with a muted Shylock, and showed his anger slowly boiling up over provocation. Emotionally, according to Simon Williams in *Shakespeare on the German Stage,* the climax came not so much in the trial scene as with "Hath not a Jew eyes?", a speech which was delivered in a manner that "must virtually have compelled the audience's sympathy."

A degree of sympathy also marked the interpretations of the first Jewish actors to play Shylock on the German stage. Ludwig Dessoir (born Leopold Dessauer) concentrated on the big passionate moments, though in a manner that was too strident for some. When Marian Evans—the future George Eliot—saw his Shylock in Berlin in 1854, she found it "perfectly disgusting." Bohumil Dawison's performance was designed to leave audiences with mixed feelings, torn between admiration for Shylock's pride and revulsion from his vindictiveness. Dawison, a leading star of the 1850s and 1860s, was a Polish Jew who had begun his theatrical career in Warsaw, but moved to Germany in 1847. In 1866 he toured America, where he was enthusiastically received by German-speaking audiences. William Winter, who saw him at the Stadt Theater in New York, praised his technique, but thought that he was insufficiently baleful: his face "did not disclose any trace of the ravages of evil passions long privately indulged."

In the later nineteenth century, the most widely acclaimed Shakespeare productions in the German theater were the work of the company created and directed by the Duke of Saxe-Meiningen. The "Meiningers" were famous for ensemble playing, for strong pictorial effects and for flowing action; every detail was carefully worked out, every figure in the crowd individualized. All these qualities were apparent in the company's production of *The Merchant of Venice*, although it was less successful when it first went on tour in 1874, with medieval-style sets and costumes, than in a later

"Renaissance" version, first seen in 1886. Within the panoramic approach which the Meiningers favored, Shylock did not play as dominant a role as he did in most productions. He was, however, allowed a certain dignity and restraint. Some critics were dissatisfied; they complained that the actor who originally took the part, Weilenbeck, failed to display a demonic streak or touches of "individual ugliness."

There was much more open rancor and rage in the Shylock of Friedrich Mitterwurzer, the foremost German actor of the *fin de siècle.* Mitterwurzer (1844–1897), who was best known for his interpretations of Ibsen, believed that acting should be "sharp and angular." He was at his best portraying troubled or divided personalities, and as Shylock he set out to provide a double focus, a mixture of the inwardly terrifying and the outwardly grotesque. According to Simon Williams, "this principle of contradiction informed the complete role, for while he was in himself a figure of fury, to the Christians he was an object of ridicule, a 'Jewish Hans Wurst.' "

In many respects Mitterwurzer's interpretation conformed to the traditional anti-Semitic stereotype, but the actor was far from displaying unfriendly feelings towards Jews himself. The only pupil he ever took on—at his own suggestion—was the Jewish actor Rudolf Schildkraut. He did all he could to further Schildkraut's career, and he would have done even more if he had not met his death in a grotesque accident. (He swallowed a glass containing poison under the impression that it was mouthwash.)

Schildkraut (1862–1930) grew up in a small town in Romania. He joined a troupe of travelling players in his teens, and eventually became a popular favorite in Vienna, specializing in comic roles in operettas—*Die Fledermaus, The Gypsy Baron.* It was not until the turn of the century that he was given a chance to prove himself as a straight actor. A theater manager who had been a friend of Mitterwurzer invited him to Hamburg, where he built up a big following for his performances in a whole range of roles, both classic and modern. Then, in 1905, Max Reinhardt invited him to Berlin. Reinhardt had just taken command of the Deutsches Theater; one of the plays with which he had decided to open his reign was *The Merchant of Venice*, and he wanted Schildkraut to play Shylock.

Reinhardt lavished all his showmanship on the production. Like other specialists in spectacle, from Charles Kean onwards, he partly used the play as an excuse for evoking Venice. His first aim was to create an aura, an atmosphere of elegance and exuberance. There were handsome sets, costumes out of Carpaccio and Veronese, street cries, snatches of song, incidental music by Humperdinck; a revolving stage reinforced the impression of a magical self-contained world given over to pleasure. And as far as the public was concerned, the spell worked. The production enjoyed a resounding popular success, and over the next thirty years it was to be presented in many other European cities, including (in 1934) Venice itself.

A few of the more demanding critics were dissatisfied. They complained that Reinhardt's approach was superficial, that he sacrificed structure to ornament; and they clearly had a case. But if the director's handling of the Venetians was excessively romantic, he went some way to compensate by assigning Shylock to a succession of exceptionally fine actors.

Schildkraut, the first of them, had already made a deep impression with his playing of the part in Hamburg. He was a short, squat, powerfully built man, with a square face and bulging eyes. In surviving photographs, his Shylock has an air of sly geniality: if it were not for the beard and sidelocks, one might have guessed that he was playing Frosch, his old part in *Die Fledermaus*. But contemporary accounts suggest something far more formidable. For much of the time his acting was matter-of-fact and understated, which only made his explosions of hatred all the more frightening. If he had learned one thing from Mitterwurzer, it was the notion of a Shylock taken aback by the force of his own anger. When he cursed Jessica ("I would my daughter were dead at my foot"), he paused and struck himself on the mouth, as though momentarily shocked by how far he had allowed himself to go. Yet he managed to convey melancholy, too, a melancholy that went much deeper than Antonio's. He was a wounded animal; he reacted, according to one critic, with "the spitefulness and simplicity of an ill-treated child."

In his later years Schildkraut moved to America, where he became a leading figure on the New York Yiddish stage. There were two parts, however, which he continued to act in German, even when the rest of the cast was speaking Yiddish; Shylock and Lear. (If it seemed odd at the time, it seems even odder in retrospect: a German Shylock, a Yiddish Antonio and Portia.) Meanwhile, back in Germany, his legend lived on. A portrait of him hung in a place of honor in the Deutsches Theater—until 1933, when it was taken down on the express orders of Goebbels and publicly burned.

Reinhardt's second Shylock was cast in a different mold. Albert Basserman (1867–1952), who came from an old-established Rhineland family, had served his apprenticeship with the Meiningen company in the 1890s. Tall, lean, a commanding presence, he was generally acknowledged to be the leading German actor of his generation. As Shylock, he wore a bushy gray beard and a hooked nose: his biographer, Julius Bab, thought that they gave him the look of a wolf in a fairy tale. True, there were also gleams of humanity in his interpretation, glimpses of a better nature that had been twisted out of shape. But the predominant effect was one of menace. *"Grimmig war er,"* wrote Bab, *"grimmig und stark"*—fierce and strong. And at the end he was completely unreconciled: he walked off the stage clenching his fists.

As with Mitterwurzer, it would be quite wrong to confuse Basserman's harsh portrayal of a character in a play with his real-life attitudes and opinions. In 1934, at the age of sixty-seven, he went into voluntary exile. He had a Jewish wife, but he also used the occasion to address an open letter to Goebbels in which he said in leaving Germany—a Germany in which the Nazis were in power—he was doing what he could to redeem the country's honor.

Other outstanding actors who played Shylock under Reinhardt's direction included Alexander Moissi (who had begun by playing Gratiano), Werner Krauss and the Austrian-Jewish actor Fritz Körtner (1892–1970). Körtner's performance in a 1924 production in Vienna was widely praised, but he himself found Reinhardt's handling of the play too lyrical, too indulgent towards Antonio and his friends. Three years later he appeared in a production in Berlin directed by Jürgen Fehling (with Elizabeth Bergner as Portia). By now he felt more strongly than ever that it was important to expose the self-seeking and intolerance that lay behind the Venetians' charm, to present a Shylock who was undeniably bitter and aggressive, but who had been made what he was by the treatment meted out to him. Fehling disagreed, and there were heated quarrels during rehearsals, but in the end a good deal of Kortner's conception came across, certainly as far as his own performance was concerned. The critic Alfred Kerr rated it above Schildkraut's or Basserman's; no one else in his long experience seemed to him to have conveyed Shylock's tragedy so simply or movingly. A tribute of another kind came from Julius Streicher's paper *Der Stürmer,* which in Körtner's words "spat poison." This was a portent; within a few years the actor was to be a refugee, scraping a living out of mediocre film-parts in England and America. After the Second World War, however, he reestablished himself in Germany. In 1969, not long before his death, he made a much-acclaimed appearance in a production of *The Merchant of Venice* on German television.

Werner Krauss (1884–1959) first played Shylock for Reinhardt as a stand-in, deputizing for Schildkraut or Basserman when they were away.* Then in 1921 the director asked him to take the lead in a new production. (By this time he had an international reputation: he had made an indelible impression as Caligari in the film *The Cabinet of Dr. Caligari* two years before.) In his memoirs he describes how he hit on a new way of interpreting Shylock now that it was, so to speak, his own part. On the first day of rehearsals, Reinhardt told him that in the Jacob and Laban speech, when he came to the lines about Jacob being the third of the patriarchs, he ought to indicate through his eyes, through his very eyelids, that he was summoning up the memory of thousands of years of Jewish history. The next day Reinhardt thought that he had not got it quite right, and remarked that, on reflection, it was something that only

**The part he normally played at the time was Lancelot Gobbo. When he took over as Shylock he was replaced in his turn by a junior member of the company, Ernst Lubitsch.*

a Jew could manage. Krauss was annoyed: if Jews could act non-Jewish parts, why could not non-Jewish actors play Jews? He stayed up half the night, brooding and drinking, and then had a sudden inspiration. He would tackle the part as Max Pallenberg might have done (Pallenberg being an actor who was famous for his comic roles and for his Mephisto in *Faust*). He would be *frech*—cheeky: when he came into court in the trial scene, for instance, he would thrust the bond under everyone's nose. At first, when this new approach was sprung on Reinhardt at rehearsal, he was speechless. Then he decided that he liked it. He gave Krauss the go-ahead, and the production was a success.

A scholar who later made a special study of Shylock, Herman Sinsheimer, formed a quite different impression of Krauss's performance. It seemed to him to produce an effect not so much of cheekiness as of madness:

> He seemed to tumble rather than walk, on old and weary feet. He was possessed and obsessed by the wrongs done to him and his like, a petulant underling who wished to argue with all and sundry on one theme only: his wrongs as a Jew. Even when he was silent, he seemed to argue on this theme. He ceased to be an actor playing a Jew and took on the perplexing appearance of a medieval player in the part of a ghost.

Sinsheimer may well have seen a different production: the actor played Shylock for a number of directors besides Reinhardt. He also appeared in a silent film of *The Merchant of Venice*, directed by Richard Oswald and shot on location in Venice in 1923.

We shall meet him again, playing the role one last time, under circumstances which no one could have foreseen in the early years of his career.

• 2 •

The French stage-history of *The Merchant of Venice* is much thinner than its German equivalent. It was not until 1830 that the play was first produced in France (and then only in a hack adaptation); not until 1917 that Shylock was portrayed by a French actor of the front rank (Firmin Gémier of the Théâtre de l'Odéon).

Yet everyone knew who Shylock was, if only by hearsay. In the words of Emile Montégut, who undertook a new translation of Shakespeare in the 1860s, he was as much the proverbial hard-hearted creditor as Don Juan was the proverbial seducer or Tartuffe the proverbial hypocrite. And everyone also knew that he was a Jew.

Among major French writers, the first to be especially drawn to *The Merchant of Venice* was Alfred de Vigny. In 1828 Vigny saw an English company perform the play in Paris, with Kean in the lead. Deeply impressed, he set about writing an adaptation, under the title *Shylock,* but failed to get it staged: the first production did not take place until long after his death. (He had better luck with his translation of *Othello,* which enjoyed a resounding success when the Comédie Française presented it the following year.)

Shylock is much shorter than *The Merchant of Venice*. Vigny trims speeches, eliminates characters, runs scenes together; in a gesture towards the classical unities, he compresses the period of Antonio's loan from three months to a helter-skelter three days. Nonetheless he preserves all the main features of Shakespeare's play—all of them, that is to say, except its essential flavor. His use of traditional rhyming couplets produces a snip-snap effect, in this context, which is far removed from the suppleness and flexibility of Shakespeare's verse, or, for that matter, his prose. Everything seems more obvious: when Shylock proposes the "merry" terms of his bond, he explains:

> *C'est un jeu, car Shylock n'est pas assassin.*

And a misplaced sense of propriety softens the physical impact that you get in the original. Antonio still abuses Shylock, but he no longer spits on him. Shylock still asks, "Hath not a Jew eyes?", but he omits "If you prick us, do we not bleed?"

Vigny's first original play, *La Maréchale d'Ancre,* was produced by the Comédie Française in 1832. Set in the early seventeenth century, it includes among its characters a court Jew, Samuel Montalto, who is a kind of up-market Shylock. At one point he claims that he is no longer a usurer: "I lend money *gratis* at present." (*Gratis,* it will be recalled, is one of the words with which Shylock taunts Antonio.) But just so that we should be in no doubt about his true nature, Vigny sums him up in the list of dramatis personae as "not too dirty on the outside, dirty enough underneath."

In part Vigny had been drawn to *The Merchant of Venice* by its romantic and musical aspects, but the fact that it also featured a villainous Jew cannot have been uncongenial to him. By the time he wrote *La Maréchale d'Ancre,* his antipathy towards Jews had sharpened. He now held them responsible for instigating the revolution of 1830 ("The Jew paid for the July revolution because he handles the bourgeoisie more easily than the nobility"), while in his later writings there are outbursts which go even further: Jews are the new masters of the world, a world in which there is no longer a place for an aristocrat like Vigny himself. Yet paradoxically he had other moods in which he could identify with them, because he thought that they were "the people who had best understood the sadness of life." He also wrote half a dozen impassioned poems on Old Testament themes. Moses, Samson, Jephthah were magic names to him: in *Servitude et Grandeur Militaires* he claimed to know the Bible by heart.

The same familiar dualism marks the attitude of Victor Hugo. In Hugo's book on Shakespeare (1864), amid a good deal of wild rhapsodizing, there is a passage of genuine eloquence about the creation of the "type," the literary figure who embodies a whole family of individuals, and yet remains an individual himself, three-dimensional and distinct. Shylock is held up as a supreme example. He is what you would get, says Hugo, if you took usurers *en masse* and extracted their concentrated essence—and popular usage, unerring as ever, has confirmed as much. In the same way, he is a Jew who brings together in one person the extremes of the Jewish character: "*Shylock est la juiverie, il est aussi le judaïsme.*" (then *Juiverie* means "Jewry," but it can also mean "a Jewish trick.") That is to say, "he represents the whole nation, high as well as low; he represents both faith and fraud"—and it is this representative quality which gives him greatness.

Some thirty-five years earlier Hugo had introduced a Jewish character into his pseudo-Shakespearean drama *Cromwell* (1827)—Manasseh Ben Israel, the rabbi who played a key part in the campaign for the readmission of Jews to England in the 1650s. The real Manasseh was a mystic, a learned biblical commentator, a friend of Rembrandt. Here (accepting for the moment the invidious distinction) was someone who could surely claim to speak for *le judaïsme* rather than *la juiverie.* But the Manassé in Hugo's play is greedy and treacherous, a cunning Jewish villain who openly announced that it is a good deed to rob a Christian. By these standards, the formulations of the passage about Shylock in the Shakespeare book represent a big advance; though we can still feel uncomfortable with them, and grateful that before he died Hugo committed himself to a whole-hearted defense of persecuted Jews in his play *Torquemada.*

Manassé had many successors. In the nineteenth century and well into the twentieth, the Shylock figure, if we use the term loosely, was as common in French literature as in English. Popular fiction was littered with Jewish scoundrels, ranging from small-scale usurers to plutocrats weaving vast sinister schemes. (One late nineteenth-century anti-Semitic novel was entitled *Le Baron Vampire,* another *Baron Jéhovah.*) At a higher level, there were the unsavory financiers in Guy de Maupassant and in Paul Bourget's *Cosmopolis;* higher still, drawn with a degree of light and shade, there were Balzac's Baron Nucingen and Gundermann, *le banquier roi, le maître de la Bourse et du monde,* in Zola's novel *L'Argent.* But none of these characters became bywords in the way that Shylock had done. In Jules Vallès's powerful autobiographical novel *Le Bachelier* (1881) a group of Parisian radicals are thinking of starting a paper. But first they need to find a printer, and one of them borrows a comparison from Shakespeare to bring home to them how difficult that is going to be:

> The printing business today! Do you know its true name? It is called *Shylock.* Shylock, the profiteer, the miser, the Jew, the man who cuts off his pound of flesh!

Shylock, *le rogneur de chair.* "Nucingen" or "Gundermann" would hardly have done as well.

The ugly, avaricious Jew was an equally familiar figure on the stage. In the 1880s Alphonse d'Ennery, a popular boulevard dramatist, explained why there were no Jewish characters in his plays:

> The first duty of an author is to please his audience; that is, to respect its tastes and habits. So if I *had* presented a Jew, I would naturally have had to make him a usurer, a swindler, a traitor, at all events a villain.

D'Ennery, who was half-Jewish, preferred not to cater to this particular taste, but there were many other playwrights ready to oblige.*

By comparison, productions of *The Merchant of Venice* itself remained a rarity. The first two adaptations were both staged in 1830; three further versions were put on in the course of the nineteenth century, but the only one of them which was of any note was *Shylock,* a verse drama by Edmond Haraucourt which was presented at the Odéon in 1889 and again in 1890. Despite the title, Haraucourt shifted the emphasis of his piece away from Shylock towards Belmont and Jessica and Lorenzo. Romance reigned, and the result, in the words of one modern commentator, was "without question closer to the French comedy of manners of its own decade than to Shakespeare's blend of fine language and social criticism." The production had two strong points in its favor, however: stylish décor, and some beautiful incidental music specially composed by Gabriel Fauré. It may have fallen well short of Shakespeare, but for those with nothing to compare it to, it could be a revelation. The future leader of the French Radical party, Edouard Herriot, who saw it when he was seventeen, was so impressed that long afterwards he was able to recite odd scraps of the text by heart.

It also prompted an essay from the veteran theater critic Francisque Sarcey. Sarcey had some kind words for Haraucourt, but his main concern was with the correct interpretation of

**It might leave a misleading impression if one did not add that, whatever prejudices there were against them, Jews enjoyed an exceptional success in the French theater from the mid-nineteenth century onwards. There is a joke in Proust about a non-Jewish theatrical producer who changes his name to Samuel in order to further his career.*

Shakespeare's play, and more especially of Shylock. He conceded that Henry Irving's portrayal of the moneylender had been both awe-inspiring and moving. He cited, at considerable length, a letter he had received from Théodore Reinach, in which Reinach—a distinguished classical scholar, and a member of one of the best-known Jewish families in France—had set down some of the by now well-worn arguments for considering Shylock a half-sympathetic character. Sarcey wanted to show his fair-mindedness, to give such arguments a hearing. But nothing could shake him in his own conviction that Shakespeare had intended Shylock to be "a grotesque monster," who deserved all he got. If that sounded unduly harsh, he added, it had to be borne in mind that the whole play was a fairy tale, or better still the equivalent of a modern operetta (with the big difference that instead of music, it had poetry—Shakespearean poetry). It was also a kind of parable, celebrating *"le triomphe de l'amour sur l'argent."* From this point of view, the fact that Shylock was a Jew was a mere incidental. But Sarcey still managed to refer twice to his receiving well-earned blows on his nose (in one case, on his hooked nose). Forgetting about his forced conversion, he also described him at the end of the play as "ridiculed, humiliated, sent back without a sou to his ghetto."*

After Haraucourt, there was nothing in the way of productions until the early twentieth century. In 1904, and again in 1906 and 1916, the Comédie Française staged a few performances of Vigny's *Shylock;* in 1912 a pioneering Shakespeare company led by Camille de Sainte-Croix presented an authentic *Merchant of Venice,* performed without scenery. But it was Firmin Gémier, in 1917, who drew the crowds. Gémier was an important figure in the French theater—Jean Vilar's Théâtre National Populaire has been described as his "godchild"—and his production was an acknowledged landmark in its time. Whether it would have the same appeal today seems doubtful. For one thing, he still preferred to follow the

**One should not read too much into this. Some two years later Sarcey protested publicly against the virulent anti-Semitism of Edouard Drumont's newly founded newspaper* La Libre Parole: *he was rewarded with a flood of hate mail for his pains.*

old tradition of using an adaptation rather than a translation, and an adaptation which took lots of liberties. For another, his interpretation of Shylock was a narrow one. According to Thornton Wilder, in his essay *Some Thoughts on Playwriting,* he portrayed him as "a vengeful and hysterical buffoon": "at the close of the trial scene, he was driven screaming about the auditorium, behind the spectators' backs and on to the stage again, in a wild Elizabethan revel." This sounds a little too "Elizabethan" for comfort, but Wilder (along with many others) greatly admired Gémier's performance. He held it up as one of two examples of the opposing extremes to which the interpretation of a major Shakespearean role could legitimately be pushed, Irving's Shylock being the other.

Despite Gémier's success, there were no further productions of *The Merchant of Venice* for a generation. In a sense, the true stage history of the play in France began only after the Second World War: over the past forty years there have been at least a dozen major productions, based on much more faithful adaptations than those used by Gémier and his predecessors.* But one earlier version will always occupy a special place. In 1913 the French director Henri Desfontaines made a film based on the play, entitled *Shylock,* with the brilliant Jewish actor Harry Baur in the main role. For Baur, it marked the beginning of a screen career which was to include appearances in such classics of the French cinema as *Poil de Carotte, Un Carnet de Bal* and *Volpone*—a career which was to be cut short in 1943, when he died as a result of being tortured by the Gestapo.

• 3 •

As Shakespeare's fame spread, Shylock's followed. By the end of the nineteenth century *The Merchant of Venice* had been translated into at least twenty languages, and since then it has been translated into a great many more. It has become familiar to Dutchmen as *De*

**For details, see the appendix to the recent translation of the play by Jean-Michel Déprats (1987).*

Koopman van Venetië, to Russians as *Venetsianskii Kupets,* to Rumanians as *Negutatorul din Venetia,* to Greeks as *Ho Emporos tes Venetias:* Shylock and Portia have been made to confront each other in Arabic and Icelandic, Zulu and Gujerati, Catalan and Welsh. A full history of the play's international progress is one which could only be written by a very large multilingual committee.

Here, we can do no more than single out a few threads from the tapestry. King Luis I of Portugal translating the play into Portuguese (in 1879). Another monarch, Rama VI of Siam, translating it into Thai. The first black Shylock, Ira Aldridge (b. New York, 1807, d. Lodz, 1865), taking audiences by storm in Riga and St. Petersburg. The Czech puppet-show versions of the play. The celebrated Italian Shylocks of the nineteenth century—Ernesto Rossi, Ermete Novelli. Nirad C. Chaudhuri, the future author of *The Autobiography of an Unknown Indian,* hearing the story for the first time as a small boy in Bengal. Geoffrey Kendal, the "Shakespeare Wallah" of the famous movie, presenting his production of *The Merchant of Venice* all over India, where it turned out to be one of the most popular works in the repertoire.

One thing is clear: *The Merchant* is a play that travels easily. Its folktalelike qualities enable it to cut across cultural boundaries, and it has proved a favorite with audiences in many different parts of the world.* In a number of cases, it has provided playgoers with their first exposure to Shakespeare. It was the first of his plays to be performed in Armenian, for example (in 1866), and the first to be performed in its entirety in Chinese—in Shanghai, in 1930.

Shakespeare's influence cannot of course be measured purely in terms of theatrical productions, or even translations. *The Merchant of Venice* was not translated into Russian until 1833, for instance, but long before that Alexander Pushkin (reading it in French and possibly, at a later stage, in English) had fallen under its spell. Shylock,

**The Flemish-speaking theater probably holds the record in this respect. Between 1884 (when Shakespeare was first presented in Flemish) and 1950 there were no less than seventeen productions of* The Merchant of Venice, *which made it easily the most popular of his plays: the runner-up was* Hamlet, *with nine productions.*

as he wrote in his *Table Talk,* seemed to him an outstanding example of Shakespeare's ability to create characters who lived independent lives, rather than being cut to a predetermined pattern:

> Shakespeare's characters, unlike Molière's, are not merely typical representatives of a certain passion or a certain vice; on the contrary, they are living beings, complete with many passions and many vices. Their varied, many-sided personalities unfold as their circumstances reveal themselves to the spectator. Molière's miser is only miserly—that is all. Shakespeare's Shylock is not only miserly, but resourceful, vindictive, child-loving and witty.

The fruits of Pushkin's admiration for Shakespeare include the "little tragedies," a series of short plays written in 1830. In one of them, *The Covetous Knight,* the central character is consumed with lust for gold, but what looks like conventional avarice on the outside is shown to conceal resplendent dreams of power. By contrast, the play also features a servile Jewish moneylender of the familiar kind, whose villainies extend as far as hinting to an heir that he can supply him with the means of poisoning his father. Given Pushkin's comments on Shylock, it is a disappointing bit of characterization.

In the course of the nineteenth century *The Merchant of Venice* became a familiar part of the Russian repertoire, and at the end of the century it was chosen by Stanislavski as the first Shakespeare play to be presented by the Moscow Art Theatre. The production failed to enjoy much success with the public, however, largely because on Stanislavski's instructions the actor who played Shylock, Yevsei Darski, adopted a Jewish accent: this was thought to be unsuitable for a serious role. Stanislavski, who had originally planned to alternate with Darski, seems to have inclined towards a poignant reading of the part. Some twenty-five years later, writing home during a visit to America, he reported that David Warfield's Shylock was the best he had ever seen.

Early in his career, he had been equally impressed by the Saxe-Meiningen production of *The Merchant,* which he had seen during one of the company's Russian tours. It is a reminder of how internationalized Shakespeare had become, even a hundred years ago, of how complex a web had been spun around his works. For another example, more pointed still, we might turn to the reflections which Jose Ortega y Gasset published in 1910 under the title *Shylock*.

They were prompted by the experience of seeing *The Merchant of Venice* performed by an Italian company, with Ermete Novelli in the main part. Ortega conceded that Novelli, "with his face like that of an enormous chimpanzee," was a gifted actor, but he was bitterly disappointed, all the same. For one thing, the rest of the cast were mediocre, so that the artistic balance that Shakespeare had achieved was lost. For another, Novelli's performance, however much technical virtuosity he showed, was disjointed and grotesque. As a result, a frivolous atmosphere spread down from the stage to the audience. The whole occasion was an affront to Shakespeare, an artist who had composed the elements in his works as carefully as Rubens composed them in his paintings, and an affront to Shylock, too. For the story of the moneylender was not just an anecdote extracted from a collection of carefree Italian tales. "The poor wandering Jew who trudges, his head bent, over the roads of history, under the weight of infinite misfortunes, is as legendary as the millennium. He is, however, alive"—and in the second half of the essay Ortega moved on to consider anti-Semitism, both as the inescapable context of the play, and as a disease that was still running its course in the real world.

He recalled his experiences while travelling in Germany, for instance—incidents like the one in a crowded railway compartment on a journey from Wittenberg to Berlin, when he had fallen into conversation with a Jewish shopkeeper. As soon as the other passengers realized that the man was a Jew, they had started directing jokes and insults at him, and Ortega confessed that the memory made him ashamed: "I was afraid that those stolid burghers would attribute a Jewish origin to my Spanish paleness and black beard. I was ashamed and did not defend him . . ." But that had been mere social anti-Semitism. Ortega also reminded his readers of what had been happening in Russia. Yesterday there had been brutal expulsions, today there were pogroms: "Kishinev, Bialystok, blood, streams of blood . . ." And then, after musing on the fate of "poor Yahweh," he worked his way back to the evening in the theater that had been his starting point:

> Signor Novelli, Signor Novelli, why transform Shylock into a picturesque figure? In the Venetian Jew Shakespeare conjured up a millennial pain: with poetic license, unflinchingly, he portrays the cruel image of hate among the races, and of enmity among their Gods.

A Spanish philosopher recording his impressions of an Italian production of an English play: Ortega's essay is a measure of how far Shakespeare had become the common property of educated Europeans everywhere. But it also underlines that there were European countries (from the perspective of 1910, Russia above all) where a production of *The Merchant of Venice* might touch a much rawer nerve than it did in England or America.

By chance, Novelli's company had been involved a few years earlier in an episode which brought this home very strikingly. In 1905 they had been due to open a season in Odessa with *The Merchant of Venice,* when Novelli was approached by a local Zionist leader, the youthful Vladimir Jabotinsky.* It was a time of violent anti-Semitic agitation, much of it officially inspired; the situation in the city was tense, and Jabotinsky appealed to Novelli to choose something less inflammatory for his opening play. To his credit, the actor agreed, though how much practical difference his decision made it is naturally impossible to say. Later that year the Jews of Odessa were subjected to the pogrom that Jabotinsky had feared: it lasted for four days and cost over 300 lives.

In non-Christian or non-Western cultures, the question of Shylock's Jewishness was far less important; sometimes it was edited

**Subsequently founder of the Revisionist branch of the Zionist movement, the breakaway group from which the present-day Likud party claims descent.*

out of the script completely. Japanese readers first got to know of *The Merchant of Venice* in the form of a story, *The Strange Affair of the Flesh of the Bosom* (1877). The anonymous adaptor transferred the action to Japan—to Sakai, a seaport near Osaka. Shylock became Yokubari Gampachi, meaning "Stubborn Close-fist," the three thousand ducats became three thousand *ryo,* Portia became Kiyoka, meaning "Odor of Purity." ("Correctly holding her fan, Kiyoka then spoke movingly of the quality of mercy.") Gampachi is hit off by the narrator with a few vivid strokes: he replies to the entreaties of Matsugae, his Antonio-like victim, "with arrogant puffs at his pipe." But there is nothing to set him apart in terms of religion, no quarrel with Matsugae over whether it is right or wrong to charge interest, and no suggestion that he has past injuries to avenge. Without such a background, his behavior seems purely sadistic, a true case of motiveless malignity.

Even in this depleted form, however, the story captured the imagination of readers and playgoers alike. *The Strange Affair of the Flesh of the Bosom* was the first Japanese tale based on Shakespeare to appear in print, and *The Merchant of Venice* was the first of Shakespeare's plays to be staged in Japan—in 1885, when a Kabuki troupe in Osaka performed a version entitled *The Season of Cherry Blossoms, The World of Money.* A second prose version, *A Lawsuit about a Pledge of Human Flesh* (1883), went through several editions.

It was not until 1911 that Japanese theaters began to present "authentic" productions of Shakespeare, but by that time a tradition of Japanese-style productions had been firmly established. This was in large part thanks to the efforts of the actor-manager Kawakami Otojiro. (The most famous of his adaptations was a version of *Othello* with Tokyo and Taiwan—then a Japanese colony—substituted for Venice and Cyprus.) In 1900 Kawakami's company visited London. One of the plays they presented was *The Merchant of Venice*, with Kawakami as Shylock and his wife, Sada Yacco, as Portia, and one of those who saw them was Desmond MacCarthy. Twenty years later, the details of their performance were still fresh in MacCarthy's mind: Kawakami in the trial scene, for instance, making faces after Portia's speeches "like a man who has swallowed bitter medicine." What impressed him most was their extraordinary emphasis on the physical. It was the only performance he had seen in which "it seemed credible that a pound of flesh was actually going to be cut from a man's breast before our eyes."*

If non-Europeans saw Shylock as a universal type, that did not necessarily prevent them from fitting him into a European context. In 1896 a young South African native, a Tswana, had his curiosity about Shakespeare aroused by a production of *Hamlet* at the local theater in Kimberley. He started reading the plays, beginning with *The Merchant of Venice*, and then recounted the stories to his friends. The characters were so realistic, he wrote, "that I was asked more than once to which of certain speculators then operating around Kimberley, Shakespeare referred as Shylock." What he failed to add, but what was fairly obviously in his mind, was that many of those speculators were Jewish.

These were exceptional circumstances, however. The general practice was to connect the story to indigenous storytelling traditions, sometimes with startling results. In *Out of Africa* (1937) Karen Blixen describes a conversation she had with her Somali steward, Farah Aden, in which she explained the plot of the play to him. Farah was a Muslim, and fully conscious of the fact that Shylock was a Jew, but that was not what interested him about this particular situation. Instead, he saw the conflict between Shylock and the Christians purely as a battle of wits:

> Here was a big, complicated business deal, somewhat on the verge of the law, the real thing to a Somali. He asked me a question or two as to the pound of flesh: it obviously seemed to him an eccentric, but not impossible agreement. And here the story began to smell of blood—his interest in it rose. When Portia came upon the stage, he pricked up his ears; I imagine that he saw her as a

**MacCarthy's reactions were no doubt intensified by his personal interest in Sada Yacco. He sent her flowers, and persuaded her to have lunch with him: "We had some delightful trivial broken talk together—but why didn't I tell her that I was in love with her?"*

> woman of his own tribe, Fatima with all her sails set, crafty and insinuating, out to outman man. Colored people do not take sides in a tale, the interest to them lies in the ingeniousness of the plot itself; and the Somali, who in real life have a strong sense of values, and a gift for moral indignation, give these a rest in fiction. Still, here Farah's sympathy was with Shylock, who had come down with the cash; he repugned his defeat.
>
> "What?" said he. "Did the Jew give up his claim? The flesh was due to him, it was little enough for him to get for all that money."
>
> "But what else could he do," I asked, "when he must not take one drop of blood?"
>
> "Memsahib," said Farah, "he could have used a redhot knife. That brings out no blood."

There was also, Karen Blixen pointed out, the problem of having to take exactly one pound of flesh, neither more nor less. But Farah was ready for that, too: he could have taken one little bit at a time, weighing the individual bits as he did. "Had the Jew no friends to give him advice?"

For the Elizabethans, Shylock had been monstrously cunning; for Farah, he had not been nearly cunning enough. It was a poor kind of a trickster who allowed himself to be outsmarted quite so easily. No doubt about it, he should have cut away the pound of flesh a bit at a time.

But in the story, Karen Blixen was finally driven to protest, he had given it up:

> "Yes that was a great pity, Memsahib," said Farah.

CHAPTER FIFTEEN

An Extended Family

· I ·

For Jews, as long as they think of themselves as Jews, *The Merchant of Venice* must always occupy a special place in the Shakespeare canon. Jewish responses to the play have been many and varied; often there has been little if anything to differentiate them from non-Jewish responses. But it would be an unusual, some would say an unnatural, Jew who could regard Shylock with complete detachment.

Of Jewish writers, the one who has left the most memorable account of his reactions to *The Merchant of Venice* is Heine. In everyday life, Heine was happy to use "Shylock" as a term of abuse: it was one of the epithets he held in reserve for Jews who incurred his enmity, especially where money was concerned. But Shakespeare's play itself aroused far more complicated feelings.

Whatever those feelings may have been to start with, they were refocussed and given greater depth by the experience of seeing Edmund Kean at Drury Lane. That was in 1827, during Heine's one visit to England—although it was not until ten years later, in the course of a series of articles about the French theater, that he described the occasion:

> The Jew of Venice was the first heroic role I saw Kean assume. I say "heroic role" deliberately, for he did not play Shylock as a broken old man, as the kind of Sheva of hatred [Sheva in Cumberland's *The Jew*] which Ludwig Devrient gave us, but rather as a hero. Thus he still lives in my memory . . .

Kean had clasped his staff in a way that made it look more like a weapon than a support. In the Jacob and Laban speech, he had first "cocooned himself, as it were, in his own words," then broken off, paused, mulled over what he wanted to say: you felt you were hearing, "not a role learned by heart, but a speech made up, thought out with effort, then and there." At the end of the speech he had smiled, "like an author happy with his own invention."

Heine's portrait of Kean is every bit as good as Hazlitt's. But it is an account of the actor rather than the role. About Shylock himself, there was more to be said.

The following year, 1838, Heine accepted a commission from a publisher to supply the text for a set of steel engravings of Shakespearean heroines. The book he produced, *Shakespeare's Girls and Women,"* was lopsided. He used up most of his space on the tragedies and histories, and when he came to the comedies, all that he had room for were a few quotations. But by that time he had already dealt with *The Merchant of Venice*, which he had decided to include among the tragedies; and his pen had run away with him. The articles on Jessica and Portia contain wide-ranging reflections, not only on the play, but on the Jews, on anti-Semitism, and (by implication) on his own deep but deeply fractured sense of Jewish identity.

His account of Jessica opens with another reminiscence of the evening when he had seen Kean.

> When I saw this piece played in Drury Lane there stood behind me in the box a pale British beauty who, at the

> end of the fourth act, wept passionately, and many times cried out. "The poor man is wronged!" She had features of the noblest Grecian cut, and her eyes were large and black. I have never been able to forget them, those great black eyes which wept for Shylock!
>
> When I think of those tears, I must include *The Merchant of Venice* among the tragedies, although the framework of the play is ornamented with laughing masks and sunny faces, satyr forms and cupids, and though the poet himself meant to make it a comedy. Originally, perhaps, Shakespeare wanted to please the mob by representing a werewolf at bay . . . But the genius of the poet, the world spirit informing and controlling him, is stronger, always, than his own will; and so it came to pass that in Shylock he presented—despite glaring elements of caricature—the justification of an unfortunate sect which Providence, from inscrutable motives, loaded with the hatred of the lower and the higher mob, and which was not invariably inclined to requite this hatred with love.
>
> But what am I saying? Shakespeare's genius also rises above the petty quarrel of two religious parties, and in fact his drama shows us neither Jews nor Christians but oppressors and oppressed, and the madly agonized exultation of the latter when they can repay their arrogant tormentors with interest for insults inflicted. There is not a trace of religious differences in this play: in Shylock, Shakespeare shows nothing but a man bidden by nature to hate his foe—just as in Antonio and his friends he surely does not depict disciples of that Divine doctrine which bids us love our enemies.

The Christians in the play, apart from Portia, are a poor lot. Lorenzo, for example: under Prussian law, he would have been sentenced to fifteen years in the penitentiary for the infamous burglary in which he was involved. And where did that leave Jessica, his partner in crime? She had done something worse—trampled on her father's affections out of sheer wantonness:

> It was no unloving father whom she left, robbed, betrayed. Shameful treachery! She even makes common cause with Shylock's enemies, and when at Belmont they speak all sorts of evil of him Jessica does not cast down her eyes, Jessica's lips do not grow white, but Jessica says the worst about her father. Horrible fault! She has no feelings, only a love of adventure.

Only once does she display true modesty—when she is ashamed of having to dress like a boy during her elopement; and only then, in Heine's view, does she display a characteristically Jewish trait. For "the Jews are a chaste, continent, I might almost say an abstract people, and in the purity of their morals"—here he launched into a new theme—"they approximate most closely to the Germanic tribes."

The idea that there might be a special affinity between Germans and Jews was one which was to reappear in many guises, some of them sinister, in the work of later writers;* it was one to which Heine himself was frequently to return. On this occasion he put the argument in highly idealized terms. The two "moral peoples" were so alike that "the Palestine of the past might be regarded as an oriental Germany, just as present-day Germany might be considered the home of the sacred word, the native soil of prophecy, the stronghold of pure spirituality." And not only Germany, but Europe as a whole, bore the stamp of Jewish moral teaching.

Given these common links, how was one to account for the fact that Jews aroused so much hatred? Heine's answer came couched in the form of a long extract from a letter he claimed to have received from an acquaintance (though recent commentators have argued that he almost certainly wrote it himself). The causes of modern anti-Semitism, according to his correspondent, were

**See, for example, the remarks of Herr Fitelberg in Thomas Mann's* Doctor Faustus *(chapter 37) on German nationalism and Judaism*—"une analogie frappante!"

essentially economic. The common people's hatred of the Jews was a misdirected hatred of the rich; their instincts were sound, but they had been led astray by centuries of false doctrine, inherited from the Middle Ages, into defining their target in the wrong terms.

We are close to the celebrated late nineteenth-century definition of anti-Semitism as "the socialism of fools"—the one difference being that the "fools," in Heine's case, are viewed with a good deal of forbearance. Such a narrowly economic diagnosis could not satisfy him for long, however. Nor could its implications for the play; and when he came to consider Portia he shifted his ground once again. If the rich, without distinction, were the villains of the piece, who more reprehensible than the lady of Belmont? But in practice it was the contrasts between Portia and Shylock that interested him. The serene good fortune that she embodied was the very opposite of Shylock's "gloomy lot." Where her words were warm and beautiful, his were "discords crashed together, shrill, hissing, acrid." And if he was "the stern Jew, hostile to all art," she represented "that after-bloom of Greek art which in the sixteenth century impregnated the world with its fragrance, from Italy outwards." What the play sets before us, in fact, is a striking instance of Heine's favorite contrast between Hellenism and Hebraism, drawn almost wholly (here, at least) in Hellenism's favor.

Yet Shylock was not so easily thrust aside. He was so vivid a presence that it was hard to believe that he could not still be found somewhere in Venice, lurking behind a pillar, or haunting the Rialto; and when Heine, a "hunter after dreams," had visited the city, he had set out in search of him.

At first, when he describes his quest, it looks as though we are launching into a piece of satire. The reason he wanted to get hold of him, he tells us, was to give him a piece of good news: his cousin, M. de Shylock of Paris—an unmistakable reference to the banker James de Rothschild—had become "the mightiest baron in Christendom," invested among other honors "with that Order of Isabella which was founded to commemorate the expulsion of the Jews and Moors from Spain." The family had come a long way.

But then the tone turns somber. After he had failed to find

Shylock on the Rialto, it had occurred to Heine that he might be at the synagogue; he had made his way there, and when he arrived he had found a service in progress. It was Yom Kippur, the Day of Atonement.

Jeffrey Sammons, in his biography of Heine, has pointed out that Heine's one visit to Venice, in 1828, took place nearly two months after the date on which Yom Kippur fell that year. The whole incident is a fantasy or a reverie—and a powerful one. As soon as Heine steps into the synagogue, any suggestion of irony drops away:

> The Jews happened just then to be celebrating their sacred Day of Atonement and stood wrapped in their white prayer shawls with uncanny noddings of their heads, looking like an assembly of ghosts. There they stood, these poor Jews, fastings and praying, since early morning: they had tasted neither food nor drink since the evening before, and had also begged the forgiveness of all their acquaintances for any wrong they might have done them during the past year, so that God might forgive them too—a beautiful custom which exists, strangely enough, among people who are supposed to have remained strangers to the teachings of Christ.

An impressive scene. But alas, as he scanned the congregation, the poet became aware of something else:

> I had visited the madhouse of San Carlo that same day, and it now occurred to me, in the synagogue, that in the glances of the Jews there flickered the same dreadful, half-staring and half-unsteady, half-crafty and half-stupid expression which I had seen shortly before in the eyes of the lunatics. This indescribable, puzzling look indicated not so much absence of mind as the supremacy of a fixed idea.

As against this macabre picture, one must set all the positive things that Heine said about Judaism (in the magnificent poem "Jehuda ben Halevy," for instance). As against *those,* there are the bitter moods of revulsion against Jewishness that can be found in a poem like "The New Israelite Hospital in Hamburg." (A hospital, we are told, that will never be able to cure the Jewish condition itself, "that thousand-year-old family disease, that plague dragged out of the Nile valley"). And in between, how many waverings, doublings back, divided feelings! The masterly survey of the poet's treatment of Jewish themes by S. S. Prawer, *Heine's Jewish Comedy,* is one long study in ambivalence.

Even the "fixed idea" that he discerned among the worshippers in Venice was not something he necessarily shuddered away from. It had its value—but it had come at too high a price: "How great a martyrdom those who hold it have already endured on its account! What greater martyrdom awaits them in the future!" And here Heine made a chilling prophecy. For all the shibboleths that divided them, Jews, Christians and Muslims (or so he claimed) did not differ in essentials. For all the persecutions that the great religions had given rise to, they had more often than not exercised a restraining influence. But suppose they lost their hold? "If one day Satan or sinful pantheism should conquer, there will gather over the heads of the poor Jews a tempest of persecution that will far surpass all they have had to endure before."

Meanwhile, there was still the question of Shylock. Heine stood looking round the synagogue. He was convinced that the old man had to be there, half-hidden under one of the white robes, praying fervently; but there was no sign of him. Then, towards evening, "when, as the Jews believe, the gates of Heaven are closed, and no further prayer can enter," the poet heard a voice—a voice "in which tears flowed that were never wept from human eyes":

> These were the sounds of agony that could only come from a heart that held locked within it all the martyrdom which a tormented people had endured for eighteen centuries . . . And it seemed to me that I knew this voice well; I felt as though I had heard it long ago, when it

> lamented, with the same tone of despair: "Jessica, my child."

Heine could of course have found a worthier or less ambiguous symbol of Jewish suffering than a vengeful moneylender. But he deliberately chose the hard case. It was an act of solidarity.

For a writer, the fact of having been born a Jew meant everything, or nothing, or (more usually) something in between. Heine is fairly easy to categorize: he was a German writer, first and last, but there were important Jewish elements in his work—elements which are obvious in terms of content and theme. Other writers, however, present more of a difficulty.

The novelist Italo Svevo, for instance. The first things any reference book is likely to tell you about him is that he was born in Trieste in 1861, that his family were Jewish, and that his real name was Ettore Schmitz. At the same time his background was a good deal more Jewish than is commonly recognized. His parents celebrated the Sabbath and the major festivals; his father attained a position of honor in the local synagogue; he and his brother attended a school run by the Chief Rabbi of Trieste. As an adult, however, he put his upbringing behind him. The whole subject of Jewishness made him uncomfortable: in an autobiographical sketch written in 1928 he described his father as "assimilated," which was at best a half-truth, and elsewhere in his writings he completely avoided Jewish topics.*

With one exception. The very first piece he published, at the age of nineteen, was an article for a Trieste newspaper, entitled "Shylock." He had been looking forward keenly to a production of *The Merchant of Venice*, with the actor Ernesto Rossi; to his dismay, he heard that it might be cancelled (for fear of offending the local Jewish community), and he was delighted to learn that it was going to be put on after all. His essay, which was designed to absolve Shakespeare from the charge of anti-Semitism, borrows its arguments straight from Heine, who is cited in the opening paragraph.

**No father bent on wholesale assimilation would have called his son "Aron," which was Svevo's (or rather Ettore Schmitz's) middle name.*

However he had started out, the playwright had risen above the prejudices of his age; he had created in Shylock *"una figura colossale, ammirabile, umana"*—a man battered by insult and contempt until the only sentiment left to him was that of revenge. How could such a character be regarded as other than tragic?

Trieste itself was a city relatively devoid of anti-Semitism, where Jews lived on close terms with their neighbors. But it was also part of the Austro-Hungarian Empire, which meant that the problem was bound to come up from time to time. It can hardly be a coincidence, as Victor Brombert has pointed out, that a few weeks before he published the Shylock article Svevo had been involved in a disagreeable incident: he had applied for a commercial job, for which he was well qualified, only to be told to his face that he could not be considered because he was a Jew.

Many critics have detected crypto-Jewish themes in Svevo's novels. Some have regretted that he did not write about them openly. In his study of Italian Jewish writers, *Prisoners of Hope,* H. Stuart Hughes gives a measured verdict. A Jewish strain is undoubtedly present in the novels, but it is a question of attitude or temperament, not something that can be pinned down too precisely. It shows itself above all in the humor of Svevo's masterpiece, *The Confessions of Zeno.* The hero of that novel is fretful and ill at ease in the world, and things are always going wrong for him. But "what starts as tragedy ends as farce." He is a resilient hypochondriac, a survivor, an example (without being specifically Jewish) of a type familiar from countless jokes and anecdotes: "the ostensibly self-denigrating Jew who in the stories he tells against himself invariably manages to come out on top." A brilliant comic equilibrium has been achieved—though at the cost of suppressing the rougher emotions that went into the essay on Shylock. Svevo has sometimes been compared, not very illuminatingly, to Proust. One thing which the two of them did have in common was Jewishness, although Proust's was far more attentuated. He was only half-Jewish, on his mother's side; he was baptized and brought up as a Catholic. Yet it was the French novelist, not the Italian, who returned again and again to Jewish themes.

Or perhaps it would be truer to say, to *one* Jewish theme, since he had no interest in Judaism, Jewish communal life or Jewish culture. He was exclusively preoccupied, understandably enough, with the situation of the assimilated Jew who cannot altogether forget his origins, and who lives in a society which won't allow him to.

There are two major Jewish characters in *Remembrance of Things Past,* Swann and Bloch. Swann's father was a stockbroker (like Proust's maternal grandfather), but Swann himself is at home in the most exclusive circles in France: he is "one of the smartest members of the Jockey Club," the confidant of duchesses, a friend of the Comte de Paris and the Prince of Wales. He is also cultivated and considerate, a man of exceptional charm and impeccable taste. What a contrast with Bloch, who is noisy, pretentious, often downright fatuous. If Swann is the "acceptable" Jew, Bloch is his unacceptable counterpart—and we are never allowed to forget his Jewish origins for long. He has a father, Solomon Bloch, whose besetting sin is avarice; the Bloch family, when they take their holiday at Balbec, form part of a tight-knit Jewish clan which the narrator describes as being "more picturesque than pleasant." Not that Bloch himself is comfortable with his Jewish identity. He, too, complains—in a characteristically loud voice—that there are too many of his correligionists staying in Balbec. ("You hear nothing but, 'I thay, Apraham, I've chust theen Chacop.' ") And when he finally achieves success as an author, along with the social success for which he has always craved, it is under the guise of "Jacques du Rozier." Du Rozier, as the narrator is at pains to point out, is his new name, not merely a pseudonym—and a name beneath which only an expert could have detected "those 'chains of Israel' with which my old schoolmate seemed definitively to have broken."

But the breaking of the chains is far from complete. In the great final episode of the novel, the reception at the Prince and Princesse de Guermantes', Bloch is one of the guests whom the narrator sees for the first time after many years. At first, he has some difficulty recognizing him. His once-curly hair is brushed flat, his moustache has gone, he sports a formidable monocle. And though his nose is still large, it no longer seems "Jewish": thanks to the surrounding alterations, it is now "scarcely more visible than is the deformity of a hunchbacked woman who skilfully manages her appearance." He also has, at first glance, an air of youthful gaiety. And why not? He is a success, a sought-after figure in drawing rooms which twenty years before he would never have been allowed to penetrate. But a few minutes later, at close quarters, he makes a different impression. In "the translucency of his face" the narrator can now discern

> another face, almost frightening, racked with anxiety, the face of an old Shylock, waiting in the wings, with his make-up prepared, for the moment when he should make his entry on to the stage and already reciting his first line under his breath.

One of the puzzling things about *Remembrance of Things Past* is why the narrator should remain as friendly with Bloch as he does: the man is a perpetual embarrassment. Or rather, it would be a puzzle, if the novel were meant to be judged by the canons of conventional realism. But in the Proustian universe, other standards apply. Bloch is not so much a friend of the narrator as an emanation. The two are bound together psychologically: Bloch is a second self who has to be ridiculed, rejected, kept at a distance, but who can never be entirely shaken off. He is also the character in the novel who bears the closest physical resemblance, albeit in caricatured form, to Marcel Proust.

In spite of his Dreyfusism, his attachment to his mother,* and the positive if rather nebulous Jewish qualities which he occasionally attributes to Swann, Proust invested a great deal of energy in a harsh inner struggle over his Jewish identity. As a novelist, he was at liberty to make the narrator-cum-hero of *Remembrance of Things Past* a non-Jew (just as he was at liberty to make him a non-homosexual). But he was too honest an artist, too true to his conflicts, to leave it at that. The repressed, in the person of Bloch, returned with a vengeance; and for Bloch, there can be no expunging the past. Even in his hour of triumph, his social mask fails to

**Jeanne Proust* (neé *Weil*) *remained nominally Jewish after her marriage out of respect for her parents.*

conceal, not merely the Bloch he once was, but the legacy of his ancestors. The detested moneylender lives on in the celebrated author, the pariah in the man of the world. Shylock has shown up in the Faubourg Saint-Germain.

The whole passage is worth looking at a little more closely. Normally the exposure of Bloch's social pretensions would be an occasion for scorn. Here, for once, the tone is serious and even sympathetic: the poor man is "racked with anxiety" (*tout anxieux*). And if his face has a "frightening" quality, it is surely because he has suddenly taken on the air of a ghost, not because he is a menacing, knife-wielding villain. Indeed, he is not Shylock at all, but an actor playing Shylock. An actor, you might almost say, who has been condemned to play Shylock.

For the bad dream which haunts him is the memory of a role, not a reality. Shylock no more represents his true nature than that of his ancestors. It was a part which was written for them by someone else, imposed on them by history; and Bloch's half-hidden anxiety is that history may not be done with it yet.

• 2 •

In 1916 Oxford University Press celebrated the tercentenary of Shakespeare's death with the publication of a massive volume edited by Sir Israel Gollancz, *A Book of Homage to Shakespeare*. It opened with a poem by Thomas Hardy ("And yet, at thy last breath, with mindless note/ The borough clocks but samely tongued the hour"), and included contributions from authors and scholars writing in at least twenty different languages, all of them reproduced—with translations appended—in the original. One of the more unexpected items was a Hebrew ode, specially composed by Rabbi Sir Hermann Gollancz (Israel Gollancz's brother, and the first English rabbi to receive a knighthood). He began by quoting a few phrases from the "Hath not a Jew" speech, rendered into Hebrew, and followed them up with a heartfelt paean: "When the days were dark, a Seer arose; lifting his voice in parable and song, he gave utterance to this plea . . ." The whole poem constituted a tribute, not only to Shakespeare, but to the happy integration of practicing Jews into mainstream English culture.

Israel Gollancz himself was a distinguished medievalist, though he was better known to the general public as the editor of J. M. Dent's Temple Shakespeare. He also wrote several papers on *The Merchant of Venice*, which were gathered together after his death in a small, privately printed book, *Allegory and Mysticism in Shakespeare.* The common theme running through them was that medieval habits of thought persisted much more strongly in Shakespeare than was generally realized, especially the traditions of moral allegory. Thus, Portia is Misericordia, Mercy personified; Antonio is a living commentary on the text, "Greater love hath no man than this, that a man lay down his life for that of a friend"; even Bassanio, in his quest for Portia, "has points of contact [not all that many, perhaps] with Spenser's Red Cross Knight in search of Una."

Such an approach naturally emphasized the Christian foundations of the play, although Gollancz took care to indicate that they might more properly be called Judaeo-Christian. He cited the rabbinical midrash which proclaimed that Mercy was one of the daughters of God; he invoked the coming together of mercy, truth, righteousness and peace described in the 85th Psalm, "the Psalm [as he reminded his readers] that belonged to Christmas Day." Shylock, however, remained a problem. An allegorical reading was almost bound to flatten him out, to leave him a wholly malign figure—Usury or Ill Nature incarnate; yet it was impossible to relinquish the feeling that he was a human being, a man whose character had been shaped by the treatment he received from other men. In the end, Gollancz was forced back on a kind of conjuring trick. He quoted Lorenzo's lines about "sweet harmony"—

> *Such harmony is in immortal souls;*
> *But whilst this muddy vesture of decay*
> *Doth grossly close it in, we cannot hear it*

and glossed them as though they contained a warrant of pardon for Shylock: "Shylock, too has an immortal soul; the muddy vesture of decay is made more muddy by the scorn and contempt of the

Antonios of the time. There, too, is the music—if it could only be heard aright."

While critics and scholars expounded the text, a number of British and American Jewish writers were tempted to fashion Shylocks of their own. Humbert Wolfe, for example, opened his first collection of verse (1920) with a dramatic monologue, "Shylock Reasons with Mr. Chesterton":

Jew-baiting still! Two thousand years are run;
And still it seems, good Master Chesterton,
Nothing's abated of the old offense.
Changing its shape, it never changes tense.
Other things were, this only was and is . . .

The notion of Shylock confronting G.K.C. is a promising one, but Wolfe lacked the necessary skill to follow it through. Either that, or the confusions of the poem reflect his own confused feelings about the subject. First, he argues that anti-Semitism produces Jews like Shylock, which in turn produces more anti-Semitism. Then he switches to a scene in a synagogue, where a mysterious voice cries out that even the innocence of Jewish children will not save them from the curse laid on them, that when Christ was on the Cross with the two thieves on either side of him, Israel was already "the fourth unseen and crucified." Then the congregation appears to accept the justice of its fate—although I must admit that at this point I find it hard to work out what is going on. And somehow (for equally obscure reasons) the scene in the synagogue is meant to symbolize a moment of potential reconciliation, one that passes all too quickly as Shylock and Chesterton resume their cycle of eternal hate.*

**Many of Chesterton's comments on Jews qualified him for the role that Wolfe assigned him, but the only reference to Shylock that I have come across in his work (no doubt there are others) is surprisingly mild, even appreciative. After praising Portia as "the most splendid and magnanimous woman in literature," he goes on to evoke the figure set over against her: "Shakespeare had conceived, with extraordinary force, humor and sympathy, a man to express the ideal of technical justice, formal morality, and the claim of a man to his rights." Admittedly this comes from an early essay, written in 1901, before Chesterton's views had hardened.*

Other writers took up the story of *The Merchant of Venice* where Shakespeare left off. The American poet Louis Untermeyer, for example, wrote a cynical epilogue, *The Merchant of Venice Act VI,* which showed Shylock and Antonio, ten years on, working together as business partners. The moral was that the religious differences between Christians and Jews were superficial: both groups were equally materialistic at heart. Untermeyer had a deep admiration for Heine—he wrote a biography of him—but he had none of Heine's sense of the tragic where Shylock was concerned.

The most ambitious of the sequels was Ludwig Lewisohn's novel *The Last Days of Shylock,* which was published in 1931, with ornate, oriental-style illustrations by the Polish-Jewish artist Arthur Szyk. Largely forgotten today, Lewisohn was a famous and controversial name in the 1920s, equally well-known as critic and novelist, as champion of European literature and apostle of outspokenness about sex, as a somewhat grandiose autobiographer and a scourge of American Main Street culture in a spirit comparable to that of Mencken and Sinclair Lewis. The child of German-Jewish immigrants, he grew up in Charleston, South Carolina, in an almost wholly assimilated atmosphere. For a time, as a student, he was attracted by Methodism, but when that phase was over he became a confirmed skeptic. In the mid-1920s, however, he embarked on a prolonged tour of Europe, which completely changed his outlook. He had gone to the Old World in love with its culture, and hoping to soak himself in its traditions. Instead, what struck him most was the intensity of the anti-Semitism he observed, above all in Poland, Austria and Germany (this last a bitter blow to a man who had published a defense of German culture in the middle of the First World War). The account of Europe he had planned to write turned into a book called *Israel* (1925), and from this time on he preached Jewish solidarity, Zionism and Judaism, though a Judaism which was as much cultural as religious.

The Last Days of Shylock was a milestone on his pilgrimage—no mere literary exercise, but a book charged with angry feelings. For much of its length it might more appropriately have been called

"The Early Days of Shylock": the first half is largely devoted to Shylock sitting alone on the night after the trial, summoning up images from his past. All this part of the story is very well done, especially the chapter called "Of Remembered Flames," an account (founded on fact) of two mass-burnings: the destruction of Jewish books which took place in Venice, in the Piazza San Marco, in 1553, and the *auto-da-fé* at Ancona in 1556 at which twenty-five Marranos who had reverted to Judaism were burned alive. Reading about such scenes, we enter more deeply into Shylock's soul, and into his point of view: *these* were the possibilities which ultimately lay behind Antonio's taunts. But Lewisohn was still saddled with Shakespeare's plot. Whatever Shylock's grounds for hating Antonio, how could the form of revenge he chose, realistically considered, seem anything other than pathological? Lewisohn was reduced to the expedient of having Shylock reflect that when it came to it, if the court had upheld his claim, "his knife would not have gone very deep into the bosom of his adversary." The sight of blood, we are told, had always sickened him.

In the second half of the story Shylock flees from Venice, sails to Constantinople, and enlists in the service of Joseph Nasi, the Sultan's Jewish counsellor. After many adventures, including a visit to Palestine, he meets Jessica, who has been deserted by Lorenzo, and is slowly reconciled to her. These chapters are less striking than the earlier ones, closer to a conventional historical romance. But they still testify to Lewisohn's saturation in his subject, and to the knowledge of Jewish customs and Jewish history that he had managed to acquire since his "return to Zion" five or six years before.*

Literary responses to *The Merchant of Venice* were of course only part of the story. For many Jews, the play was quite simply a sore point; and even those who found it acceptable when it was read or seen by adults were often troubled by its widespread use as a school text. In 1912 Jewish groups in the United States (the only country where Jews were in a position to bring to bear the necessary

**For some post-World War Two sequels to the play, see below, p. 334.*

pressure) began campaigning to have it removed from the curriculum. In 1927 E. E. Stoll reported with satisfaction—since it confirmed his own view of how Shylock should be interpreted—that "the Jewish Anti-Defamation League is more and more successful in its endeavors to keep the play out of the schools." By 1930 it had been banned by school superintendents in some ninety American cities.

I must admit to mixed feelings in the matter. Books should not be banned, except for the most compelling reasons; once you start, you never know where it will stop. On the other hand, school texts are a special case, and it is not hard to imagine circumstances in which being made to read *The Merchant of Venice* in a classroom could be genuinely inflammatory or hurtful. It depends on so many things: on the teacher, on the reactions of the children, on the prevailing attitudes of society at large. But with less and less literature being studied in schools anyway, perhaps the problem will solve itself. Perhaps it already has.

The advent of Hitler inevitably made the whole subject far more sensitive. The Nazis themselves, as we shall see, were well aware of the opportunities that *The Merchant of Venice* offered them. But there was also at least one satirical attack on Nazism which drew on the play to subtle effect.

To Be or Not to Be (1942) was one of Ernst Lubitsch's last films. Set in occupied Poland, it is the story of a troupe of Polish actors who outwit the Nazis and neutralize a Nazi agent with a series of quick-change tricks and stratagems (including an impersonation of Hitler). Much of the humor is directed at the vanity of actors; much of it is boulevard wit of a familiar Lubitsch kind. But the film's lightness of touch should not be mistaken for flippancy. Unlike most Hollywood black comedies of a later era, it does not take place in a moral vacuum. It makes its own wry affirmations, and the evils it lampoons lose none of their horror for being ridiculed.

Lubitsch was a German Jew. His star, Jack Benny, had been born Benjamin Kubelsky; but the only overtly Jewish character in the film is Greenberg, played by another German Jew, Felix Bressart, who had arrived in Hollywood as a refugee only a few years before. (Lubitsch had previously cast him as one of the Soviet trade delegates in *Ninotchka.*) Greenberg is a minor member of the Polish troupe, who is constantly reminded of his humble status. But he never allows himself to be crushed,* and Lubitsch assigns him one of the most important motifs in the film. Early on, while he is waiting backstage during a performance of *Hamlet,* we see him practicing the "Hath not a Jew" speech. The effect is comic and Walter Mitty-ish: he is a bit player fantasizing about what it would be like to be a star. Later on, he comes back to the speech, this time while standing amid the debris of a bombed street in Warsaw. The context naturally gives the lines a new resonance, but you also realize how wise Lubitsch was to have prepared the ground. If he had begun by serving up the speech straight, it might easily have seemed a facile and rather hackneyed attempt to play on our feelings. As it is, the gap between the first and second versions is itself a source of pathos, a measure of how much everything has been transformed by the war. And when the speech comes round again, Lubitsch builds still further on what has gone before. By this time the situation is desperate, and Greenberg, forced to recite in front of an audience of German soldiers, gives the performance of his life. Between the first and second renderings of the speech, he acquired depth; between the second and the third, he has acquired strength. The lines now burn with anger as well as sorrow; they contain a warning as well as a plea. But given the circumstances under which they are delivered, it is not really revenge that they proclaim, but resistance—resistance, and the will to survive.

• 3 •

The German-Jewish novelist Karl Emil Franzos (1845–1904) devoted much of his work to evoking the world of the small-town Galician Jews among whom he had spent his childhood. In one of

*GREENBERG: *Would you like to hear my opinion?*
THE DIRECTOR OF THE THEATER: *No, Mr. Greenberg, I do not want to hear your opinion.*
GREENBERG: *All right then, let me give you my reaction.*

his novels, *Der Pojaz* ("The Clown"), a village wagoner who is visiting the city of Czernowitz is persuaded to apply for a job with a theatrical company. He is a natural mimic, but he has never been to a theater before; indeed, he has no real idea what a theater is. The director of the company, whom he describes as "a long 'Deitch' " (German), receives him amiably, and tells him that first he had better watch the play being performed that evening.

Some of the wagoner's comments on the performance are naive, some are shrewd, all of them relate the play as well as he can to his own familiar world. There is a merchant called Anton who keeps clicking his tongue and wagging his head, "just as if he were very sad." Then it turns out that he has no money and has to borrow some, which explains why he is sad. There is an old Jew whom everyone calls "Shylock"—but then Gentiles are always getting Jewish names wrong, and in all probability it should be "Shyeh" (Isaiah). There is a servant who eats Shyeh's bread and curses him behind his back. ("But if you think that surprised me you're wrong. Take Yanko, our Dr. Schlesinger's coachman—he does the same thing exactly.") Sometimes you feel sorry for Shyeh, and other times his behavior is unintelligible or even detestable. But the final injustice of forcing him to become a "meshumed" (a convert) is more than the wagoner can bear. He shouts out in protest, and it is just as well that at that point the curtain comes down and everyone starts leaving.

Afterwards he tells the director that he is puzzled. Is the author (whom he has never heard of) a friend of the Jews, or isn't he? Surely the director can settle the matter—he must be acquainted with him, after all. Everyone bursts out laughing, and the director explains that the poet who wrote the play has been dead three hundred years; that he was a noble, great man, and could therefore recognize the injustice done to the Jews, but that in those days Jews had been hated everywhere, "as much as they are in Poland today," and that he had tried to please his audience. The wagoner persists: in that case, why not improve the ending? " 'God forbid!' said the Herr Direktor. 'I know some day you'll understand what a sin that would be.' "

Sholem Aleichem would no doubt have made a good deal

more of such a episode. Franzos, writing from the outside, is a little too quaint, a little too deliberately humorous. But the picture he paints is recognizable in essentials, and it gives one some idea of how remote the theater was from the experience of most East European Jews until the late nineteenth century. Folk traditions existed, but the early pioneers of the professional Yiddish theater had to overcome enormous obstacles, including the disapproval of Jewish religious leaders. It was not until 1876 that the first professional company was established (at Jassy, in Romania). Others quickly followed; but in 1883 the Czarist authorities issued a decree banning theatrical performances in Yiddish throughout the Russian empire, and Yiddish players began to join the great migration westward. It was in America, a few years later, that Shakespeare entered the Yiddish theater, first in the form of Judaized adaptations (most notably, Jacob Gordin's *The Jewish King Lear,* 1892), and then with attempts to present his work on its own terms.

The first Yiddish translation of Shakespeare, published in Warsaw in 1886, was a prose version of *Julius Caesar.* The second, published in New York in 1899, was Joseph Bovshover's verse translation of *The Merchant of Venice*. Bovshover, one of the so-called "sweatshop poets," was a young anarchist who had undergone many hardships, and who eventually succumbed to mental illness: he saw the play as a protest against social injustice, with Shakespeare using Shylock as an outlet for his own bitterness. The translation had its admirers at the time, but according to the literary historian Leonard Prager it is stiff and heavy, "a victim of a period when elegance meant Germanisms." There is no record of its ever having been performed.*

It was the most celebrated of Yiddish actors, Jacob Adler, who finally brought Shylock to the Yiddish stage. Adler (1855–1926) was

**Translation isn't everything. Yiddish-speaking Jews knew something of Shakespeare and his legend before they knew his actual works, and there were some East European Jews—the intelligentsia—who read him in other languages. In one of the earliest novels written in Hebrew, Peretz Smolenskin's* The Reward of the Righteous *(1874), a bigoted father burns the books belonging to his emancipated daughter. They include a Polish translation of* The Merchant of Venice.

one of the great legends of the Lower East Side in the decades when Jewish immigration was at its peak—a man renowned for his masterful ways, his regal bearing, his love of good living, his womanizing, and the total hold he had over his audience. In many respects he was an actor-manager in the familiar mold, but the conditions under which he worked made him a culture hero as well. For in a few short years the theater had become one of the central institutions of the immigrant Jewish community, a source of gossip, excitement and social cohesion. A gifted non-Jewish observer, Hutchings Hapgood, made it clear in his book *The Spirit of the Ghetto* (1902) just how special its role was:

> In the three Yiddish theaters of the Bowery is expressed the world of the ghetto—that New York City of Russian Jews, large, complex, with a full life and civilization. In the midst of the frivolous Bowery, devoted to tinsel variety shows, "dive" music-halls, fake museums, trivial amusement booths of all sorts, cheap lodging houses, ten-cent shops and Irish-American tough saloons, the theaters of the chosen people alone present the serious as well as the trivial interests of an entire community.

Adler was not only the foremost star of this particular firmament; he was also the actor most closely associated with efforts to raise the level of the plays that were presented. His success in *The Jewish King Lear* (which was melodramatic, but a big improvement on the melodramas that had preceded it) marked a major breakthrough. The play was set in nineteenth-century Russia: the "Lear figure" was a rich merchant who was cast out by two hardhearted daughters, though not before the "Kent" figure had told him the story of Shakespeare's *King Lear* by way of a warning. Fifty years later people who had seen him could still remember the intensity of Adler's performance: his easy opulence in the opening scenes, his scorn, his bitter cry as he finally went into the street to beg his bread. It was a performance which, among other things, redoubled Shakespeare's prestige among Yiddish-speaking playgoers, and helped to pave the way for Adler's *Merchant of Venice*.

Adler had a lofty conception of Shylock. He saw in him a man of "high intellect and proud convictions," with a certain grandeur "imparted to him by the sufferings and traditions that have been his teachers." A man, too, "who is rooted in life and has grown strong in it." There was anguish in the performance: when the curtain came down on the scene (the non-Shakespearean scene) where Shylock discovers that Jessica has fled, all that could be heard was the sound of cloth being torn—the forsaken father rending his garment. But the keynote of the interpretation was pride. In the courtroom scene, Adler tried to put across the idea that Shylock did not intend to go through with his claim, that "the desired climax," as he put it, "was to refuse the pound of flesh with a gesture of divine compassion." In the event, the high point came as he was about to leave. Gratiano seized his arm and forced him down to the ground; for a moment, in the words of Adler's biographer, Lulla Rosenfeld, "Shylock, crouching, sobbing, was the very picture of the terrified ghetto Jew." But the moment passed: he rose, shook the dust of the court from his sleeves, and made the proud exit.

At a safe remove from the ghetto, Jews might have been able to live with the idea of a villainous Shylock, but for Adler's audiences it was out of the question. He gave them not so much what they wanted as what they needed, and his production—first presented in December 1901—was a great success. Two years later, he played the part on Broadway, speaking his lines in Yiddish while the rest of the cast spoke English. He was highly praised by the New York reviewers, but it was his first and last appearance (by choice) on the English-language stage.

There were many subsequent Yiddish productions of *The Merchant of Venice*, in both America and Europe. The first Yiddish actor to play Shylock in England (preceding Maurice Moscovitch) was Sigmund Feinman, who made his home in London between 1906 and his death in 1909. Other Yiddish actors who played the part included Maurice Schwartz, the Polish-born Isaac Samberg and Alexander Granach (a well-known actor on the German stage before 1933: his Yiddish performance in New York in 1938 marked a return to his first language). A particularly highly regarded production, starring Isaac Samberg, was that of the Vilna Troupe, in 1929. The troupe was noted for its uncompromising artistic standards; the translation, specially commissioned, was by a fine poet, Israel Stern. (There are some English translations of his work in *The Penguin Book of Modern Yiddish Verse.*) Both Stern and Samberg perished during the Holocaust.

Yiddish-speaking Jews responded strongly to Shakespeare, whenever they were given a chance to. This is not to say that *The Merchant of Venice* did not present them with difficulties. It did, and numerous Yiddish essayists and critics nagged away at "the Shylock problem." One of them, Shlomo Bickel, summed up his divided feelings (and those of many other Jewish readers and theatergoers) in an essay published in 1947:

> We can't make up our minds what to do with Shylock. We feel the moral grandeur of the Shylock figure, but we are afraid to accept it completely. We admire his challenging agressiveness, but we shrink from its logical consequences. We are repelled by the subterfuge with which Portia obtains her verdict, but we applaud her, so that we should not ourselves be accused of Shylockism . . .
>
> So we are prepared to deny Shylock. Yet we know that he is putting forward in our name such a justified and fundamental historic grievance and complaint that it must not be left unsaid.

An earlier critic, H. D. Nomberg (1876–1927), had been much more shocked by Shakespeare's use of the revenge theme, and in voicing his dismay he had put his finger on a basic weakness of attempts to "justify" Shylock, including Shakespeare's own.* "How could that towering genius," he asked, "have imagined so incredible a savage?" The answer he gave was twofold. First, the Shylock story had deep roots: he had no doubt that it went back to the medieval blood-libel.

**Nomberg, who lived in Warsaw, was an associate of the great Yiddish writer Y. L. Peretz. Shakespeare was one of his idols: his Yiddish translation of* Romeo and Juliet *is said by Leonard Prager to be of considerable merit.*

Secondly, he believed that the playwright had tried to imagine how an ordinary individual would have reacted to Shylock's place:

> Shakespeare found it all so obvious and natural. Read Shylock's monologue, how he recounts the suffering of his tribe, the humiliations inflicted on him and his, and you will see the hatred and revenge that were to Shakespeare the logical, inescapable consequence of the position in which the Jew had been placed among the nations.

Yet the facts of Jewish existence, had the poet but known them, were quite otherwise. Jewish vengefulness was a Christian myth: on the contrary, Nomberg insisted, it was something to be proud of "that we have been inhumanly treated, yet our humanity is undiminished."

An unusual case of a Jewish man of the theater completely turning against *The Merchant of Venice* was that of Maurice Schwartz. Schwartz, the director and principal actor of the Yiddish Art Theater in New York, was the most controversial of the major personalities of the Yiddish stage, a flamboyant combination of idealist, huckster, vainglorious showman and theatrical genius. (James Agate said that his production of Andreyev's *Seven Who Were Hanged* contained "more great acting than I have ever seen on any stage in any place.") In 1959, he explained to an interviewer why he had recently refused an invitation to play Shylock that he had received from a theater in Cleveland, Ohio:

> It's an anti-Semitic play. When Moscovitch did it in New York I realized why they had the Kishinev pogroms. Shakespeare was a good businessman. He knew that Barabas (he borrowed Shylock from Marlowe) would make money. But it's definitely an anti-Semitic play, and I wouldn't do it.

This was not long before Schwartz's death, however. Earlier in his career he had had no problems about playing the part. He had performed it in Yiddish in 1921; then years later he had appeared in selected scenes in English on one of the big vaudeville circuits. And in 1947 he had had one of his last popular successes in a Yiddish play (based on a Hebrew novel) called *Shylock's Daughter*—although admittedly his choice of this particular piece might be said to have signalled that his disenchantment with *The Merchant of Venice* itself was already well advanced. A grotesque rewrite of the original, it featured such attractions as an Antonio who is married to Portia, a Lorenzo who is being blackmailed by Lancelot Gobbo, and a Jessica who goes to Rome to intercede for some imprisoned Jews and then gets deflected into marrying Lorenzo in a kind of hypnotic trance. The whole affair was pure hokum, but at least it allowed Schwartz to pull out all the stops as a saintly and sorely abused Shylock. (One of his colleagues said that the play should really have been called *Shylock's Daughter's Father*.)

Shortly before Schwartz set about misapplying his gifts in this fashion, Yiddish playgoers in London were given an opportunity to see *The Merchant of Venice* plain and unadorned. The New Yiddish Theatre Company's production of the play was presented in Adler Hall, Whitechapel (no connection with Jacob Adler) in September 1946, with Meier Tselniker as Shylock and his daughter Anna as Portia.* The translation, which kept close to the text, was by Abish Meisels, who had arrived in Britain as a refugee from Austria in 1938; the director was a non-Jew, Robert Atkins, a veteran of the Old Vic and Stratford-upon-Avon who is best remembered for his work as director of the Open Air Theatre in Regent's Park.

Securing Atkins's services was a bold move in itself. It also gave notice that the production was going to aim at a fair degree of fidelity to Shakespeare, which in practice chiefly meant not taking too soft a line with Shylock. Tselniker endowed the character with humanity—it could hardly have been otherwise—but critics were

**Tselniker, who was born in Bessarabia, first came to London in 1927 and established his own company in 1936. He later became well-known as a character actor in such British films of the 1950s as* Make Me an Offer *and* Expresso Bongo.

The part of Bassanio—something which I must admit rejoices my heart—was played by an actor called Yidel Goldberg.

also impressed by his toughness, and by the mean streak that he displayed. There is an excellent account of how the occasion as a whole struck an outsider by Siriol Hugh-Jones (a gifted journalist, who sadly died young). The acting, she wrote, was "emphatic, often remarkably audience-conscious, highly colored, vocally energetic, hyper-articulate," while "the two-piece orchestra, the indomitable audience and the overwhelming strenuous interval" were an important part of the performance.

The Adler Hall production was the last Yiddish production of *The Merchant of Venice* to be staged in Britain. It was a small, one is almost tempted to say a small-town affair, but under the circumstances this is what gave it a heroic quality. The actors simply got on with their job, without any great fuss. But little more than a year had passed since the end of Hitler's war; it was as though they were also saying, "We are still here. And we are not afraid to confront *The Merchant of Venice*, with all its problems. We can take it."

• 4 •

The earliest full-length translations of Shakespeare plays into Hebrew were of *Othello* (1874) and *Romeo and Juliet* (1878). (They were both the work of Isaac Salkinson, a Jewish convert to Christianity who ended his days as a Presbyterian minister in Glasgow.) The first translation of *The Merchant of Venice*, by the poet Simon Halkin, did not appear until 1929, but only seven years after that, in May 1936, the play was produced by the Habimah Theatre (which later became the National Theatre of Israel) in Tel Aviv. The director, Leopold Jessner, had been a leading theatrical figure in pre-Hitler Berlin, famous for his pioneering Expressionist productions at the Schiller Theater and elsewhere.

Jessner's approach was as serious-minded as one would expect, given the time and the place. Not that the production was lacking in lively detail: the opening scene, for example, took place in a bustling Venetian café. But there was a conscious decision to make Shylock a representative or symbolic Jew, brought low by his enemies. The two leading actors of the Habimah company, Aharon

Meskin and Shimon Finkel, alternated in the part. According to Avraham Oz (who was later to translate the play himself), "Meskin was a heroic figure, making use of his commanding physical stature and resounding voice: Finkel emphasized Shylock's spiteful bitterness." Where they were at one was in denying the character "any trace of its inherent comic potential."

Inevitably the production aroused controversy, and Jessner agreed to take part in a mock trial at which the author, the director and the theater itself were all arraigned. One of the witnesses for the prosecution, a left-wing poet called Alexander Penn, accused Jessner of glossing over Shylock's economic activities: "the show should have been a sharp reminder, an acute warning against all those petty Shylocks, those speculators and profiteers penetrating our country." (This was a reference to the "petit bourgeois" immigrants who had begun to arrive in Palestine in the mid-1920s, in the wake of the original Zionist pioneers.) Penn also complained that the production had failed to make clear that Shylock's lust for revenge was alien to the Jewish spirit; and here again, as Avraham Oz explains, a local theme began to creep in. The Arab Revolt in Palestine had broken out a few weeks earlier, in April 1936. Jews were being killed, but although there were isolated reprisals, the Jewish community as a whole had already committed itself to the strictly defensive policy of "Havlagah," or self-restraint. At such a time the myth of Jewish vengefulness rankled more than ever.

The second Hebrew production of *The Merchant of Venice* took place in what was by now the state of Israel, in 1959. It was directed by Tyrone Guthrie, who tried as far as possible to treat the play as a romantic comedy. The actors wore modern dress; Shylock (once again played on alternate nights by Meskin and Finkel) was described by one critic as looking like "a liberal Rabbi with a well-trimmed beard and a clever and pleasant expression." The production struck a much lighter note than Jessner, in 1936, could have afforded, even if he had wanted to; but a strong element of what Meskin called "the national, pathetic element" still remained.

It was not until 1972 that an unsympathetic Shylock appeared on the Hebrew-speaking stage. On this occasion the director was a native-born Israeli, Yossi Yzraely; the production, at the Cameri Theatre in Tel Aviv, featured a background accompaniment of puppets, which pointed up the argument, and the symbolic use of black and white costumes throughout (white for Christians, black for Jews, black and white stripes for Jessica after she had eloped). The actor who played Shylock portrayed him as ignoble, furtive and unprepossessing, a Jew to gladden anti-Semites, but Yzraely was equally unyielding in his presentation of the Christian characters as persecutors. At one level he was undertaking an anatomy of prejudice, which showed both groups locked into their own crippling preconceptions; at another, the message was that a victim of persecution is no less a victim for being personally unpleasing or morally flawed. And on both counts the production was intended to serve as a signal that, for Israelis at least, the old apologetic tradition was at an end.

CHAPTER SIXTEEN

Economic Man

· I ·

Shylock is a usurer. For some commentators, that is the essential point about him: everything else is secondary or incidental. Others have gone further, and seen in him nothing less than the personification of capitalism.

The first and greatest English writer to approach him in this spirit was John Ruskin. In 1862 and 1863 Ruskin published a series of articles on political economy in *Fraser's* magazine. They confirmed his recently acquired reputation as a fierce critic of the economic status quo, and the indignation they provoked was so intense that the magazine decided to cut short publication. Ten years later, in 1872, they were published in book form under the title *Munera Pulveris.*

The fourth paper in the series was devoted to distinguishing between two kinds of commerce. "Commerce in kindness" meant trading for "mere pay." "Commerce in unkindness" meant trading for profit, which was "one of the essential, and quite the most fatal, forms of usury." For usury "merely means taking an exorbitant sum for the use of anything; and it is no matter whether the exorbitance is on loan or exchange, on rent or on price—the essence of the usury being that it is obtained by advantage of opportunity or necessity, and not as due reward for labor." (Ruskin eventually came to oppose the charging of *any* interest on money, but he regarded other forms of "usury" as even worse.)

The inhumanity of trading for gain also seemed to him "a fulfilment of the law that the corruption of the best is the worst." For if the government was the head of the body politic, and the laboring classes were the limbs, the mercantile class, "presiding over circulation and communication of things," was the heart; and if that hardened, everything was lost:

> And this is the ultimate lesson which the leader of English intellect meant for us (a lesson, indeed, not all his own, but part of the old wisdom of humanity) in the tale of *The Merchant of Venice*; in which the true and incorrupt merchant—*kind and free, beyond every other Shakespearian conception of men*—is opposed to the corrupted merchant, or usurer; the enmity being deepened by the expression of the strange hatred which the corrupted merchant bears to the pure one, mixed with intense scorn—
>
> "This is the fool that lent out money gratis; look to him, jailor" (as to lunatic no less than criminal); the enmity, observe, having its symbolism literally carried out by being aimed straight at the heart, and finally foiled by a literal appeal to the great moral law that flesh and blood cannot be weighed.

Munera Pulveris is a strange book, which works as much by free association as by sustained argument. One of its features is a constant dwelling on the root meanings (or supposed root meanings) of words and names—so that "Portia," for example, is meant to summon up suggestions of fortune, of a gate, of a portion, and so on. Matthew Arnold singled out this aspect of Ruskin as demonstrating, "to the highest excess, the note of provinciality," and it is true that many of the verbal connections he makes are strained and fanciful. But others are acute: his pointing out, for instance, that "gratis," a contemptible word to Shylock, is the more precious to us because it comes from "the mighty 'Gratia,' " meaning Grace. We may even be willing to follow him as he plunges into a tangle of associations linking grace with gratitude, gratitude with *merci,* and *merci* with mercy—mercy, which is given freely, as opposed to *merces,* the Latin for a reward.*

Ruskin saw *The Merchant of Venice* as a myth, built around a simple opposition between good and bad. And perhaps this is how Shakespeare saw it—but hardly on the terms that Ruskin implies. For, however admirable Antonio's refusal to charge interest, there is certainly nothing in the play to suggest that he conducts his main business, buying and selling goods, for mere pay rather than profit. Ruskin has simply imposed the full Ruskinian ideal on him. He is the perfect, incorruptible, deliberately non-profit-making merchant—assuming that such a prodigy exists. (Elsewhere in his disquisition Ruskin came close to arguing that trade and deceit were inseparable. "Sin sticks so fast between the joinings of the stones of buying and selling," he wrote, that the very term "to trade" had "warped itself, by the instinct of the nations, into their worst word for fraud . . . and 'trader,' 'traditor' and 'traitor' are but the same word." Like a good deal of his homemade etymology, this is not the case: "traitor" does indeed derive, via the French, from the Latin *traditor,* but "trade" comes from an unconnected Germanic word, cognate with "tread."**)

As for Shylock, he is equally an "ideal type." Ruskin did not believe that Victorian businessmen went around gouging out pounds of flesh, any more than the cartoonist who portrays a bloated capitalist believes that all capitalists are literally bloated; but

**The original idea behind "mercy" was the reward you got in Heaven for compassion you showed on earth. It is curious to reflect that the word has the same root as "mercenary," and that it is related, indirectly, to "merchant."*

***Gerard Manley Hopkins showed a finer sense of linguistic links in his poem "God's Grandeur," when he followed up the line "Generations have trod, have trod, have trod" with "And all is seared with trade."*

he thought badly enough of the market economy to treat Shylock—the traditional, wholly villainous Shylock—as its appropriate symbol.

He had little interest, on the other hand, in Shylock as a dramatic character. Finer shades and mixed motives were not the business of an interpreter of myths, and the experience of seeing Henry Irving play the part only left him more deeply entrenched in his views—though not before he had been somewhat farcically embroiled in the world of theatrical publicity.

He went to see Irving in November 1879, in the company of his youthful disciple Oscar Wilde. (This was about a month after the production opened.) One of the actors spotted him in the stalls, and Irving set him a note inviting him to come backstage. "So I went," he reported to a friend, "and made him a pretty little speech," offering his congratulations on a performance that was "noble, tender and true." He did not altogether mean it, but no one is on oath paying compliments to an actor in his dressing room. The next morning, however, it occurred to him that his words might be quoted out of context, and he penned a letter to Irving in order to forestall possible misunderstandings:

> My dear Mr. Irving,
>
> The kind interest you shewed in what I was too awkwardly imperfect in saying when you received me on Friday evening, leads me to write to you with more accuracy and frankness if I can, and may, on what I felt—namely, this, that you were a most true and tender and noble actor—but that you had not yet as much love for Shakespeare as for your art, and were therefore not careful enough to be wholly in harmony with his design.

He was careful not to say anything further about Irving's own performance; instead, he complained that there had been an imbalance, that neither "your opponent's part of Antonio" nor "the brightly opponent part of Bassanio" had been given their proper weight. Even Ellen Terry had been too playful; he was surprised that Irving had not taught her "a grander reading of the part."

His letter arrived too late. The kind words he had spoken were already on their way to the journal *The Theatre,* where they duly appeared. Ruskin then took the rather roundabout course of writing to a friend, a Mr. Laister, and getting him to write to Irving on his behalf. "I have no doubt," he told Laister,

> that whatever Mr. Irving has stated that I said, I *did say.* But in personal address to an artist to whom one is introduced for the first time, one does not usually say all that may be in one's mind . . . I did and do much admire Mr. Irving's own acting as Shylock: but I entirely dissent (and indignantly as well as entirely) from his general reading and treatment of the play.

Laister quoted this passage in his letter to Irving; he also passed on Ruskin's request for the full text of his original letter to the actor to be published in *The Theatre,* a journal which he assumed that Irving controlled. Irving, ruthless as ever, took advantage of this oblique approach and declined to enter into correspondence with a stranger. He also denied that he had any connection with *The Theatre,* which was only partly true: he had been the proprietor until a few weeks before, and still exercised influence behind the scenes. In the end, Ruskin was forced to write to the journal himself, giving the gist of his letter to Irving, but leaving out his criticisms of individual members of the cast.

Shylock the capitalist was what mattered to him, not Shylock the Jew. But he could not altogether ignore the Jewish aspects of *The Merchant of Venice*, and he was not happy with them. In 1873, delivering the lectures on Tuscan art which he published under the title *Val D'Arno,* he threw out the suggestion that medieval resistance to the spread of usury (i.e., capitalism) had been neutralized by being deflected into prejudice against Jews—a prejudice which (unlike his master Carlyle, to whom *Munera Pulveris* had been dedicated) he utterly condemned. "All wholesome indigation against usurers," he told his audience, "was prevented, in the Christian mind, by wicked and cruel religious hatred of the race of Christ." And this confusion carried over into the post-medieval world, so that "in the end, Shakespeare himself, in his fierce effort against the madness, suffered himself, to miss his mark by making his usurer a Jew."

Ruskin has had little if any direct influence on Shakespeare criticism, but a good deal of what has been written about *The Merchant of Venice* in the twentieth century has been broadly Ruskinian in its assumptions. A succession of commentators have seen the play as a conflict between Shylock's economic philosophy (which they naturally condemn) and "traditional values" or "love's wealth" or "the grace of community." Few of them have paused to ask whether the profit motive might not be an engine of social progress—whether Adam Smith might not have had a point; but then as long as they confine themselves to the play that Shakespeare wrote, as opposed to economic life in general, there is no particular reason why they should.

The most forceful twentieth-century restatement of Ruskin's position can be found in an essay by Max Plowman (1883–1941).* Not that Plowman was a disciple of Ruskin; but his contention that *The Merchant of Venice* "was designed to throw the life-value and the money-value into the strongest possible contrast" is entirely in the spirit of the Victorian writer's celebrated dictum that "there is no wealth but life." His essay (written in 1931) goes on to characterize Shylock as the enemy of the "good-fellowship" which is the ruling principle elsewhere in the play—the enemy "because he would check the free flow of money, which should move as healthfully as blood in the human body, and by incision play the vampire." To sentimentalize such a figure was "not merely to damage but to destroy the action of the play," and the moral of that action, Plowman insisted, had lost none of its relevance over the centuries: "Money is today what Shylock was to the world of Venice—the forbidding aspect, the dark principle, the shadow in the sun, the grim necessity. Its logic is inhuman."

Plowman was an impassioned, single-minded idealist. "The

**Pacifist, editor of the* Adelphi, *authority on Blake, friend and early encourager of George Orwell.*

star by which he steered his course," Middleton Murry wrote of him after his death, "was one absolutely fixed in the heavens"; he believed in Imagination, in the full Blakean sense, and he used *The Merchant of Venice* primarily as a text for preaching against materialism. His sermon was an eloquent one; he was good at evoking (and deploring) the magical powers of money in the fallen world in which we live. An ordinary reader, however, is still entitled to ask where that leaves those aspects of Shylock which cannot be reduced to a question of money, above all his role as Jew and outsider. The answer, for Plowman, is almost nowhere: such incidentals simply help to flesh out the essential, money-centered fable. But at one point, early on in the essay, he does allow himself a curious aside. "Yes," he writes, "money is a great mystery"—and then adds, darkly, "only one race can understand it."

If this means what I think it does, it is a regrettable lapse. It is also a reminder of how difficult Shakespeare and the whole weight of Western tradition have made it to separate the racial or religious aspects of Shylock from the economic. We can continue to interpret *The Merchant of Venice* as a fable of false wealth and true wealth if we choose to (many excellent critics do). But there is no wishing Shylock's Jewishness away, and no point in pretending, even if we put the economic issues first, that it isn't a large complicating factor.

• 2 •

In the early history of socialism—which mostly means its early history in France and Germany—anti-capitalist and anti-Jewish themes were often entwined. In France, the utopian socialist Charles Fourier returned again and again to the subject of the Jews and their supposed pernicious influence. His disciple Alphonse Toussenel wrote a book entitled *Les juifs, rois de l'époque* (1844). The socialist-cum-anarchist Pierre-Joseph Proudhon gave vent in his notebooks to anti-Semitic remarks which were worthy of Hitler, and concluded them by affirming that "what the peoples of the middle ages hated by instinct, I hate upon reflection." Proudhon spoke more truly than he knew. The identification of blood-sucking exploiter and Jew can only be explained as a carryover from the medieval identification of Jew and usurer, and from earlier stereotypes still: when Fourier wrote a fable about a German Jew arriving in France and embarking on a career of fraud, he called him "Iscariot."

Given this background, it was inevitable that Shylock should have occupied a place in socialist mythology. The revolutionist Auguste Blanqui, for example, talked casually of "Shylocks" and Jewish "swindlers." The Christian Socialist Pierre Leroux looked forward to a time when Jews would be redeemed; but if he discerned in them positively Christlike potentialities, their present sunken condition was more aptly symbolized in his eyes by the Jew of Venice. "We will not always see that unsightly countenance it has today," Leroux wrote of the Jewish people, in an article published in 1846:

> It will recapture a more cheerful, younger, smiling countenance; it will cease to look like the Jew Shylock; and I hope to see it resurrected in the features of the Nazarene whom the Jews have crucified and whom they are still crucifying today by gambling and capital.

The novelist Jules Vallès, who has already been quoted (see p. 246), could equally well have been cited here. He was a former Communard, an ardent socialist, the editor (until 1885) of the paper *Le Cri du Peuple.* It was not until the closing decades of the century that the anti-Semitic component in French socialism began to fade; and even after the Dreyfus affair it did not entirely disappear.

The situation in Germany, where a socialist movement first emerged around 1840, was more complicated, not least because several of the key figures in early German socialism (Marx, Lassalle, Moses Hess) were Jews themselves. And even before the theoreticians began hammering out their doctrines, German Jewish writers had advanced a literary critique of capitalism—one in which Jews were assigned an uncomfortably prominent position.

Heine wrote, half banteringly, that "money is the god of our time, and Rothschild is his prophet." In a more splenetic mood, he went as far as to describe finance capital as "Jewish poison." But these were by no means fixed opinions. He knew too much about both Jews and capitalists to swallow the suggestion that they were somehow one and the same, and he flatly rejected the more insidious idea there was an essential affinity between Judaism and commercialism. In his later writings he emphasized the ethical values of the Jewish religion, and criticized the prejudice and superficiality of those German thinkers of his own time who had subjected it to a wholly negative appraisal—both "godless self-gods" such as Ludwig Feuerbach and Bruno Bauer, and "my obdurate friend" Karl Marx.

Marx's views about the significance of Judaism were much more consistently foreshadowed by Ludwig Börne (1786–1837). Börne, who was born Loeb Baruch in the Frankfurt ghetto, was a brilliant political journalist and theater critic. He was also, in the words of Orlando Figes, "the first radical Jew," a man equally alienated from both the Jewish world he had abandoned and a Germany that refused to accept him, even after baptism, as a full German. The starting point of his radicalism was the conviction (no doubt colored by conflicts with his father, a prosperous merchant and money changer) that Judaism was the religion of enslavement to money; he then extended his critique to cover European society as a whole, which he saw as becoming steadily more "Judaized." Unlike Marx, he tried his best to distinguish between Judaism in the abstract—Judaism as he conceived of it—and flesh-and-blood Jews. In practice, he acknowledged, contemporary worshippers at the Golden Calf were at least as likely to be Christians. But the Calf itself remained unmistakably Jewish.

A good deal of this fantasy found its way into Börne's essay on *The Merchant of Venice* (published in 1828), but with an added twist. Shylock was at one and the same time a symbol of ingrained Jewish subservience to the "gold-devil," and an "avenging angel," bent on exacting retribution for the injuries inflicted on his "despised, downtrodden race." His quest for vengeance had its admirable aspects. It was selfless; for once he was pursuing something that meant more to him than profit. It was also appalling—or would have been, if he had been allowed to carry his scheme through. In the event, however, it was no more than a phase in his moral education. If he had never embarked on it, he would have spent the rest of his days continuing to amass wealth; but by the end of the play he had been given an opportunity to overcome his "Jewish egoism," to learn that love rather than gold ought to be the master of the world.

And what would Shakespeare have said if he could have returned to earth in 1828? The second half of Börne's essay is devoted to a biting account of the latter-day Shylocks, the big bankers and speculators. They inhabit a paper universe, a world within which God is the supreme finance minister, the Fall of Man was the first stock-market crash, and the Day of Judgment is the close of the current account. Some of them formally subscribe to the faith of the Old Testament, some to that of the New, but the latter can hardly be called Christians: they are all ruthless despoilers, ready to sacrifice whole nations to their greed. Compared to them, the original Shylock was "a lamb."

Börne was playing with dangerous ideas. Not only did the myth of Judaization—*Verjudung*—presuppose a fixed, unchanging "Jewish spirit"; it also implied that Jews had an almost supernatural ability to impose that spirit on the societies among which they lived. Before emancipation, the enemies of the Jews had at least been able to regard them as a containable force. Now their influence could be made to seem more pervasive, and more corrosive. In its full-blown form, the Judaization myth was eventually used by anti-Semites to account for any social or cultural development which they hated. In its purely economic version, it received its classic formulation in the early writings of Karl Marx.

Marx's essay *On the Jewish Question* (1844) was initially prompted by a pamphlet of the same name by the left-wing Hegelian Bruno Bauer. Bauer had argued that as long as Prussia was a Christian state, it was both selfish and illogical of Prussian Jews to demand full civil rights; what they ought to be doing instead was agitating for the abolition of religion in general, so that everybody could be emancipated. Marx, for his part, saw the question in social and economic terms, which cut across religious categories. He had no objection to Jewish emancipation as such, so long as one recognized that it was mere political emancipation, the right to enjoy unrestricted access to bourgeois society, as opposed to true emancipation—emancipation *from* bourgeois society. In other respects, however, he and Bauer were at one. He accepted Bauer's hostile characterization of the Jews without demur, and extended it by applying the concept of Judaization. A few sentences, excerpted from different points in the essay, will convey the gist of his argument: "Money is the jealous god of Israel, beside which no other god may exist." "The god of the Jews has been secularized and become the god of this world." "The Jews have emancipated themselves in so far as the Christians have become Jews." "In the final analysis, the emancipation of the Jews is the emancipation of mankind from Judaism."

The most surprising thing about *On the Jewish Question* is that anyone should ever have taken it for a piece of serious social analysis. In his introduction to the volume in which the first English translation appeared (1963), the translator, T. B. Bottomore, comments that "the cast of Marx's mind was fundamentally scientific." If so, it is a fact which would be hard to gather from the essay itself. On the contrary, its dogmatic assertions and unsubstantiated generalizations are unscientific to the last degree. So is its manifest bias. Under the guise of discovering historical laws, Marx was simply fashioning a new version of the old myth equating Jews with usury; and his tone was often correspondingly vicious. He could write, for example, that Judaism had been preserved "not in spite of history, but by history"—that "it is from its own entrails that civil society ceaselessly engenders the Jew."

Marx's pose of objectivity is a measure of how deep his hatred of his Jewish origins ran. He had to keep himself right out of the picture: he could never have permitted himself anything like Lassalle's sardonic admission that "I hate Jews and I hate journalists; unfortunately I am both."* And though some of his views in this

**As a precocious and "difficult" schoolboy in Leipzig, Lassalle had been told by an exasperated headmaster that he ought to become an actor, because then he would be able to play Shylock.*

area had been anticipated by Börne and Heine, there were major differences. Heine's negative judgments were tempered by affection, regret, irony, a desire to examine the evidence. Börne, while he was moving towards a "Marxist" position, had a far more generous sense of the concrete human issues involved. And both men were writers, who did not claim to do more than follow the dictates of personal feeling and inspiration. Neither of them set up as a law-giver—or a scientist.

This is not to say that Marx himself did not have powerful literary gifts, or that he was not steeped in imaginative literature. One of the authors he knew best was Shakespeare, and one of the Shakespeare plays that meant the most to him was *The Merchant of Venice*—or rather that part of it which concerned Shylock. Only *Timon of Athens* came more pat to this purpose, with its superb denunciations of the omnipotence of money (the "common whore of mankind," the "yellow slave" that can "knit and break religions").

Very early in his career, in 1842, Marx wrote a series of articles for the *Rehinische Zeitung* about a bill making it a crime to gather firewood from forests (an immemorial right of the peasants). To demonstrate the inhumanity of the proposal, and the perversion of justice which it involved, he quoted at length from the trial scene in *The Merchant of Venice*. As S. S. Prawer observes, "the implied identification of Gentile, feudal landowners with Shylock the Jew no doubt gave Marx, and readers attuned to him, a malicious species of pleasure."

Most of Marx's other references to Shylock follow a similar pattern. In an essay on Hegel's *Philosophy of Right,* published at the same time as *On the Jewish Question,* he drew on the (not very obvious) parallel with the moneylender to denounce the conservativism of the Historical school of law associated with the jurist Karl von Savigny: "A Shylock, but a servile Shylock, it swears upon its bond, its historical, Christian-Germanic bond, for every pound of flesh cut from the hearts of the people." In *Das Kapital,* he referred to British landowners as "aristocratic Shylocks." During the aftermath of the Franco-Prussian War he wrote of "the Prussian

Shylock, there with his bond," completing the ruin of France by demanding a huge indemnity and interest on the unpaid instalments. In all these cases, the comparison was meant to be demeaning: it was aimed at social pretensions—pretensions to be any better than the despised Jew—as well as economic and political practice.

Elsewhere, discussing the idea of financial confidence, Marx commented that "the person who exhibits such confidence equates—like Shylock!—a 'good' man with a man who can pay." And there is one passage in *Das Kapital,* as Prawer has pointed out, where "capital itself takes on the likeness and speaks with the very voice of Shylock." Marx reminds his readers that, having discovered that there was nothing in the Factory Act of 1844 compelling them to do so, British factory owners refused to give child laborers any kind of rest period or break for food:

> Workmen and factory-inspectors protested on hygienic and moral grounds, but Capital answered:
>
> *My deed upon my head! I crave the law,*
> *The penalty and forfeit of my bond.*

Later on rubbing in the reference, he quotes from the play a second time ("Ay, his heart; so says the bond") and talks of the owners' "Shylock-like clinging" to the law.

There is one thing that all Marx's invocations of Shylock have in common. None of them refers specifically to Jews; there is no equivalent among them to Heine's dubbing James de Rothschild "M. de Shylock." But it would be wrong to suppose that Marx was held back in this respect by considerations of delicacy. If anything, the Shylock references serve to amplify the thesis of *On the Jewish Question.* Western society has been thoroughly Judaized. Shylock is everywhere—running banks, factories, landed estates; making money wherever there is money to be made.

Not all apologists for Marx are embarrassed by *On the Jewish Question* but those who are generally emphasize that he was still very young when he wrote it (only twenty-five), that he had not yet worked out his fundamental ideas, and that he appears to have lost interest in theorizing about Jews after the mid-1840s. As against these undoubted truths, three points ought to be borne in mind. First, he never repudiated *On the Jewish Question,* either directly or obliquely. Second, he indulged in a good deal of obnoxious anti-Semitic abuse in his correspondence, and he was not far behind in some of his journalism. Third, in all his voluminous writings there is nothing to counterbalance his antipathies—"not a single expression of concern," as Robert Wistrich has noted, "at the plight of persecuted and oppressed Jews anywhere."

It remains true that by the late 1840s he had transferred the main thrust of his animus from Shylock to Shylock's pupils, from the Jew to the *Christjude.* But that should hardly afford us much consolation. The ugliest feature of *On the Jewish Question,* in retrospect, is that it provides the groundwork for Marx's later thought. The mature Marx went after bigger game: where it was once only Jews that had to be eliminated, it was now the bourgeoisie. But the attitudes he displayed are already fully apparent in the early essay—the arrogance, the brutal contempt, the determination to put human beings through a metaphysical mincing machine. We can already say of its author, in words once used of him by Golo Mann, that "such a man cannot better the world."

Marx died in 1883. In the generation following his death, a number of factors, beginning with the rise of political anti-Semitism, compelled his followers to define their position in relation to Jewish issues. The story is extremely complicated, but roughly speaking (and setting aside the actual practice of Communist regimes) Marxists in the twentieth century have been committed to opposing a) anti-Semitism; b) the Jewish bourgeoisie (in so far as it is bourgeois); and c) anything which they construe as Jewish nationalism. Not surprisingly, they have often been caught up in contradictions.

Some of these contradictions are reflected in Marxist responses to *The Merchant of Venice*. Shylock is a victim of prejudice, but he is also the most ruthless capitalist in the play. He is a scapegoat of the bourgeoisie, but he is also, first and last, a member of the bourgeoisie. In the end his conflict with Antonio is a nuisance, a distraction from the class struggle; but it cannot be reduced to purely personal terms.

The play does not in fact lend itself readily to Marxist purposes. The German author Walter Mehring implied as much when he wrote a play called *The Merchant of Berlin,* which was staged in Berlin in 1929, in an elaborate production by Erwin Piscator. The title held out the prospect of a parallel with Shakespeare, but what Mehring and Piscator offered was the approved Communist paradigm of relations between Jewish capitalist and anti-Semitic capitalist—a paradigm that Shakespeare had failed to provide. Mehring's merchant is a penniless East European Jew called Simon Chaim Caftan (which is about as subtle as calling a Scots character Jock Kilt). He arrives in Berlin during the inflation of 1923, sets up in business with an unscrupulous German lawyer called Mueller, and makes a fortune speculating in scrap metal. Eventually he comes to grief, while Mueller and his cronies, all of them good right-wing German nationalists, are left free to continue with their depredations. They are the true villains of capitalism; Caftan is a mere surface phenomenon—or so we are given to understand. But the fable rests on an absurdity. It is no more plausible that a man like Caftan and a man like Mueller should have teamed up together than that Shylock should have gone into partnership with Antonio.*

Mehring at least wrote his own play. There were also Marxist attempts to wrench *The Merchant of Venice* itself in the desired direction, and here the prize must surely go to the Czech director Emil Burian. In the Burian version, which was staged in Prague in 1934, the conflict at the heart of the play was shown to be the class struggle, as embodied by Antonio and Shylock on the one hand and Launcelot Gobbo and Tubal, no less, on the other. The enmity between Antonio and Shylock was a secondary affair: they were essentially birds of the same capitalist feather.

**When Piscator directed* The Merchant of Venice *in West Berlin after the war, in 1963, he tried to combine a "materialistic" reading with what he called a "more or less 'philosemitic' approach." Ernst Deutsch's Shylock was widely admired, but there were many complaints that the production as a whole had been politicized at the expense of the poetry.*

In recent decades, rigid ideology has been largely replaced in the theater by a more diffuse leftism, which seldom calls itself explicitly Marxist. In the academic world, on the other hand, Marxism (of an increasingly esoteric kind) continues to find its exponents. Much of the literary criticism they have produced is unreadable, but some of it has its rewards. In *A Marxist Study of Shakespeare's Comedies* (1979), for instance, Elliot Krieger takes the familiar theme of the contrast between aristocratic Belmont and bourgeois Venice, and still manages to make a number of fresh points—about the exchange of rings, about Portia's apparent determination to treat the trial as a game. You don't have to be plugged into Kriger's belief system to find many of his individual comments illuminating. Yet it is curious to see how little he has to say about the most famous character in the play. In the course of an essay of some thirty pages, Shylock is seldom in the spotlight, and when he is, it is mostly in the role of representative bourgeois. Not quite *Hamlet* without the Prince, perhaps—but a reminder that even a sophisticated Marxist often finds it hard to put the emphasis where it properly belongs.

CHAPTER SEVENTEEN

A Father Figure

The *Merchant of Venice* has attracted a good deal of attention from psychoanalysts and psychoanalytic critics, beginning with Freud himself. In 1913 he published a paper entitled "The Theme of the Three Caskets," which had been initially prompted by his sudden conviction, the previous year, that Portia's riddle was based on the same underlying motif as the opening scene of *King Lear* and the story of the Judgment of Paris. The caskets, he decided, were "symbols of the essential thing in women, and therefore of a women herself"; his eventual conclusion, which he arrived at after considering not only Cordelia and Helen of Troy but numerous other figures, including Cinderella, was that in myths involving a choice between three women, the one whom the hero chooses (or whom in the case of *Lear* he ought to have chosen) ultimately represents death—the earth mother waiting to receive man back, as opposed to the mother who gave him birth and "the beloved who is chosen after her pattern." True, the "right" woman is generally the fairest of the three, or the youngest, or the most faithful. But this, he argued, is exactly the kind of "replacement by the opposite" which occurs in fantasies and dreams. The deadlier the reality, the more innocent the disguise.

"The Theme of the Three Caskets" raises a number of puzzles. Why, for example, did Freud feel impelled to begin his enquiry with Portia and Bassanio? The casket theme is only tangential to his real subject, which is myths involving a choice between women: *Lear* would have been a much more appropriate starting point. And given that he *did* begin with *The Merchant of Venice,* it is odd that he should have had nothing at all to say about those aspects of the play which are richest in psychological interest. The theme of morality in *Lear* is one thing; but has anyone's understanding of *The Merchant* been seriously deepened by being told that in choosing the lead casket Bassanio is somehow, at some level, opting for death? On the other hand it seems reasonable to ask, as Marjorie Garber does in her book *Shakespeare's Ghost Writers,* why Freud should have backed away from an opportunity to write about the two most interesting characters in the play—"Shylock and Portia, the Jew and the independent woman." Professor Garber supplies her own answer, in an essay of some length. Briefly, she sees "The Theme of the Three Caskets," which is ostensibly a study of substitution, as an exercise in substitution itself: the feelings which lay behind it, she suggests, were centered on Freud's third daughter, the dutiful Anna, who was then eighteen years old. It may be so. It may also be true, as she argues, that Freud was more comfortable writing about *Lear* than about *The Merchant of Venice* partly because "by turning the Jew into the partriarch, Shylock into Lear," he was able to "universalize and ennoble his own patriarchal position." Readers will have to decide such matters for themselves; but certainly it is tantalizing, for anyone aware of how deep Freud's Jewish roots ran, that he should have come as close to writing about Shylock as he did and then said nothing.

Over the years his followers have made good the omission. The first psychoanalytic study of Shylock was published by an American analyst, Isadore Coriat, in 1921. Coriat—I quote from the summary in Norman Holland's invaluable survey, *Psychoanalysis and Shakespeare*—found in the moneylender

> the three characteristics which psychoanalysts associate with those people whose psychic development was repeatedly irritated during the period of childhood when a lot of attention is focused on the process of defecation: anal characters, in other words, who react to events in later life as though they were being forced or had been forced to deliver some very precious part of themselves.

Such persons are fond of children because they associate them with lost purity. (Coriat was surely reading much to much into Shylock's feelings for Jessica.) They are miserly, and think of money as a means of exerting control over other people; and they tend to be irritable and explosive.

Later psychoanalytic critics, keeping closer to the play's imagery, have diagnosed Shylock as an "oral" rather than an "anal" personality. Both Theodore Reik and Robert Fliess, for example, have pointed out how often he falls into the language of biting, devouring, attacking with his mouth. Not that one set of character traits necessarily rules out the other. "Realistically," as Norman Holland reminds us—realistically in terms of psychoanalytic theory—"aggression from the earliest or oral stage of infancy tends to carry over into the next stage, the anal."

Either way, aggression is the key word. Psychoanalytic accounts of Shylock seldom pay much attention to the injuries he has received; the emphasis is on the injuries he intends to inflict. He is the man who wields the knife, and inevitably his determination to cut a pound of flesh from Antonio's breast has come to be seen as a displaced threat of castration.

Theodore Reik was the first, though by no means the last, to carry this interpretation a stage further. Behind the image of Shylock as castrator, he argued, there lay a more general fear of Jews associated with the ritual of circumcision:

> Circumcision is, as psychanalytic experiences teach us, conceived as a milder form of castration. The Jew thus appeared to the Gentiles as a dangerous figure with whom the threat of castration originated. Consciously, to Shakespeare and his contemporaries (as to many of

> our own time), the Jew appears as a money-taking and -grasping figure who takes financial advantage of the Gentiles. Unconsciously, he is the man who threatens to damage them by cutting off the penis.

Somewhat inconsistently (but then symbolism in psychoanalysis is famously fluid) Reik saw the pound of flesh device not only as a symbolic castration, but as a symbolic circumcision too. Shylock had planned to turn Antonio into a Jew, which meant that it was poetic justice—an eye for an eye—that at the end of the trial he himself should be turned into a Christian.

Taken by itself, this interpretation may well sound unduly schematic. But it makes a rather different impression when you come across it in its original context.

Reik (1888–1969) had had literary ambitions as a young man, but he gave them up when Freud encouraged him to concentrate all his energies on the practice of analysis. The books which he published after he moved to America in 1938 represented a revival of the author *manqué*: they were discursive, anecdotal, aimed at a popular audience. From a professional view, this laid him open to the charge of lowering his standards, but for the lay reader there is something reassuringly human about an analyst who refused to keep himself out of the picture, who did not present his views as though he had arrived at them in a laboratory sealed off from the outside world.

His most extended reflections on *The Merchant of Venice* can be found in his book *The Search Within* (1956).* They open with an account of him lying on his couch in his apartment in New York, at the end of a long, tiring day. His seventeen-year-old daughter Theodora—"Thody"—comes in to say goodnight. She is going out on a date, though he knows better than to ask her with whom. In his day, in Austria, children were not so independent, but now things are different . . .

His thoughts drift off to a patient he had seen earlier that day,

* *They are adapted from an earlier version in* The Secret Self *(1953).*

a homosexual with a drinking problem called Bill. At one point Bill had mentioned that one of his homosexual friends was Jewish, and added that, unlike most people in the southern state where he had grown up, he did not harbor feelings of racial prejudice. A few minutes later, however, he had spoken contemptuously of Jews and "niggers." He had also told a story about an antique dealer who had tried to cheat him, rounding it off with the observation, "Once a Jew, always a Jew."

Further thoughts float into Reik's head. He starts jotting them down. Feeling sleepy, he finds a list of names crowding in on him: Jones . . . Jericho . . . Jephthah . . . Jessica . . . Jehovah . . . Jesus . . . Trying to work out what they might mean, he is swept along by a rich stream of associations: Ernest Jones, who wrote about *Hamlet,* Eugene O'Neill's *The Emperor Jones, Othello,* the old Jewish crook called Jericho in *Les Enfants du Paradis,* the scenes from *Othello* (Jews and blacks) in the same film . . . Then he pauses over Jephthah, judge of Israel, who was forced by a rash row to sacrifice his daughter. (There is an allusion to the story in *Hamlet.*) Jephthah in turn reminds him of Shylock, who loved Jessica and cursed her, who even wished to see her dead at his feet when he learned that she had stolen his money. Critics, he reflects, have marvelled that any father could express such a feeling. They do not understand that is it the "Oriental temper" which burst forth in Shylock, just as it did in Jephthah—that excitable temper which flares up suddenly and is often enough followed by severe remorse. "Yes, those ancient Jews were afraid of themselves and of the intensity of their passions." So afraid, in fact, that in one of their most sacred prayers—Kol Nidre, recited on the eve of the Day of Atonement—they asked God to consider oaths spoken in moments of rage as invalid.

Recalling Shylock, Reik feels an urge to reread the scene where he curses Jessica, but when he takes up the book, even though it is now late at night, he finds himself rereading the entire play. Stray thoughts nag at him, the sense of something momentous that is conveyed without being spoken. Antonio and Shylock grow in his mind to "gigantic figures standing against each other silently." At first he tries to solve the mystery by resorting to a conscious analytic interpretation—and it is here that he unfolds his theory of castration, circumcision and the imagined threat to Gentile masculinity.

Even this, however, seems no more than an isolated scrap of interpretation until it blends in with other impressions. He thinks about Shylock again, and about his overriding thirst for revenge. The God of the Old Testament was vengeful, too, and Reik has a sudden intimation of Jahweh Himself descending to earth, "diminished and dressed up as a Jewish money-lender." But the thought has not yet properly crystallized, and he turns to Shylock's rival. Antonio—where have we met him before? He is the man of sorrows, the sacrificial lamb; the more Reik considers him, the more he takes on, in reduced form, the lineaments of Christ. And if he reveals an unexpected vein of hatred in the way he rates Shylock about "his money and his usances," that merely confirms the parallel. Did not Jesus Himself abuse and whip the money changers and drive them out of the Temple?

Now the picture is complete, and Shylock and Antonio once again stand counterpoised—two small people in Venice, "but their conflict shakes the world." One is the emissary of the jealous Old Testament God, God the Father, the other represents the milder Son-God of the Gospels who suffered death and became God Himself afterwards. Starting out with a trivial plot about three thousand ducats, Shakespeare had worked his way back to stuff of which the world's great legends are made.

Reik is filled with a pleasurable sense of discovery, but then doubts set in. Haven't the connections that he has just teased out been made before? He rummages in his memory. When did he first see *The Merchant of Venice?* In Vienna, when he was sixteen or seventeen. At the time, his favorite author was not Shakespeare, but Heine. He recalls a sketch by Heine in which the gods of Greece and Rome are pictured as living on in humdrum human disguise after they have been dethroned by Christianity—Apollo becoming an Austrian shepherd, Mercury a prosperous Dutch merchant, and so forth. But Heine also wrote about Shylock. He described searching for him in Venice, and hearing a voice in the synagogue, sob, "Jessica, my child!"

How have all these complicated trains of thought (and there are others, which I have left out) come to be triggered off by the memory of the morning's session with Bill? There were Bill's anti-Semitic remarks, but beyond that Reik feels blank. It is very late; he ought to go to bed. It is after midnight. Thody is not home yet . . . Suddenly the penny drops, and he can trace back his reverie to its starting point. When Thody came in to say goodnight, he must have had some uncomfortable thought that he had tried to brush aside. Who was her date? Suppose she became infatuated with some worthless playboy; suppose he made off with the funds—representing years of work on her father's part—that have been earmarked for her college education. Knowing her for the sensible girl she is, Reik recognizes that these are groundless fears. On the other hand she had a life of her own to live. She had recently expressed dissatisfaction with the modest family apartment; she sometimes gets impatient with her father's old-fashioned ways. Reik is afraid of losing her, and he does not doubt that his thoughts have been fuelled by powerful subterranean emotions: genuine love and concern, but also "jealousy, possessiveness, fury against the unknown young man who will take her away from me."

The main weight of his interpretation falls on such feelings.* But while they certainly help to explain why his thoughts should have wandered in the direction of Shylock and Jessica, they do not adequately account for the fact that he has spent even more time musing about Shylock and Antonio. His reverie must surely have had its origins in the coming together of two different sets of feelings: his anxieties about Thody and his reactions to the session with Bill. What gives his comments on Shakespeare's characters their force, even at those points where he has been anticipated by earlier writers, is the extent of his personal involvement. It is as though he were saying, "Shylock is cruel, vindictive, thoroughly repugnant, yet I find myself forced to identify with him twice over. I identify with him as a father, and I identify with him as a Jew."

The second identification—even setting aside Shylock's per-

* *Feelings, one might note in passing, for a daughter—Theodora—on whom he had bestowed a feminine version of his own name.*

sonal malignity—needs to be as heavily qualified as the first. Reik described himself as "an infidel Jew." He was a rationalist, for whom all religions were equally illusory. But as his writings make clear, he was still bound to the Jewish past by small customs and traditions, vestigial loyalties, family ties, occasional habits of speech, and a considerable knowledge of the rites he no longer practiced. Those were the positive elements in his Jewishness; but even if he had wished to discard them, there was still anti-Semitism to contend with—and that very morning Bill had spelled out the message of anti-Semitism in its most succinct form. "Once a Jew, always a Jew."

The image of Shylock as father and the image of Shylock as Jew reinforce one another: Judaism represents the "old" order, Christianity the "new." But even if the theological or cultural elements are minimized, Shylock remains far the most obvious father figure in the play. Needless to say he represents "the bad father"; and in Portia—as an American psychoanalyst, A. Fodor, was the first to point out—he is complemented by "the good mother," Shylock's world is not only threatening, but harsh and restricted, a world of rules and prohibitions. Portia, by contrast, offers love, comfort and sustenance. In psychoanalytic terms, as Norman Holland observes, Belmont, "the beautiful mountain," suggests "the bountiful mother breast"—and by extension, one might add, the milk of human kindness.

There is more to the story than that however. Portia is also a daughter, subject to the whimsical decrees of a dead father. Her relationship with Bassanio is complicated by Bassanio's relationship with Antonio. When she takes charge of events at the trial, it is in male disguise; she is a tough adversary, and there are distinct limits to her benevolence.

Over the past twenty years or so psychoanalytic criticism has geared itself up to deal with just such complexities, and in place of simple contrasts, a study like Leonard Tennenhouse's "The Counterfeit Order of *The Merchant of Venice*" (1980) posits a whole network of criss-crossing sympathies and antipathies. Tennenhouse is mainly concerned with those aspects of the play which he sees as having been designed to resolve "oppositions within Shakespeare's culture," yet which at the same time signal "disturbance, conflict and anxiety." Male friendship was idealized by the Elizabethans, he claims, precisely because actual relations between men were so competitive, while the cult of romantic love was an attempt to deny the realities of a world riddled with sexual antagonism and mistrust. In the latter stages of the play the two romantic ideals collide, as Portia comes between Antonio and Bassanio, and by the end disenchantment has begun to set in: the language of the final act is "saturated with metaphors of cuckoldry, treachery, and disguise." Tennenhouse also argues that Shakespeare felt ambivalent about Jessica's flight: the poet could not wholly approve of any father being betrayed by his child, even a Jew. Shylock himself, on the other hand, commands relatively little attention in the essay—partly, perhaps, because there is not much new to say about him. He is still, first and foremost, the menacing father figure. But psychoanalysis has a way of getting around to all the permutations sooner or later, and Tennenhouse does make at least one original point: along with Shylock's more familiar characteristics, he discerns in him "malevolent maternal qualities.' The influence of Freud on the interpretation of literature naturally extends far beyond formal psychoanalytic criticism. For the greater part of the twentieth century, it has been "in the air"; it has encouraged critics to look below the surface, to search for hidden impulses and connections. In the case of *The Merchant of Venice* that has often meant scrutinizing the motives of the virtuous characters, with a view to "unmasking" them; and nowhere have amateur Freudians been more enthusiastic than in proclaiming that Antonio is a homosexual.

Not that the professionals would disagree. Many of them have made the same point: the earliest instance that Norman Holland cites is an article by T. A. Ross, which appeared in the *British Journal of Medical Psychology* in 1934.* Even before Freud, in fact, there were

** Ross concluded that Antonio was in love with Bassanio but continent, which is why he speaks of himself as a "wether" (a castrated ram), and that Shakespeare regarded continent homosexuality as noble and admirable. But this doesn't mean that Antonio didn't find it a depressing condition. He compares himself to a* tainted *wether, and to "the weakest kind of fruit" that is the first to drop to the ground.*

critics who felt that the relationship between Antonio and Bassanio had its unexplained aspects. But it was left to the post-Freudian age to come up with the explanation—to come up with it and sometimes, in the theater especially, to spell it out and underline it three times. I have seen one production, for example, which closed with Portia dancing with Bassanio, Antonio cutting in and taking over from Portia, Portia taking over again and leaving Antonio out in the cold.

Cheap stuff. We are a long way at such moments from the "godlike amity" of which the play speaks, and in recent times historically minded critics have often been moved to protest that an exalted, purely platonic friendship between men was one of the great Renaissance ideals. Certainly Antonio's relationship with Bassanio needs to be seen in its original Renaissance context, however much of a strain that puts on some earthbound twentieth-century imaginations. Yet it is far from being an image of perfect concord, of soul speaking to soul. One of the chief points about it is that it is an unequal friendship, that Antonio's feelings are so much more intense than Bassanio's. To W. H. Auden, they seemed "an example of that inordinate affection which theologians have always condemned as a form of idolatory."

Auden's essay on *The Merchant of Venice* (which can be found in *The Dyer's Hand)* takes Antonio's homosexuality for granted, though chiefly for the purpose of drawing a somber parallel with Shylock. "There is no reason to suppose that Shakespeare had read Dante," he writes "but he must have been familiar with the association of usury with sodomy of which Dante speaks in the Eleventh Canto of the Inferno." (In their different ways both usurers and sodomites were supposed to scorn Nature.) "It can, therefore, hardly be an accident that Shylock the usurer has as his antagonist a man whose emotional life, though his conduct may be chaste, is concentrated upon a member of his own sex."

We may properly object that Antonio is nonetheless good and that Shylock is bad; that Antonio's homosexuality is a mere supposition, and that Shylock's usury is the first thing we learn about him. But Auden insists on reminding us how much the two men have in common. They are both members of an acquisitive society, the merchant no less than the moneylender. They are both sober men, who "avoid the carnal music of this world." Above all, they are both outsiders. Shylock is vanquished at the end of the fourth act, "and will trouble Arcadia no more." At the end of the fifth act, Antonio is left "standing alone on the darkened stage, outside the Eden from which, not by the choice of others, but by his own nature, he is excluded."

All of which is true; and yet the antagonism remains, far stronger than any affinity. Or perhaps we should say that the shared need for antagonism is the strongest affinity of all. In a subtle recent study, *Avec Shakespeare* (1988), the French psychonalayst Daniel Sibony describes "Shylock-Antonio" as "a perverse coupling" (like "Othello-Iago"). The conjunction of the two men represents the coming together of two worlds which are just complementary enough to form an unstable compound, "*un couple total et explosif.*" And though each of them leads on the other, the initiator of their lethal partnership is Antonio. He doesn't merely approach Shylock, he provokes him, seduces him, offers him as prey to a hungry man; and when Shylock proposes his terms, he is seduced in his turn, thrilled by the idea of becoming a sacrificial victim. Nor is there any inconsistency, in the realms of fantasy at least, between the masochism which drives him on and his urge to destroy a hated enemy. On the contrary, he dreams of taking possession of that enemy in the very act of surrendering to him.

Sibony's Antonio is more masochist than homosexual, although he is both, and both conditions (or their intertwining) are closely related to his depression. He feels the need for someone to be cruel to him, in order to bring him fully to life, and he finds just such a person. In principle, his choice of enemies is completely open: it might have led anywhere. But in practice it is culturally determined. The private neurosis of this otherwise courteous and kindly man finds a public outlet in anti-Semitism.

CHAPTER EIGHTEEN

Anti-Semites

· I ·

Histories of anti-Semitism often contain a passing reference to Shakespeare. In Robert Wistrich's *Anti-Semitism: The Longest Hatred,* for instance, we are told that despite the playwright's skill in humanizing certain qualities of Shylock, "his portrait served to crystallize and reinforce an anti-Semitic literary stereotype for centuries to come." A bleak verdict, but in the context within which Wistrich is writing, an inescapable one. We can console ourselves with the thought that there is so much more to *The Merchant of Venice* than *that*; we can argue forever about whether Shakespeare was expressing anti-Semitic sentiments, or merely describing them. But when it comes to the question of influence, there can be no serious dispute: Shylock has a prominent place in anti-Semitic mythology.

"To crystallize and reinforce": Wistrich chooses his words with care. The stereotype was flourishing hundreds of years before Shakespeare, and it would have gone on flourishing for hundreds of years without him. But he endowed it with his fame and prestige, and in a sense his humanizing it only made it seem more plausible.

Israel Zangwill used to tell a story about a Victorian gentlewoman who explained, speaking for her social class, that "of course Shylock is the only Jew most of us know personally."

It must also be borne in mind that most people first get to hear of Shylock at an early age, when the seeds of prejudice are most readily sown. In their celebrated study *The Lore and Lanuage of Schoolchildren,* Iona and Peter Opie recorded that "today"—in the 1950s—"children colloquially refer to a Jew as a Yid, Shylock or Hooknose." In a Mass-Observation survey carried our during the Second World War, *The Merchant of Venice* was regularly cited by respondents who were asked to name the influences that had done most to shape their attitudes to Jews when they were young. Present-day researchers, it is true, might well come up with different results. But this is how things still stood forty or fifty years ago, as they had for generations before.

A good deal of the material which has already been discussed in this book has its anti-Semitic aspects, but in most cases those aspects are secondary, or incidental, or offset by other considerations. Something more remains to be said about Shylock in relation to plain, unalloyed anti-Semitism, which naturally includes anti-Semitism in its organized form.

A systematic survey would keep a research team busy for years, but a few examples will, I think, be enough. Take, for instance, a recent article on the history of anti-Semitism in Australia by Sol Encel, a sociologist at the University of New South Wales. It should first be made clear that anti-Semitism has played only a very minor part in Australian life—in the words of Professor Encel, it has never been more than "a slight background noise." But it has always existed, and in the course of the article, brief though it is, Shylock makes an appearance on three separate occasions. The earliest comment Encel cites comes from a newspaper in Tasmania, which in 1832 railed at newly arrived Jewish immigrants as "Shylocks" and "incubuses." A second quotation is an interesting example of how useful Shylock could be when anti-Semites were looking for a purely secular symbol of "the eternal Jew." In 1894, in an attack on Jewish financial interests, the Melbourne *Age* informed its readers that "the Hebrew is a mark of the obloquy of the world, not on account of his fidelity to the Mosaic dispensation, but because he is and must remain the Shylock of the nations." Finally, from among various anti-Semitic writings inspired by the First World War, Encel singles out *The Kingdom of Shylock* (1915), a pamphlet by a left-wing Australian Labour M.P. who claimed that the war was the result of an imperialist plot hatched in Britain and financed by Jewish money.

Five years later, in 1920, an Englishman called E. S. Spencer (in this case, a man of the extreme right) published a small book entitled *Democracy or Shylocracy?,* which he described as "a graphic exposure of Jewish corruption in Finance, Politics and Society." On both sides of the world, Shylock served as a synonym for the sinister international financier—and on both sides of the Atlantic, too. In the United States, according to the historian Richard Hofstadter, "the Shylock image pervades money crankery from the Greenbackers to Father Coughlin and Ezra Pound." It is true that making use of the Shylock image seldom entailed mentioning Shylock by name, but occasionally it did. Hofstadter's observation occurs in the course of an essay about the free-silver pamphleteer William "Coin" Harvey, and although Harvey sometimes denied that he had any prejudice against Jews, he did not hesitate to identify one of the faces of the enemy, in his bestseller *Coin's Financial School* (1894), as that of "a Jewish Shylock clutching his gold." (He also published a lurid novel, *A Tale of Two Nations,* about a plot to undermine the American economy organized from London by a Rothschild-like banker called Baron Rothe.)

If the modern Shylock was the financier who pulled all the strings, he was also the successful Jew trying to break into social circles where he wasn't wanted. In June 1877 the banker Joseph Seligman was refused admission to the Grand Hotel in Saratoga Springs on the instructions of the hotel's executor-proprietor, Judge Hilton. Seligman was probably the best-known Jew in America at the time; the affair aroused enormous interest, and Hilton defended his decision in a newspaper interview during which he attacked Seligman in violent terms. The banker was "as audacious as he is vulgar." He was "to the Hebrew" [the upright Jew—Hilton disavowed anti-Semitism] "what the Shyster is to the law profession: he is the 'Sheeny.'" And if he had nonetheless achieved social prominence, "he owed some of his most vaunted offices to the practice of the veriest Shylockian meanness."

Most of the newspapers of the day rallied to Seligman's support. He was a man of great influence (President Grant had offered him the post of Secretary of the Treasury) and the incident cannot have done him any great harm. But it was a landmark, even so: the clearest sign up until then of the spread of discriminatory practices which had been largely unknown in America before the Civil War. It was also an episode calculated to disturb any Jew who read about it, whatever his social class. For anti-Semitism cut across economic divisions, and "Shylockian" was a term that could just as readily have been used to smear a poor Jew as a rich one. In 1882, the *New York Times* carried a story by its Paris correspondent advising readers not to waste their sympathy on the victims of the anti-Jewish persecutions that had broken out in Russia. Such people, he wrote, had brought their troubles on themselves. They were pariahs who proved that "Shylock was not the mere creation of a poet's fancy.' *

The Shylock of anti-Semitic folklore is first and foremost the usurer.** The phrase "pound of flesh" has most commonly been employed as a metaphor for the ruthless exaction of money, the enforcing of a hard bargain. But in the play it is a literal pound of flesh that Shylock seeks, and the darker myth of the avenger has always been there, waiting to be put to wider use. In his autobiography, the German novelist and dramatist Karl Gutzkow (1811–1878) gives an account of the anti-Jewish prejudice which he himself managed to transcend, but which was all around him when he was growing up in the 1820s:

**These were only one man's views: elsewhere the paper praised Russian Jews as "thrifty and hard-working," and denounced the "heart-rending crimes" being committed against them.*

***As recently as October 1991 a man was convicted under the Public Order Act for displaying racially inflammatory placards on a street in Bethnal Green, East London. One of them bore the phrase "Shylockian usury."*

> In school I got to know the Jew as a traitor and a braggart. What was feared by all was a hunchbacked monster from Poland, as vengeful as Shylock.

The hump, in this fantasy, was a symbol of social disadvantage as well as moral deformity; but social disadvantage—poverty and oppression—only made the supposed Shylocks of Eastern Europe even more dangerous than their prosperous kinsmen in the west, even more hostile and resentful.

The notion of Jewish vengefulness was no less entrenched in Eastern Europe itself. In a study of the depiction of Jews on the nineteenth-century Polish stage, the historian Michael Steinlauf cites a revealing passage from the memoirs of the Polish actor Wincenty Rapacki (published in 1905). Rapacki describes going into a synagogue while he was preparing to play the part of Shylock, and in the course of the service witnessing "old men, so serious, so calm a moment ago, suddenly transformed into thundering titans awakening heaven in order to rouse it to vengeance with them." An innocent remark, as Steinlauf says, but a momentous misconception—and one which *The Merchant of Venice* reinforced.

Shylock was also one of the great exemplars of "Jewish legalism." In 1896 an Austrian priest named Deckert, who had been summoned before the courts on a charge of defaming the Jews in his sermons, successfully defended himself in the following terms:

> I know that in almost all European countries the Jews are at present emancipated . . . and that formally this emancipation is legally established. It is granted to them in accordance with the constitution, and the Jews insist on it, like Shylock on his bond. But Christian society has not yet ratified this total equalization of Jews with Christians, and will not, as long as a spark of Christian belief and national self-consciousness glows within it.

These were ominous words. They were meant to remind modern Jews that, like Shylock, they were still creatures of *le pays légal* rather than *le pays réel*; that emancipation was as perverse a misuse of the law as Shylock's bond, and that bad laws could always be revoked.

Deckert's was an old-style clerical anti-Semitism. The nineteenth century also saw the rise of newer, much deadlier anti-Semitic ideologies. They defined the Jew in terms of race rather than religion, and held him responsible for all the vices, real or supposed, of modern civilization. In some respects, Shylock was ill-suited to serve their needs. He was a figure from the traditional, pre-industrial past, while *The Merchant of Venice* promised him salvation through baptism—something which no up-to-date racial anti-Semite would have countenanced. But there was still ample scope for him, since the old prejudices continued to flourish alongside the new ones. Shylock the usurer became Shylock the banker; Shylock the avenger was transformed into Shylock the conspirator. Nor did anti-Semitic abuse necessarily have to go into particulars. When Louis-Ferdinand Céline described New York, in *L'Ecole des Cadavres* (1938), as "the most clamorous Shylockery in the world," he was simply adding a decorative twirl to what was already a prolonged anti-Jewish diatribe.

Other comparisons were more pointed. In 1893 an anonymous pamphlet published in Berlin jeered at German Conservatives ("Cohnservatives") for their feebleness in failing to come to grips with the Jewish question. Restrictive legislation, it went on to argue, would be useless, since the Jews would merely go through the formalities of conversion and stay on, like the Marranos in Spain. The only effective way to drive them out was to seize their wealth: "Just as Portia once destroyed Shylock, so now Germania destroys this nation of international speculators." To invoke Portia was to invest a plan for mass-robbery with high moral authority—although the pamphleteer was proposing to go a lot further than the court in Venice, which had in the end left Shylock with half his goods. There was added menace, too, in the fact that he talked not merely of confiscation, but of destruction.

With the Russian Revolution and the lesser upheavals that followed, the demonology of modern anti-Semitism was complete. Jews had been denounced as subversives from the days of Marx and Lassalle, but in the nineteenth century they had been more conspicuous as money-makers. Now, after 1917, the Jewish devil became a Bolshevik and a plutocrat in equal measure. That Jewish capitalists and Jewish communists appeared to be on opposite sides of the political divide was a blind; that most Jewish revolutionaries were determined to slough off their Jewishness was beside the point. Even so, Shakespeare's moneylender might have seemed a poor candidate for the role of revolutionary bogeyman. But anti-Semitism has its own logic. Kurt Eisner, president of the short-lived Bavarian Republic at the end of the First World War, was a left-wing intellectual, an ascetic, an orator, a student of Kant and Nietzsche, but that did not prevent a Nationalistic opponent from denouncing him as "a Shylock with a dirty little hat on his head." Eisner (who was assassinated in 1919) was also regularly described as a Galician Jew who was only pretending to be a German, even though he in fact came from Berlin. Both slurs amounted to much the same thing, since by now Shylock himself was almost always pictured as an *Ostjude,* a Jew from Eastern Europe—at worst, as the "monster from Poland" of Karl Gutzkow's schoolboy nightmare.*

In the same year that Eisner was gunned down, the veteran anti-Semite Theodore Fritsch was advising his readers, in a book entitled *The Origins and Nature of Jewry,* that if they wanted a faithful representation of a Jew, they should read Shakespeare rather than Lessing: the true Jew was not Nathan the Wise, he was Shylock. And at this point, we draw close to the Nazi era. Fritsch's career as an anti-Semitic agitator and publisher spanned over fifty years. The author of a frequently reprinted *Handbuch der Judenfrage* ("Handbook of the Jewish Question"), he had been one of the founders of the German Anti-Semitic League in the 1880s; he was active to the last, and when he died, in September 1933, he received a glowing official tribute from Julius Streicher. He had lived long enough to see the advent of a regime which was committed to putting the most extreme anti-Semitic ideas into practice.

* *When a leading member of the Jewish community in Munich begged Eisner to stand down as president for the sake of his fellow-Jews, he replied: "I have greater concerns than to consider such obsolete 'questions of tact' for a single minute."*

• 2 •

Whatever other cultural changes they inflicted, the Nazis retained the traditional German respect for Shakespeare—"unser Shakespeare." During the period they held power, almost all his plays were produced in Germany, some of them many times over; in September 1939 he was the one author exempt from the official ban on enemy dramatists. Germans were encouraged to take pride in the idea that they had appropriated him, that they alone had done him full justice. At the same time, it was emphasized that he himself had been essentially Germanic in spirit: his works were extolled for the lessons they offered in patriotism, the need for strong leadership, the overriding claims of the State. Eventually, it is true, a number of them were supressed: *Othello,* for example, on racial grounds, *Antony and Cleopatra* because it was "too perverse and effeminate." But in general the esteem in which he was held never wavered.

The Merchant of Venice enjoyed special popularity from the outset. In 1933 there were no less than twenty separate productions; between 1934 and 1939 there were another thirty. The emphasis was in every case strongly anti-Semitic (how could it have been otherwise?), and there were commentators on hand to make sure that audiences did not miss any of the implications. In 1935, for instance, a newspaper in Koenigsberg carried an essay to coincide with a production in the local theater. The writer conceded that at first sight there was something worrying about a play in which a Jew was portrayed as hard-working and thrifty, and the Christians could easily be mistaken for irresponsible idlers. But Shylock, properly understood, was cowardly and malicious, while in the trial scene both Antonio and his friends acted with a selflessness that proved their true worth. At the climax, two opposing worlds stood revealed, and "the secret of these worlds has only now become clear to us, since we now know that they are the expression of racial opposites." Without being fully aware of what he was doing, Shakespeare had depicted the essence of the situation, "and unfurled a problem that is of the highest relevance to us today."

With their famous thoroughness, the Nazis also pressed Christopher Marlowe into service. One of the attractions of the Easter festival at Weimar in 1939 was an adaptation of *The Jew of Malta* by the artistic director of the Weimar theater, Otto zur Nedden. According to a monograph published at the time, zur Nedden improved on his original by turning Barabas into "a logically stylized, racially determined portrait of a real Jew." Between them the combination of modern accuracy and Elizabethan energy produced an "ideal portrait" of "a pitiless, vengeful, Christian-hating Jew, who is incapable of exercising power even with the resources available to a governor, who can do nothing but destroy."

In the case of Shakespeare, updating and tampering with the text were generally frowned on. One exception was the Jessica and Lorenzo subplot: as the story of an interracial marriage, it presented directors with a problem, which they circumvented as best they could.* In other respects, however, productions of *The Merchant of Venice* were largely based on tradition, or at any rate on one tradition, that of the wholly vicious Shylock. There was no need, after all, to resort to textual innovations or directorial tricks in order to raise the tension inside the theater. It was enough to recall events in the world outside: the same hostile portrayal of Shylock was liable to seem far more highly charged after 1933 than it would have done before.

When the director Paul Rose staged the play in Berlin in 1942, he nonetheless felt it necessary to whip up additional animosity. Rose's production had a *commedia dell' arte* flavor; it emphasized the festive aspects of the story—so much so that for a time the critic of the official Nazi newspaper, the *Volkischer Beobachter,* was afraid that the playwright's message was going to get lost in "the play of hands, feet and bodies." But everything turned out well. In the trial

**The compromise favored by Lothar Müthel (see below) was to make Jessica the child of an adulterous union between Shylock's wife and a Gentile. From the point of view of Nazi doctrine, this represented only a slight improvement. The real-life child of such parents would still have been classified as a mongrel—a* "Mischling *first class,"* *subject to persecution and marked down for eventual extermination.*

scene the message reasserted itself, "like an accusation against the race." Rose had scattered a number of extras in the audience, to shout and curse when Shylock appeared: "the voice of the people chimed in from the gallery, their angry cries and shrill whistles echoed from the stalls."

The most notorious *Merchant of Venice* of the Nazi years was the production which opened at the Burgtheater in Vienna in May 1943. The play was put on at the express command of the Gauleiter for Vienna, Baldur von Schirach. The director, Lothar Müthel, had been a member of the Nazi party since 1933. Shylock was played by Werner Krauss.

By 1943 there were very few Jews left in Vienna. In the course of the previous year most of them had been deported, amid horrifying and pitiful scenes. And Baldur von Schirach was proud of the part he had played in their removal (which in the great majority of cases meant sending them to their deaths). In a widely reported speech in September 1942, he told his audience that

> every Jew active in Europe is a danger to European culture. If people want to criticize me for deporting tens of thousands of Jews from this city—which was once the European metropolis of Jewry—to the eastern ghetto, I can only answer that I see it as a positive contribution to European culture.

In ordering *The Merchant of Venice* to be performed, Schirach (whose father, incidentally, had been a theater director) was in effect decreeing a celebration.

Nor was there anything fortuitous about the choice of Werner Krauss for the leading role. Krauss, as we have seen, had been a much-acclaimed Shylock in the 1920s, but even more to the point was the fact that he had lent his talents to the film *Jew Süss* (1940), in which he had played all the Jewish roles—one nastier than the next—apart from that of Süss himself. For *Jew Süss* marked a new stage in Nazi propaganda. It had been made, on Goebbels's instructions, when the Final Solution was already taking shape; it was repeatedly shown in occupied territories on the eve of roundups and "actions," in order to intensify anti-Jewish feeling and dispel any possible sympathy for the victims.

Lothar Müthel claimed that he wanted to present *The Merchant of Venice* as a "fantastical comedy, and Krauss ensured that it was comedy of the most sinister kind. According to one critic, his first entrance was enough to make the entire audience shudder: "With a crash and a weird train of shadows, something revoltingly alien and startlingly repulsive crawled across the stage." Another account was more specific about the supposed racial aspects of the performance:

> The pale pink face, surrounded by bright red hair and beard, with its unsteady, cunning little eyes; the greasy caftan with the yellow prayer-shawl slung round; the splay-footed, shuffling walk; the foot stamping with rage; the claw-like gestures with the hands; the voice, now bawling, now muttering—all add up to a pathological image of the East European Jewish type, expressing all its inner and outer uncleanliness, emphasizing danger through humor.

This particular article was headed "Shylock der Ostjude."

It would be curious to know exactly what was going on in Krauss's mind. Before 1933 many of his closest colleagues had been Jews, most notably Max Reinhardt.* Had he always secretly hated them? Had he undergone a genuine conversion to Nazi ideas after Hitler came to power? One place where you will not find the answer to such questions is in the memoirs he published in 1958. As far as his wartime activities are concerned, these are highly evasive—and, on occasion, positively slimy. In an effort to counter accusations that the characters he played in *Jew Süss* were evil and ugly, he claimed that he had simply based them on "a wonderful film" he had seen featuring the Hebrew-speaking actors of the Habimah company. As for Shylock, he had been under pressure from Müthel to play the

* *A particular* bête noire *of the Nazis, who generally referred to him—rubbing in the fact that he had changed his name—as "Reinhardt-Goldmann."*

part in a different manner from the way he played it for Reinhardt, and he had hit on the idea of making the character out to be "rather stupid" (stupid enough to have thought that he could get away with the bond). This suggestion of stupidity, he added, was something that the Jews "took very badly"—as though they did not have worse things to worry about in 1943.

In 1948 Krauss appeared before a de-Nazification Court in Stuttgart. One of the documents he produced in his defense was a letter he had received from Bernard Shaw, asserting that to hold him responsible for the crimes of the regime he had served was "vindictive stupidity." In spite of this, he was convicted as a "minor offender" and fined the equivalent of £125, but it did not take him long to work his way back to respectability. During the 1950s he received a number of high honors, both from the state and from the German theatrical profession.

By the time Krauss played Shylock in Vienna, the Final Solution was well advanced. The nightmare continued to rage throughout Europe for a further two years, and one place which it eventually reached was Venice. In December 1943 a team of Italian police and Fascist agents raided a Jewish hospital in the former ghetto and arrested all the patients, including those too old or sick to move. A number of private homes were also raided, with police sirens wailing to drown the cries of the victims. The following August there were two further roundups, conducted on this occasion by the SS; finally, in October 1944, the SS spent five days combing hospitals and mental institutions for Jewish patients who might have eluded them. All in all, 212 Jews were deported, out of a community numbering some 2,000. Most of them were sent to Auschwitz; fifteen of them survived.

CHAPTER NINETEEN

Since 1945

· 1 ·

Some nine million Jews lived in the European countries that fell under Nazi rule during the Second World War; around six million of them were murdered. As the full enormity of what had happened sank in, Shylock became a much more problematic character. The problems he raised were still of the same kind as they had been before, but they had grown altogether more disturbing.

It was a long time before actors and directors felt obliged to take the new situation into account. This is not to single them out for criticism, however. On the contrary, other groups with a more obvious responsibility for coming to terms with the Holocaust were far more remiss—professional historians, for instance.* And the question of exactly *how* a production of *The Merchant of Venice* is meant to reflect terrible events that took place 350 years after it was written does not admit of an easy answer. There are times when one feels that it does not admit of an answer at all.

**For some shocking examples of the neglect or trivialization of the Holocaust in post-war historiography, see Lucy Dawidowicz's* The Holocaust and the Historians *(1981).*

During the war itself, British audiences had two major opportunities to see the play. Shylock was one of Donald Wolfit's big touring parts: he played him, according to his biographer, as a "villain full of venom and hatred, spitting on the Christians at the end of the trial scene." Frederick Valk gave a more balanced though no less powerful performance at the Old Vic in 1943—bullnecked, growling, austere in his pride, formidable in his anger. Valk himself was a German Jewish refugee (he had once played Tubal alongside the Shylock of Fritz Kortner), but he refused either to romanticize the part or to tone it down.*

The principal British Shylocks of the post-war years were conventional villains, of one type or another. Michael Redgrave, for example, gave a blood-curdling, over-the-top performance at Stratford in 1953; Emlyn Williams, in 1956, was "small, greasy and insect-like." In America, too, the most highly praised Shylock of the 1950s, Morris Carnovsky, was an undoubted "heavy," though an incisive and serious one. There was only one attention-grabbing (and not very happy) innovation when he played the part at Stratford, Connecticut, in 1957: he delivered "Hath not a Jew?" in a spotlight, as though it were an operatic aria.

Michael Langham's production at Stratford-upon-Avon in 1960 was widely felt at the time to mark a turning point. Peter O'Toole's Shylock was handsome, dignified, heroic; set against him were "a gushing, nervous, trivial band of Christians." Here was one way of trying to redress old injustices.

Amid a chorus of acclaim, Nigel Dennis, who was a gifted occasional commentator on the theater as well as a novelist, remained unmoved. The production, he wrote, was a popular success because it confirmed the critics and the audience in a sense of their own virtuousness. The director had seen it as his duty

> first to assume that Shakespeare was on Shylock's side and, second, to create, in support of this assumption,

* *Returning to the role twelve years later—in Canada, under the direction of Tyrone Guthrie—he invested it with more grandeur. "In the trial scene," his widow wrote in a memoir, "we saw a Shylock sketched who might have come striding down from some mercantile Mount Sinai, ready to crack the tables of stone on the skulls of his tormentors."*

> whatever "business" is needed to put it over. Anti-Semitism, as we know it today, must somehow be projected creatively backwards nearly four hundred years, in order that Shakespeare may be brought seriously forward over the same period. Anything in the text that hinders this recreation must be so played as to make it innocuous.

The ladies of Belmont, for example, had to be "chickens and kittens, all fluff and chatter: even a little dignity might steal some of Shylock's thunder." Portia, "dressed as Buttons, the bell-hop," had to present her case against Shylock "with irreproachable emptiness. And as for Peter O'Toole, he was "so absolutely right by modern standards" that the audience was ravished, as though by its own reflection:

> It was with admiration that we watched him putting a fine cutting edge on his knife and testing it on a handkerchief held up by Tubal: whatever might happen to Antonio's heart, our own was in the right, contemporary, compassionate place.

A satirist by temperament, Dennis enjoyed taking a tough line. He went on to argue that the only wholly satisfying way to play Shylock was as "the sort of villain that we find in Sweeney Todd, or Captain Hook, or Svengali." At which point I part company from him; but in his negative criticisms, he seems to me to have been entirely justified.

By later standards, it is true, the Langham production was relatively orthodox. So were the other major productions of the 1960s. In Britain, Eric Porter's Shylock (1965) was sharp and rancorous. "He pounced upon his thoughts like a bird of prey," Robert Speaight reported. "There was indeed something vulturelike in his whole treatment of the part." In New York, Joseph Papp chose *The Merchant of Venice* to inaugurate his Shakespeare Festival in Central Park (1962). There were a few "modernizing" touches—the masquers wore robes reminiscent of the Ku Klux Klan—but for the most part Papp stuck to a traditional Renaissance setting, and left it to his actors to provide the thrills. George C. Scott's guttural-voiced Shylock was a man bitterly conscious of his wrongs, and implacable in his hatreds—an outstanding performance, according to those who saw it, full of self-mocking wit and coiled-up power.

And then came Jonathan Miller. Miller's production of the play, with Laurence Olivier as Shylock, was presented by the National Theatre in 1970, and filmed for television in 1973. If one had to nominate the key production of its period, it is the one that—however reluctantly—one would have to choose.

The most immediately obvious break with tradition was the decision to set the play in the late Victorian period, in a world of top hats, frock coats and heavy upholstery. On the face of it, this created a major problem with respect to the story of the bond. The notion of cutting a pound of flesh is ugly enough even in the context of a folktale, but when it is transposed to a realistic modern or semi-modern setting, it is liable to seem positively obscene. In his book on Venice, it will be recalled, William Dean Howells observed that if an Antonio and a Shylock had tried to draw up their agreement in the nineteenth century, they would have been taken straight to the nearest mental hospital.

In the Miller production, however, the potential horrors were largely neutralized. The bond story assumed secondary importance; instead, there was an attempt to rewrite the play as a study of a half-assimilated Jew brought up against the tenacity of upper-class anti-Semitism. Olivier's Shylock longed for social acceptance, but when it came to it, he found that the old prejudices were still bubbling away. And the bigotry of the well-bred Christian characters was meant to be all of a piece with their other vices. They were portrayed as corrupt, cold-hearted frauds.

Much of this was achieved by straightforward burlesque. When Bassanio described Portia in the first act—"In Belmont is a lady richly left"—a café violinist launched into a lush accompaniment of the word "richly." The song "Tell Me Where Is Fancy Bred" was warbled by a pair of absurd Victorian sopranos, ogling at the lead casket to make sure Bassanio made the right choice.

Lorenzo was a complacent bore who kept interrupting his moonlit speeches in Act V with puffs at his pipe, until Jessica finally fell asleep. Naturally the lesser characters were sent up with equal abandon: Arragon, for instance, was turned into a doddering octogenerian who kept dropping lumps of sugar into his coffee and then tried to pocket the tongs. And even where the point being made was compatible with the text, it tended to be heavily overdone. It is permissible to show Portia half-ignoring Jessica, but not to show her making no attempt to conceal the fact that she cannot even be bothered to learn Jessica's name.

If Shylock's enemies were travestied, Shylock himself enjoyed the benefit of some judicious cuts. His opening speech about Antonio was omitted ("I hate him for he is a Christian . . ."); so was "were he out of Venice I can get what merchandise I will." Instead, he only had one real motive for revenge: a mixture of rage and grief at the loss of his daughter.

In the street scene, Olivier lashed himself into a heroic fury. In the trial scene, when he realized that he had lost, he slumped across the table in a posture suggesting an upside-down crucifixion. But for the most part he exercised his talents for grotesque comedy: his Shylock was a glossy, highly conspicuous parvenu, with features inspired by George Arliss's portrayal of Disraeli, and an impossible clipped accent. Part of the character's outlandishness arose from his maladroit efforts to imitate the Gentiles, part of it was pure theatricality. He was constantly prodding people with his silver-headed cane, and one wonders what quirk it was that made Olivier model the triumphant little jig that he broke into when he heard about Antonio's losses on the newsreel of Hitler executing a similar dance outside his railway carriage at Compiègne, after the fall of France.

Looking back some fifteen years later, Jonathan Miller argued that "allowing Shylock to appear as one among many businessmen, scarcely distinguishable from them . . . made sense of his claim that, apart from his customs, a Jew is like anyone else." In fact Shylock needs no such help from a director. His claim to common humanity is based on much more fundamental attributes than similarities of dress or social manner; he did *not* say "Doth not a Jew wear a top hat?" But then the whole theme of assimilation and rejection was something which the production tried to graft on to the play from outside, and the result was a high degree of incoherence. Even Olivier's magnetism could not lend credibility to a Shylock who did not grow out of either Jewish history or Shakespeare's text, but who had been specially manufactured for the occasion. The "authentic" Jewish touches—the skullcap under the top hat, the flourish of a prayer shawl, the final off-stage chanting of the Kaddish or memorial prayer—rang particularly false in the context.

If I call Miller's *Merchant* the key production of its period, it is not because it was necessarily the best, but because it was the one which established the principle that a director is free to do whatever he likes with the play—to bend it, twist it, advertise his boredom with it; to spice it up with anachronisms; to steamroller the poetry; to hit the audience over the head with what ought to be subtle implications. Virtually all Shakespeare's plays have been subjected to this kind of treatment in the past thirty years, but *The Merchant of Venice,* given its subject matter, has proved an especially popular candidate.

The most effective way of making the play acceptable to post-Holocaust sensibilities, in the view of many directors, is to underscore the prejudices of the Christian characters, and generally show them in an ugly light. Sometimes this has taken a decidedly primitive form. In the 1980 BBC television production, for instance, Solanio emphasized the nastiness of his joke about Shylock's "flesh"—"Rebels it at these years?"—by grabbing him by the crotch at the same time. In the 1984 Royal Shakespeare Company production, even though it was broadly traditional, the masquers wore pig masks during the elopement scene, and Solanio donned the caricature mask of a Jew while gloating over Shylock's distress. But the most thoroughgoing attempt to downgrade the Christians so far—by belittling them, rather than by making them seem wicked—must surely be the modern-dress production by Ellis Rabb at Lincoln Center in New York in 1973. Belmont became a luxury yacht anchored in a lagoon. Most of the guests were bored jet-setters. The homosexual motif was heavily played up. Antonio, under the impression (according to one commentator) that he was speaking Yiddish, bade Shylock farewell at the end of the third scene with a limp *"Auf Wiedersehn."* During the love duet at the beginning of Act V, Lorenzo had a drunken quarrel with Jessica and slapped her across the face. During the game of rings, Portia slapped Bassanio—but perhaps by then she had become as irritated with him as the critic John Simon, who described him as "strutting about like a male model showing off the latest Bill Blass collection while mumbling his lines in a barely audible, breakneck monotone, like some lobotomized valedictorian at an idiot school."

With enemies like these, almost anyone would enjoy a certain amount of sympathy, and the Shylock in the Rabb production was more sympathetic than most—a dignified Jewish professional man, in a dark suit and homburg. Recent British directors, on the other hand, have tended to fight shy of ennobling the part, feeling that it is enough if the anti-Semitism of the other characters stands condemned; and in 1978 the Royal Shakespeare Company production by John Barton risked what was by then the novelty of a thoroughly unpleasant Shylock. The setting was Edwardian; the moneylender, played by Patrick Stewart, was mean, shabby, commonplace, a tyrant at home, servile out of doors, arrogant as soon as he thought he had Antonio in his clutches. At the end, when he had been defeated, he tried to ingratiate himself with everyone, even laughing at Gratiano's jokes. He was a survivor, but at what a cost! Here and there, especially in his rough handling of Jessica, Stewart may have gone beyond anything the text warranted, but critics agreed that he offered a valid reading of the part, and a powerful one; that he had justified his description of it as "a tragic role, but a curiously small-scale, *domestic* tragic role."

That still left the question of Shylock's Jewishness. Writing about the production, Stewart made it clear that he was trying to portray the faults and false values of an individual, not of a type. This was a Shylock with few obviously Jewish traits, a Shylock who was only incidentally a Jew. But to the extent that the performance succeeded, it was by muting or toning down everything that connects the character to a wider history than his own. The role was small-scale because its significance had been reduced.

David Suchet, the Jewish-born actor who took the part in John Barton's second production of the play, in 1980, restored the missing dimension. His aim, he wrote, was to present a Shylock who was an outsider *because* he was a Jew: the two aspects of the man's character were inseparable. Suchet adopted a slight accent, tried to suggest the humor of a member of a minority group, registered the pressures acting on Shylock as well as the pressures building up inside him. And he was not afraid of contradictions. His Shylock (unlike Partrick Stewart's) showed Jessica a good deal of paternal tenderness, for example, but that did not mean she was necessarily wrong to find her life with him oppressive. As Suchet explained in an interview, "it is part of Shakespeare's brilliance as a writer that you can see the relationship from either point of view. His characters are full of inconsistencies, and if you flow with the man you will, hopefully, end up with something like he intended."

Suchet's other comments show a similar willingness to "flow with the man." He is a welcome reminder that there are still actors who see their job as trying to do justice to the text, rather than using it as a trampoline for self-display. By contrast, Bill Alexander's production for the Royal Shakespeare Company (1987), with Antony Sher as Shylock, stands out as an example of how far the urge to be different can go. It was a dire occasion throughout, but the low point was undoubtedly the trial scene, during which Antonio was tied to a pole while Shylock descended on him like a blood-crazed fanatic, chanting a Hebrew prayer. I quote from an admiring account by James C. Bulman:

> As he chanted, he doffed his black gaberdine and donned a tallis [prayer shawl], sprinkled a few drops of blood from a horn case with his hand on to a white cloth, then poured out the rest, lifted the cloth to heaven, and swept upstage to place it at Antonio's feet as though in preparation for a ritual slaughter. As the chants grew more cacophonous, Shylock made a wide arc, swinging his arms in rhythm; then, with a startling violence, he ran at Antonio to tear his shirt off. Like one possessed, he circled behind Antonio cupped one hand around his

victim's neck, and in the other raised a dagger above his head—

at which point Portia called out "Tarry a little." The scene naturally showed Shylock at his most gruesome, but it was consistent with the general presentation of him as the kind of caricature "oriental" that a white racist might dream of on a bad night: half-wheedling, half-offensive, unsavory in appearance and manner. The dubious theory behind this approach was that it was supposed to ruffle the complacency of liberal audiences by stirring up their buried prejudice—prejudice which they then had to unlearn. At the same time, the Gentile characters were shown behaving even more odiously, pelting Shylock with stones, prodding him with sticks, threatening to push him into the canal. And both sides conducted minor hostilities by means of an epidemic of spitting. Antonio spat at Shylock while bidding him farewell ("Hie thee, gentle Jew"); Shylock spat at Antonio while he was on his way to jail; the spitting never seemed to stop. As Henry James wrote, apropos of the inferior Shakespeare productions of his own day, there is something monstrous in seeing the most precious intellectual inheritance of the human race so fearfully knocked about." *

By making Shylock a Levantine Jew, a kind of "Third World" Jew, Alexander and Sher were partly hoping to get away from an exclusively European focus. As Sher explained, "we didn't want our production to be about anti-Semitism only but about racism more generally." And stressing his own South African origins, he added that Shylock's response to barbarous treatment seemed to him "to have applications to South Africa and the Middle East today." Not that the Holocaust was forgotten. A yellow Star of David was aerosol-sprayed on the wall at the back of the stage; Shylock and Tubal had yellow stars stitched to their coats.

British productions have on the whole fought shy of direct allusions to Nazi crimes. In Germany, on the other hand, the yellow

**There was an equally regrettable outbreak of spitting in Peter Hall's 1989 production. In other respects this was a sound conventional staging of the play, although Dustin Hoffman's Shylock very much belonged in the "small-scale" category.*

star had already figured prominently in a production by Arie Zinger, in 1979. At his first meeting with Antonio, in a coffeehouse, Shylock had drawn a star on a table; Antonio had chalked the word *"Jude"* in the center of the star; the table had been rolled over on its side so that everyone could see. And the previous year, 1978, German audiences had been confronted with an ambitious attempt to weld the story of Shylock and the history of the Holocaust firmly together—George Tabori's *I Would My Daughter Were Dead at My Foot, and the Jewels in her Ear (Ich wollte, meine Tochter läge tot zu meinen Füssen und hätte die Juwelen in den Ohren).*

Tabori, a Hungarian-born Jew whose father had been murdered in Auschwitz, had worked in England and America after 1933, and an earlier, English-language version of *I Would My Daughter . . .* had been staged at the Stockbridge Playhouse in Massachusetts in 1966. The basic device of the piece was that of a play within a play: a group of Jewish concentration-camp prisoners were being forced to perform a version of *The Merchant of Venice* for the amusement of their guards. Ninety percent of the words were still Shakespeare's, but in addition to cuts and interpolations, constant use was made of expressionist techniques. At one point the entire cast scattered among the audience, wearing false beards and crooked noses that made them look like caricatures out of *Der Stürmer.* Jewish puppets were subjected to ferocious mutilation. When Shylock submitted to baptism, he stood in a pool of blood while his hair was sprayed blond.

Tabori's target was Shakespeare as well as the Nazis—or rather, whatever it was in Shakespeare that enabled the Nazis to make use of him. As an account of *The Merchant of Venice, I Would My Daughter . . .* is plainly unfair, but that is not how it should be judged. It is a play in its own right, a comment on the course of European history.

There was an understandable reluctance to portray Shylock unfavorably in the post-war German theater, but in 1972 the taboo was broken by the controversial director Peter Zadek (himself of Jewish origin) in a production at Bochum. According to the critic Volker Canaris, Zadek's purpose—rather like Antony Sher's—was "to provoke the public into examining its repressed prejudices." To that end, his Shylock, played by Hans Mahnke, was mean, cringing, malicious, a walking compendium of anti-Semitic clichés. Other aspects of the production attracted almost as much attention, however—the mazelike set, for example, and a Lancelot Gobbo who bore a strong resemblance to Danny Kaye. (The spirit of Komisarjevsky still lives.)

Zadek returned to the play in 1989, in a production for the Vienna Burgtheater. It was another tract for other times. The main set was a bank, all glass and steel and high tech; the Venetians were yuppies with cordless phones: Shylock, "just into middle age, blond and brylcreemed," reminded the reviewer in the *Financial Times* of Michael Douglas in the film *Wall Street.* He was also, to start with, fully at home in his surroundings: "a dealer as straight or crooked as the rest—tense, speech clipped, the guy in the office who makes black jokes about bonds in pounds of flesh. And though his schemes ultimately led to his downfall, the audience was left in no doubt that he would survive, "that he would be back at his desk before long."

It sounds like an interesting evening, but there must have been all kinds of inconsistencies and loose ends in the script. If Shakespeare had really wanted to write a play about the boom years of the 1980s, he could surely have made a better job of it.

• 2 •

A number of recent writers have been tempted to create their own versions of *The Merchant of Venice,* or to find new roles for its characters.

Charles Marowitz, in *Variations on The Merchant of Venice* (1977), follows George Tabori in largely using lines lifted from Shakespeare, although they are chopped up, shuffled around and supplemented with borrowings from *The Jew of Malta.* The action of the play, which takes place in Palestine in 1946, towards the end of the British mandate, is introduced and rounded off by reports of the bombing of the King David Hotel in Jerusalem by Jewish extremists. Antonio, in a pin-stripe suit, is meant to embody the views of the Foreign

Office. Bassanio wears the uniform of a British lieutenant. Shylock, Tubal and Jessica (under a pretense of loving Lorenzo) are all working for the Jewish underground. The moral ought to be simple—persecution drives men and women to seek extreme remedies; but the effect of trying to superimpose a tale of ducats and caskets on the complexities of modern Middle Eastern politics is one of ever-deepening confusion.

The Shylock portrayed in Arnold Wesker's *The Merchant* (1976) is scholarly, impetuous and warm-hearted: he has a sister called Rivka who warns him that his enthusiasms will get him into trouble. Wesker, writing in naturalistic prose, attempts to convey the liveliness and the cultural attainments of the sixteenth-century ghetto (one of the characters he introduces is the playwright Salomon Usque). He also throws into relief the anti-Semitism of most of the Venetians, although Antonio and Portia are both exceptions: indeed, Antonio is one of Shylock's closest friends. When we first meet the two of them, they are sitting in Shylock's study, cataloging his books, and when Antonio needs money, Shylock wants to lend it to him without interest or security. The necessity of drawing up a formal agreement is imposed on them by the law; they both enter into their "nonsense bond" like giggling children, and they are horrified by its consequences.

As a humanistic sermon, *The Merchant* has much to recommend it. As a play, it lacks bite; even though it ends sadly, it leaves one with a predominant sense of wishful thinking.

In *Shylock's Revenge,* by David Henry Wilson, Shylock has become a Christian, but he is still smarting. He lays charges against Lorenzo and Jessica for stealing his money and jewels, and against Antonio, Bassanio iand Gratiano for abetting them; he wins the case, gets back his possessions and becomes a Jew again. Then Lorenzo, Salerio and Solanio plot to kill him, and inadvertently kill Tubal instead. But Portia has a black maid, and the maid has a brother who helps to bring them to justice. His name is Othello.

Amid a good deal of broad burlesque, the play (which was first produced at the University of Hamburg in 1989) sets out to make serious points—about racism, the law, the power of money. Usury, for example, is shown achieving respectability when it is practiced behind the impersonal facade of a bank, the "Venetian Finance Company." And as for Shylock, he arouses mixed feelings. He is a far better man than his enemies, but he is still a hard man, unforgiving and unyielding. The author, in his preface to the play, draws a contemporary parallel. Our ambivalence towards Shylock, he writes, is

> a perfect image for the world's attitude toward Israel. There is sympathy for the outsider surrounded by hostile forces, and solidarity with a nation that has survived unspeakable and unimaginable horrors. There is also fear of and resentment at the harsh intransigence Israel/Shylock shows towards those in its/his power.

Within a few short years Marowitz's freedom-fighter has become—on this showing—an oppressor. Either way, the comparison between Israel and Shylock seems to me profoundly unhelpful; but I suspect that it is one we may hear of again.

Writing a play on a Shakespeare theme means setting up in competition with Shakespeare on his own ground—a foolhardly enterprise. Fiction offers greater freedom, and it is a freedom of which Erica Jong takes full advantage in *Serenissima* (1987). The heroine of this elaborate fantasy is an American movie star, Jessica Pruitt, who has come to Venice to make a film based on *The Merchant of Venice*. Transported back in time, she assumes the identity of Jessica in the play; she also catches the fancy of Shakespeare—a young Shakespeare, with most of his life's work still ahead of him, who is visiting Italy in the company of his patron, the Earl of Southampton. They meet when he wanders into the ghetto, meet again when he returns to negotiate a loan from her father Shallach (five ducats at 5 percent interest), and then embark on a series of colorful adventures. Their lovemaking is described in detail ("Fie on't! Was Will Shakespeare good in bed? Let the reader judge"); the poet also tries to save her from Southampton, who has led her into an empty synagogue for the purpose of raping her.

Meanwhile, her father is half-mad with grief at the loss of his daughter. Shallach is a proud, outwardly forbidding figure, embittered at being confined in the ghetto, but for all his sternness he has usually been ready to indulge his only child. (" 'What are ducats compared to a daughter?' he liked to say.") By the time she is reunited with him, she has a better sense of his true worth. The modern Jessica, the movie star, knows it, too; in fact she knows it already, since she also knows "the Jewish play" that Shakespeare finally came to write. About Shylock, she observes, the playwright was "unerring." He is "a great soul, despite his defects," who is not to be compared with Portia ("that Miss Priss, that WASP debutante"), or with any of his antagonists—except, in a small way, Antonio:

> Against our wills, we leave the theater feeling Shylock's deep humanity. And Jessica's. How did the playwright know to put it there?
>
> He knew.

And one reason he knew, we are meant to conclude, is on account of the experience recorded in *Serenissima.*

Shylock has also won admiration from those who relish the fact that there is no nonsense about him, no compunction about seeking revenge. "I like Shylock," Fiona Pitt-Kethley announces at the beginning of a poem that bears his name. She goes on to tell us that she first learned to sympathize with his point of view when she played him at the age of eleven:

> *My version was more Sweeney Todd than Jew.*
> *I pulled my hair round, tied up as a beard,*
> *wore a loose preaching-gown and velvet cap*
> *and brandished mother's bread knife in the Court.*

He had "more guts and more integrity," she decided then, "than all the Gentile bastards in the play." Now, twenty-four years later, she thinks of him again. The man she loved—"a bastard-Gentile type"—has rejected her as "too eccentric." ("Though not a Jew, I am a Jew to him.") Yet he still craves sympathy from her on account of the bad time he has been given by his wife. Unbearable! There seems nothing for it but to follow Shylock's example, and to better his instruction:

> *Revenge is sweet—almost as sweet as sex.*
> *No smart-arse Portia'll spring to his defense.*
> *"The quality of mercy is not strained . . ."*
> *Mercy? I've not seen much of it around,*
> *"strained" or unstrained. I'll get my pound of flesh.*
> *I've learned my lesson from poor Shylock's case—*
> I'll *settle for the bastard's blood as well.*

The anonymous moneylender of *Il Pecorone* has undergone some strange transformations since he was first put on the stage four hundred years ago. But perhaps none is stranger than the one that has ended with him serving as a vehicle for the *chagrin d'amour* of Fiona Pitt-Kethley.

• 3 •

In 1942 C. S. Lewis delivered the British Academy's annual Shakepeare Lecture. His subject was *Hamlet,* but in the course of his remarks he also found room for some reflections on *The Merchant of Venice.* It was a play, he told his audience, which was particularly liable to be "twisted out of recognition" by character criticism, by approaching it as though it were a realistic novel. Nothing was easier, for example, than to "disengage and condemn the mercenary element in Bassanio's original suit to Portia, to point out that Jessica was a bad daughter, and by dwelling on Shylock's wrongs to turn him into a tragic figure." But what was the point of the play that you were left with? Why should anyone enjoy "such a confused and depressed piece of work"? No, the real play was "not so much about men as about mentals":

> The important thing about Bassanio is that he can say, "Only my blood speaks to you in my veins", and again, "all the wealth I had ran in my veins" . . . The whole contrast is between the crimson and organic wealth in

> his veins, the medium of nobility and fecundity, and the cold, mineral wealth in Shylock's countinghouse.

At one level, no doubt, the charge that he was "a mercenary wooer" could not be refuted, but it was the wrong level, the level of "prosaic analysis":

> The play is much nearer the *Märchen* level than that. When the hero marries the princess we are not expected to ask whether her wealth, her beauty or her rank was the determining factor. They are all blended together in the simple man's conception of Princess.

And on this occasion, Lewis himself was happy to be included among the simple men. Readers were welcome to disagree with his interpretation of the play, but he asked them, whatever else they did, not to dismiss it as farfetched, since it represented his "immediate and spontaneous reaction":

> A wicked ogre of a Jew is ten thousand times nearer to that reaction than any of the sad, subtle, realistic figures produced by the critics. If I err, I err in childishness, not in sophistication.

Lewis made out his case with characteristic vigor, but there was nothing particularly new about it. It was the traditional view of the play, in one of its major variants—*The Merchant* as fairy tale. It was also the view which predominated among critics, in other variants, for the first twenty years or so after the Second World War. In 1950, for example, Nevill Coghill published an account centered on the opposition between Justice and Mercy, the Old Law and the New. For John Russell Brown, in 1957, the essential contrast was between the bounty of "love's wealth" and the sterility of material wealth pursued as an end in itself. C. L. Barber, in *Shakepeare's Festive Comedy (1959)*, put the stress on communal values: "The whole play dramatizes the conflict between the mechanisms of wealth and the masterful, social use of it." It is true that Barber also expressed reservations about how far a thematic reading could encompass the play's variety: in Shylock, in particular, there was a quite different kind of play waiting to be worked out. But the final note, the Belmont note, was one of celebration, and "the more one is aware of the comedy's high seriousness in its concern for the grace of community, the less one wants to lose the play Shakespeare wrote for the sake of the one he merely suggested."

It was left to Frank Kermode, writing in 1961, to present the case for an allegorical reading at its most clear-cut in a manner that brooked no disagreement:

> *The Merchant of Venice* is "about" judgment, redemption and mercy; the supersession in human history of the grim four thousand years of unalleviated justice by the era of love and mercy. It begins with usury and corrupt love; it ends with harmony and perfect love. And all the time it tells its audience that this is its subject; only by a determined effort to avoid the obvious can one mistake the theme of *The Merchant of Venice.*

How far Kermode would subscribe to the same views today I do not know. Coming from such an urbane critic, the tone of the passage is oddly pugnacious; perhaps because he sensed that the dissenters were massing just over the horizon.

For the time being, however, the critical climate still encouraged readers to think of Shakespeare's plays as poems, myths, "extended metaphors." They were to be taken on their own terms, or as products, however distinguished, of their own time—reflections of the Elizabethan world-picture. And character analysis, except in small doses, was still frowned on. The overall design was the thing.

Much of the criticism of that era still seems to me admirable: closer in spirit to Shakespeare than the kinds of criticism that have flourished since, better calculated to enhance our appreciation of his work. But in the case of *The Merchant of Venice,* the myth expounders found themselves confronted with a problem with which they did not properly engage. Can a modern reader really be expected to settle contentedly for the idea that Shylock is "a wicked ogre of a Jew," and leave it at that? C. S. Lewis's account of the play is stirring in its simplicity, but I must admit that I shiver a little when I recall the date—1942—at which Lewis was writing.

One myth-expounding critic who cast at least a glance at the contemporary world was M. C. Bradbrook, in *Shakespeare and Elizabethan Poetry* (1951)—and one rather wishes she had not. For Miss Bradbrook, *The Merchant of Venice* is "in the best sense artificial": "the symbolism is almost blatant, the violence of the contrasts almost glaring." And those contrasts are irremediably weakened if Shylock is sentimentalized, as he has so often been, by "modern humanitarianism," and if his crime is seen as "anything less than damnable." As a purely literary exposition of the play, this will pass; but in making her case, Miss Bradbrook unfortunately felt impelled to appeal to history as well:

> The present generation has been taught by bitter examples that persecution breeds criminals, and sometimes criminals of so violent and perverted a nature that their only end, in a world that does not believe in the efficacy of forcible baptism, would seem to be despair. The concentration camps of Nazi Germany bred many heroes and martyrs but also a few Shylocks.

I must admit that I do not fully understand this passage, but I do not like what I do understand. No doubt persecution *sometimes* breeds criminals, but is that the first, second or hundredth point that one wants to make about the Nazi camps, least of all in the context of a comparison with Shylock? Nor of course should the desire for revenge which those who suffered in the camps may have felt while they were there be confused with criminality. Nor can I see anything that remotely merits the label "Shylock-like" about the subsequent treatment of those who organized and ran the camps. Who exactly are the "violent and perverted" criminals Miss Bradbrook has in mind, anyway? And where does forcible baptism come in?

•

As we enter the 1960s, the picture grows more complicated. Publications proliferate. New readings multiply. Theorists set up their stands. Common-sense assumptions about the nature of literature are called into question; radicals proclaim the universal primacy of politics. And criticism in general becomes far more narrowly academic, far more of a closed shop.

Under the circumstances, it would be hopeless to attempt a brief summary of everything that has been written about *The Merchant of Venice* over the past thirty years. But one broad tendency is unmistakable. The comparative consensus achieved by the critics mentioned so far in this section—what one might call the neo-traditional view—has been rejected. In its place, we have been increasingly asked to think of *The Merchant* as a play which cannot possibly mean what it appears to say, a play which constantly subverts its own surface values and throws doubt on the purported motives of its characters. Where the key words were once "justice" and "mercy," "gold" and "love," they are now (among others) "sceptical," "tension," "discrepancy," "distancing" and "demystify."

A. D. Moody drew a useful distinction in his book *Shakespeare: The Merchant of Venice,* published in 1964. There was the "prima facie" reading of the play, and there was the "ironic" reading; and for Moody, the ironic reading was indisputably the right one. The Christians, he argued, repeatedly fail to live up to their principles. Shylock's humanity is "larger in scope and depth than theirs," and his defeat at their hands feels like "a reversal of the right order of things." We can take pleasure in the end of the play if we choose—it is one of the most disturbing things about it—but only if we are content with illusions: to the clear-sighted, Belmont is a parody of what it claims to represent.

Coming when it did, Moody's book was a refreshing challenge to current orthodoxy. By contrast, René Girard's "To Entrap the Wisest," first read as a paper at the English Institute in New York in 1978, shows the ironic reading firmly in the ascendant. Girard makes some of the same points as Moody, but his tone is much more dogmatic. The play, he maintains, works at two different levels:

Shakespeare appears to join in the general scapegoating of Shylock, but he is constantly sending out signals that in reality he condemns it. Either you see this, or you belong to "the larger and coarser part of the audience," in which case you don't:

> If irony were demonstrable it would cease to be irony. Irony must not be explicit enough to destroy the efficiency of the scapegoat machine in the minds of those fools for whom the machine was set up in the first place.

This is the language of intimidation. Girard dares you not to agree with him, at the cost of proclaiming yourself an idiot, that "the symmetry between the explicit venality of Shylock and the implicit venality of the other Venetians cannot fail to be intended by the author." He is equally insistent that the bond is a "spectacular instance of that complete interpretation between the financial and the human that is characteristic less of Shylock than of the other Venetians"—so that "in his efforts to teach Antonio a lesson, Shylock becomes his grotesque double." Nor is it any defense of the Christians that, most of the time, they do not *sound* cruel or venal. One of the principal lessons of the play is spelled out for us (a further irony) by Bassanio, who speaks more truly than he realizes when he makes his choice between the caskets. "The world is still deceived with ornament": we must beware of appearances—especially, in this play, "the appearances of beautiful language." The "prosaic analysis" against which C. S. Lewis set his face could hardly go further.

Or could it? Terry Eagleton, for whom Bassanio is "a self-loving parasite," undertakes a more brutal form of demystification in the name of Karl Marx:

> The bourgeoisie have always pretended that sex transcends utility, at the very moment they debase it to a commodity. The Romantic is in this respect just the flipside of the Utilitarian, fetishizing a realm (the love of a good woman) supposedly free of his own squalid limitations.

Eagleton is also tempted to rewrite the play, in the manner of an "innovative" director—to speculate, for instance, that in the trial scene Shylock "never really expected to win in the first place":

> One can imagine him waiting with a certain academic interest to see what dodge the Christians will devise to let one of their own kind off the hook. Perhaps he throws the audience a knowing wink when Portia produces her knockdown argument.

What one *can* imagine, all too easily, is a scene like this on the contemporary stage.

Most recent criticism, without indulging in Eagletonian winks, is in fact fairly relaxed about Shylock. The pressure to present him as a noble or heroic figure is off. It is enough to establish that he is not as bad as the Christians; and if you are convinced from the start that they are a nasty lot, and deceitful into the bargain, that is no very hard task.*

This reversal of yesterday's values is part of a general tendency to demythologize and deconstruct, to search out a more radical Shakespeare (or, alternatively, to punish him for not being radical enough). But in the case of *The Merchant of Venice,* there are also special circumstances at work. The downgrading of the Christian characters would probably have taken place anyway, but awareness of the Holocaust has undoubtedly helped to make it something that readers and theatergoers are willing to accept.

Meanwhile, the traditionalists have largely fallen silent. Perhaps they feel that there is nothing more to be said, that the grand dichotomies of the play (Justice versus Mercy, and so forth) have been described and expounded once and for all. Recently, however, a French critic, Pierre Spriet, has had the courage to restate the traditional view, and then ask how far it can still be made to work

* *Feminist critics have tried to treat Portia as a separate case—pointing out, for instance, that like Shylock she is a victim (of her father's will; of the need to disguise herself as a man before she can show her true mettle). But in the end, if you accept a radical or ironic reading of the play, it is impossible not to align her with Shylock's persecutors.*

in the present-day theater. Spriet himself has no doubt that the framework of the play is Christian moral theology, as St. Paul taught it, and as the Elizabethans understood it. Within this framework, Shylock is a quintessential Jew, who clings to the Law rather than seeking salvation through Christ. He may merit a certain amount of pity as a man, but his creed is the very negation of Christianity: no Elizabethan audience could have thought otherwise, and it is surely more sensible to assume that Shakespeare shared the beliefs of his contemporaries than to suppose that he was a crypto-modern, "one of us"—that anything in his work that threatens to offend us must be interpreted as "a subtle form of irony."

At the same time, Renaissance Christianity is very remote from us. It was already growing remote a hundred years ago: many of its doctrines would have seemed intolerable if they had been advocated with the same fervor that they once were, or in some cases if they had been advocated at all. And in the past fifty years, an even bigger gulf has opened up:

> If nineteenth-century audiences found it difficult to give a Christian meaning to *The Merchant,* post-Second World War ones have become, understandably, utterly unable to read in *The Merchant* any message other than the prefiguration of the Holocaust . . . It is unthinkable to imagine that today's audiences could adopt, even for the brief moment of a performance, the Christian vision of the world which prevailed in medieval and Renaissance times.

Yet it is no answer to distort the play, in an effort to make it conform to modern standards, and then claim that what you are offering the public is still Shakespeare. The sad truth, Spriet concludes (he had just seen the Bill Alexander-Antony Sher production) is that *The Merchant of Venice* is a play that can no longer be adequately performed. With Shakespeare's other plays, we can suspend judgment, if necessary: any gap between his moral assumptions and our own can be overcome. But in this case the distance is too great. "The play must be abandoned."

•

Spriet presents his readers with too stark a choice, however. There is room for something between an "Elizabethan" production and the excesses of a Bill Alexander: compromises are possible, and most people would, I think, agree that intelligent compromises are worthwhile. Fortunately, too, not all recent critics write as though the only alternative to a rigidly prima facie reading was a systematically ironic reading. The best of them are more flexible, more prepared to "flow with the man."

Two examples stand out: the chapter on *The Merchant of Venice* in Norman Rabkin's *Shakespeare and the Problem of Meaning* (1981), and a short book on the play by John Lyon (1988).

Rabkin (an American) uses *The Merchant* as a test case for his argument against narrowly thematic readings of Shakespeare. "Ambivalent signals," he writes, "are built into the play"; "at every point at which we want simplicity, we get complexity"; our shifting responses to the characters are a reflection of the inconsistencies and uncertainties that we normally experience in life itself. Lyon (an Englishman) is more cautious. He points out that the celebration of multiplicity for its own sake, if it is pushed too far, can be used to justify inconsistencies that are simply artistic flaws. But with that proviso, his approach is essentially the same as Rabkin's: an exploration of the constant emotional adjustments that the play demands, of the ways in which a Shylock or a Portia can arouse two different feelings at once, and a dozen different feelings in succession.

Openness in literature brings with it the obvious risk of shapelessness. If the approach advocated by Rabkin and Lyon were to be universally adopted, we would soon start hankering for something simpler and stronger. But as it is, strong views of *The Merchant of Venice* abound; for the moment, qualified and multifaced views seem more rewarding.

• 4 •

We have no way of knowing what was in Shakespeare's mind when he began writing *The Merchant of Venice.* Even if we had, what he intended and what he accomplished are not necessarily the same thing. "Never trust the artist, trust the tale."

Still, we can take a reasonable guess at his intentions, and we can reasonably assume that they were at least partly fulfilled. The remarks that follow simply represent what I believe myself—although I am reinforced in my belief by the fact that many critics and commentators, perhaps the majority, have held roughly similar views.

Shylock is meant to be a villain. There can be arguments about his motives and his personality, but there can be no serious argument about his behavior. Given the opportunity—an opportunity which he himself has created—he attempts to commit legalized murder.

He is also a Jewish villain. He did not have to be: Christians were moneylenders too, and the story would have worked perfectly well with a Christian villain. What would be almost inconceivable, on the other hand, would be for him to be Jewish—in a play written in the sixteenth century—and for it not to count, except in some minor or attenuated sense. Jewishness is one of his primary characteristics: he emphasizes it himself, and it is emphasized for him by everyone with whom he has dealings.

His Jewish villainies, moreover, are strictly traditional. He is a usurer; he is cunning and cruel; he pursues a vendetta against Christians—or against their noblest available representative. Behind his plot against Antonio lie fantasies of ritual murder, ultimately going back to the Jews' supposed role in the Crucifixion.

How much weight Shakespeare would have wanted us to attach to the religious motifs in the play is uncertain. He was writing an Elizabethan comedy, not a medieval morality. But Elizabethan England was a society that was still pervaded by Christian beliefs and assumptions; and Shylock's role, in its main outlines, was a product of Christian folklore. It must be remembered, too, that the playwright went out of his way to impose a religious solution (or so it would have seemed to his audience) on the problem of Shylock. As far as we know, there was no precedent in his sources for the forcible conversion.

As a villain, Shylock was supposed to be a hate figure. As the villain in a comedy, whose designs were thwarted, he was paradoxically, with Macklin's decision in the eighteenth century (prefigured by Rowe's description of the play as a tragedy) that he ought to be played a pure villain, someone to be taken seriously. But even for the Elizabethans, I suspect, the comedy was never more than skin deep. The reference to his "extreame crueltie" on the title page of the First Quarto suggests that the threatening aspects of his character were always uppermost.

Invested with Shakespearean power and, in time, with Shakespearean prestige, Shylock the Jewish villain became part of world mythology. He may not have added anything to existing stereotypes, but as the most famous Jewish character in literature he helped to spread them and to keep them vigorously alive. He belongs, inescapably, to the history of anti-Semitism.

Yet Shakespeare, though he may often have started out with stereotypes, seldom ended up with them. He individualized Shylock; he provided him with motives—not pseudo-motives, but motives that anyone can understand; he equipped him with a private life, with compelling powers of self-expression, with senses, affections, passions. Shylock might easily have been a small character—someone, say, like the villainous Don John in *Much Ado About Nothing.* But he is a big character, like Falstaff—someone who bursts the bounds of the play in which he appears.

In building him up, Shakespeare was no doubt first and foremost obeying his professional instincts. A contemptible Shylock would have meant a one-sided conflict, a one-sided conflict would have meant a weak play. At the same time, he did not feel impelled to come up with a Napoleon of crime like Marlowe's Barabas. In his outward circumstances, Shylock remains a prosaic, commonplace moneylender, which according to Elizabethan literary convention should have been enough in itself to ensure that he was irredeemably petty and sordid. That he is so much more than that was put down by James Joyce to an element of concealed autobiography on Shakespeare's part: "He drew Shylock out of his own long pocket." Novelists are allowed to indulge in this kind of speculation, critics and biographers do so at their peril—which does not mean that the idea may not have something in it. We know that in real life Shakespeare was a shrewd and successful businessman, and it is perfectly possible that he had a lurking sympathy with Shylock's economic realism. Antonio's altruism may have been preferable in principle, but that was not the way the world worked.

One thing we can be sure of: he was not a secret twentieth-century liberal, animated by programmatic opposition to racial prejudice. (If he had been, he would have done better not to have written *The Merchant of Venice* at all.) He simply tried to imagine, within the confines of his plot, and within the limits that his culture set him, what it would be like to be a Jew. But dramatic imagination, when it is pitched at the Shakespearean level, becomes a moral quality, a form of humanism, and I agree with what Israel Davis wrote over a hundred years ago: it was a greater step for him to have created Shylock in the sixteenth century than for George Eliot to have written *Daniel Deronda* in the nineteenth century. The seeds of sympathy are there. Actors who have portrayed a tragic or sorely misused Shylock may often have gone too far, but it is Shakespeare himself who gave him their opening.

To sympathize with Shylock at all means that we cannot *totally* sympathize with the Christians. But does imperfect sympathy have to harden into antipathy? Do we have to end up agreeing with those who find them worthless?

I don't think so.

It is a mistake for criticism to try to emulate poetry, but it is sometimes necessary to remind ourselves of the spirit of Shakespeare's plays as well as their substance, of the level at which he wrote, the tone and color of the effects which he created. For the Austrian poet Hugo von Hofmannsthal, the essential Atmosphere of his work (Hofmannsthal spelled it with a capital "A") was one of "nobility in the sense of the Cinquecento," a nobility that was

> infinitely freer, infinitely more human than anything we are accustomed to associate with this notion. It is not only the characters and their feelings born out of

> Shakespeare's soul which are imbued with this nobility, but precisely and above all the Atmosphere, the air of life, *ce grand air* pervading everything.

This may seem some way away from *The Merchant of Venice.* A Shakespeare play is not the same thing as a Giorgone painting; unlike a painting, it is a work in which things happen. But it can still have the equivalent of Giorgonesque qualities; and those qualities, or their equivalent, help to make *The Merchant of Venice* what it is—help to make it still worth reading or seeing.

Strip away the atmosphere from the scene in which Bassanio chooses between the caskets, for instance, and you are left with a piece of childishness. But this is what Portia actually says:

> *Now he goes*
> *With no less presence, but with much more love*
> *Than young Alcides when he did redeem*
> *The virgin tribute paid by howling Troy*
> *To the sea-monster. I stand for sacrifice.*
> *The rest aloof are the Dardanian wives,*
> *With bleared visages come forth to view*
> *The issue of the exploit.*

And again, as he finally makes his choice:

> *How all the other passions fleet to air:*
> *As doubtful thoughts, and rash-embraced despair*
> *And shuddering fear, and green-eyed jealousy!*
> *O love, be moderate, allay thy ecstasy,*
> *In measure rain thy joy, scant this excess!*
> *I feel too much thy blessing: make it less*
> *For fear I surfeit.*

Of course, noble words do not necessarily imply noble deeds; but the Christian characters have admirable ideals, and on the whole—in their dealings among themselves, as opposed to their dealings with Shylock—they live up to them.

As for the view that they are meant to be taken ironically, it cannot be disproved; but then neither can the view that they are meant to be taken completely at face value. The chief arguments against the pure-irony interpretation are that great stretches of the play do not feel ironic; that when you have been told that they are, and go back and read them again, they *still* do not feel ironic; and that wholesale irony, running right through a play, is not Shakespeare's practice anywhere else (though there are doubtless critics ready to maintain that it is).

We do not have to go to the other extreme. The Christians have their dubious aspects, their potential conflicts, their mixed motives. If the play is a fairy tale, it is a fairy tale for grown-ups, a fairy tale with depths and shadows. But the fantasy, though it is sometimes shaken, is never shattered. The lovers are true lovers; the prima facie virtues turn out to be real virtues.

Which still leaves Shylock. In a sense, it is foolish to complain about the treatment meted out to him. The trouble lies in the very concept of his character, in the moneybags and the knife. How can the other characters fail to hate him? And if the question of his Jewishness did not come into it, I doubt whether the rough handling he receives would cause us much distress.

But that is an impossible "if." In the eyes of the other characters, the fact that he is a Jew is an offense in itself. The ways in which they express their feelings on the subject are brilliantly differentiated—they range from the coarse to the high-minded, from the glacial to the vitriolic; but at no point does anyone suggest that there might be a distinction to be drawn between his being a Jew and his being an obnoxious individual. The result is ugly, whether Shakespeare himself saw it that way or not.

If all this were simply one more nastiness on the part of nasty people, there would be nothing more to be said. What is tragic about the anti-Semitism in the play is that it coexists with so many admirable or attractive qualities. Antonio, Portia and Bassanio; Lorenzo in his speeches at Belmont; even Gratiano, in the speech he makes early on in his own defense ("Let me play the fool")—between them they represent, at their best, some of the leading values of their civilization. Unfortunately, though, their prejudice against Jews is as deeply ingrained as any of their virtues.

It is worth repeating that they are not racists in the full

modern sense. Shylock can save himself (in principle) through baptism, and Jessica's genes do not prevent her from having always been a Christian at heart, an *anima naturaliter Christiana.* But from the perspective of the late twentieth century, neither fact can afford us more than very limited consolation.

Exactly where the play now stands depends on one's wider reading of European history. I personally think it is absurd to suppose that there is a direct line of descent from Antonio to Hitler, or from Portia to the SS, but that is because I do not believe that the Holocaust was in any way inevitable. I *do* believe, on the other hand, that the ground for the Holocaust was well prepared, and to that extent the play can never seem quite the same again. It is still a masterpiece; but there is a permanent chill in the air, even in the gardens of Belmont.

Notes

Place of publication is London except where indicated.

PART ONE: SHAKESPEARE'S SHYLOCK

CHAPTER ONE: *WHERE DOES HE COME FROM?*

15 the tale of Giannetto: an English translation can be found in the Arden edition of *The Merchant of Venice* (1955), ed. John Russell Brown, pp. 140–53, and in Geoffrey Bullough, *Narrative and Dramatic Sources of Shakespeare,* vol. i (1958), pp. 463–76.

18 *Komoedia gennandt* . . . : there is a detailed description in Herman Sinsheimer, *Shylock: The History of a Character* (1947), pp. 59–61.

18 *The Ballad of Gernutus*: reprinted in the Arden edition, pp. 153–66.

22 a once-celebrated book: Werner Sombart, *The Jews and Modern Capitalism* (*Die Juden und das Wirtschaftsleben,* 1911; English translation 1913).

23 "The Theology of Marlowe's *The Jew of Malta*": Hunter, *Dramatic Identities and Cultural Traditions* (Liverpool, 1978), pp. 60–102.

23 terribly serious, even savage . . . : T. S. Eliot, "Christopher Marlowe," *Selected Essays* (1951), p. 123. The essay was written in 1919.

27 The Jew of medieval myth: see in particular Joshua Trachtenberg, *The Devil and the Jews* (New Haven, 1943).

28 a play entitled *Moschus*: described in Sinsheimer, op. cit., pp. 76–7.

CHAPTER TWO: *JEWS*

32 worse than Judas himself . . . : Lopez's trial is described in detail in Sidney Lee, "The Original Shylock," *Gentlemen's Magazine* 246 (1880).

33 all events brought grist . . . : James Joyce, *Ulysses,* the "Scylla and Charybdis" or Library section (1960 ed., p. 262).

33 "Lopez," it has been pointed out . . . : by John Dover Wilson in *The Merchant of Venice,* ed. Arthur Quiller-Couch and John Dover Wilson (Cambridge, 1926), p. 117.

34 Roger Prior: see his article "A Second Jewish Community in Tudor London," *Jewish Historical Studies* vol. xxxi (1990), pp. 137–52.

35 the Jewish wolves . . . : Emilia Lanier, *The Poems of Shakespeare's Dark Lady,* with an introduction by A. L. Rowse (1978), p. 100.

36 Shylock could only have been a member . . . : see Cecil Roth, "The Background of Shylock," *Personalities and Events in Jewish History* (Philadelphia, 1953), pp. 237–47.

37 social and cultural vitality: see, for example, Riccardo Calimanni, *The Ghetto of Venice: A History,* trs. Katherine Silberblatt Wolfthal (New York, 1987).

38 a play called *Esther*: see Calimanni, op. cit., p. 143.

38 *The Life of Judah*: there is a recent translation, *The Autobiography of a Seventeenth-Century Venetian Rabbi,* trs. and ed. Mark R. Cohen (Princeton, 1988).

39 Is discrepant from Shylock . . . : Natalie Zemon Davis, "Fame and Secrecy: Leone Modena's *Life* as an Early Modern Autobiography," in Mark R. Cohen's edition of *The Autobiography,* p. 68.

39 On the Jews and Renaissance music, see Cecil Roth, *The Jews and the Renaissance* (Philadelphia, 1959), pp. 271–304.

43 Ruskin thought . . . : John Ruskin, *Munera Pulveris* (1872), par. 134.

44 In the "Bishop's Bible": quoted by W. Moelwyn Merchant in his notes to the New Penguin edition of *The Merchant of Venice* (1967), p. 174.

44 They shall awake as Jacob did . . . : John Donne, sermon preached on 29 February 1627/8 (*XXVI Sermons,* 1660).

45 It is often said . . . : Harold Fisch, *The Dual Image* (1959), p. 34.

CHAPTER THREE: *THREE THOUSAND DUCATS*

47 *The Merchant of Venice* is discussed by Nelson on pp. 86–9 and pp. 141–51.

48 The whole weight of Christian teaching . . . : For the general background, see Benjamin Nelson, *The Idea of Usury: From Tribal Brotherhood to Universal Otherhood* (Princeton, 1949).

48 in itself a proof . . . : R. H. Tawney, introduction to Thomas Wilson's *Discourse upon Usury,* 1572 (1925), p. 19.

48 agriculture, industry and foreign trade . . . : ibid, p. 86.

49 They were also familiar figures on the stage: see Celeste Turner Wright, "Some Conventions Regarding the Usurer in Elizabethan Literature," *Studies in Philology* (1934), pp. 176–97, and "The Usurer's Sin in Elizabethan Literature," *Studies in Philology* (1938), pp. 178–94.

52 many of the most famous courtiers: see Tawney, op. cit., pp. 32–3.

57 setting aside these Jewish dreams . . . : *The Works of Francis Bacon* III *New Atlantis* (1887), p. 138.

57 The American historian Lewis Feuer: see his article "Francis Bacon and the Jews: Who was the Jew in the New Atlantis?", *Jewish Historical Studies* vol. xxix (1988), pp. 1–26.

59 he found himself taken to court: see S. Schoenbaum, *William Shakespeare: A Compact Documentary Life* (revised edition, 1987), pp. 322–3.

60 in an age without credit cards . . . : ibid., p. 241.

60 The Quiney correspondence: see E. A. J. Honigmann, *Shakespeare and his Contemporaries* (1982), pp. 8–9. See also Honigmann's article "There is a World Elsewhere: William Shakespeare, Businessman," in *Images of Shakespeare,* eds. Werner Habicht, D. J. Palmer and Roger Pringle (1988), pp. 40–6.

62 we were just in a financial position . . . : John Maynard Keynes, *A Treatise on Money,* vol. ii (1971), p. 137.

62 On James Burbage and the financing of the Theatre, see E. K. Chambers, *William Shakespeare: A Study of Facts and Problems,* (1930) vol. ii, pp. 65–6.

CHAPTER FOUR: *"Shylock Is My Name"*

65 other speech habits . . . : see Otto Jespersen, *Growth and Structure of the English Language* (Anchor Books edition, New York, 1956), pp. 232–4.

65 as Brian Vickers has pointed out . . . : see *The Artistry of Shakespeare's Prose* (1968), pp. 82–8.

CHAPTER FIVE: *Wife and Daughter*

69 monkeys symbolized lechery . . . : for further discussion, see Ruth Nevo, *Comic Transformations in Shakespeare* (1980), p. 118.

70 An American scholar . . . : see Beatrice Brown, "Medieval Prototypes of Jessica and Lorenzo," *Modern Language Notes,* April 1929, pp. 227–32.

71 the women of the Jewish race . . . : quoted in Léon Poliakov, *The History of Anti-Semitism: Vol. III, From Voltaire to Wagner,* trs. Miriam Kochan (1975), p. 326.

71 the dogmatic compromise . . . : Leslie Fiedler, *The Stranger in Shakespeare* (1973), p. 117.

CHAPTER SIX: *"I Stand for Judgment"*

76 a survey published in 1972: O. Hood Phillips, *Shakespeare and the Lawyers* (1972), pp. 91–118.

77 Rudolf von Ihering: *The Struggle for Law* (1872), cited in the Variorum edition of *The Merchant of Venice,* ed. H. H. Furness (Philadelphia, 1888), pp. 410–11.

78 Sir Frederick Pollock: see Hood Phillips, op. cit., p. 105.

79 In *The Merchant of Venice,* William Shakespeare . . . : W. Nicholas Knight, "Equity, *The Merchant of Venice* and William Lambarde," *Shakespeare Survey* 27 (1974), p. 95.

79 the judicial problems arising . . . : E. F. J. Tucker, "The Letter of the Law in *The Merchant of Venice*," *Shakespeare Survey* 29 (1976), p. 94.

80 In the trial scene . . . : ibid., p. 97.

80 the concept of equity . . . : Richard A. Posner, *Law and Literature: A Misunderstood Relation* (1988), p. 96.

81 personified the spirit of equity . . . : ibid., p.96.

84 have all the infantile violence . . . : Robert Fliess as summarized in Norman Holland, *Psychoanalysis and Shakespeare* (New York, 1964), pp. 240–2.

86 no protest against the traditional theory . . . : David Brion Davis, *The Problem of Slavery in Western Culture* (Pelican edition, 1970), p. 126.

86 The Devil makes his appearance . . . : G. W. Keeton, *Shakespeare's Legal and Political Background* (1967), p. 141.

CHAPTER SEVEN: *CHRISTIANS*

93 The Cross his stage was . . . : quoted in *The Shakespeare Allusion-Book*, ed. C. M. Ingleby (second edition, 1932), vol. i, p. 237.

95 saccharine banalities . . . : Leslie Fiedler, *The Stranger in Shakespeare* (1973), p. 131.

97 a more or less abstract . . . : Jacob Katz, *Exclusiveness and Tolerance: Studies in Jewish-Gentile Relations in Medieval and Modern Times* (Oxford, 1961), p. xiv.

98 the best flesh-shambles . . . : John Day, *Humour Out of Breath* (1608). Quoted in Murray J. Levith, *Shakespeare's Italian Settings and Plays* (1989), p. 12.

PART TWO: *INTERPRETATIONS (1600–1939)*

CHAPTER EIGHT: *FROM COMICAL TO TRAGICAL*

105 If with the Jew . . . : for Mynshull, see *The Shakespeare Allusion-Book*, ed. C. M. Ingleby (1932), p. 269.

106 *The Travels of the Three English Brothers*: for a fuller discussion see H. Neville Davies, "*Pericles* and the Sherley Brothers," in *Shakespeare and his Contemporaries*, ed. E. A. J. Honigmann (Manchester, 1986).

107 A. H. Bullen: *The Works of John Day* (1881), notes to *The Three English Brothers*, p. iii.

107 Your English Jews . . . : quoted by M. J. Landa, *The Jew in Drama* (1926), p. 99.

107 Jew tricks . . . : ibid., pp. 101–2.

108 Shakespeare's sacred name . . . : Dryden, Prologue to *Aureng-Zebe* (1675).

110 very aspectabund . . . : John Downes, *Roscius Anglicanus* (first printed, 1789). Cited by Toby Lelyveld, *Shylock on the Stage* (1961), p.18.

110 though we have seen that play . . . : Nicholas Rowe, *Some Account of the Life of Mr. William Shakespeare* (1709), p. xix.

111 He made daily visits . . . : *The Connoisseur*, January 1754; cited by William W. Appleton, *Charles Macklin: An Actor's Life* (1961), p. 46.

111 Jews, their history. . . . : Appleton, p. 45.

112 a great fives player . . . : ibid., p. 17.

112 By God, sir . . . : William Cook, *Memoirs of Charles Macklin* (1804), cited by Appleton, p. 49.

112 there was such an iron-visaged look . . . : Cook, op. cit., quoted in the Variorum edition, p. 374.

113 Vat you tink . . . : Carola Oman, *David Garrick* (1958), p. 32.

113 Shylock is not one . . . : Lichtenberg, *Letters from England.* Adapted from the translation in the Variorum edition, pp. 374–5.

114 "stood like a TOWER" . . . : James Boaden, *Memoirs of the Life of John Philip Kemble* (1825), cit. Appleton, p. 51.

114 as rough and husky . . . : John Bernard, *Retrospections of the Stage* (1830), cit. Appleton, p. 197.

115 If God writes . . . : cit. Appleton, p. 36.

116 It cannot be denied . . . : Lichtenberg, as above.

116 I'll call to Simon . . . : Maria Edgeworth, *Harrington* (1817), p. 3.

117 the most celebrated Jew . . . : ibid., p. 101.

117 No power of imagination . . . : ibid., p. 153.

117 the genius of the greatest poet . . . : ibid., p. 165.

118 to destroy it, my dear . . . : ibid., p. 270.

118 to the provinces . . . : in *Strolling Players and Drama in the Provinces 1660–1765*, Sybil Rosenfeld gives details of performances before 1765 in all four of the provincial centers she studies, Norwich, York, Bristol and Canterbury.

119 George Colman on Henderson: William Winter, *Shakespeare on the Stage* (New York, 1911), pp. 144–5.

120 Cooke, a square-faced . . . : Leigh Hunt, *Autobiography* (1860), ch. 6.

121 the toe-bone story: Barry Cornwall, *Life of Edmund Kean* (1835), vol. ii, pp. 195–202.

122 The Jew's argument . . . : Johnson's edition of Shakespeare, note on *Merchant of Venice*, iv. i. 90.

122 In other comments . . . : see, for example, the note on *The Jew of Venice* in the life of Granville in *Lives of the Poets.*

122 "An Apology for the Character and Conduct of Shylock": in *Essays by a Society of Gentlemen at Exeter* (Exeter, 1796). Substantial extracts are reprinted in the Variorum edition.

124 a decrepit old man . . . : Hazlitt, *Characters of Shakespear's Plays* (1817).

CHAPTER NINE: *Romantics and Revisionists*

125 The Jew, or nothing . . . : John Doran, *Their Majesties' Servants* (1865), p. 428.

126 a stroller needed . . . : Giles Playfair, *Kean* (1950), p. 30.

126 For Kean's first performance of Shylock at Drury Lane, see particularly Doran, op. cit.

127 Hazlitt's reviews of Kean were reprinted in his *View of the English Stage* (1818), and subsequently in *Hazlitt on Theatre* (1895), ed. William Archer and Robert Lowe.

127 At the exclamation . . . : W. J. Fox in *The People's Journal,* 1846; quoted by Authur C. Sprague, *Shakespeare and the Actors* (Cambridge, Mass., 1944), p. 24.

128 Shylock is in Venice . . . : F. W. Hawkins, *Life of Kean* (1869), p. 126.

129 on the Jewish boycott: see Tucker Brooke, "The Reputation of Christopher Marlowe" (*Transactions of the Connecticut Academy of Arts and Sciences,* 1922), p. 402–3.

129 during the whole of the fifth act . . . : quoted by Playfair, op. cit., p. 266.

130 he exaggerated everything . . . : quoted in *William Allingham's Diary* (1907), p. 247.

130 Anything more impressive . . . : G. H. Lewes, *Of Actors and the Art of Acting* (1875 ed.), p. 11.

131 He was nothing . . . : "On Shakespeare and Milton," *Lectures on the English Poets* (1818).

132 We suspect that the main feeling . . . : *Leigh Hunt's Dramatic Criticism,* ed. Lawrence Hustin Houtchens and Carolyn Washburn Houtchens (1950), p. 290.

132 clothing his dry bones . . . : ibid., p. 197.

133 on whom the world had been spitting . . . : Barry Cornwall, *Life of Edmund Kean* (1835), vol. ii, p. 47.

133 Representing the persecutor . . . : Charles Armitage Brown, *Shakespeare's Autobiographical Poems* (1838), p. 278.

133 In fact Shakespeare . . . : *Dramatic Works of Shakespeare* (1838), ed. Thomas Campbell, p. xxxv.

134 The equipment . . . : quoted by Alfred Rubens, "Jews and the English Stage, 1667–1850," *Transactions of the Jewish Historical Society of England,* vol. xxiv (1975).

134 I have not got the key . . . : *Reminiscences and Selections from his Diary and Letters,* ed. Frederick Pollock (1875), vol. ii, pp. 153–4.

135 It was a Jew wheedling . . . : quoted by Alan S. Downer, *The Eminent Tragedian: William Charles Macready* (Cambridge, Mass., 1966), p. 211.

136 abject, sordid . . . : G. H. Lewes, *Dramatic Essays Reprinted from the Examiner,* ed. William Archer and R. W. Lowe (1894), p. 115.

136 Mr. Lewes never for one instant . . . : quoted by Archer and Lowe, ibid., p. xviii.

137 Shaw's article, "Sullivan, Shakespeare and Shaw": reprinted in *Shaw on Theatre,* ed. E. J. West (New York, 1959).

137 chiefly selected . . . : Charles Kean's acting edition of *The Merchant of Venice* (1858), quoted by Lelyveld, op. cit., p. 59.

138 There are no tears . . . : *Of Actors and the Art of Acting,* p.19.

138 a pudding voice . . . : see William Winter, op cit., pp. 152–3.

139 There was an old Jew . . . : *Pineywoods Tavern, or Sam Slick in Texas* (1858). Quoted by Louise Mayo, *The Ambivalent Image: Nineteenth-Century America's Perception of the Jew* (1988), p. 78.

139 the representative Hebrew . . . : quoted by Lelyveld, op. cit., p. 65. For an amusing English account of Junius Brutus Booth, which suggests that Gould greatly exaggerated his importance, see Dutton Cook, *Hours with the Players* (1881).

141 nothing but a pair of eyes . . . : quoted by Arthur Colby Sprague, *Shakespearian Players and Performances* (1954), p. 132.

141 I believe you hold . . . : *Between Actor and Critic: Selected Letters of Edwin Booth and William Winter,* ed. Daniel J. Watermeier (Princeton, 1971), p. 256.

142 a majestic Hebrew . . . : Winter, op. cit., p.156.

143 If we side with him . . . : *A New Variorum Edition of The Merchant of Venice,* ed. Horace Howard Furness (Philadelphia, 1888), p. 384.

143 an un-Jewlike action . . . : ibid., p. 384.

143 "Shylock Not a Jew": there are quotations from the article in Mayo, op. cit., pp. 77–8 and in Lelyveld, op. cit., p. 75 (though Lelyveld does not attribute them to Bryant by name).

CHAPTER TEN: *HENRY IRVING*

146 He was never undignified . . . : Joseph Hatton, *Henry Irving's Impressions of America* (1884), p. 269.

146 I suppose he was the coolest actor . . . : Edward Gordon Craig, *Henry Irving* (1930), p. 21.

147 The tendency of the play . . . : the *Theatre,* December 1879 (writing as "An Actor"). Quoted by Furness, op. cit., p. 433.

147 I look upon Shylock . . . : Hatton, op. cit., p. 265.

147 his best, I think . . . : John Morley, *The Life of William Ewart Gladstone* (1903), vol. ii, p. 604.

148 the horrible stillness . . . : quoted by Sprague, op. cit., p. 115 and Lelyveld, op. cit., p. 8.

148 even Portia . . . : Clement Scott, *From "The Bells" to "King Arthur"* (1897), p. 167.

148 How small and mean . . . : W. Graham Robertson, *Time Was* (1930), p. 55.

149 the stage was empty . . . : *Ellen Terry's Memoirs,* with notes and additional material by Edith Craig and Christopher St. John (1932), p. 147.

149 For absolute pathos . . . : ibid., p.146.

149 his final exit . . . : my account is chiefly based on Laurence Irving, *Henry Irving: The Actor and his World* (1951), pp. 343–4, and Alan Hughes, *Henry Irving, Shakespearean* (Cambridge, 1981), pp. 238–9.

149 a mystical belief . . . : Laurence Irving, op. cit., p.344.

150 Here is an usurer . . . : *Spectator,* 8 November 1879.

151 For the old Jew . . . : Austin Brereton, *The Life of Henry Irving* (1908), vol. i, p. 315.

151 if Mr. Irving chose . . . . Percy Fitzgerald, *Henry Irving: A Record of Twenty Years at the Lyceum,* p. 140 (1893).

151 a result which he . . . : Brereton, op. cit., vol. i, p. 317.

152 very clever, very natural . . . : Squire Bancroft, *The Bancrofts* (popular edition, 1911), p. 231.

152 it was *nothing* . . . : Ellen Terry, op. cit., p. 87.

153 I knew that I had "got them" . . . : ibid., p. 86.

153 as though it were made of gossamer . . . : Laurence Irving, op. cit., p. 339.

153 too free and familiar . . . : Henry James, *The Scenic Art: Notes on Acting and the Drama 1872–1901,* ed. Allan Wade (1949), p. 143. Originally published in *Scribner's Monthly,* January 1881.

153 Your whole conception . . . : quoted by Ellen Terry, op. cit., p. 145.

154 *Et tu, Brute* . . . : quoted by Laurence Irving, op. cit., p. 357.

154 the popular myth . . . : Hughes, op. cit., p. 227.
154 a noble kinsman . . . : Ellen Terry, *Four Lectures on Shakespeare* (1932), p. 121.
154 The Duke and Portia . . . : the *Theatre* (writing as "An Actor"), December 1879.
155 a bit of a loafer . . . : quoted by Hughes, op. cit., p. 235. The discrepancies between the published text of the lectures and the manuscript notes are discussed by Betty Bandel in "Ellen Terry's Foul Papers," *Theatre Survey,* May 1969.
155 the sympathy enjoyed . . . : the *Theatre,* November 1879, p. 194.
155 "An Actor" . . . : the *Theatre,* December 1879, pp. 253–61.
156 simply hideous . . . : quoted by Laurence Irving, op. cit., p. 256.
157 Of his Shylock last winter . . . : James, *The Scenic Art*, pp. 140–1.
158 He was utterly unlike . . . : *Ellen Terry and Bernard Shaw: A Correspondence* (1931), p. xx.
159 His first success . . . : "Blaming the Bard," *Saturday Review,* September 1896. Reprinted in *Our Theatre in the Nineties* (1931), vol. iii, p. 198.
159 a matyred saint . . . : letter to Henry Murray, 2 November 1930. Reprinted in *Collected Letters,* vol. iv. (1988), p. 213.
159 played Shylock for sympathy . . . : quoted by Laurence Irving, op. cit., p. 500.
159 from observation at rehearsal . . . : J. H. Barnes, "Irving Days at the Lyceum," *The Nineteenth Century and After,* January 1923, p. 104.
160 When Irving first acted . . . : Winter, op. cit., pp. 177–8.
160 unbending arrogance . . . : Humbert Wolfe, *Portraits by Inference* (1934), p. 68.
161 in the name of all the Jews . . . : Eliza Aria, *My Sentimental Self* (1922), p. 85.
161 The Lincoln Handicap Story . . . : ibid., p. 28. For a sketch of Mrs. Aria in her later years, see Osbert Sitwell, *Noble Essences* (1950), pp. 158–60.
162 the Jew idealised . . . : A. B. Walkley, *Playhouse Impressions* (1892) p. 259.
162 Wa thane . . . : quoted in *Ellen Terry's Memoirs,* p. 210.
164 When I saw the play . . . : George Sampson, *Seven Essays* (Cambridge, 1947), p. 179.

CHAPTER ELEVEN: *STAGE AND STUDY*

166 the effect was more humorous . . . : Hesketh Pearson, *Beerbohm Tree* (1956), p. 133. Pearson played the part of Balthasar.
166 the beautiful Jewish hymn . . . : Maud Tree, in *Herbert Beerbohm Tree: Some Memories of Him and of His Art,* collected by Max Beerbohm (n.d., c. 1920), p. 148.
167 Among the Elizabethans . . . : Max Beerbohm, *More Theatres* (1969), p. 345.
168 study of racial strength . . . : ibid., p. 518.
168 much more of imagination . . . : ibid., p. 345.
168 Another admirer . . . : Gordon Crosse, *Shakespearean Playgoing 1890–1952* (1953), p. 31.
168 was written at a time . . . : Arthur Bourchier, *Some Reflections on the Drama—and Shakespeare* (Oxford, 1911), p. 37.
169 a revengeful and uncomplicated usurer . . . : J. C. Trewin, *Shakespeare on the English Stage 1900–1961* (1964), p. 36.
169 This reading . . . : Matheson Lang, *Mr. Wu Looks Back* (1940), p. 216.

169 For Zangwill on Lang, see "Shylock and Other Stage Jews" in *The Voice of Jerusalem* (1920).

170 a fairy tale . . . : Winter, op. cit., p. 197.

170 he made Shylock . . . : ibid., p. 199. On Mansfield's Shylock see also Lelyveld and the references in Arthur C. Sprague, *Shakespeare and the Actors* (Cambridge, Mass., 1945).

170 The public wanted a star . . . : Joseph Francis Daly, *The Life of Augustin Daly* (New York, 1917), p. 632.

171 neither as tragic nor as comic . . . : Lelyveld, op. cit., p. 105.

171 Mr. Southern's Shylock . . . : quoted by Sheridan Morley, *The Great Stage Stars* (1986), p. 265.

172 not feeble . . . : Robert Speaight, *William Poel and the Elizabethan Revival* (1954), p. 41.

173 the religious character . . . : ibid., p. 140.

174 not primarily . . . : William Poel, *Shakespeare in the Theatre* (1913), p. 77.

174 the tragical Historie . . . : ibid., p. 48.

175 One reason . . . : A. C. Bradley, *Shakespearean Tragedy* (1904), p. 21.

175 Shylock had the best of the argument . . . : George Saintsbury reviewing *Daniel Deronda* in 1876. Cited in *George Eliot and Her Readers,* ed. Laurence Lerner and John Holmstrom (1966), p. 141.

175 engage the interest . . . : Walter Raleigh, *Shakespeare* (1907), p. 149.

175 Antonio and Bassanio . . . : ibid., p. 150.

176 mean, mercenary . . . : Stopford Brooke, *On Ten Plays of Shakespeare* (1905), pp. 136–7.

176 in an odd recess . . . : ibid., p. 140.

176 Shakespeare, the man . . .: C. H. Herford, *Shakespeare* (1912), p. 38.

176 builded better . . . : Brander Matthews, *Shakespeare as a Playwright* (1913), p. 150.

177 it must assuredly . . . : F. C. Boas, *Shakespeare and his Predecessors* (1896), p. 218.

177 On the Boas family, see Louis Hyman, *The Jews of Ireland* (1972).

177 magnificent outburst . . . : ibid., p. 226.

178 a savage greed . . . : Sidney Lee, *The Life of William Shakespeare* (1915 edition), p. 133.

179 Yes, yes . . . : Arthur Quiller-Couch, *Shakespeare's Workmanship* (1931 edition), p. 75.

179 Being such Christians . . . : ibid., p.76.

179 a man of intellect . . . : John Masefield, *William Shakespeare* (1911), p. 104.

180 Here for the first time . . . : Frank Harris, *The Man Shakespeare and His Tragic Life Story* (revised edition, 1911), p. 188.

180 the pressure from the outside . . . : ibid., p. 200.

180 A brutal insult . . . : ibid., p. 201.

181 all critical insights . . . : W. K. Wimsatt. *The Verbal Icon* (1954), p. 56.

182 except at popular performances . . . : Elmer Edgar Stoll, *Shakespeare Studies* (1927), p. 335–6.

183 That Hebraic and picturesque figure . . . : ibid., p. 336.

CHAPTER TWELVE: *Between the Wars*

184 Writing in 1936 . . . : John Middleton Murry, *Shakespeare* (1936), p. 211.
185 the audience at the Pavilion . . . : M. J. Landa, *The Shylock Myth* (1942), p. 38.
185 For deprecating movements . . . : Desmond MacCarthy, *Drama* (1940), p. 15.
186 what I have said . . . : ibid., p. 16.
186 You might equally well . . . : W. A. Darlington, *Through the Fourth Wall* (1922), p. 20.
186 a fiend incarnate . . . : Reginald Denham, *Stars in My Hair* (1958), p. 93.
187 came to serve . . . : Irving Howe, *World of Our Fathers* (1976), p. 402.
187 studies of the Hebrew race . . . : ibid., p. 403.
188 as I have been sometimes . . . : Stark Young, *Immortal Shadows* (New York, 1948), p. 39.
188 Biologically, even . . . : ibid., p. 40.
189 I have always believed . . . : *George Arliss by Himself* (1940), p. 10.
190 a Shylock *intime* . . . : James Agate, *Brief Chronicles* (1943), p. 52.
191 he spoke in the accent . . . : quoted in John Casson, *Lewis and Sybil* (1972), p. 142.
191 a mean little miser . . . : quoted in Diana Devlin, *A Speaking Part: Lewis Casson and the Theatre of His Time* (1982), p. 166.
191 magnificence . . . : ibid., p. 166.
191 a depraved exquisite . . . : review in the *Daily Telegraph,* quoted in James C. Bulman, *Shakespeare in Performance: The Merchant of Venice* (Manchester, 1991), p. 58.
192 dissipated, fast . . . : quoted in Bulman, op. cit., p. 65.
192 a wicked old scamp . . . : quoted in Bulman, p. 68.
192 the political doctrines . . . : Theodore Komisarjevsky, *The Theatre and a Changing Civilization* (1935), p. x.
193 all bathed alternately . . . : Bulman, op. cit., p. 56.
194 the most thrilling performance . . . : Alec Guinness, *Blessings in Disguise* (1985), p. 171.
194 Proud and inflammably racial . . . : Trewin, op. cit., p. 133.
194 a thunderclap . . . : *The Times,* 29 April 1932.
194 Of course . . . the blessed memory . . . : *Letters from Graham Robertson,* ed. Kerrison Preston (1953), p. 270.
195 The Merchant of Venice is a fairy tale. . . . : Harley Granville-Barker, *Prefaces to Shakespeare: Second Series* (1930), p. 67.
196 that constant calling . . . : ibid., p. 95.
196 is no more a mere means . . . : ibid, p. 95.
197 greater powers . . . : G. Wilson Knight, *Shakespearean Production* (revised edition, 1963), p. 188.
198 In them the Dionysian principle . . . : ibid., p.196.
198 In the later scenes . . . : ibid., p. 198.
199 hardly a hint . . . : Audrey Williamson, *Theatre of Two Decades* (1951), p. 61.
200 The squalor of a Transylvanian usurer . . . : *The New Statesman,* 7 May 1938.
201 the proposals of Shakespeare's deliberate will . . . : H. B. Charlton, *Shakespearian Comedy* (1938), p. 160.

201 an entirely indefensible exhibition . . . : ibid., p. 124.
202 Shylock may have taken him . . . : John Dover Wilson, *Shakespeare's Happy Comedies* (1962), p. 110.
203 the kind of story-teller . . . : Mark Van Doren, *Shakespeare* (British edition, 1941), p. 2.
203 Where Shakespeare's sympathies lay . . . : ibid., pp. 104–5.

PART THREE: *A Citizen of the World*

CHAPTER THIRTEEN: *A Legend and Its Legacy*

209 And every child . . . : *Epistle to Lord Cobham,* lines 114–5.
210 the *Gray's Inn Journal* . . . : see Thomas W. Perry, *Public Opinion, Propaganda, and Politics in Eighteenth-century England* (Cambridge, Mass., 1960), p. 106 and p. 166.
210 I observe with much concern . . . : quoted by Stanley Thomas Williams, *Richard Cumberland: His Life and Dramatic Works* (New Haven, Conn., 1917), p. 215.
211 the widow's friend . . . : *The Jew,* act V, scene 2.
211 a Harpagon . . . : James Picciotto, *Sketches of Anglo-Jewish History* (reprinted, 1956), p. 230.
211 act like a *Christian* . . . : *The Lady's Magazine,* May 1794. Quoted by Williams, op. cit., p. 236.
212 We cannot be surprised . . . : cited by Landa, *The Jew in Drama,* p. 140.
212 Divine Rebecca . . . : Francis Jeffrey, *Contributions to the Edinburgh Review,* vol. iii (1844), p. 477.
212 When Israel . . . : *Ivanhoe,* ch. 39.
212 I think Miss Edgeworth's . . . : *The Letters of Scott,* ed. H. J. C. Grierson (1932–1937), vol. iv, p. 478.
214 Ehud, or Ahab . . . : Scott's Journal, entry for 1 Nov. 1827.
214 their pound of flesh . . . : Scott's Journal, entries for 31 Oct. 1827 and 3 Nov. 1827.
214 a charming letter . . . : for the exchange between Byron and Nathan, see *Anglo-Jewish Letters (1158–1917),* ed. Cecil Roth (1938), pp. 244–5.
215 Wilson Knight has argued . . . : see *Byron and Shakespeare* (1966), pp. 205–11.
215 I know the precise worth . . . : letter to Murray, 6 April 1819.
215 Who hold the balance . . . : *Don Juan,* Canto XII, stanza 5.
215 How rich is Britain! . . . : *The Age of Bronze,* lines 668–703.
216 At the heart of the problem . . . : Edgar Rosenberg, *From Shylock to Svengali* (1961), pp. 187–8.
218 Unflattering references . . . : for a detailed account of the subject see Harry Stone, "Dickens and the Jews," *Victorian Studies,* March 1959, pp. 223–53.
218 In the errant fancy . . . : "An Italian Dream," *Pictures from Italy* (1846).
219 You'd better get somebody . . . : Anthony Trollope, *The Prime Minister,* ch. 46.
221 Miss Shylock . . . : quoted in Edward Coleman, *The Jew in English Drama: An Annotated Bibliography* (New York, 1943), p. 76.
221 He was gifted . . . : Edmund Wilson, *Canon Barham and the Devils* (1973), p. 11.

223 What is the cannibal . . . : "Famine and Fashion," *Punch* (1843), p. 203. The article also quotes from the leader in *The Times.*

223 the cruel, revengeful . . . : quoted in *Benjamin Disraeli: Letters 1835–1837,* ed. J. A. W. Gunn et al. Toronto, 1982), p. 49.

223 On the playbills for *Shylock!*: see M. C. N. Salbstein, *The Emancipation of the Jews in Britain* (1982), p. 216.

224 I think that your being . . . : W. F. Monypenny and G. E. Buckle, *Life of Disraeli* (1910–1920), vol. iii, p. 137.

224 Emily Wharton's irate father: see *The Prime Minister,* ch. 3.

224 Shylock is dead . . . : William Dean Howells, *Venetian Life* (1866), p. 207.

225 Over *The Merchant of Venice* . . . : Peter Fleming, theater review in the *Spectator,* 16 December 1932.

225 On Disraeli as Gratiano: Monypenny and Buckle, op. cit., vol. i, p. 20.

225 The statistics about American high schools are quoted by Gary Taylor, *Reinventing Shakespeare* (1990), p. 204.

226 Basil Rathbone's memoirs: *In and Out of Character* (1956), p. 33.

227 A well clad Jew . . . : James Joyce, *The Critical Writings,* ed. Ellsworth Mason and Richard Ellmann (1965), p. 34.

228 A useful tribe . . . : Wyndham Lewis, *Self Condemned* (1954), p. 62.

228 It's too true Dick . . . : Wyndham Lewis, *The Apes of God* (1930), p. 48.

229 And you forgive all . . . : St. John Ervine, *The Lady of Belmont* (1923), p. 95.

230 "Dirge": printed in Valerie Eliot, ed., *The Waste Land: A Facsimile and Transcript of the Original Drafts* (1971), p. 121.

231 The Bard of Avon . . . : Ezra Pound, Canto XCIII.

232 It is something . . . : T. S. Eliot, *Selected Essays* (1951), p. 123.

232 Barabas from Shylock . . . : ibid., p. 157.

232 a more complex tissue . . . : ibid., p. 158.

232 On the top of the books . . . : Philip Larkin, *Jill* (1964 ed.), p. 38.

CHAPTER FOURTEEN: *Other Voices, Other Cultures*

235 On the Raspe translation, see Edward Coleman, op. cit., p. 28.

235 It is easy for the poet . . . : A. W. Schlegel, *Lectures on Dramatic Art and Poetry*, trs. John Black (1815), vol. ii, p. 169.

236 The letter of the law . . . : ibid., p.169.

237 the relation of man to property . . . : reprinted in *The Merchant of Venice: A Casebook,* ed. John Wilders (1969), p. 34.

237 In principle . . . he had no intention . . . : Karl Mantzius, *History of Theatrical Art,* trs. C. Archer (1921), vol. vi, p. 324.

238 must virtually have compelled . . . : Simon Williams, *Shakespeare on the German Stage 1586–1914* (Cambridge, 1990), p. 141.

238 perfectly disgusting . . . : quoted by Gordon Haight, *George Eliot: A Biography* (1968), p. 171.

238 did not disclose . . . : Winter, *Shakespeare on the Stage,* p. 163.

239 individual ugliness . . . : quoted by John Osborne, *The Meiningen Court Theatre* (Cambridge, 1988), p. 72.

239 this principle of contradiction . . . : Simon Williams, op. cit., p. 145.

240 the spitefulness and simplicity . . . : Herman Sinsheimer, *Shylock: The History of a Character* (1947), p. 142.

241 a wolf in a fairy tale . . . : see Julius Bab, *Albert Basserman* (Leipzig, 1929), p. 165.

241 For Körtner's views on Reinhardt and his dispute with Rehling, see Fritz Körtner, *Aller Tage Abend* (Munich, 1959), pp. 377–9.

242 For Kerr's review of Körtner, see Alfred Kerr, *Mit Schleuder und Harfe* (Berlin, 1981), pp. 394–8.

242 On Krauss, Reinhardt and Shylock, see Werner Krauss, *Das Schauspiel meines Lebens* (Stuttgart, 1958), pp. 206–8.

243 He seemed to tumble . . . : Sinsheimer, op. cit., p. 142.

244 In the words of Emile Montégut . . . : see Shakespeare, *Oeuvres Complètes*, vol. i (1868), p. 370.

245 The Jew paid . . . : cited by Léon Poliakov, *The History of Anti-Semitism*, trs. Miriam Kochan, vol. iii (1975), p. 360.

245 the people who had best understood . . . : ibid., p. 363.

245 *Shylock est la juiverie* . . . : Victor Hugo, *William Shakespeare* (Paris, 1869 ed.), p. 188.

246 The printing business today! . . . : Jules Vallès, *Le Bachelier* (Paris, 1950 ed.), p. 100.

247 The first duty of an author . . . : cited by C. Lehrman, *L'Element Juif dans la Littérature Française: De la Révolution à nos Jours* (Paris, 1961), p. 41.

247 without question closer . . . : Jean-Michel Nectoux, *Gabriel Fauré: A Musical Life* (Cambridge, 1991), p. 143. On page 164 of his book Nectoux reproduces the 1889 costume designs for Shylock and Antonio.

247 Edouard Herriot . . . : see his memoirs, *Jadis* (Paris, 1948), vol. i, p. 93.

247 For Sarcey's essay, see Francisque Sarcey, *Quarante Ans de Théâtre* (Paris, 1900), vol. iii, pp. 380–8.

248 For Sarcey and *La Libre Parole*, see Nelly Wilson, *Bernard-Lazare* (Cambridge, 1978), pp. 187–8.

249 Gémier and Jean Vilar, see Jean-Albert Bédé, article on "France" in *A Shakespeare Encyclopedia*, ed. Oscar Campbell and Edward Quinn (1966), p. 245.

249 a vengeful and hysterical buffoon . . . : Thornton Wilder, "Some Thoughts on Playwriting" (1941), quoted by Robert Hapgood, *Shakespeare, The Theatre-Poet* (Oxford, 1988), p. 77.

250 On Shakespeare in Flemish, see D. de Gruyter and Wayne Hayward, "Shakespeare on the Flemish Stage of Belgium, 1876–1951," *Shakespeare Survey*, vol. 5 (1952), pp. 106–9.

250 The first Armenian production, see Edward Alexander, "Shakespeare's plays in Armenia," *Shakespeare Quarterly*, vol. ix (1958), p. 390.

250 The first Chinese production, see Qi-Xin, He, "China's Shakespeare," *Shakespeare Quarterly*, vol. xxxvii (1986), p. 151.

251 Shakespeare's characters . . . : quoted by Paul Debreczeny, *The Other Pushkin* (Stanford, 1983), p. 7. See also Tatiana Wolff, "Shakespeare's Influence on Pushkin's Dramatic Work," *Shakespeare Survey*, vol. 5 (1952), p. 101.

251 On Stanislavski and David Warfield, see Jean Benedetti, *Stanislavski* (1988), p. 271.
252 The poor wandering Jew . . . : Jose Ortega y Gasset, "Shylock," in *Shakespeare in Europe,* ed. Oswald LeWinter (1963), p. 331.
253 Signor Novelli . . . : ibid., p. 333.
253 On Jabotinsky and Novelli, see Joseph Schechtman, *The Jabotinsky Story,* vol. i, *Rebel and Statesman* (New York, 1956), p. 74.
254 Correctly holding her fan . . . : quoted in Toyoda Minoru, *Shakespeare in Japan: A Historical Survey* (1940), p. 87.
254 like a man who has swallowed bitter medicine . . . : Desmond MacCarthy, *Drama* (1940), p. 20.
255 we had some delightful trivial broken talk . . . : quoted in Hugh and Mirabel Cecil, *Clever Hearts* (1990), p. 63.
255 I was asked more than once . . . : "A South African's Homage," in *A Book of Homage to Shakespeare,* ed. Israel Gollancz (Oxford, 1916). The article is anonymous.
255 Here was a big, complicated business deal . . . : Karen Blixen, *Out of Africa* (Penguin edition, 1954), pp. 222–3.

CHAPTER FIFTEEN: *An Extended Family*

258 The Jew of Venice . . . : quoted by S. S. Prawer, *Heine's Jewish Comedy* (Oxford, 1983), p. 275.
258 When I saw this piece . . . : ibid., p. 292. (The paragraph beginning "But what am I saying" is taken from Heinrich Heine, *Works of Prose,* ed. Herman Kesten, trs. E. B. Aston [New York, 1943], p. 185).
260 It was no unloving father . . . : adapted from *Works of Prose,* trs. Ashton, p. 190.
262 The Jews happened just then . . . : quoted by Prawer, op. cit., p. 294.
263 These were the sounds of agony . . . : ibid., p. 296.
264 an article . . . entitled "Shylock" . . . : it is reprinted in Italo Svevo, *Saggi e Pagine Sparse* (Milan, 1954), pp. 11–13.
265 as Victor Brombert has pointed out . . . : see "Svevo's Witness," *The American Scholar,* Summer 1991, p. 428.
265 what starts as tragedy . . . : H. Stuart Hughes, *Prisoners of Hope* (Cambridge, Mass., 1983), pp. 44–5.
266 You hear nothing but . . . : Marcel Proust, *Remembrance of Things Past,* trs. Terence Kilmartin (1981), vol. i, p. 793.
266 those "chains of Israel" . . . : ibid., vol. iii, p. 995.
266 scarcely more visible . . . : ibid., p. 996.
267 another face, almost frightening . . . : ibid., p. 1012.
268 When the days were dark . . . : *A Book of Homage to Shakespeare* (Oxford, 1916), p. 307.
269 has points of contact . . . : Israel Gollancz, *Allegory and Mysticism in Shakespeare* (1931), p. 56.
269 Shylock, too, has an immortal soul . . . : ibid., p. 34.

270 Jew-baiting still . . . : Humbert Wolfe, *Early Poems* (Oxford, 1930), p. 57.

270 the most splendid and magnanimous woman . . . : G. K. Chesterton, "The Heroines of Shakespeare" (1901), reprinted in *A Handful of Authors* (1953), p. 74.

272 his knife would not have gone . . . : Ludwig Lewisohn, *The Last Days of Shylock* (1931), p. 4.

273 the Jewish Anti-Defamation League . . . : E. E. Stoll, op. cit., p. 255.

275 a village wagoner who is visiting the city of Czernowitz: see Karl Emil Franzos, "Shylock in Czernowitz," trs. Nathan Ausubel, in *A Treasury of Jewish Humor*, ed. Ausubel (Garden City, N.Y., 1952), pp. 657–88.

276 a victim of a period . . . : Leonard Prager, "Shakespeare in Yiddish," *Shakespeare Quarterly* (Spring, 1962), pp. 149–63.

276 *The Reward of the Righteous*, see David Pattison, *The Hebrew Novel in Czarist Russia* (Edinburgh, 1964), p. 227.

277 In the three Yiddish theaters . . . : Hutchins Hapgood, *The Spirit of the Ghetto* (New York, 1965 reprint), p. 118.

278 high intellect and proud convictions . . . : Lulla Rosenfeld, *Bright Star of Exile: Jacob Adlre and the Yiddish Theatre* (New York, 1977), p. 303.

278 Shylock, crouching, sobbing . . . : ibid., p. 305.

279 We can't make up our minds . . . : Shlomo Bickel, "The Argument about Shylock," in *Great Yiddish Writers of the Twentieth Century,* trs. and ed. Joseph Leftwich (Northvale, New Jersey, 1987), p. 255.

280 Shakespeare found it all so obvious . . . : H. D. Nomberg, "Shylock and the Blood Libel," ibid., p. 291.

280 more great acting . . . : James Agate, *Red Letter Nights* (1944), pp. 111–12, quoted by Irving Howe, op. cit., p. 489.

280 It's an anti-Semitic play . . . : quoted in David Lifson, *The Yiddish Theater in America* (New York, 1965), p. 320.

282 emphatic, often remarkably audience-conscious . . . : Siriol Hugh-Jones, the *New Statesman,* 24 September 1949, pp. 204–5. For further details connected with the production see Leonard Prager, *Yiddish Culture in Britain* (Frankfurt-on-Main, 1990) and David Mazower, *Yiddish Theatre in London* (1987).

283 Meskin was a heroic figure . . . : Avraham Oz, "Transformations of Authenticity: *The Merchant of Venice* in Israel 1936–1980," *Deutsche Shakespeare-Gesellschaft, Jahrbuch 1983* (Bochum), p. 171.

283 the show should have been . . . : ibid., p. 170.

283 a liberal Rabbi . . . : ibid., p. 173.

284 On Yzraely's production, see Oz, op. cit., and Gershon Shaked, "The Play: gateway to cultural dialogue," in *The Play Out of Context,* ed. Scolnikov and Holland (Cambridge, 1989), pp. 22–3.

CHAPTER SIXTEEN: *Economic Man*

285 merely means taking . . . : John Ruskin, *Munera Pulveris* (1872), p. 99.

286 And this is the ultimate lesson . . . : ibid., p. 102.

286 Matthew Arnold singled out . . . : in "The Literary Influence of Academies," *Essays in Criticism: First Series* (1865).

287 sin sticks so fast . . . : Ruskin, op. cit., p. 100.

288 He went to see Irving . . . : for this episode, and the passages quoted, see Laurence Irving, op. cit., pp. 345–9.

289 All wholesome indignation . . . : John Ruskin, *Val D'Arno* (1882), p. 210.

290 was designed to throw . . . : Max Plowman, "Money and the Merchant," *The Adelphi* (1931); reprinted in *The Merchant of Venice: A Casebook,* ed. John Wilders (1969), p. 79.

290 because he would check . . . : ibid., p. 79.

291 The star by which . . . : quoted in F. A. Lea, *The Life of John Middleton Murry* (1959), p. 294.

291 Yes, . . . money is a great mystery . . . : Plowman, op. cit., p. 77.

291 Proudhon gave vent . . . : see George Lichtheim, "Socialism and the Jews," *Collected Essays* (New York, 1973), p. 425.

292 For Blanqui's remarks, ibid., p. 428.

292 We will not always . . . : quoted by Léon Poliakov, *The History of Anti-Semitism,* translated by Miriam Kochan (1975), vol. iii, p.372.

292 money is the god . . . : quoted by Julius Carlebach, *Karl Marx and the Radical Critique of Judaism* (1978), p. 80.

292 Jewish poison . . . : quoted (from *The Baths of Lucca*) by Jeffrey Sammons, *Heinrich Heine: A Modern Biography* (1979), p. 249.

293 godless self-gods . . . : quoted (from the preface to the second edition of *On the History of Philosophy and Religion in Germany*) by Carlebach, op. cit., p. 190.

293 the first radical Jew . . . : see Orlando Figes, "Ludwig Börne and the Formation of a Radical Critique of Judaism," *Leo Baeck Institute Yearbook,* 29 (1984), pp. 351–82.

293 Börne's essay on *The Merchant of Venice: "Der Jude Shylock im Kaufmann von Venedig,"* in Börne, *Sämtliche Schriften,* ed. Inge and Peter Rippmann (Dusseldorf, 1964), vol. i, pp. 499–504.

294 On *Verjudung,* see Steven E. Ascheim "The Jew Within: The Myth of 'Judaization' in Germany" in *The Jewish Response to German Culture,* ed. Jehuda Reinhartz and Walter Schatzberg (1985), pp. 212–41.

295 Money is the jealous god . . . : Karl Marx, *Early Writings,* trs. and ed. T. B. Bottomore (1963), pp. 34–7.

295 The cast of Marx's mind . . . : ibid., p. xiii.

295 it is from its own entrails . . . : ibid., p. 36.

295 I hate Jews and I hate journalists . . . : cited by Julius Carlebach, *Karl Marx and the Radical Critique of Judaism* (1978), p. 340.

295 For the incident of Lassalle and his headmaster see Edmund Wilson, *To the Finland Station* (new edition, 1972), p. 273.

296 the implied identification . . . : S. S. Prawer, *Karl Marx and World Literature* (Oxford, 1976), p. 51.

296 a Shylock, but a servile Shylock . . . : Marx, *Early Writings,* ed. Bottomore, p. 45.

296 aristocratic Shylocks . . . : *Capital,* vol. i, ch. 23; cit. Prawer, p. 328.

296 the Prussian Shylock . . . : cit. Prawer, p. 353.
297 the person who exhibits . . . : ibid., p. 72.
297 capital itself takes on . . . : ibid., p. 327.
297 workmen and factory-inspectors . . . : *Capital,* vol. i, ch. 8; cit. Prawer, p. 327.
298 not a single expression . . . : Robert S. Wistrich, *Revolutionary Jews from Marx to Trotsky* (1976), p. 39.

CHAPTER SEVENTEEN: *A FATHER FIGURE*

301 symbols of the essential thing . . . : Sigmund Freud, "The Theme of the Three Caskets," reprinted in *The Merchant of Venice: A Casebook,* ed. John Wilders (1969), p. 60.
302 Shylock and Portia . . . : Marjorie Garber, *Shakespeare's Ghost Writers* (1987), p. 85.
302 by turning the Jew . . . : ibid., p. 86.
303 the three characteristics . . . : Norman Holland, *Psychoanalysis and Shakespeare* (New York, 1966), p. 237.
303 Realistically, . . . aggression . . . : ibid., p. 238.
303 Circumcision is . . . : Theodore Reik, *The Search Within* (New York, 1956), p. 359.
304 They open with an account . . . : see Reik, op. cit., pp. 349–71.
308 "The Counterfeit Order of *The Merchant of Venice*": see *Representing Shakespeare: New Psychoanalytic Essays,* ed. Murray M. Schwartz and Coppelia Kahn (1980), pp. 54–69.
309 malevolent maternal qualities . . . : ibid., p. 68.
310 an example of that inordinate affection . . . : W. H. Auden, *The Dyer's Hand* (1963), p. 231.
310 There is no reason to suppose . . . : ibid., p. 231.
311 Standing alone on the darkened stage . . . : ibid., p. 233.
311 *un couple total* . . . : Daniel Sibony, *Avec Shakespeare* (Paris, 1988), p. 153.

CHAPTER EIGHTEEN: *ANTI-SEMITES*

312 his portrait served . . . : Robert Wistrich, *Anti-Semitism: The Longest Hatred* (1991), p. 102.
313 today, . . . children colloquially . . . : Iona and Peter Opie, *The Lore and Language of Schoolchildren* (Oxford, 1959), p. 346.
313 a Mass-Observation survey . . . : see Tony Kushner, *The Persistence of Prejudice: Antisemitism in British Society During the Second World War* (Manchester, 1989), p. 111.
313 a recent article . . . : see Sol Encel, "Anti-Semitism and Prejudice in Australia," *Patterns of Prejudice* vol. 23, no. 1, (Spring 1989), pp. 16–27.
314 The Shylock image pervades . . . : Richard Hofstadter, *The Paranoid Style in American Politics* (1966), p. 301.
314 A Jewish Shylock . . . : quoted by Louise A. Mayo, *The Ambivalent Image: Nineteenth-Century America's Perception of the Jew* (1988), p. 130.

314 as audacious as he is vulgar . . . : ibid., p. 94.
315 Shylock was not the mere creation . . . : ibid., p. 151.
316 As recently as October 1991 . . . : for a full account, see the *Jewish Chronicle,* 4 October 1991, p. 6.
316 in school I got to know . . . : quoted by Sander L. Gilman, *Jewish Self-Hatred* (1986), p. 172.
316 old men, so serious . . . : quoted in Michael C. Steinlauf, "Mr. Geldhab and Sambo in Peyes," in *Polin: A Journal of Polish-Jewish Studies,* vol. iv (Oxford, 1989), p. 108.
316 I know that in almost all European countries . . . : quoted in Peter Pulzer, *The Rise of Political Anti-Semitism in Germany and Austria* (1954), p. 132.
317 the most clamorous Shylockery . . . : Louis-Ferdinand Céline, *L'Ecole des Cadavres* (Paris, 1938), p. 48.
317 Just as Portia once . . . : quoted in Donald L. Niewyk, "Solving the 'Jewish Problem,'" *Leo Baeck Institute Year book,* 35 (1990), p. 361.
318 a Shylock with a dirty little hat . . . : quoted in Steven Ascheim, *Strangers and Brothers: The East European Jew in German and German Jewish Consciousness 1800–1923* (1982), p. 233.
318 I have greater concerns . . . : quoted in Donald E. Niewyk, "German Jews in Revolution and Revolt," *Studies in Contemporary Jewry IV,* ed. Jonathan Frankel (Oxford, 1988), p. 47.
318 Theodore Fritsch was advising his readers . . . : see Christina von Braun and Ludger Heid ed., *Der Ewige Judenhass* (Stuttgart, 1990), p. 208.
319 the secret of these worlds . . . : quoted in Joseph Wulf, *Theater und Film im Dritten Reich: Ein Dokumentation* (Gutersloh, 1964), p. 257.
320 a logically stylized . . . : ibid., p. 255.
321 the voice of the people chimed . . . : ibid., p. 258.
321 every Jew active in Europe . . . : ibid., p. 11.
321 Werner Krauss on *Jew Süss* and Shylock: *Das Schauspiel meines Lebens* (Stuttgart, 1958), pp. 199–209.
322 The pale pink face . . . : ibid., p. 259.
323 vindictive stupidity . . . : see Bernard Shaw, *Collected Letters,* vol. iv: 1926–1950, ed. Dan H. Laurence (1988), pp. 808–9.
323 On the deportations from Venice, see Susan Zuccotti, *The Italians and the Holocaust* (1987), pp. 188–9, 197, 200.

CHAPTER NINETEEN: *Since 1945*

325 a villain full of venom . . . : Ronald Harwood, *Sir Donald Wolfit* (1971), p. 155.
325 In the trial scene . . . we saw a Shylock . . . : Diana Valk, *Shylock for a Summer* (1958), p. 65.
325 small, greasy and insect-like . . . : Samuel L. Leiter, ed., *Shakespeare Around the Globe* (New York, 1986), p. 431.
325 a gushing, nervous, trivial . . . : ibid., p. 433. (quoting John Russell Brown).
325 first to assume that Shakespeare . . . : Nigel Dennis, *Dramatic Essays* (1962), p. 50.

326 It was with admiration . . . : ibid., p. 51.

326 He pounced upon his thoughts . . . : quoted in Leiter, op. cit., p. 424.

327 On Jonathan Miller, see particularly the accounts of his production in James C. Bulman, op. cit., and Bill Overton, *Text and Performance: The Merchant of Venice* (1987).

328 allowing Shylock to appear . . . : Jonathan Miller, *Subsequent Performances* (1986), p. 155.

330 under the impression . . . that he was speaking Yiddish . . . : see Bernard Grebanier, *Then Came Each Actor* (New York, 1975), p. 530.

330 strutting about . . . : quoted in Grebanier, op. cit., p. 530.

330 a tragic role, but . . . : quoted in Judith Cook, *Shakespeare's Players* (1983), p. 82.

331 His aim, he wrote . . . : see Overton, op. cit., p. 53.

331 it is part of Shakespeare's brilliance . . . : quoted in Cook, op. cit., p. 83.

331 Bill Alexander's production . . . : for a full account, see Bulman, op. cit., pp. 117–42.

331 As he chanted . . . : Bulman, op. cit., p. 118.

332 there is something monstrous . . . : Henry James, *The Scenic Art* (1949), p. 145.

332 we didn't want our production . . . : interview in *Drama,* 4, 1947; quoted in Bulman, op. cit., p. 120.

334 to provoke the public . . . : Volker Canaris, "Style and the Director" in *The German Theatre,* ed. Ronald Hayman (1975), p. 273.

334 just into middle age . . . : Jackie Wullschlager, the *Financial Times,* May 1990.

336 a perfect image . . . : David Henry Wilson: appendix to Dietrich Schwanitz, *Shylock* (Hamburg, 1989), p. 237.

336 Fie on't! . . . : Erica Jong, *Serenissima* (1987), p. 172.

337 What are ducats . . . : ibid., p. 151.

337 Against our wills . . . : ibid., p. 212.

337 My version was . . . : Fiona Pitt-Kethley, "Shylock," *London Review of Books,* 25 January 1990.

338 to disengage and condemn . . . : C. S. Lewis, "Hamlet: The Prince or the Poem?", *Selected Library Essays* (Cambridge, 1969), p. 95.

338 The important thing . . . : ibid., p. 96.

339 A wicked ogre . . . : ibid., p. 97.

339 Nevill Coghill published an account: "The Basis of Shakespearian Comedy," reprinted in Anne Ridler, ed., *Shakespeare Criticism 1935–1960* (1963).

339 For John Russell Brown . . . : see "Love's Wealth and the Judgment of *The Merchant of Venice,*" reprinted in *Shakespeare and His Comedies* (1962).

339 The whole play dramatizes . . . : C. L. Barber, *Shakespeare's Festive Comedy* (Princeton, 1959), p.170.

340 the more one is aware . . . : ibid., p. 191.

340 *The Merchant of Venice* is "about" judgment. . . : Frank Kermode, *Shakespeare, Spenser, Donne* (1971, p. 215.

341 in the best sense artificial . . . : M. C. Bradbrook, *Shakespeare and Elizabethan Poetry* (1951), p. 178.

341 The present generation . . . : ibid., p. 175.
342 larger in scope . . . : A. D. Moody, *Shakespeare: The Merchant of Venice* (1964), p. 15.
343 If irony were demonstrable . . . : René Girard, "To Entrap the Wisest," *Literature and Society: Selected Papers from the English Institute, 1978*, ed. Edward W. Said (1980), p. 112.
343 the symmetry between . . . : ibid., p. 100.
343 spectacular instance . . . : ibid., p. 104.
343 the bourgeoisie have always pretended . . . : Terry Eagleton, *William Shakespeare* (Oxford, 1986), p. 46.
344 One can imagine him waiting . . . : ibid., p. 38.
345 If nineteenth-century audiences . . . : Pierre Spriet, "*The Merchant of Venice's* Doom," *Cahiers Elizabéthains* 24 (1988), p. 54.
346 a short book by John Lyon, *Harvester New Critical Introductions to Shakespeare—The Merchant of Venice* (1988).
346 Ambivalent signals . . . : Norman Rabkin, *Shakespeare and the Problem of Meaning* (1981), p. 28.
349 nobility in the sense of the Cinquescento . . . : "Shakespeare's Kings and Noblemen" (1905), in LeWinter, op. cit., p. 320.

Index